IF YOU THINK JEWISH COOKING IS MOSTLY MATZOH BALLS AND CHICKEN SOUP: THINK AGAIN! FEW CUISINES ARE AS ETHNICALLY VARIED AS JEWISH FOOD . . . AND NO ONE KNOWS JEWISH COOKING BETTER THAN FAYE LEVY. THE CRITICS AGREE: "YOU DON'T HAVE TO BE JEWISH TO DELIGHT IN AND USE THIS TEMPTING COOKBOOK!"*

FAYE LEVY'S INTERNATIONAL JEWISH COOKBOOK

"Good, solid, practical-minded . . . can easily be followed by cooks unfamiliar with the terrain."
—*Los Angeles Times*

"A treasure! . . . It is chock-full of mouthwatering dishes. I recommend this book to anyone who loves great food." —*Nina Simonds, author of China's Food*

"There has been a need for a really fine Jewish cookbook . . . and this is the book."
—*Joyce Goldstein, Square One Restaurant, San Francisco*

"With her usual attention to every detail, Faye Levy has given us a wonderful mixture of sophistication and tradition from the Jewish kitchen." —*Haim Shapiro, The Jerusalem Post*

"Ms. Levy draws on her exciting food and travel experience to open up a world of enticing new tastes in Jewish cuisine." —*Cookbook Digest*

"A treasure . . . a great book for browsers . . . a fascinating exploration of the way Jewish cuisine has drawn from cultures all over the world." —*New York Post*

"The authoritative guide to contemporary international Jewish cuisine. . . . Good modern Jewish cookbooks are few and far between: recommended." —*Library Journal*

"More than a collection of Jewish recipes: It's a cultural history as well. It far transcends [Levy's] intent . . . by the breadth and depth of its contents." —*Chicago Tribune*

"Faye Levy has studied and taught cooking in France, Israel, and the United States. She ranks among the most imaginative and careful of all cookbook authors, so her recipes are inspirational and accurate."
—*Boston Herald*

"Excellent contemporary holiday recipes. I highly recommend FAYE LEVY'S INTERNATIONAL JEWISH COOKBOOK." —*Baltimore Sun*

"A deliciously vivid tapestry of real-life contemporary Jewish cooking with its deep and varied ethnic roots intact." —*Alice Medrich, author of Cocolat*

"Encourages browsers of any background to incorporate some new ideas into their own traditional meals . . . Levy's recipes are 'high class' in their fidelity to fresh ingredients, traditional standards, and contemporary taste." —*Kirkus Reviews*

OTHER BOOKS BY FAYE LEVY

Fresh from France: Dessert Sensations
Fresh from France: Dinner Inspirations
Fresh from France: Vegetable Creations
Sensational Pasta
Faye Levy's Chocolate Sensations
Classic Cooking Techniques
La Cuisine du Poisson (in French, with Fernand Chambrette)
Faye Levy's Favorite Recipes (in Hebrew)
French Cooking Without Meat (in Hebrew)
French Desserts (in Hebrew)
French Cakes, Pastries and Cookies (in Hebrew)
The La Varenne Tour Book

FAYE LEVY'S INTERNATIONAL JEWISH COOKBOOK

Faye Levy

WARNER BOOKS

A Time Warner Company

Warner Books, Inc., 1271 Avenue of the Americas,
New York, NY 10020

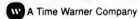 A Time Warner Company

Printed in the United States of America
First Trade printing: September 1995
10 9 8 7 6 5 4 3 2 1

Originally published in hardcover by Warner Books, Inc.

Library of Congress Cataloging-in-Publication Data

Levy, Faye.
    [International Jewish cookbook]
    Faye Levy's international Jewish cookbook / Faye Levy.
        p.   cm.
    Includes index.
    ISBN 0-446-67126-6
    1. Cookery, Jewish.   2. Cookery, International.   I. Title.
TX724.L413   1991   91-50083
641.5′676—dc20   CIP

Book Design by Giorgetta Bell McRee

For my mother, Pauline Kahn Luria
And my mother-in-law, Rachel Levy

And to the memory of my father, Louis Kahn

CONTENTS

ACKNOWLEDGMENTS *ix*
INTRODUCTION *xiii*

PART I: HOLIDAY MENUS AND RECIPES *1*

1. Passover: The Springtime Holiday *3*
2. Shavuot: The Cheesecake Holiday *53*
3. Rosh Hashanah: The Jewish New Year *63*
   A Note About Yom Kippur *80*

vii

4. Succot: The Harvest Holiday *81*
5. Hanukkah: The Festival of Lights and Latkes *101*
6. Purim: The Hamantaschen Holiday *123*
7. Sabbath: The Weekly Feast *131*

PART II: EVERYDAY JEWISH DISHES *147*

8. Appetizers *149*
9. Salads *167*
10. Soups *183*
11. Blintzes, Pancakes, and Egg Dishes *197*
12. Fish *209*
13. Poultry and Meat *223*
14. Vegetables *249*
15. Noodles, Rice, and Other Grains *269*
16. Breads *285*
17. Desserts, Cakes, and Cookies *303*
18. Menus for Celebrations *333*
19. Cooking Techniques *345*
20. A Brief Guide to Keeping Kosher *349*

CONVERSION CHART *351*
INDEX *353*
ABOUT THE AUTHOR *363*

ACKNOWLEDGMENTS

I am grateful to Geula Resh and Yehiel Limor of *At* magazine, Israel's most prestigious women's magazine, for inviting me to write the magazine's main cooking column four years ago, thus giving me the opportunity to keep in close touch with Israeli readers through my monthly articles.

Similarly, I appreciate the chance given to me by *Jerusalem Post* editors Matt Nesvisky, Haim Shapiro, and Faye Bittker during the past two years to write a biweekly cooking column for the newspaper.

One of the people who helped me most in my food writing career is Ruth Sirkis, the most prominent cooking expert and cookbook author in Israel, my mentor and presently the publisher of four books of mine in Hebrew. I wish to express my deep appreciation to her for teaching me about all types of Jewish cooking and fine cuisine in general. During the two years I worked for her, I learned a great deal from her about writing articles and cookbooks. The high standards of her work have always been a source of inspiration to me.

Sometimes it seems that I've been getting ready to write this book for my whole life and that everyone who has contributed to my Jewish eduction deserves to be thanked—my teachers at the Hebrew Academy of Washington, D.C., where I went to elementary school, and at Midrasha Hebrew High School in Washington as well as my parents' friends and our relatives. They taught me the meaning of Jewish culture, and without this knowledge this book would have been impossible to write.

But this book is about cooking, and so I will limit my thanks here to those who directly taught me how to cook Jewish specialties.

First I wish to thank my mother, Pauline Kahn Luria, who lovingly prepared traditional Ashkenazic Jewish food when I was growing up, not just for holidays but every day. Kosher cake mixes and prepared foods were not available, and even if they had been, she probably would have made everything from scratch anyway. And I thank her for agreeing with enthusiasm to teach me Jewish cooking when I was already an adult. Like many people of my generation, I hadn't realized that I should have been learning this while I was growing up.

I am grateful to my mother-in-law, Rachel Levy, for introducing me to the exciting specialties of Yemenite Jewish cooking and for sharing culinary tips with me during the last twenty-one years. I'm sure that for her it seemed strange that a woman could reach the age of nineteen without knowing how to cook. (She already knew how to bake pita bread when she was only six!)

Many other relatives, friends, neighbors, and colleagues at the various places I worked during the seven years I lived in Israel taught me about Jewish cooking, each in his or her own way —by teaching me personally in her own kitchen; by giving me good recipes; by inviting me to dinner; or by giving me information regarding who is the best cook of a particular style of cooking and where are the best markets and the most interesting restaurants.

Thanks to Mati Kahn, my brother Tzvi's wife, who was born in India and who, together with her sister Kathleen, taught me about the wonderful style of cooking of Jews from that country; Hedva Cohen, my sister-in-law, and her husband David, who introduced me to many fine Moroccan specialties; my sisters-in-law Nirit and Etti Levy, who taught me about modern Israeli cooking; my husband's cousin, Saida Avraham, who built her own traditional Yemenite kitchen, including large clay wood-fired ovens, to preserve the authentic ways of cooking she learned in Yemen; my mother-in-law's sister, Mazal Cohen, also a wonderful Yemenite cook; and my aunt, Sylvia Saks, for teaching me about Ashkenazic specialties.

I sincerely appreciate the help of my friend Ronnie Venezia of Jerusalem and her mother Suzanne Elmaleh, who gave me lessons in Lebanese Jewish cooking; Jaklyn Cohen of Holon, Israel, who taught me to prepare dishes of the Jews of Iraq; Ninette Bachar from Tunisia, a neighbor of my husband's parents in Israel, who showed me how to prepare a couscous feast and other North African specialties; Paule Tourdjman, who worked with me at La Varenne Cooking School in Paris, France, and taught me much about the cuisine of Moroccan Jews; Dvora Cohen, a relative of my husband who lives in Paris and who contributed to my knowledge of both Moroccan and Yemenite cooking; my friend Greg Dinner who lives in London, England, and who showed me how to make his grandmother's delicious potato kugel; Perla Abergel of Rishon Lezion, Israel, and her daughter Shulamit, from whom I learned wonderful Moroccan dishes as well as the warmth of North African Jewish hospitality.

At the Tel Aviv University Library, where I worked, I learned about many styles of Jewish cooking from Mrs. Yehudai, an American married to a Yemenite; Mrs. Wasserman, from Vienna; Mrs. Berman, from Romania; and Margaret, from Egypt. At the same time, my neighbors in Bat Yam, a suburb of Tel Aviv where I lived for six years, and who were from Morocco, Algeria, and Yemen, all gave me tips about cooking and recipes. I appreciate their advice and I enjoyed their enthusiasm for good food.

I am grateful to Sarah Keinan, my teacher at the Tel Aviv Seminary of Nutrition and Home Economics and to all the teachers of the WIZO cooking courses I attended for their instruction in Jewish holiday cooking.

I wish to thank Haim Shapiro of the *Jerusalem Post* for his many fine articles on cooking and dining in Israel, which inspired me for many years.

I would like to thank the magazine and newspaper editors who published my articles and recipes on Jewish cooking and thus enabled me to turn my passion into my métier:

Zanne Zakroff of *Gourmet* magazine; Barbara Fairchild of *Bon Appétit* magazine; and Larry Levine of *Western Chef* magazine.

Russ Parsons of the *Los Angeles Times* Syndicate, and formerly of the *Los Angeles Herald Examiner*; Manuel Chait of the *Jewish Bulletin*; Charles Britton of Copley Los Angeles Newspapers; Maureen Clancy of the *San Diego Union*; Michael Bauer and Tom Sietsema of the *San Francisco Chronicle*; Helen Dollaghan of the *Denver Post*; Rosemary Black of the *New York Daily News*; Bob Kelleter and Phyllis Richman of the *Washington Post*; Carol Haddix of the *Chicago Tribune*; Evelyn Kramer and Gail Perrin of the *Boston Globe*; Iris Bailin of the *Cleveland Plain Dealer*; Barbara Gibbs Ostmann of the *St. Louis Post-Dispatch*; Susan Puckett of the *Atlanta Journal-Constitution*; Ginger Johnston and Barbara Durbin of the *Portland Oregonian*; Nanette Wiser of Copley News Service; Dale Curry of the *New Orleans Times-Picayune*; Mary Maushard of the *Baltimore Evening Sun*; Susan Wyland of the *Detroit News*; Muriel Stevens of the *Las Vegas Sun*; Kathy Lindsley of the *Rochester Times-Union*; Toni Cashnelli of the *Cincinnati Enquirer*; George Anderson of the *Pittsburgh Post-Gazette*; Donna Lee of the *Providence Journal-Bulletin*; Candy Sagon of the *Dallas Times Herald*; Linda Giuca of the *Hartford Courant*; Teresa Rousseau of the *Waterbury Republican*; James Gray of the *Albany Times-Union*.

Former food editors Ken Bookman of the *Philadelphia Inquirer*; Kit Snedaker of the *Los Angeles Herald Examiner*; Pucci Meyer of the *New York Post*; Taffy Jacaway of the *Miami News*; the late Pat Baldridge of the *Baton Rouge Sunday Advocate*; Winnifred Jardine of the *Salt Lake City Deseret News*; Ann Hoffman of the *Norfolk Virginian-Pilot*; the late Peggy Daum of the *Milwaukee Journal*; and Cynthia David of the *London, Ontario, Free Press*, now at the *Toronto Sun*.

I am grateful to Liv Blumer, my editor, for her creative ideas for making the book much better, for her support and for her having gently pushed me to do my best; and to Maureen and Eric Lasher for finding a good home for my book.

I sincerely appreciate the creative work of photographers Tommy Miyasaki and David Wong of deGennaro Studios and of food stylist Annie Horenn. Thanks also to Ronnie Venezia for helping us cook for the photographs.

Thanks to Gallery Judaica, Westwood, California, for loaning us the following items, all of which can be purchased at the store: the blue plate, candlesticks, and goblet, created by Bonita

Goodberg, which appear in the *Shabbat* photograph, as well as the challah cover; the Seder plate and Glasscrafters small goblets in the Passover photo; the Sara Mann platter in the Hanukkah photo; the LaRosh tallit and matzo cover; and the shofar, ''hai'' kiddush cup, apple-shaped honey container, Torah pointer, and small Torah.

Thanks to the Jewish Quarter in Beverly Hills, California, for loaning us the Sandra Kravitz Hanukkah menorah, the dreidel, *etrog* box, challah knife, prayer book, and Passover haggadah for the photographs.

Thanks to Julia Child for giving me the idea for this book, in a letter she wrote to me seventeen years ago, when I was living in Israel, suggesting I write a ''high-class book on Jewish cooking.'' Thanks also to Grace Kirschenbaum of the World of Cookbooks Newsletter for encouraging me to write this book.

Most of all I wish to thank my husband Yakir, who is the main reason I moved to Israel in the first place! Yakir helped me to research and write the book and test the recipes and, of course, to eat all the dishes.

INTRODUCTION

During the seven years I spent in Israel, the melting pot of Jewish cooking, I was so impressed and intrigued by the extraordinary diversity of the Jewish culinary heritage that I decided to change careers and turn my hobby into my profession.

At the time I was a student of sociology and anthropology at the Hebrew University in Jerusalem and at Tel Aviv University. As soon as I graduated, I became the assistant to Israel's foremost culinary personality and cookbook author, Ruth Sirkis, and worked with her for two years.

It was fascinating to learn to prepare Jewish specialties beyond matzo ball soup, gefilte fish, and blintzes. I discovered a rich and varied international cuisine of many wonderful dishes and exotic flavors. When I married Yakir, an Israeli-born Jew of Yemenite origin, I feasted at his mother's house on many superb dishes with Mediterranean flair—delectable stuffed vegetables, spicy meats, aromatic soups, tasty salads, a variety of cakes and breads, and both savory and sweet pastries.

I felt that in a way Yakir and I symbolized the Israeli experience, which has contributed to the shaping of modern Jewish cuisine. We came from different worlds: I was born in the United States, my father's parents came to America from Russia, and my mother was born in Poland;

Yakir was born and raised in Israel, and his parents were born in the Middle East (in the southern part of the Arabian Peninsula). All these areas were important Jewish centers with distinct styles of cooking.

Jewish cooking is what we both grew up with, although each of us was raised on totally different dishes. The major branches of Jewish cooking, the Ashkenazic, or eastern and central European, and the Sephardic, or Mediterranean and Middle Eastern, are well represented in our families. My mother, who spent most of her life in Washington, D.C., and has been a Jerusalem resident for over twenty years, cooks traditional eastern European Jewish cuisine, the style most widely known in the United States. Yakir's mother lives near Tel Aviv and cooks in the Yemenite style, the delicious cuisine of the Jewish community of Yemen. My sister-in-law, who lives in Jerusalem, was born in India, where another popular style of Jewish cooking developed. Other in-laws are from Morocco and their aromatic Mediterranean cuisine is a favorite in Israel. We have enjoyed learning cooking from all of them, as well as from friends and neighbors from Romania, Tunisia, Iraq, and other countries.

From Israel, I went to study cooking in Paris, the city with the largest Jewish population in western Europe. Yakir and I lived there for six years and while I studied French cuisine, we also learned first-hand about the culinary customs of European Jewry.

When I returned to the United States in 1982 and settled in Los Angeles, I became the Jewish cooking columnist of the *Los Angeles Herald Examiner* and the *Los Angeles Jewish Bulletin*. I also began to teach classes and to write articles on cooking for the Jewish holidays for newspapers throughout the country in which I presented the dishes that I learned abroad.

I have often been asked to define Jewish cuisine. I feel that describing Jewish cooking is quite similar to defining American cooking. Both America and the Jewish world comprise a great variety of ethnic groups. At an exhibition of the culture and cuisine of the Kurdish Jews, which we went to see in Israel's capital, the mayor of Jerusalem pointed out that "the Jewish people have *always* been a nation of tribes."

In each of the countries where Jews have lived, there has naturally been a resemblance between their cooking and the local cuisine, owing to cultural influences and available ingredients. Jewish cooks have adopted dishes like the Middle Eastern falafel, just as Americans adopted the Italian pizza. Jews have also popularized such specialties as eastern European rye bread with caraway seeds and Hungarian strudel in countries outside the area in which they were created, and these are today known to many people as part of Jewish cooking.

Traditional Jewish cooking is kosher, of course. Because of the requirements of keeping kosher and of following the Jewish holiday customs, the Jews also developed unique dishes of their own. For example, cold fish dishes and delicious, slow-baking stews and kugels were all created to fit in with the laws of the Sabbath.

Kosher cooking originated in the eastern Mediterranean area, at the convergence of the Middle Eastern and Mediterranean styles of cooking and dining. In this region the eating habits and tastes are often naturally in accord with the rules for keeping kosher. Pork is hardly used in the area; oil is the main cooking fat rather than butter or animal fat; and meat and poultry are rarely cooked with dairy products. Today, thousands of years later, thanks to the Jewish State, the

Mediterranean birthplace of Judaic culture serves once again as an inspiration for Jewish cooking everywhere.

ASHKENAZIC AND SEPHARDIC JEWS—CULINARY PROFILES

From a cultural and culinary standpoint, the Jews are divided into two major groups: Ashkenazic and Sephardic. This is a simplification, however, since neither category is homogeneous.

The name Ashkenazic comes from the word *Ashkenaz*, a former Hebrew name for Germany, and refers to the Jews from eastern and central Europe. Sephardic comes from *Sepharad*, the Hebrew word for Spain, and stands for Jews from the Mediterranean area and the Middle East.

A large number of Sephardic Jews are indeed descendants of the Spanish Jews who were forced to leave Spain in 1492 and were dispersed throughout the Mediterranean region and eventually to other areas such as Holland and the New World. Many of the countries to which they moved already had non-Spanish Jewish residents, however, who had arrived during the Roman Empire and other periods. Some Jews were exiled to ancient Babylon (now Iraq) in the eighth century B.C.E. when the Assyrians conquered Israel, and from there many migrated to Iran. Historians are not sure where the Jews from Yemen, Ethiopia, and India came from. They are also included in the Sephardic group, although their origins were not in Spain. In Hebrew the Sephardic Jews are also called *Edot Hamizrach*, or "the communities of the East."

Ashkenazic Jews are also made up of several groups, notably the German, Austrian, Hungarian, Polish, and Russian Jews. Because Russia is so vast, some Jews from the southern and Asian parts of the Soviet Union have a cuisine totally unlike that of the western Russian style. The Jews from the Soviet areas of Georgia near the Turkish border, from the Caucasus area near the border with Iran, and from Bukhara near Afghanistan are Sephardic in a culinary sense.

The various branches of Jewish cooking are different from regional cuisines, such as those of France and Italy, owing to the movement of Jews from place to place throughout history, resulting in a mixture of Jews of different backgrounds in some countries. This was the case, for example, in Greece, Italy, France, Turkey, and Syria. Thus different dishes and customs crept from a Jewish group's collective memory into each local cuisine and merged to varying degrees with the cooking of their Jewish and non-Jewish neighbors. This was true in ancient times and continues in the modern age.

Of course, Jews live in other parts of the world, too. Jews in North America are mainly Ashkenazic, although the first Jews to arrive were Sephardic. There are Sephardic and Ashkenazic Jews in South and Central America as well as in South Africa.

The fact that traditional Jewish cooking is kosher affects the choice of ingredients and how the dishes are combined in a menu, and is another way in which Jewish cooking is often different from that of their neighbors in any given country.

ASHKENAZIC COOKING

The principal culinary difference between the two major branches of Jewish cuisine lies in the use of flavorings. Ashkenazic cooks prefer simple seasonings and are more likely to use a small number of herbs and spices, while Sephardic cooks are more inclined to sprinkle foods with mixtures of spices or herbs and to add these in larger amounts.

Onions are important in all branches of Jewish cooking, but in Ashkenazic cooking they are frequently the main flavoring of a dish. Depending on the recipe, the onions might be raw, lightly sautéed, or deeply browned.

A technique by which Ashkenazic cooks accent their dishes is to add thoroughly sautéed onions and paprika, and sometimes sautéed mushrooms as well. The mushrooms are usually button mushrooms, but for special occasions are wild mushrooms like cèpes or chanterelles that Americans normally associate with French cooking.

Popular fresh herbs are dill, parsley, and occasionally chives; nutmeg, allspice, and bay leaves are also used. Garlic is well liked, although it is utilized with greater restraint than in Sephardic cooking. Dill-scented pickled cucumbers are a favorite condiment and add zest to salads. Horseradish is served as a spicy accompaniment for fish and meat.

The theme of sweet and sour runs through Ashkenazic cuisine, for cooking fish, meat, and some vegetables. Sweet-and-sour sauces are made with sugar, honey, or raisins as the sweetener, and with vinegar, lemon juice, or sour salt as the sour agent.

Well-made Ashkenazic food can be delicate but is not bland. In fact, the Hungarian branch can be surprisingly spicy, because of the sweet and hot paprika and the peppers that enter their soups and stews. Cooks of Polish and Russian origin, however, mostly prefer subtly flavored foods over spicy ones and might season a dish only with salt, pepper, and paprika so that the taste of the main ingredient is emphasized rather than that of the spices. Still, even dishes with fruit or sweet seasonings are balanced with the sharpness of black pepper. Traditional cooks used chicken or goose fat for sautéing for meat meals and butter for dairy meals, but most modern cooks have replaced the poultry fats with vegetable oil and margarine.

Chicken and meat often are roasted or braised or stewed with winter vegetables—carrots, turnips, potatoes, and onions. Veal, goose, and duck are reserved for special occasions. Freshwater fish are preferred, since they are familiar from central Europe. Smoked and cured fish, such as lox, smoked whitefish, and pickled herring, are choice items for brunch, light meals, and appetizers. Spreads made with creamy cheeses are also brunch favorites.

Ashkenazic Jews are fond of egg noodles—fine noodles for clear soups, short noodles called farfel for bean soups, bowties and any other shape of noodles served as a side dish with sautéed onions and mushrooms. Potatoes appear often on the menu and are the basis of creamy salads, crisp pancakes, and hearty kugels. Asparagus, carrots, beets, cauliflower, and cabbage are popular, and so is sauerkraut. Fruit is used extensively, not just for dessert but in first-course soups and to complement main courses.

Ashkenazic Jews are renowned in America for their baking, which is done mostly in the Hungarian or Austrian style. The light tortes, rich strudels, luscious cheesecakes, buttery yeast cakes, marble cakes, honey cakes, bread puddings, and delicious blintzes all have their counterparts in eastern Europe. Cakes and desserts are flavored with walnuts, fruit, poppy seeds, and wine. Challah, bagels, rye bread, and pumpernickel are the best-loved breads.

Poland and Russia

Jews from Poland and Russia opt for simple seasonings—mainly onion, garlic in small amounts, bay leaves to flavor soups, and sometimes sweet-and-sour tomato sauces. Pearl barley and kasha (buckwheat groats) are frequently served grains. Combinations of vegetables cooked with fruit, such as potatoes with prunes, are favorite side dishes for holidays. Sour cream enriches and accompanies dairy dishes.

Alsace and Germany

The Jews of Alsace in eastern France share their compatriots' love for sweet and savory tarts, foie gras, and wine. They use the French bouquet garni of thyme, bay leaves, and parsley as a flavoring for soups and stews, in which they also simmer a whole onion studded with cloves, in the French manner. They add fresh herbs like tarragon and chives to sauces, and nutmeg to meat dishes and stuffings. Jews from Germany like similar flavorings. Prunes and raisins are frequent partners for meat or poultry, and dumplings are classic accompaniments for meats and additions to soups.

Hungary, Austria, and Romania

Hungarian Jewish cooks are famous for their beef goulash prepared with paprika and caraway seeds, served with noodles or dumplings, and both they and Austrian Jews bake wonderful tortes, pastries, and other desserts. Hungarian and Romanian Jews prepare some spicy dishes with peppers and eggplants, which may have been influenced by the Sephardic tradition of their neighbors farther south in Bulgaria and Turkey.

SEPHARDIC COOKING

Generous use of herbs and spices makes this style of cuisine aromatic and, in some cases, quite hot. Olive oil, garlic, and lemon are prominent seasonings throughout most of the Sephardic world.

In some Sephardic Jewish communities, fresh herbs are the dominant flavorings, whereas in others, especially those from North Africa and the Middle East, the emphasis is on pungent spices, a heritage from the days when the spice caravans passed through much of the area. Dill is popular among some Sephardic Jews, especially those from Greece and Turkey, but is seldom found in the saucepans of those from the Maghreb countries of Morocco, Algeria, Tunisia, and Libya. On the other hand, cumin, dried ginger, and fresh coriander (cilantro) are preferred by Jews from North Africa and the eastern Mediterranean, but rarely enter the kitchens of those from the countries north of the Mediterranean. A touch of cinnamon perfumes the casseroles of Sephardic Jews from Greece, Turkey, Lebanon, Iraq, and North Africa.

Lamb is a choice meat among most Sephardic Jews and rice is a favorite accompaniment. Saltwater fish are the preferred type. Pita is the best-loved bread, especially among Jews from the Middle East. Olives are used extensively as appetizers and garnishes.

Vegetables are prepared in a great variety of ways, and a lavish spread of vegetable salads is a typical way to begin a festive Sephardic meal. Mediterranean vegetables such as eggplant, zucchini, artichokes, tomatoes, peppers, fava beans, and okra appear frequently on the tables of Sephardic Jews. Vegetables are often served with tomato sauce and, for special occasions, are stuffed and braised.

Desserts are based on nuts (especially almonds, pistachios, and pine nuts), sugar, eggs, and filo dough rather than dairy products, but desserts in general are less central to Sephardic than to Ashkenazic cooking. Orange flower water, cinnamon, and dates are beloved Sephardic dessert flavorings.

North Africa

North African cooks make liberal use of garlic and herbs, especially fresh coriander (cilantro) and Italian parsley, followed by mint. Hot pepper in the form of cayenne powder or fresh and dried chilies is well liked, and is often paired with garlic in spicy stews and tomato sauces. A great variety of spices flavor meats, fish, and vegetables, and many dishes contain a blend of several spices. Couscous is the favorite side dish.

Moroccan cooking is the most varied and refined of the cuisines of the Jews of North Africa. It is sometimes hot and sometimes delicate, but always aromatic. Saffron is especially popular, as are copious amounts of fresh herbs and garlic. Lemon juice and salt-preserved lemons impart a tangy accent to some dishes. Meat main courses might be flavored with cumin, fresh coriander, and hot and sweet paprika, or with fruit and a mixture of "sweet spices"—ginger, cinnamon, nutmeg, mace, and allspice.

The Jews of Algeria and Tunisia prefer a seasoning trio of cumin, hot pepper, and garlic for main courses. Libyan Jews have a reputation for hot food. They are fond of chilies, which they often ally with garlic and sometimes also with cumin or turmeric.

Southern Europe and Turkey

Lemon juice is used generously in the Greek and Turkish Jewish kitchen. Unlike many other Sephardic Jews, Greek Jews cook with white and red dry wine. A hint of honey or sugar adds a sweeet touch to some meat and fish dishes as well as tomato sauces, and sometimes is balanced with lemon juice.

Jews from Greece and Turkey regularly use dill, parsley, mint, and green onions to flavor cheese and meat dishes, and also like rosemary and oregano. Cinnamon and coriander seeds occasionally accent meat stews. Walnuts and almonds sometimes enrich sauces for fish and meat. Turkish cooking can be quite peppery, with generous amounts of cayenne added to some dishes.

Feta and parmesan cheeses enhance dairy dishes. Yogurt is a frequent accompaniment to pastries and vegetable dishes, both here and among Jews from the Middle East. Filo dough is used in dessert pastries, with fillings of nuts and dried fruit. Jews from Bulgaria, which borders Greece and Turkey, share many of the same culinary characteristics.

The cooking of the Jews of Georgia, an area of the Soviet Union near Turkey, bears a certain resemblance to that of the Turkish Jews. Eggplant and other Mediterranean vegetables are favorities, as are dishes flavored with plenty of garlic and sauces made with walnuts, and pastries with spicy meat fillings.

The Jews of Italy cook in the general Sephardic fashion but, like their compatriots, prepare many pasta dishes and use the seasonings popular in Italian cooking, such as rosemary, sage, basil, garlic, olive oil, and fresh tomato sauce.

Middle East and India

The aromatic cuisine of the Jews from Syria and Lebanon relies mainly on the tastes of lemon, olive oil, fresh coriander, mint, and garlic. The emphasis is on fresh flavorings rather than on spices. Tahini (sesame sauce) plays an important part in the kitchens of Jews from the eastern Mediterranean countries and is loved in Egypt as well.

The cooking of the Jews from Egypt resembles that of Jews from Syria and Lebanon more than those from the rest of North Africa. The food is flavorful but not fiery. Cooks have a fondness for lemon juice, garlic, and allspice. They use cumin or turmeric in discreet amounts but do not usually combine them in the same dish. For seasoning meat or poultry, turmeric is often paired with lemon juice, or cumin with garlic. Cardamom and fresh and dried coriander are other well-liked spices.

The cooking of the Yemenite Jews is simple, direct, and hearty. The most popular seasoning is a mixture of cumin, turmeric, and black pepper and is sprinkled liberally into soups, meat, fish, and vegetable dishes. Garlic is used abundantly, and sometimes dishes are accented with fresh coriander (cilantro). Hot peppers might be added to the food but generally appear on the table as hot pepper–garlic chutney, for each person to add to taste. Cardamom sometimes seasons meat, and also appears in a spice blend with ginger, cinnamon, and cloves to flavor coffee. From a culinary standpoint, the Jews of Ethiopia have quite a lot in common with the Jews of Yemen.

Jews from Iraq and from Kurdistan, an area that is now part of Iran, Iraq, and Turkey, use fresh herbs and greens in lavish quantities, both wild ones and common ones like dill, Italian parsley, fresh coriander, celery leaves, and spinach. Garlic, hot pepper, cumin, and a spice mixture resembling curry powder also add zest to main courses, which are accompanied by wheat berries, bulgur wheat, or rice.

Plenty of fresh herbs go into the pots of Iranian Jews—dill, mint, coriander, celery leaves, parsley, and scallions, often several in the same dish. These flavor soups, as well as meat stews with dried beans. Spices used include saffron, cumin, turmeric, coriander seeds, cardamom, and hot red pepper, but are generally added in discreet amounts. Prunes, dates, and quinces are occasionally cooked with poultry and meat, and fruit sometimes garnishes rice.

The Jews of India are divided into three groups: those of Bombay, also known as Bene Israel; those of Cochin; and those whose families originated in Iraq and arrived in India during the last century. As with the general cooking of India, spices are very important to all the groups. A single dish might include cumin, cinnamon, cloves, nutmeg, turmeric, cardamom, bay leaves, and coriander seed, as well as garlic, hot peppers, ginger, and fresh coriander (cilantro). Of course, there are also dishes with just a few flavorings. The cooking of the Indian Jews from Iraq is influenced by both Indian and Iraqi cuisines. A popular seasoning combination for their soups and main courses is cumin, garlic, and fresh dill.

In this book I present recipes for the kinds of dishes that are being cooked today in Jewish households throughout the world, from Jerusalem to Paris to Los Angeles. They include traditional Ashkenazic favorites as well as Sephardic specialties, that together make up a cuisine that is colorful, fresh, and delicious.

Bon appétit, or as we say in Hebrew, *"Bétéavon!"*

Faye Levy

PART 1

Holiday Menus and Recipes

1

PASSOVER: THE SPRINGTIME HOLIDAY

 Of all the Jewish holidays, Passover is the one most associated with good eating. Paradoxically, on Passover there are extra regulations beyond the usual rules of keeping kosher. It seems that Jewish cooks set out to prove that, in spite of these additional restraints, for Passover they can produce the most delicious cuisine of the year.

Passover, or *Pesach* in Hebrew, is a celebration of the ancient Hebrews' deliverance from slavery in Egypt. The holiday is observed for eight days (seven days in Israel) and takes place in the spring. The food customs of Passover exist to commemorate this historic event in a concrete way, to encourage everyone to identify with the joyous experience of his or her ancestors' liberation.

A Passover Primer

On the Passover table matzo is served instead of bread, as a reminder of the Hebrews' hurried escape. The Torah, or Jewish bible, relates that in their haste to leave Egypt about 3,000 years ago, the Hebrews did not have time to let their bread, which was most likely a form of sourdough bread, rise. The resulting flat bread became the first matzos.

From this arose the prohibition against eating leavened bread during the week of Passover, and against using wheat flour, because it can leaven, or ferment, naturally upon contact with liquid. (This is the sourdough principle, that a mixture of flour and water left to sit catches wild yeast from the air.)

Matzo itself is made from wheat flour but the regulations surrounding its baking ensure that the dough will be mixed as quickly as possible and baked immediately, to prevent it from fermenting. Cakes, cookies, and dumplings for Passover are made from either potato starch or matzo meal made from ground matzos, or a more finely ground version called cake meal.

Things are not quite so simple, however. Because the Jews were scattered throughout much of the world, different communities developed varying interpretations of the Passover laws over time. Thus, most Ashkenazic Jews (from eastern and central Europe) will not eat corn, rice, or beans (which are known collectively as *kitniyot*) during Passover, since these can ferment. Many Sephardic communities do eat these foods during the holiday, however. This leads to interesting labeling of kosher products in those areas where members of both communities live, such as Israel and France. Some products will be labeled Kosher for *Pesach* for Those Who Eat *Kitniyot*, which basically means "Kosher for Passover for Bean Eaters."

In Orthodox homes, Passover involves plenty of preparation. When I was growing up, a few days before the holiday my parents went down to the storage room to bring up both sets of Passover dishes, pans, and silverware—those for dairy meals and those for meat, which replaced the usual dairy and meat dishes of the rest of the year. Eating on these special plates, that appeared on the table during just one week of the year, added to the feeling of festivity.

The Seder

The Seder, or ceremonial Passover dinner, takes place throughout the world on the first and second nights of the holiday, but in Israel on the first night only. On a special decorative Seder plate, which is divided into sections, are displayed small portions of the foods for the ritual. Each section is labeled with a word, usually in Hebrew, denoting where to place each food. These symbolic foods recall the Jews' lives as slaves, escape to freedom, and establishment as a community in the land of Israel. "Bitter herbs," usually grated fresh horseradish on Ashkenazic Seder plates and bitter lettuce on Sephardic ones, symbolize the bitterness of life during the period of slavery. A roasted lamb shank or chicken neck is a reminder of the sacrifices at the Temple in Jerusalem. A hard-boiled egg also appears on the plate to commemorate the offerings brought to the Temple on holidays. To celebrate spring, a stick of celery or a sprig of parsley also has its place on the Seder plate.

The best-loved of the Seder foods is undoubtedly haroset, a spread or condiment made of apples, sometimes dried fruits, nuts, and cinnamon. Its reddish brown color recalls the mortar and bricks the Hebrew slaves were forced to make in Egypt. The tasting of haroset is part of the Seder ceremony before dinner, but it remains on the table so everyone can enjoy it throughout the meal. Some families make enough haroset for the entire week of Passover, and serve it as a sweet and satisfying snack with matzo.

After tasting the ritual foods and drinking wine in the order explained in the Haggadah, the special book of procedures and prayers of the Seder, the dinner itself begins.

Passover Menus

On many tables, a fish dish is a frequent choice for a Passover appetizer, often followed by chicken soup. Roast chicken is a popular main course among most Jews, and Ashkenazic cooks often like to add a matzo-based stuffing. Roast lamb is another frequent choice on the Sephardic holiday menu.

Passover cakes and cookies are often flavored with nuts, which give them an appealing richness, yet at the same time they are light because they do not contain flour. It is amazing how well this age-old culinary custom fits the food trends of today!

Sweet red wine is practically synonymous with Passover wine, but today dry Passover wines are gaining in popularity. At a Seder that my husband and I attended in Paris, we enjoyed a kosher-for-Passover dry red Bordeaux. I find it best to provide both sweet and dry wine to satisfy everyone's taste. For the blessings before dinner, most people are used to sweet wine and tend to prefer it.

Other ideal Passover dishes:

Artichokes with Lemon Dressing (page 159)
Ashkenazic Chicken Soup with Fresh Dill and Light Matzo Balls
(made without baking powder) (page 84)
Spicy Roast Chicken with Matzo-Onion Stuffing (page 230)
Potato Kugel with Asparagus and Broccoli (page 250)
Sweet Carrot Kugel (page 253)

Matzo and Apple Kugel (page 331)
Moist Coconut Macaroons (page 319)
Nut and Chocolate-Studded Meringues (page 320)

Following are some menu suggestions and descriptions of Passover Seders that I have particularly enjoyed, that can be re-created using recipes from this book.

PASSOVER IN PARIS

During the six years my husband and I spent in France, we were glad to have the chance to attend Parisian Passover Seders and to explore French Jewish cuisine. Most of the Jews in France are either of North African or eastern European origin, and the taste of both groups is reflected in the holiday fare. Although much of the Passover menu is dictated by tradition and some dishes are standard throughout the world, the French influence is also evident.

One time we went to a Seder given at a Parisian synagogue, where the menu was especially intriguing. It featured time-honored Jewish dishes alongside classic French ones, and was the inspiration for our menu here.

For a first course, we were offered a choice of either *saumon en gelée, sauce verte* (French salmon in aspic with herb sauce), or gefilte fish (Ashkenazic light fish dumplings). Next were delicate leek fritters in the Sephardic Jewish tradition. Serving roast lamb is a Passover custom dating from biblical times; ours was flavored with garlic and onions Mediterranean style, and was accompanied by roasted potatoes and a zucchini casserole. The haroset featured a delightful mélange of three nuts, apples, and wine.

Since the Passover Seder is one of the most festive dinners of the year, we were served two desserts: one was a light matzo-raisin kugel from Alsace, and the second was a luscious French chocolate hazelnut gâteau, made with a small amount of potato starch instead of flour.

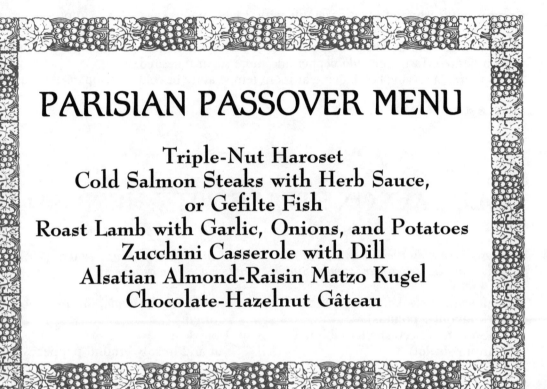

PARISIAN PASSOVER MENU

Triple-Nut Haroset
Cold Salmon Steaks with Herb Sauce,
or Gefilte Fish
Roast Lamb with Garlic, Onions, and Potatoes
Zucchini Casserole with Dill
Alsatian Almond-Raisin Matzo Kugel
Chocolate-Hazelnut Gâteau

TRIPLE-NUT HAROSET

Toasted hazelnuts combine with walnuts, almonds, apples, cinnamon, and wine to give this haroset, prepared in the Ashkenazic manner, an intriguing flavor.

⅓ cup walnuts
⅓ cup almonds
⅓ cup hazelnuts
2 to 3 tablespoons sugar
1 medium or large apple, peeled, halved, and cored
¾ cup pitted dates, chopped

¾ teaspoon ground cinnamon
2 to 4 tablespoons red wine
2 to 3 tablespoons strained fresh orange juice (optional)
pinch of black pepper (optional)
matzos, for serving

Grind walnuts, almonds, and hazelnuts with 2 tablespoons sugar in a food processor until fairly fine, leaving a few small chunks. Transfer to a bowl. Coarsely grate apple, then add to nut mixture. Stir in dates, cinnamon, and 2 tablespoons wine. Add orange juice or more wine if desired. Taste, and add pepper and more sugar if desired.

Spoon into a serving bowl. Serve at room temperature or cold, accompanied by matzos.

Makes 8 servings

COLD SALMON STEAKS WITH HERB SAUCE

This tasty French dish makes an elegant first course for the Seder or can be served as a refreshing summer main course for four, accompanied by sliced tomatoes and cucumbers.

8 small salmon steaks, about 1 inch thick (about 2 pounds)
1 tablespoon minced shallot (about 1 medium shallot)
½ cup dry white wine

2 sprigs fresh thyme, or ½ teaspoon dried
1 bay leaf
salt and freshly ground pepper

Herb Sauce

20 spinach leaves, stems removed, leaves rinsed well
⅓ cup watercress leaves
¼ cup small parsley sprigs
2 tablespoons tarragon leaves (optional)

1 cup mayonnaise
salt and pepper
2 to 3 tablespoons warm water (optional)
lettuce leaves, for serving

Preheat oven to 425°F. Remove any scales from fish steaks. Generously grease a 10-cup oval gratin dish or other heavy shallow baking dish with soft margarine. Cut an oval piece of parchment paper to size of dish and grease paper. Sprinkle base of dish with chopped shallot. Arrange fish pieces in dish in one layer. Pour wine over them and add thyme and bay leaf. Sprinkle fish lightly with salt and pepper. Set greased paper directly on fish.

Bake fish for 12 minutes. To check if done, insert a cake tester or thin skewer into thickest part of fish for about 5 seconds and touch tester to underside of your wrist; it should be hot to touch. If fish is not quite done, bake another 2 minutes and test again.

Remove fish carefully to platter with 2 wide slotted spatulas. Cool to room temperature.

To make sauce, plunge spinach and watercress into a medium saucepan with boiling water. Return to a boil and drain. Rinse under cold water and drain thoroughly. Squeeze to remove excess liquid.

Puree the spinach, watercress, parsley, and tarragon in a food processor until smooth. If necessary, add 2 or 3 tablespoons of mayonnaise to help make a smoother puree. Add remaining mayonnaise and process until smooth. Taste, then add salt and pepper if needed. If sauce is very thick, beat in warm water 1 tablespoon at a time until it is just thin enough to be poured. (Sauce can be kept, covered, for 1 day in refrigerator.)

Serve cold, or at cool room temperature.

Remove skin from fish by scraping with paring knife and pulling it with your fingers. Serve salmon steaks on lettuce leaves, accompanying each serving with a spoonful of sauce. Serve any remaining sauce separately.

Makes 8 servings

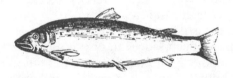

GEFILTE FISH

Gefilte fish means ''filled fish,'' and in some old-fashioned versions of the recipe the ground fish mixture is actually stuffed into fish slices. Now most people shape the ''filling'' into ovals or balls and omit the fish slices. Traditionally the dish is made from a mixture of equal quantities of three freshwater fish—carp, pike, and whitefish—but today cooks vary the fish according to what is available where they live. I use mostly whitefish with a little halibut, since the result is very delicate in flavor and has an appealing white color.

Gefilte fish is generally served on a bed of lettuce, with each piece garnished with a carrot slice. Sharp horseradish is the accompaniment de rigueur in most homes, but the family of a friend of mine from Mexico City serves gefilte fish with spicy chiles chipotles or hot salsa! Either way, it makes a refreshing appetizer that is low in calories.

1 3-pound whitefish (including bones
   and head), filleted

Fish Stock

3 pounds additional fish bones and
   head (optional)
2 medium onions, sliced

3 sprigs parsley
1 teaspoon salt
6 cups water

¾ pound halibut fillets
2 large eggs
2 medium onions, finely chopped
2 teaspoons salt
½ teaspoon ground pepper

2 tablespoons matzo meal
2 large carrots, peeled and sliced

bottled horseradish prepared with
 · beets, for serving

Set whitefish fillets on a board, skin side down. Slip blade of a flexible knife between flesh and skin and use it to remove skin of fish, sliding knife away from you with one hand and pulling off skin with other. Run your fingers carefully over fish fillets and remove any small bones remaining in flesh. Set fillets aside.

Rinse bones and heads of fish under cold water for at least 5 minutes. Combine all ingredients for stock in a large, deep saucepan or pot. Bring to a boil and skim off foam as it accumulates. Cover and simmer 30 minutes. Strain and return to pan. Taste for seasoning.

Grind whitefish and halibut fillets in 2 batches in a food processor until very fine. Return half the fish to food processor and add 1 egg, half the chopped onions, 1 teaspoon salt, and ¼ teaspoon pepper. Process well, then transfer to a large bowl. Repeat with remaining fish, egg, onions, salt, and pepper. Transfer to bowl and mix with first batch. Stir in matzo meal.

Add carrots to strained stock and bring to a simmer. With moistened hands, shape fish mixture into ovals or balls, using ¼ to ⅓ cup mixture for each. Carefully drop fish balls into simmering stock. Add enough hot water to barely cover them, if necessary, pouring it carefully into stock near edge of pan. Return to a simmer, cover, and simmer over low heat about 1 hour. Let cool in stock. Refrigerate fish and carrots in stock for at least 4 hours before serving. (Can be kept for 3 days in refrigerator.)

To serve, garnish each fish ball with a carrot slice. Pass horseradish separately.

Makes 18 to 20 pieces; 9 or 10 servings

ROAST LAMB WITH GARLIC, ONIONS, AND POTATOES

To facilitate the preparation of this succulent dish, a favorite of Jews in southern France, ask the butcher to trim the fat and skin from the lamb, and then to bone it, roll it, and tie it. Zucchini with Tomatoes and Dill (page 265) also makes a good accompaniment.

8 garlic cloves
5½-pound lamb shoulder, boned and
   tied in a rolled roast (about 3½
   pounds after boning), bones
   reserved if possible
salt and pepper

8 medium baking potatoes
2 medium onions, sliced
⅔ cup water
1 large tomato, peeled, seeded, and
   chopped
¼ cup chopped fresh parsley

Preheat oven to 375°F. Cut 12 very thin lengthwise slivers from garlic; chop remaining garlic. Pierce lamb with point of a sharp knife. With aid of knife, hold a slit open and insert a garlic sliver. Repeat with remaining garlic slivers, spacing them fairly evenly. Sprinkle lamb with salt and pepper. Put lamb bones in center of a large roasting pan and set roast on top of them; or set it on a rack.

Peel and quarter potatoes and put in pan around meat.

Sprinkle potatoes with remaining chopped garlic, salt, and pepper. Add sliced onions and water to pan.

Cover and bake 1 hour. Uncover and stir potatoes gently. Bake 30 minutes. Add tomato to pan juices and stir. Roast lamb until it is very tender and an instant-read or meat thermometer registers 150°F. for medium or 160°F. for well done, about 1 hour and 10 to 15 minutes; during roasting, baste lamb and potatoes occasionally, turn potatoes once or twice, and add a few tablespoons water to pan if it becomes dry.

Let meat rest on a board 10 to 15 minutes before carving. Meanwhile, spoon pan juices over potatoes and keep them warm in low oven. If bones are meaty, cut meat from bones. Remove strings from meat. Carve lamb into ½-inch slices, using a very sharp large knife. With a small knife, remove excess fat from slices.

Sprinkle potatoes and lamb with parsley and serve hot. Season pan juices to taste with salt and pepper; serve separately.

Makes 8 servings

ZUCCHINI CASSEROLE WITH DILL

A Sephardic-style kugel, or baked vegetable casserole, this makes a nice accompaniment for roast lamb or chicken.

2 pounds medium zucchini
1 large onion
5 large eggs
¼ cup chopped fresh parsley

2 tablespoons snipped fresh dill
⅓ cup matzo meal
4 tablespoons olive oil
salt and pepper

Preheat oven to 375°F. Grate zucchini and onion on large holes of grater. Put both in a strainer and squeeze firmly to remove excess liquid. Transfer zucchini and onion to a bowl. Add eggs, parsley, dill, matzo meal, and 1 tablespoon oil. Season quite generously with salt and pepper so mixture will not be bland. Mix well.

   Heat 2 tablespoons oil in a shallow 8-inch square baking dish in oven for 3 or 4 minutes. Add zucchini mixture to hot dish. Sprinkle with remaining oil. Bake 50 minutes to 1 hour or until set. Let stand about 5 minutes before serving. Serve hot.

Makes about 8 servings

ALSATIAN ALMOND-RAISIN MATZO KUGEL

The province of Alsace in eastern France has long been the home of a large Ashkenazic Jewish community and also happens to be one of the best regions of France for desserts, such as this unusually light matzo kugel, with crunchy chopped almonds, dark raisins, and a cinnamon-brandy glaze.

6 matzos
½ cup dark raisins
⅔ cup whole almonds
½ cup sugar

5 large eggs, separated
pinch of salt
1¼ teaspoons ground cinnamon

Glaze

¼ cup sugar
2 tablespoons brandy, plus 1 teaspoon
   if needed
½ teaspoon ground cinnamon

Preheat oven to 375°F. Grease a 9-inch square baking dish with margarine. Break matzos in small pieces and put in a bowl. Cover with hot water and let stand for 2 minutes. Put in a strainer and squeeze out as much water as possible. Put in a large bowl. Cover raisins with hot water. Let stand 5 minutes and drain.

Grind almonds in a food processor with 2 tablespoons sugar until fine. Add to bowl of matzo, then stir in egg yolks, salt, cinnamon, raisins, and 4 tablespoons sugar.

Beat egg whites until just stiff. Add remaining 2 tablespoons sugar and beat at high speed another ½ minute or until glossy. Gently fold egg whites, in 4 portions, into matzo mixture.

Spoon mixture into greased dish. Bake in preheated oven about 25 minutes or until firm.

Meanwhile prepare glaze: combine sugar, 2 tablespoons brandy, and cinnamon in small bowl and stir until well blended. If mixture is too thick to pour, add an additional teaspoon brandy.

When kugel is done, remove from oven and spoon glaze evenly over top. Brush glaze gently over cake. Cut in squares and serve hot or warm.

Makes about 8 servings

CHOCOLATE-HAZELNUT GÂTEAU

This cake is very rich, moist, and delicious without frosting. For a meatless dinner, you can substitute butter for the margarine and serve the cake with whipped cream (see Variation). Potato starch is often used in Passover cakes like this one and produces a tender, slightly crumbly texture.

1 cup (about 4½ ounces) hazelnuts (filberts)
½ cup sugar
5 ounces semisweet chocolate, chopped
2 tablespoons water

½ cup (1 stick) unsalted nondairy margarine, cut into 8 pieces, at room temperature
4 large eggs, separated, at room temperature
1 teaspoon vanilla extract
2 tablespoons potato starch

Preheat oven to 350°F. Toast hazelnuts in a shallow baking pan in oven about 8 minutes or until skins begin to split. Transfer to a strainer. While nuts are hot, remove most of skins by rubbing nuts energetically with a towel against strainer. Cool nuts completely.

Reduce oven temperature to 325°F. Lightly grease an 8-inch springform pan with 2½-inch sides, line its base with parchment paper or foil, and grease paper or foil.

Grind hazelnuts with 2 tablespoons sugar in a food processor until as fine as possible. Transfer to a bowl.

Place chocolate and water in a large bowl and set above hot water over low heat to melt. Stir until smooth. Add margarine and stir until blended. Remove from pan of water.

Whisk egg yolks to blend. Gradually add yolks to chocolate mixture, whisking vigorously. Stir in ¼ cup sugar, followed by vanilla, nuts, and potato starch. Mix well.

Whip egg whites in a large bowl until soft peaks form. Gradually beat in remaining 2 tablespoons sugar and whip at high speed until whites are stiff and shiny but not dry. Gently fold whites into chocolate mixture in 3 batches. Fold lightly but quickly, just until batter is blended.

Transfer batter to prepared pan and spread evenly. Bake about 1 hour or until a cake tester inserted in center of cake comes out clean.

Cool in pan on a rack for about 10 minutes. Run a thin-bladed flexible knife or metal spatula carefully around side of cake. Invert cake onto rack, gently release spring, and remove side and base of pan. Carefully remove paper and cool cake completely. Invert cake onto another rack, then onto a platter so that smooth side of cake faces up. (Cake can be kept, wrapped, up to 2 days at room temperature or in refrigerator.) Serve it at room temperature.

Makes 8 servings

VARIATION: For a dairy meal serve with whipped cream.

Whipped Cream and Garnish

1 cup heavy cream
2 teaspoons sugar
1 teaspoon vanilla extract

grated semisweet chocolate, for
sprinkling

Whip cream with sugar and vanilla in chilled bowl until stiff. Spread over top and sides of cake and sprinkle lightly with grated chocolate; or serve whipped cream separately. Chill frosted cake at least 1 hour before serving.

PASSOVER IN JERUSALEM

Passover has always been my favorite holiday. But I liked it more than ever during the years I lived in Israel as a college student. Back in my old home in Washington, D.C., Passover used to be a time for a family get-together and good traditional Ashkenazic food. In Israel there was the excitement of discovering the holiday specialties of my many new Sephardic in-laws. To me their food was exotic and fascinating.

One memorable Passover I celebrated was at my mother's new home in Jerusalem. We decided to prepare the Seder together with several of my new in-laws. Each person promised to cook a favorite dish. This would make it easier for everyone and would give us all the chance to taste each other's food.

First my mother and I went to the bustling Mahaneh Yehudah market to buy produce for the dinner, including the ritual foods for the Seder—celery, horseradish, and apples and nuts for haroset. This was the busiest time of the year, as everyone was getting ready for the Jewish festival with the greatest focus on cooking. Women were discussing their Passover menus while trying to keep their children from handling the fruit. There was a certain feeling of anticipation and, even though our shopping took longer than usual, it was great fun.

On the morning of the Seder we began cooking. My sister-in-law, of Moroccan origin, prepared a colorful, exuberant first course—a salad of sweet and hot peppers sautéed with tomatoes and garlic, often referred to in Israel simply as "Moroccan salad." Another sister-in-law made a delicious Israeli eggplant salad enriched with the local olive oil. A diced vegetable salad was the responsibility of my Israeli-born brother-in-law, since he has the patience to cut the vegetables in very tiny cubes, and everyone in the family agrees that his version of this refreshing Mediterranean salad is the best.

For the main course, we decided on turkey, and my mother-in-law, who is from Yemen, made a wonderful, aromatic matzo-and-mushroom stuffing seasoned with garlic and fresh coriander. Her sister brought an unusual treat—round homemade matzos, and an elegant embroidered cloth to cover them.

To serve with the turkey, my mother, who was born in Poland, baked an eastern European potato and vegetable kugel, a delicate casserole of potatoes, carrots, squash, and sautéed onions.

For dessert, my mother and I prepared an Austrian-style almond cake and topped it with a fluffy orange frosting. The cake gained its body from a generous amount of almonds and a little matzo meal, and was light textured and intensely flavored with almonds.

JERUSALEM PASSOVER MENU

Haroset with Dates and Pine Nuts
Zesty Pepper-Tomato Salad
Roasted Eggplant Salad with Olive Oil
and Garlic
Israeli Vegetable Salad
Roast Turkey with Matzo-Mushroom Stuffing
Potato and Vegetable Kugel
Passover Almond Cake with Orange Frosting

HAROSET WITH DATES AND PINE NUTS

Dates are a frequent addition to haroset in Israel, especially among Jews from North Africa, Iran, and Italy, and date juice flavors a version of haroset from India. In certain Sephardic recipes for haroset there are no apples; instead, a larger proportion of dried fruits is used, for a concentrated fruit taste. Sometimes the haroset is very thick and is rolled into balls or small log shapes. A Moroccan style of presenting haroset is to spread the mixture on plates and garnish it with toasted pine nuts, as in this recipe.

½ cup pecans or walnuts
3 to 4 tablespoons sugar
2 medium apples, peeled and cored
2 to 3 tablespoons lemon juice
1 teaspoon ground cinnamon

½ teaspoon ground ginger
½ cup almonds, chopped
12 pitted dates, chopped
¼ cup pine nuts
matzos, for serving

Grind pecans or walnuts with 3 tablespoons sugar in a food processor until fine. Grate apples and add 2 tablespoons lemon juice. Stir in ground nuts, cinnamon, ginger, almonds, and dates. Taste and add more sugar or lemon juice if desired.

　To serve, spread on a flat dish and sprinkle decoratively with pine nuts. Serve as a spread with matzos.

Makes 8 servings

ZESTY PEPPER-TOMATO SALAD

This spicy salad, regarded by Jews of Morocco, Algeria, and Turkey as their own, is one of my favorite appetizers. It is made of sautéed bell peppers that are then simmered gently with tomatoes, garlic, and chilies. It is great for Passover but also for Rosh Hashanah, when tomatoes and bell peppers are at the peak of their season. Cooking mellows the flavors, so that the garlic and hot peppers add sparkle but do not overwhelm the dish. SEE PHOTOGRAPH.

5 to 6 tablespoons olive oil
2 large green bell peppers, diced in ½-inch pieces
2 large red bell peppers, diced in ½-inch pieces
3 pounds ripe tomatoes, peeled, seeded, and diced; or 3 28-ounce cans plum tomatoes, drained and diced

salt to taste
4 jalapeño peppers, finely diced
12 medium garlic cloves, chopped

Heat 4 tablespoons oil in a large skillet over medium-low heat. Add bell peppers and sauté until softened, about 15 minutes. Remove with slotted spoon.

Add tomatoes to oil, sprinkle with salt, and cook over medium-low heat about 15 minutes or until thickened. Add sautéed peppers, jalapeño peppers, and garlic and cook over low heat about 10 minutes or until peppers are tender and mixture is thick. Remove from heat and stir in remaining 1 or 2 tablespoons oil. Taste and adjust seasoning. Serve at room temperature.

Makes 6 to 8 servings

ROASTED EGGPLANT SALAD WITH OLIVE OIL AND GARLIC

Variations on this delectable appetizer, which is also known as "eggplant caviar," are prepared throughout the eastern Mediterranean, from a Greek version flavored with oregano to a Lebanese with yogurt and mint to an Egyptian with tahini (sesame paste). In Israel this is called salad but it is really more like a spread.

Instead of being baked, the eggplant can be grilled so it acquires a smoky flavor, as on page 171. Serve it with matzos during Passover, and with bread or pita during the rest of the year. We sometimes add chopped fresh coriander, although it's not traditional, and serve the salad on baked potatoes, garnished with coriander sprigs.

4 medium eggplants (about 4½ pounds total)
2 or 3 medium garlic cloves, minced
3 to 4 tablespoons extra-virgin olive oil
1 to 2 teaspoons strained fresh lemon juice (optional)

2 to 3 tablespoons chopped fresh coriander (cilantro) (optional)
salt and freshly ground pepper
fresh parsley sprigs, for garnish

Preheat oven to 400°F. Pierce each eggplant a few times with a fork to prevent it from bursting. Bake whole eggplants on a large baking sheet lined with foil for 30 minutes. Turn eggplants over and bake them 30 to 40 minutes or until very tender when pricked with a fork. Leave eggplants until cool enough to handle. Holding cap, peel off skin of each eggplant. Drain eggplants in a colander for 1 hour.

Cut off eggplant caps. Chop the flesh, using a knife, until it is a chunky puree. In a large bowl combine eggplant puree, garlic, oil, lemon juice, coriander, and salt and pepper to taste; mix well—salad should be highly seasoned. Refrigerate at least 30 minutes before serving. (Salad can be kept, covered, up to 3 days in refrigerator.)

Spoon salad into a shallow bowl and garnish with parsley sprigs.

Makes 8 to 10 servings

NOTE: If you like, make this a smooth puree. Puree the eggplant with the garlic in a food processor until smooth. With machine running, pour in olive oil, then add lemon juice. Stir in remaining ingredients.

ISRAELI VEGETABLE SALAD

Recently I read a prediction in a major paper that Mediterranean salads of diced raw vegetables will become a hot item in American restaurants. What surprises me is that it has taken us so long to discover them. In Israel this salad of diced raw vegetables is a must at all kinds of meals, from the most festive party to the simplest supper. Cubes of tomato and cucumber are the basic ingredients but frequent additions are diced bell peppers, shredded green or red cabbage, diced radishes, or a small amount of diced celery or chopped red or yellow onion. For a pretty presentation, cut the vegetables in dice no larger than ½ inch and serve the salad in a glass bowl.

8 medium tomatoes, cut into small dice

1 long (European) cucumber or 2 medium cucumbers, cut into small dice

2 medium red or green bell peppers or fresh pimientos, cut into small dice

3 tablespoons chopped fresh parsley

3 tablespoons chopped fresh coriander (cilantro) (optional)

3 tablespoons chopped green onions (optional)

2 to 3 tablespoons extra-virgin olive or vegetable oil

2 to 3 teaspoons strained fresh lemon juice

salt and freshly ground pepper

Mix the diced tomatoes, cucumber, peppers, parsley, coriander, and green onions. Add oil, lemon juice, and salt and pepper to taste. Serve at cool room temperature.

Makes 8 servings

ROAST TURKEY
WITH MATZO-MUSHROOM STUFFING

This turkey is a good choice for entertaining, whether for Passover or Thanksgiving! For Rosh Hashanah, I like turkey with a fruity rice stuffing, as in the chicken recipe on page 75. Potato and Vegetable Kugel makes a delicious accompaniment.

Matzo-Mushroom Stuffing (recipe follows)
10- to 12-pound fresh or frozen turkey, thawed
salt and freshly ground pepper
½ cup (1 stick) nondairy margarine, softened

3 cups chicken soup or stock
½ cup dry white wine
4 teaspoons potato starch, dissolved in 3 tablespoons dry white wine
2 tablespoons chopped fresh coriander (cilantro) or parsley

Prepare stuffing. Preheat oven to 425°F. and remove top rack. Sprinkle turkey inside and out with salt and pepper. Spoon some stuffing into neck cavity. Fold neck skin under body and fasten with a skewer. Pack body cavity loosely with stuffing and cover opening with a crumpled piece of foil. Truss turkey if desired with a trussing string and needle or close it with skewers. Spoon remaining stuffing into an oiled 1-quart baking dish.

Spread turkey with ¼ cup margarine and set it, breast side up, on a rack in a large roasting pan. Roast for 30 minutes, basting twice. Melt remaining ¼ cup margarine in a medium saucepan and put an 8-inch double piece of cheesecloth in saucepan of margarine.

Reduce oven temperature to 350°F. Cover turkey breast with soaked cheesecloth, then roast turkey for 1½ hours, basting with pan juices and any remaining margarine every 15 minutes. If pan becomes dry, add ¼ cup chicken soup or stock.

Put dish of extra stuffing in oven and baste with a little of turkey juices. Cover with foil; bake about 45 minutes. Meanwhile, continue roasting turkey, basting occasionally, until juices run clear when leg is pricked or instant-read meat thermometer inserted into thickest part of thigh registers 180°F., about 20 to 45 minutes. Transfer turkey carefully to platter or large board. Discard strings, skewers, and cheesecloth. Baste once with pan juices, and cover turkey.

Skim excess fat from juices in pan. Add wine and ½ cup soup and bring to a boil, stirring and scraping to dissolve any brown bits in pan. Strain into a saucepan. Add remaining soup and bring to a boil over medium heat. Whisk in potato starch mixture then return to a boil, whisking, and simmer until thick enough to lightly coat a spoon. Add coriander or parsley. Taste and adjust seasoning.

Carve turkey and arrange on platter. Spoon stuffing onto platter or into a serving dish. Reheat sauce briefly, then pour into a sauceboat and serve alongside turkey.

Makes 6 to 8 servings

Matzo-Mushroom Stuffing

Although this stuffing is designed for Passover, it makes a great partner for poultry all year round. In addition to the mushrooms, the stuffing owes its good taste to onions, garlic, and a generous amount of fresh coriander.

8 matzos
1½ cups hot chicken soup or stock
5 tablespoons olive oil
2 large onions, chopped
salt and pepper

8 ounces small button mushrooms,
  quartered
4 large garlic cloves, minced
3 large eggs, beaten
⅓ cup chopped fresh coriander
  (cilantro) or parsley

Crumble matzos into a large bowl and pour hot soup over them.

Heat 4 tablespoons oil in a large skillet and add onions and a pinch of salt and pepper. Sauté over medium heat, stirring often, about 7 minutes or until onions begin to turn golden. Add remaining tablespoon oil, then add mushrooms and sauté 5 minutes or until tender. Remove from heat and stir in garlic. Add mushroom mixture to matzo mixture and let cool. Stir in eggs and coriander or parsley and taste for seasoning.

Makes about 7 cups

POTATO AND VEGETABLE KUGEL

For better color and a more interesting flavor, my mother often adds shredded carrots and squash as well as sautéed onions to the familiar grated potato kugel.

2 tablespoons plus 1 teaspoon
  vegetable oil
1 large onion, chopped
1 pound yellow squash
2 large carrots, peeled
2 large baking potatoes

3 large eggs
1 teaspoon salt
¼ teaspoon ground pepper
⅓ cup chopped fresh parsley
1 teaspoon paprika
¼ cup matzo meal

Preheat oven to 350°F. Heat 2 tablespoons oil in a skillet, add onion, and sauté over medium-low heat until softened, about 10 minutes.

Coarsely grate squash and carrots. Transfer to a large bowl and add sautéed onion. Peel and coarsely grate potatoes, put in large strainer, and squeeze out excess liquid; add to bowl of vegetables. Add eggs, salt, pepper, parsley, paprika, and matzo meal.

Generously grease an 8-inch square pan or a 7-cup baking dish. Heat briefly in oven, then add vegetable mixture. Sprinkle with 1 teaspoon oil, then shake a little paprika on top. Bake about 1 hour or until brown and set.

Makes 6 to 8 servings

PASSOVER ALMOND CAKE WITH ORANGE FROSTING

As is typical in Passover baking, a generous quantity of ground almonds is used to give this cake flavor, richness, and body. The cake is wonderful on its own, but the luscious fresh citrus frosting and the sprinkling of toasted sliced almonds make for a festive look. Serve the cake with fresh strawberries or orange segments.

1½ cups (about 8 ounces) whole
   unblanched almonds
¼ cup matzo meal

1 cup granulated sugar
4 large eggs, separated

Orange Frosting

¾ cup (1½ sticks) unsalted nondairy
   margarine, softened slightly
⅓ cup superfine sugar
1 tablespoon finely grated orange rind

3 tablespoons strained fresh orange
   juice
2 tablespoons toasted sliced almonds,
   for garnish (optional)

Preheat oven to 350°F. Grease a 9-inch springform pan with margarine and flour pan with a little matzo meal.

Grind almonds with matzo meal and ¼ cup granulated sugar in food processor until fine. Beat egg yolks with ½ cup sugar at high speed of mixer until light and fluffy. Set aside.

In clean bowl, whip egg whites to soft peaks. Gradually beat in remaining ¼ cup sugar, beating until stiff and shiny.

Alternately in 3 batches, fold whites and almond mixture into yolk mixture. Transfer to pan and bake about 35 minutes or until a cake tester or toothpick inserted in center of cake comes out dry. Cool slightly, then run a metal spatula gently around cake and remove sides of springform. Cool on a rack. Cake will sink slightly.

For frosting, cream margarine and superfine sugar until smooth. Add grated orange rind, then gradually add juice and beat until smooth and fluffy. Spread frosting on sides and top of cake. Sprinkle top with toasted sliced almonds. (Cake can be kept, covered, for 2 days in refrigerator but remove 1 hour before serving.) Serve at room temperature.

Makes 8 to 10 servings

PASSOVER IN CALIFORNIA

Many of the Passover dishes most familiar in this country come from eastern and central Europe and are based on ingredients that were available there. Since we are lucky to be blessed with an extraordinary variety of fresh vegetables and fruits, we now use them in our traditional dishes to add a touch of elegance, color, and lightness for a festive Seder menu.

In addition, we like to cook some of the specialties of the Mediterranean and Middle Eastern Jews to add new flavors to our Passover menus. These dishes are perfectly suited to southern California, since the climate and produce are similar.

In this spirit, the familiar matzo ball soup is transformed into a chicken soup with asparagus and almond matzo balls. Roast lamb, a favorite for the Seder menu, comes with a fresh spinach stuffing and is served with Sephardic cauliflower in an aromatic tomato sauce. Haroset, the apple and nut spread served with matzo, is prepared in the Moroccan style—flavored with the tang of citrus juice and garnished with pine nuts. A pecan and cocoa torte, using the New World's pecans as the basis for a rich European-style cake, makes a grande finale for the Passover feast.

ECLECTIC PASSOVER MENU

Haroset with Dates and Pine Nuts (page 17)
**Chicken Soup with Asparagus
and Almond Kneidlach**
Roast Lamb Shoulder with Spinach Stuffing
Cauliflower in Tomato Sauce
Green Salad
**Pecan-Cocoa Torte with
Chocolate-Cinnamon Frosting**

CHICKEN SOUP WITH ASPARAGUS AND ALMOND KNEIDLACH

Passover is the holiday of spring, so asparagus is a natural, fresh addition to the customary chicken soup. Ground almonds and a surprise blanched almond in the center of each kneidel (matzo ball) add a festive note.

2 pounds chicken wings	2 celery stalks, including leafy tops
9 cups cold water	5 parsley sprigs
1 large onion, peeled	salt and pepper
1 large carrot, peeled	16 asparagus spears

Almond Matzo Balls

2 large eggs	½ teaspoon salt
1 tablespoon vegetable oil	pinch of ground ginger
½ cup matzo meal	2 tablespoons water
2 tablespoons finely chopped blanched almonds	12 to 15 blanched almonds, cut in half lengthwise

To make chicken soup, combine chicken wings, water, onion, carrot, celery, parsley and salt in a large saucepan and bring to a boil. Skim thoroughly. Partly cover and simmer 1½ to 2 hours, skimming occasionally. Skim off excess fat. (Chicken soup can be kept 3 days in refrigerator; skim fat again and reheat before serving.) Add pepper and taste for seasoning.

Peel asparagus and cut off white bases. Cut stalks in 1-inch pieces and leave tips whole.

To make matzo balls, lightly beat eggs with oil in a medium mixing bowl. Add matzo meal, chopped almonds, salt, and ginger and stir until well blended. Stir in water. Let mixture stand for 20 minutes so matzo meal absorbs liquid.

Bring about 2 quarts salted water to a boil in a large saucepan. With wet hands, take about 1 teaspoon of matzo ball mixture and roll it between your palms into a ball; mixture will be soft. Set balls on a plate. Push half a blanched almond into center of each, letting one end of almond show. With a rubber spatula, carefully slide balls into boiling water. Cover and simmer over low heat about 30 minutes or until firm. Keep them warm and covered until ready to serve. (Matzo balls can be made 2 days ahead and kept covered, in their cooking liquid, in refrigerator; reheat gently in cooking liquid or in soup before serving.)

Discard onion, carrot, celery, and parsley from soup. Shortly before serving, add asparagus to soup and simmer about 7 minutes or until tender. To serve, ladle soup into bowls and add a few asparagus pieces to each. With a slotted spoon, add 2 or 3 matzo balls, with their almonds showing. Serve hot.

Makes 8 servings

ROAST LAMB SHOULDER WITH SPINACH STUFFING

Lamb is the meat of choice for Passover in many Sephardic communities. Here it is spread with an Italian-style garlic-accented spinach matzo stuffing, then rolled and roasted.

Spinach and Matzo Stuffing

4 matzos
1 cup hot chicken soup or stock
¼ cup vegetable oil
2 medium onions, finely chopped
salt and pepper

4 garlic cloves, minced
3 pounds fresh spinach, or 2 10-ounce
 packages frozen leaf spinach
3 large eggs
freshly grated nutmeg to taste

5½- to 6-pound lamb shoulder, boned,
 with a pocket cut for stuffing (about
 4½ pounds after boning)

1 garlic clove, halved
salt and pepper

Preheat oven to 450°F. To make stuffing, crumble matzos into small pieces in a bowl and pour soup over them. Mix well. Let stand about 15 minutes. Heat oil in a large skillet and add onions, salt, and pepper. Sauté over medium heat, stirring often, about 10 minutes or until softened. Add garlic and cook ½ minute.

If using fresh spinach, remove stems and rinse leaves well. Cook spinach, uncovered, in a very large saucepan of boiling salted water over high heat until tender, about 3 minutes; or cook frozen spinach 2 minutes. Rinse with cold water and squeeze by hand until dry. Chop with knife or in food processor.

Add onion mixture, spinach, and eggs to matzo mixture and season to taste with salt, pepper, and nutmeg. Mixture should be generously seasoned so it will stand up to flavor of lamb.

Fill pocket in lamb shoulder with stuffing, packing it in firmly; you will need about half the stuffing. Close pocket with skewers or sew it closed with trussing needle and kitchen string. Set lamb in a medium roasting pan. Rub lamb vigorously with cut garlic clove and sprinkle it with salt and pepper. Roast 15 minutes to sear lamb, then reduce oven temperature to 350°F. and continue roasting until very tender, about 1¾ to 2 hours longer or until a meat thermometer inserted in meat registers 155–160°F.

Meanwhile, spoon the remaining stuffing into a greased deep 4- to 5-cup baking dish; bake alongside lamb at 350°F. for about 30 minutes or until firm.

Let meat rest on a cutting board for 15 minutes. Carve into ½- to ¾-inch slices, using a very sharp large knife. With a small knife, remove any excess fat from each slice. Use a broad spatula to transfer slices to each plate. Serve extra stuffing separately.

Makes 8 to 10 servings

CAULIFLOWER IN TOMATO SAUCE

Sephardic Jews prepare many vegetables in tomato sauce and in general prefer them cooked until very tender rather than crunchy. When this dish is prepared the old-fashioned way, the cauliflower is dipped in batter and fried before being simmered in tomato sauce, but this is a lighter version, more in keeping with today's style.

2 tablespoons olive or vegetable oil
½ medium onion, chopped
2 large garlic cloves, minced
2½ pounds ripe tomatoes, peeled, seeded, and chopped; or 2 28-ounce cans plum tomatoes, drained and chopped
1 tablespoon tomato paste

½ cup water
1 bay leaf
½ teaspoon dried oregano
salt and pepper to taste
1 large cauliflower, divided into medium florets
1 tablespoon chopped fresh parsley (optional)

Heat oil in a large saucepan over medium heat. Add onion and sauté, stirring occasionally, about 5 minutes or until it begins to brown. Add garlic, tomatoes, tomato paste, water, bay leaf, oregano, salt, and pepper. Cook over medium heat, stirring often, about 30 minutes or until tomatoes are soft and mixture is thick and smooth. Discard bay leaf. Taste and adjust seasoning. (Sauce can be kept, covered, 2 days in refrigerator. Reheat before continuing.)

Cook cauliflower uncovered in a large pan of boiling salted water over high heat about 3 to 4 minutes or until nearly tender. Drain, rinse with cold water, and drain thoroughly.

Add cauliflower to tomato sauce, cover, and simmer, gently turning florets occasionally, about 5 minutes or until very tender. Taste and adjust seasoning. Serve hot or at room temperature. Sprinkle with parsley when serving.

Makes 4 to 6 servings

PECAN-COCOA TORTE
WITH CHOCOLATE-CINNAMON FROSTING

For an impressive Passover dessert, this layer cake is often my choice. The luscious cinnamon-accented frosting is wonderfully rich and chocolatey but not overly sweet.

3½ cups (12 ounces) pecans
1½ cups granulated sugar
5 tablespoons matzo cake meal or
 sifted matzo meal

2 tablespoons unsweetened cocoa
1 teaspoon ground cinnamon
6 large eggs, separated, at room
 temperature

Chocolate-Cinnamon Frosting

5 ounces semisweet chocolate,
 chopped
1 cup (2 sticks) unsalted nondairy
 margarine, at room temperature
½ cup superfine sugar

1 tablespoon unsweetened cocoa
½ teaspoon ground cinnamon
2 large eggs, at room temperature
8 to 10 pecan halves, for garnish

Preheat oven to 350°F. Using margarine, grease two 9-inch round cake pans about 1½ inches deep. Line base of each with parchment paper or foil and grease parchment or foil. Use a little matzo cake meal to flour sides of pans and lined bases, tapping to remove excess.

In a food processor grind pecans with ½ cup granulated sugar in 2 batches to a fine powder. Transfer to a bowl. Sift cake meal with cocoa and cinnamon. Add to pecan mixture and stir until blended.

Beat egg yolks with ½ cup sugar in a large bowl for about 5 minutes or until mixture is pale yellow and very thick.

Beat egg whites in another large bowl until soft peaks form. Gradually add remaining ½ cup sugar and whip at high speed about ½ minute or until whites are very stiff and shiny but not dry. Sprinkle one-third of pecan mixture over yolks and fold gently until nearly blended. Spoon one-third of whites on top and fold gently. Repeat until all pecan mixture and whites are added. Fold just until blended and no white streaks remain.

Pour into prepared pans and quickly spread evenly. Bake about 30 minutes or until a cake tester inserted in center of cakes comes out clean. Without releasing cakes, set a rack on each pan, turn over, and leave upside down for 10 minutes, with pan still on each cake. Turn back over. Run a thin-bladed flexible knife around sides of each cake. Turn out onto racks, carefully peel off paper, and let cool completely.

To make frosting, melt chocolate in a small saucepan set above hot water over low heat. Let cool. Cream margarine in a large bowl until very soft and smooth. Add superfine sugar, cocoa, and cinnamon and beat until smooth. Beat in eggs one by one at high speed, then beat in melted chocolate.

Spread about one-third of the frosting on one cake layer. Set second layer on top. (Carefully trim top layer if necessary, using a serrated knife, so cake is even.) Spread frosting on sides and top of cake and smooth with a long metal spatula. Garnish top with a circle of pecan halves near edge of cake. Refrigerate at least 1 hour before serving. (Frosted cake can be kept 2 days in refrigerator.)

Makes 12 servings

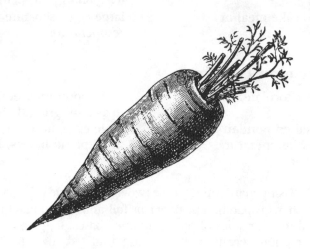

DAIRY PASSOVER MENU

For the first night of Passover, the Seder is usually planned around a main course of roast meat or poultry. The second night is often more casual. When I was growing up, my mother always prepared a *milchig* dinner, featuring dairy foods, for the second Seder. To us, as children, this dinner was even more fun than the Seder of the first night because we were allowed to spread butter on our matzos.

On this night we could enjoy our favorite treats: Passover cheese kugel topped with sour cream, Passover pancakes, and fried matzo with eggs. Sometimes my mother even made special Passover rolls that could double as cream puffs. For dessert, we could look forward to a rich chocolate-nut cake frosted with real whipped cream. It was a true feast that we would remember for the rest of the year.

DAIRY PASSOVER MENU

Orange-Scented Haroset with Wine
Gefilte Fish (page 9)
Passover Cheese Pancakes,
or Fried Matzo with Eggs
Savory Mushrooms with Thyme and Olive Oil
Steamed Broccoli or Other Green Vegetable
Passover "Rolls"
Lemon-Scented Cheese Kugel with Raisins
Ashkenazic Walnut Torte
with Chocolate Glaze,
or Chocolate Hazelnut Gâteau
with Whipped Cream (page 14)

ORANGE-SCENTED HAROSET WITH WINE

This is a fresh-tasting haroset, made of apples and nuts and flavored with orange juice and zest. Other fresh fruit can be added as well. Iranian Jews sometimes add bananas and pears to their haroset, and season it with saffron and pepper as well as wine.

½ cup hazelnuts (filberts)
½ cup walnuts
¼ cup sugar
2 large apples, peeled, halved, and
  cored

3 tablespoons sweet red wine
2 tablespoons strained fresh orange
  juice
grated zest of ½ orange
matzos, for serving

Grind hazelnuts and walnuts with sugar in a food processor until fairly fine, leaving a few small chunks. Transfer to a bowl. Chop apples in food processor until fine, then add to nut mixture. Stir in wine, orange juice, and grated zest.

Spoon into a bowl. Serve at room temperature or cold, accompanied by matzos.

Makes 8 servings

PASSOVER CHEESE PANCAKES

Serve these for brunch with a mixture of cinnamon and sugar or with a bowl of sour cream. Alternatively, serve them as an appetizer with a topping of sautéed vegetables, especially mushrooms or leeks.

1 cup (8 ounces) cottage cheese
4 large eggs, beaten
½ cup matzo meal
2 tablespoons (¼ stick) butter, melted

pinch of salt
pinch of black pepper (optional)
¼ cup (½ stick) butter and ¼ cup
  vegetable oil, for frying

Mix cottage cheese with eggs, matzo meal, melted butter, and salt and pepper to taste.

Heat 2 tablespoons butter and 2 tablespoons oil in a large heavy skillet. Add about 1 tablespoon batter for each pancake and fry over medium heat until lightly browned on each side, about 2 minutes per side. Use 2 slotted spatulas to turn them carefully. Remove with a slotted spoon when done and continue frying remaining batter, adding more butter and oil as pan becomes dry; reduce heat if fat begins to brown. Serve hot.

Makes 4 to 6 servings

FRIED MATZO WITH EGGS

Originally a Passover dish, known in Yiddish as matzo brei, *this simple preparation has become a favorite of many Ashkenazim throughout the year. There are various ways to cook the matzo and egg mixture—as an omelet, as scrambled eggs, or as small pancakes. It makes a good breakfast, brunch, or light supper dish. Serve it alone or accompanied by applesauce, sugar, or jam.*

4 matzos
4 large eggs

½ teaspoon salt
3 to 4 tablespoons (½ stick) butter

Soak matzos in cold water for about 10 minutes and drain. Break them into bite-size squares or larger. Beat eggs with salt and pour over matzos. Stir until matzos are coated.

Melt butter in a heavy skillet and add batter. Cook the mixture as you like, frying it until done to your taste: either add all the mixture and brown it on both sides, like a flat omelet; fry by tablespoonfuls, like small pancakes; or fry, stirring, like scrambled eggs.

Makes 4 servings

SAVORY MUSHROOMS
WITH THYME AND OLIVE OIL

A mushroom first course or side dish like this one, flavored with the Moroccan seasoning combination of garlic, cumin, paprika, and thyme, can be found in many Israeli homes and is the mushroom dish we cook most often. We use olive oil on its own for cooking the mushrooms for a meal that includes meat, or a mixture of olive oil and butter for a fish dinner. The cooking time is relatively long so the mushrooms absorb the seasonings well.

¼ cup olive oil or 4 tablespoons (½ stick) butter
1 medium onion, chopped
1 pound fairly small button mushrooms, quartered
salt and freshly ground pepper

1 teaspoon dried leaf thyme, crumbled
½ teaspoon paprika
1 teaspoon ground cumin
cayenne pepper to taste
1 tablespoon chopped fresh parsley

Heat oil in a large skillet over medium heat. Add onion and sauté about 7 minutes or until tender. Add mushrooms, salt, pepper, thyme, paprika, and cumin. Sauté, stirring often, for

15 to 20 minutes or until mushrooms are well coated with spices and any liquid that accumulated in pan has evaporated; reduce heat toward the end of cooking time if necessary. Add cayenne; taste and adjust seasoning. (Mushrooms can be kept, covered, for 2 days in refrigerator. Reheat over medium heat.) Add parsley and serve.

Makes 4 servings

PASSOVER "ROLLS"

These rolls are a traditional recipe among Ashkenazic Jews, and are sold in Paris by Jewish bakeries in the "European Jewish" section of the city on and around rue des Rosiers. The rolls are actually made of cream puff dough, or pâte à choux, with matzo meal used instead of flour. Like cream puffs, they are hollow in the center. They can also be split, filled, and served as appetizer or dessert cream puffs.

1 cup water	1 teaspoon salt
½ cup (1 stick) unsalted margarine or butter	1½ cups matzo meal
	5 large eggs

Preheat oven to 400°F. Grease 2 baking sheets. Heat water, margarine, and salt in a medium saucepan over medium-low heat until margarine melts. Raise heat and bring to a boil. Remove from heat and add matzo meal all at once. Mix well. Return pan to low heat and cook, stirring, for 1 minute. Remove from heat and cool about 5 minutes.

Beat in 1 egg. When mixture is completely smooth, beat in a second egg. Continue adding eggs one by one, beating thoroughly after each addition.

Drop batter by heaping tablespoons (measuring about 2 tablespoons each) onto baking sheets, allowing about 1½ inches between them. Bake about 40 minutes or until golden brown and firm.

Makes about 20 rolls

LEMON-SCENTED CHEESE KUGEL WITH RAISINS

During Passover, matzos replace the usual noodles in kugel. For a meatless Passover menu, this slightly sweet baked pudding enriched with cottage cheese and studded with nuts and raisins can play the role of either main course or dessert.

4 matzos
2 cups (16 ounces) cottage cheese,
   preferably small curd
3 large eggs
½ teaspoon salt
⅓ cup sugar
1 tablespoon lemon juice

grated rind of ½ lemon
½ cup raisins
½ cup broken or coarsely chopped
   walnuts
6 tablespoons (¾ stick) unsalted
   butter, melted
sour cream, for serving

Preheat oven to 325°F. Soak whole matzos in cold water to cover until slightly softened but not mushy, about 1½ minutes. Drain thoroughly. Mix cottage cheese, eggs, salt, sugar, lemon juice, lemon rind, raisins, and walnuts.

Pour about 3 tablespoons melted butter into an 8-inch square baking dish or 2-quart cake pan. Set 1 whole matzo in pan, filling in any spaces with pieces from another matzo. Spread half the cheese mixture in pan. Cover with another layer of matzos. Spread remaining cheese mixture in pan. Top with a layer of matzos. Sprinkle remaining melted butter on top. Bake for about 1 hour or until set and top is browned.

Serve hot or lukewarm. Cut in squares and serve with sour cream.

Makes 6 servings

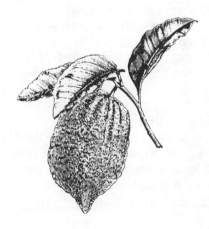

ASHKENAZIC WALNUT TORTE
WITH CHOCOLATE GLAZE

Ground nuts and matzo meal instead of flour give body to this rich Hungarian-style sponge cake. Matzo meal is made from ground matzos; matzo cake meal is more finely ground.

After baking, the cake is cooled upside down in the pan so it won't sink. The cake should be baked in a tube pan that has small "feet" to enable the air to circulate under the cake while it cools. If your tube pan does not have feet, you can cool the cake on a rack. The pan is not greased, or the cake would fall out. For the same reason, nonstick pans should not be used.

1¾ cups walnuts
¼ cup matzo cake meal or matzo meal
1 cup plus 2 tablespoons sugar
7 large eggs, separated

grated rind ½ orange
1 tablespoon orange juice
tiny pinch of salt

Chocolate Glaze (optional)

3 ounces bittersweet or semisweet
   chocolate
3 tablespoons water
3 tablespoons unsalted margarine

3 tablespoons sugar

8 to 10 walnut halves, for garnish

Preheat oven to 350°F. Have ready a 10-inch tube pan with 4⅛-inch sides and a removable bottom. Do not grease pan.

In a food processor, finely grind the walnuts with matzo cake meal and 3 tablespoons sugar, using an on/off motion. Transfer mixture to a bowl.

In a large bowl, beat yolks until blended. Gradually beat in ½ cup plus 2 tablespoons sugar. Beat at high speed about 5 minutes or until yolk mixture is very thick and light in color. Beat in orange rind, then gradually beat in orange juice.

In another large bowl whip egg whites with a pinch of salt until soft peaks form. Gradually beat in remaining 5 tablespoons sugar. Whip at high speed about ½ minute until glossy. Fold one-third of the nut mixture into yolks, followed by one-third of whites. Continue with remaining mixtures, adding last batch of whites before nuts are completely blended in. Fold as lightly but as quickly as possible.

Transfer batter immediately to pan and smooth top. Bake in center of oven about 1 hour and 5 minutes or until a cake tester inserted into cake comes out dry. (Cake rises more at sides than in center but will look fine when it's turned out.) Turn cake upside down in pan and leave about 2 hours or until completely cool.

To remove cake from pan, run a thin-bladed knife around sides of cake. Push up bottom and remove sides of pan. Slide knife around tube, then very carefully under cake. Turn cake over onto a large platter. (Cake can be kept, covered, for 2 days in refrigerator.)

To make glaze, combine all ingredients except nuts in a small heavy saucepan and heat over low heat, stirring until smooth. Spoon slowly over cake and allow glaze to drip down sides. Decorate with walnut halves. Refrigerate briefly so glaze sets.

Makes about 10 servings

A SEPHARDIC SEDER

For the majority of Jews in America, who are of Ashkenazic, or eastern and central European, origin, Passover menus begin with gefilte fish, followed by chicken soup with matzo balls and roast chicken as a main course. This had been my own experience when I was growing up, and I always looked forward to the holiday dinners. But Passover menus became even more exciting for me when I moved to Israel and discovered the flavorful Sephardic, or Mediterranean Jewish, cuisine.

Sephardic Seders also feature fish as an appetizer, but it is likely to be baked with olive oil, garlic, and saffron. Chicken soup appears, too, but it is embellished with spring vegetables—artichokes, young leeks, spring onions, and fava beans.

Lamb, a Mediterranean favorite, is a popular choice for the main course on the Sephardic holiday menu, but braised beef, chicken, or even both might be offered instead. In keeping with the Mediterranean tradition, a colorful assortment of salads—of both cooked and uncooked vegetables—adorns the Seder table. Dessert is usually fresh fruit, fruit salad, or a light cake.

The following menu is for a Seder in the Sephardic tradition, and includes Moroccan and Yemenite Jewish specialties. To make cooking easier, virtually the entire meal can be prepared ahead. Only a few finishing touches need be done before the dinner.

A SEPHARDIC SEDER MENU

Date-Almond-Walnut Haroset
Baked Fish with Saffron and Red Bell Peppers
Spring Vegetable Soup with Fresh Herbs
Mediterranean Vegetable Salad
Carrot and Asparagus Salad
Yemenite Beef and Chicken Casserole,
or Yemenite Braised Lamb with
Cumin and Garlic
Moroccan Potato Casserole
Passover Almond Cake with Strawberry Sauce

DATE-ALMOND-WALNUT HAROSET

Sephardic versions of haroset have an intense fruit flavor, as in this recipe, which contains a generous amount of dates. While Ashkenazic haroset has a large proportion of apples, Sephardic versions may or may not contain them.

8 ounces pitted dates, preferably dark
 ones
½ cup almonds
½ cup walnuts
about ¼ cup sweet red wine
 (traditional Passover wine)

¾ teaspoon ground ginger
½ teaspoon ground cinnamon
pinch of freshly ground black pepper
2 pinches ground cloves
1 medium apple

Halve dates and remove any remaining pits or pit fragments. Finely chop almonds and walnuts in food processor and remove. Add dates, ¼ cup wine, and spices to processor and grind until fairly smooth. Mix with nuts. Grate apple coarsely and stir in. Add more wine by teaspoons if necessary to make a mixture that is spreadable but still thick.

Makes 1¾ cups; 8 to 12 servings

BAKED FISH WITH SAFFRON AND RED BELL PEPPERS

Moroccan Jews make this dish with whole fish, but fillets make it easier to prepare and to eat. Serve it hot or at room temperature. SEE PHOTOGRAPH.

6 tablespoons extra-virgin olive oil
1 large red bell pepper, diced in ½-
 inch pieces
5 large garlic cloves, chopped
¼ teaspoon saffron threads
cayenne pepper to taste

2 pounds halibut, cod, scrod, or sea
 bass steaks or fillets, about ½- to ¾-
 inch thick, cut into 8 pieces
½ teaspoon dried thyme, crumbled
salt and freshly ground pepper
4 teaspoons chopped fresh parsley

Preheat oven to 400°F. Heat 4 tablespoons olive oil in a large ovenproof skillet. Add bell pepper and cook over low heat 10 minutes or until tender. Add garlic, saffron, and cayenne and cook ½ minute.

Divide mixture between 2 skillets if necessary, so that fish will form a single layer; heat second skillet a few seconds. Set fish on pepper mixture, folding under any thin "tails"; turn fish to coat with seasoning mixture. Sprinkle fish with remaining 2 tablespoons oil, then with thyme, salt, and pepper. Cover with foil and bake 15 minutes or until fish can just be flaked but is not falling apart. Taste liquid and adjust seasoning.

Serve fish hot or lukewarm. Sprinkle with parsley, then spoon some of the cooking juices with peppers over each piece.

Makes 8 servings

SPRING VEGETABLE SOUP WITH FRESH HERBS

North African Jews prepare this light soup for Passover with fresh fava beans. If your family doesn't eat beans for the holiday, substitute the zucchini.

6 cups chicken stock
2 cups water
1 large onion, diced
2 garlic cloves, chopped
2 celery stalks, peeled and sliced thin
salt and freshly ground pepper
2 large leeks (about 1 pound), split
   and cleaned
1½ pounds fresh fava beans, shelled;
   or 1 10-ounce package frozen baby
   lima beans (about 2 cups) or butter
   beans; or 2 small zucchini, diced

4 fresh artichokes or 16 pieces frozen
   artichoke hearts
1 lemon (if using fresh artichokes)
⅓ cup chopped fresh mint
⅓ cup chopped fresh parsley
⅓ cup chopped fresh coriander
   (cilantro)
cayenne pepper to taste
matzos, as accompaniment

Combine stock, water, onion, garlic, celery, salt, and pepper in saucepan. Bring to a boil. Cover and cook over low heat 20 minutes. Slice the white, light green, and 2 inches of dark green parts of leeks and add to soup. Add beans or zucchini and frozen artichoke pieces, if using, and return to a boil. Cover and cook over low heat 30 minutes or until vegetables are tender.

If using fresh artichokes, prepare artichoke hearts and cook them separately (see page 346). Quarter them and add to soup.

Add mint, parsley, coriander, and cayenne to soup. Taste and adjust seasoning. Serve with matzos.

Makes 8 servings

MEDITERRANEAN VEGETABLE SALAD

Versions of this salad are enjoyed in Israel all year round, but for Passover it includes spring onions and small radishes. SEE PHOTOGRAPH.

4 large green onions, chopped (1⅓ cups)

8 small red radishes, diced in about ¼-inch pieces

12 plum tomatoes, diced (5 cups)

1 long (European) cucumber or 2 medium cucumbers, peeled and diced in ⅜-inch pieces (3½ cups)

½ cup chopped fresh parsley

salt and pepper

cayenne pepper to taste

2 tablespoons plus 2 teaspoons extra-virgin olive oil

1 tablespoon plus 1 teaspoon fresh lemon juice

green onion fan (optional)

Mix vegetables and parsley in a bowl. Sprinkle with salt, pepper, and cayenne and mix well. Sprinkle with olive oil, mix, then sprinkle with lemon juice and mix again. Taste and adjust seasoning.

To make a green onion fan, cut off all but 3 inches of the white part of a green onion. Make several parallel, lengthwise cuts outward from the center of the white part, beginning an inch up from the bottom. Put in ice water in refrigerator for about an hour. Ends will curl.

Makes 8 servings

CARROT AND ASPARAGUS SALAD

Moroccan and Tunisian Jewish cooks prepare a great variety of salads of cooked vegetables. This dish is usually made with carrots alone, or sometimes with carrots and artichokes. SEE PHOTOGRAPH.

2 pounds medium carrots (about 10), peeled
salt
1½ pounds medium asparagus, peeled and cut into 2-inch pieces
6 tablespoons vegetable oil
2 medium onions, halved and thinly sliced

½ teaspoon hot red pepper flakes
½ teaspoon caraway seeds
½ teaspoon paprika
½ teaspoon ground cumin
¼ cup strained fresh lemon juice
cayenne pepper to taste

Cut carrots in 2-inch lengths and quarter the pieces. Halve any pieces that are wider than the others. In a saucepan, cover carrots with water and add a pinch of salt. Bring to a boil and simmer over medium heat 15 minutes or until just tender. Remove with slotted spoon. Add asparagus to cooking liquid and boil uncovered for 3 to 4 minutes or until just tender. Remove asparagus, reserving cooking liquid. Rinse asparagus with cold water; drain well.

Heat oil in a large skillet over medium heat. Stir in onions and sauté 10 minutes or until tender. Add ½ cup vegetable cooking liquid, pepper flakes, caraway seeds, paprika, cumin, and a pinch of salt. Bring to a boil, stirring. Reduce heat to low.

Add carrots. Simmer, uncovered, for 5 minutes or until sauce is reduced and coats carrots thoroughly. Add asparagus and mix gently. Serve hot, warm, or cold. Add lemon juice just before serving. Taste and add more salt and cayenne if necessary; salad should be fairly spicy.

Makes 8 servings

YEMENITE BEEF AND CHICKEN CASSEROLE

My Israeli mother-in-law prepares this aromatic "meal in one dish" of chicken and beef when several relatives arrive for lunch or dinner, since this way each person has his or her choice of beef or chicken. And the resulting cooking juices, accented with garlic and cumin, are heavenly. At home we refer to this dish as "Yemenite daube*" because it is prepared by a method similar to that of the traditional southern French* daube—*the meat is simply put in the casserole without preliminary sautéing, and browns slowly as it bakes. Unlike the French version, which is moistened with wine, this dish requires only a few tomatoes, and the meat cooks mainly in its own juices. If you prefer, you can use only beef or chicken, and in this case, double the quantity of either one.*

2 tablespoons vegetable oil or chicken
   fat
2 medium onions, chopped
8 medium garlic cloves, chopped
3 tablespoons ground cumin
1½ teaspoons turmeric
1 tablespoon tomato paste
1 cup water
2 pounds boneless beef shoulder or
   beef for stew, excess fat removed,
   cut in 1- to 1½-inch cubes

3 pounds chicken pieces
8 medium (about 2 pounds) boiling
   potatoes, peeled
⅓ cup coarsely chopped fresh parsley
salt and freshly ground black pepper
¾ pound ripe tomatoes, chopped; or 1
   14-ounce can plum tomatoes,
   drained and chopped

Position rack in lower third of oven and preheat to 300°F. Heat oil in a large, deep, heavy flameproof casserole over medium-low heat, add onions, and sauté until golden, about 12 minutes. Remove from heat. Stir in garlic, cumin, turmeric, tomato paste, and ½ cup water.

Add beef, chicken, potatoes, parsley, salt and pepper, and tomatoes to casserole and mix well; meat and chicken should be well coated with spices. Cover tightly and bake about 3 hours or until beef is very tender; check occasionally and add remaining water, if necessary, so there is just a little sauce but meat does not get dry. Taste sauce and adjust seasoning. (Casserole can be kept overnight in refrigerator and reheated, covered, in low oven or over low heat.) Serve hot.

Makes 8 servings

YEMENITE BRAISED LAMB WITH CUMIN AND GARLIC

This type of aromatic braised meat is a favorite of my in-laws from Yemen. I find it convenient to cook the lamb one day ahead so the flavors can blend and the chilled sauce can be more thoroughly skimmed of fat.

2 tablespoons vegetable oil
2 medium onions, chopped
6 large garlic cloves, chopped
4 teaspoons cumin, freshly ground if
   possible
1 teaspoon turmeric
1 tablespoon tomato paste
¾ pound ripe tomatoes, chopped; or 1
   14-ounce can plum tomatoes,
   drained and chopped

8 lamb shoulder chops (about 4
   pounds total), excess fat trimmed
salt and freshly ground black pepper
½ cup water
6 tablespoons chopped fresh coriander
   (cilantro) or parsley

Position rack in lower third of oven and preheat to 350°F. Heat oil in a large, heavy flameproof casserole over medium-low heat, add onions, and sauté until golden, about 20 minutes. Remove from heat and stir in garlic, cumin, turmeric, tomato paste, and tomatoes. Remove about two-thirds of the mixture from pan, and reserve it.

Sprinkle lamb with salt and pepper on both sides. Put pieces in casserole in layers, scattering some of seasoning mixture over each and rubbing seasoning mixture into meat. Add any remaining seasoning mixture to casserole. Pour water into pan.

Cover tightly and bake 45 minutes. Turn meat over, baste it, and continue baking about 1 hour more or until meat is tender when pierced with a knife; check occasionally and add water if necessary so pan does not become dry. Remove meat from pan, then skim fat from sauce. If sauce is too thin, boil it for 3 or 4 minutes to reduce slightly. Taste sauce and adjust seasoning. (Meat can be kept overnight in refrigerator; skim the sauce of fat, then reheat meat in sauce, covered, in low oven or over low heat.)

Add 4 tablespoons coriander or parsley to sauce. Serve hot, with some of sauce spooned over each meat piece. Sprinkle with remaining herb.

Makes 8 servings

MOROCCAN POTATO CASSEROLE

If your family does not serve peas for Passover, substitute the combination of celery and zucchini. Sometimes diced cooked chicken or other meat is added to this casserole to turn it into a festive main-course lunch during Passover week.

2 pounds white potatoes, scrubbed
1 medium carrot, peeled and halved crosswise
1 cup fresh shelled or frozen peas; or ½ cup peeled, diced celery and ½ cup diced zucchini
4 tablespoons vegetable oil

2 large onions (1 pound total), chopped
6 large eggs
¼ teaspoon turmeric
1 teaspoon salt
½ teaspoon ground black pepper
½ cup chopped fresh parsley

Preheat oven to 350°F. Put potatoes and carrot in saucepan, cover with water, and add a pinch of salt. Bring to a boil and cook about 20 minutes or until carrot is tender. Remove with a slotted spoon. Cook potatoes 10 minutes more or until tender, then remove. Add peas or celery and zucchini mixture to liquid; boil frozen peas 1 minute, fresh peas or zucchini 2 to 5 minutes, or until just tender. Rinse peas or zucchini mixture with cold water and drain. Dice carrot.

Heat 3 tablespoons oil in a large skillet over medium heat, add onions, and sauté until they begin to brown, about 20 minutes.

Peel potatoes and finely mash with potato masher. Add eggs to potatoes one by one, beating well after adding each. Stir in turmeric, salt, pepper, parsley, and onions with their oil. Taste and adjust seasoning. Fold in carrot and peas.

Heat remaining 1 tablespoon oil in a 2-quart casserole in oven for 2 minutes or until hot. Remove with pot holders and swirl casserole carefully so oil coats sides. Carefully add potato mixture; do not mix in oil from sides of pan. Bake 50 minutes or until a knife inserted in center comes out dry. Serve hot or cold.

Makes 8 servings as part of large menu; 4 to 6 servings in regular menu

PASSOVER ALMOND CAKE
WITH STRAWBERRY SAUCE

The traditional light cakes made for Passover, such as this Italian Jewish almond cake, are often flavored with nuts, which give them an appealing richness, and contain a little matzo meal as a substitute for flour. For a modern presentation, the cake is accompanied by fresh strawberries tossed with strawberry sauce and sprinkled with mint. SEE PHOTOGRAPH.

1⅔ cups (about 8½ ounces) whole
   unblanched almonds
¼ cup matzo cake meal or matzo meal
1 cup sugar
4 large eggs, separated
1¼ teaspoons grated lemon rind
salt

double recipe of Strawberry Sauce
   (page 59)

2 cups sliced fresh strawberries
4 teaspoons very thin strips fresh mint
   (optional)
mint sprigs, for garnish (optional)

Preheat oven to 350°F. Grease a 9-inch springform pan with margarine.

Grind almonds with matzo meal and ¼ cup sugar in food processor until fine. Beat egg yolks with ½ cup sugar at high speed of mixer until light and fluffy. Beat in lemon rind just until blended. Set aside.

In a clean bowl whip egg whites with a pinch of salt to soft peaks. Gradually beat in remaining ¼ cup sugar, beating until stiff and shiny.

In 3 batches, alternately fold whites and almond mixture into yolk mixture. Transfer to pan and bake about 35 minutes or until a cake tester or toothpick inserted in center of cake comes out dry. Cool slightly, then run a metal spatula gently around cake and remove sides of springform. Cool on a rack. Cake will sink slightly. (Cake can be kept, covered, for 1 day at room temperature or in refrigerator.) Serve at cool room temperature.

Make double recipe of strawberry sauce, using granulated sugar instead of confectioners' sugar. Mix ½ cup sauce with the sliced berries.

To serve, cut cake in wedges and put on dessert plates. Spoon a few sliced berries on one side of cake and sprinkle with mint strips. Spoon sauce on other side of cake. Garnish with mint sprigs.

Makes 8 servings

A FESTIVE PASSOVER SABBATH MENU

Since Passover lasts for eight days, there are plenty of meals to prepare besides the Seder menus of the first two nights. The Sabbath dinner menu is especially festive, although with fewer items than the Seder menu, and each family has its favorite dishes. For the following menu, the first and main courses are North African, the dessert is European style, and the almond macaroons are Passover favorites of Jews of all origins.

A FESTIVE PASSOVER SABBATH MENU

Spicy Potato Salad
Israeli Vegetable Salad (page 20)
Spring Lamb Stew with Many Vegetables
(Msouki)
Strawberry Cream Puffs for Passover,
or Chocolate Mousse for Passover
Citrus-Scented Almond Macaroons

SPICY POTATO SALAD

If you think potato salads need a large quantity of a rich dressing to be good, try this tasty appetizer from the Tunisian repertoire. The intriguing combination of caraway, cumin, and cilantro in a light, tangy dressing make this aromatic potato salad one of the best.

2 pounds red-skinned potatoes, scrubbed but not peeled	½ teaspoon paprika
salt to taste	1 tablespoon water
3 tablespoons fresh lemon juice	2 tablespoons olive oil
2 teaspoons ground cumin	¼ teaspoon caraway seeds
½ teaspoon hot pepper sauce	1 tablespoon chopped fresh coriander (cilantro)

Put potatoes in large saucepan, cover with water by about ½ inch, and add salt. Bring to boil, cover, and simmer over low heat about 25 minutes, or until a knife can pierce center of the largest potato easily and potato falls from knife when lifted.

Meanwhile prepare dressing. In a bowl large enough to contain potatoes, whisk lemon juice with cumin, a pinch of salt, hot pepper sauce, paprika, and water. Add olive oil and caraway seeds and whisk again.

Drain potatoes and leave just until cool enough to handle. Peel them and cut in 1-inch dice. Add potatoes to bowl and mix gently but thoroughly with dressing. Leave to cool. Serve cold or at room temperature. Just before serving, sprinkle with coriander.

Makes 5 or 6 servings

SPRING LAMB STEW WITH MANY VEGETABLES (MSOUKI)

We enjoyed this Passover stew, a specialty of Jews from Algeria and Tunisia, at restaurants in the North African Jewish section of Paris near rue Montmartre. It is a slightly spicy, colorful stew made with a great variety of vegetables and either lamb or beef, and it is thickened with crumbled matzo. In Paris they use a special round ''Tunisian'' matzo that is decorated with a lacy pattern and is thicker than the familiar square matzos; these pretty matzos are also served on the side. Some people serve the stew for the Seder, while others prefer it for dinners during Passover week.

Like many traditional dishes, msouki comes in many forms—it can be a soup, a stew, or a plate of vegetables topped by a piece of braised meat. Usually it has many vegetables, but some cooks prefer to add only artichokes, spring onions, spinach, and fava beans. North African Jews do not avoid beans for Passover, but Ashkenazim who wish to omit them will still find this stew to have an interesting medley of textures and tastes.

2 pounds lamb shoulder, excess fat
   removed
salt and freshly ground pepper
1 teaspoon paprika
3 tablespoons olive oil
2 cups water
1 tablespoon tomato paste
2 medium onions, halved and sliced
6 medium garlic cloves, chopped
2 medium carrots, diced
1 celery stalk, diced
1½ pounds fresh spinach, or 1 10-
   ounce package frozen spinach,
   thawed and squeezed
1½ pounds fresh fava beans, shelled;
   or 1 10-ounce package frozen lima
   beans (about 2 cups)

1 leek, split, cleaned, and sliced
4 fresh artichoke hearts (see page 346
   for preparation), or 1 9-ounce
   package frozen artichoke hearts
1 lemon (if using fresh artichokes)
2 medium zucchini, diced
⅓ cup chopped fresh parsley
⅓ cup chopped fresh coriander
   (cilantro)
⅓ cup chopped fresh mint
cayenne pepper to taste, or 1 teaspoon
   hot pepper sauce
2 matzos, broken into about 1-inch
   pieces

Cut lamb into 1-inch pieces. Sprinkle lightly with salt, pepper, and paprika.

Combine oil, water, and tomato paste in a large enamel casserole and whisk to blend. Add onions, garlic, carrots, celery, salt, and pepper and mix well. Set seasoned lamb pieces on top. Bring to a boil, cover, and cook over low heat, stirring from time to time, for 30 minutes. Add spinach, fava or lima beans, leek, frozen artichoke pieces if using, and zucchini and return to a boil. Cover and cook 30 minutes or until meat is tender.

Taste stew and adjust seasoning. Reserve 1 tablespoon parsley and 1 tablespoon coriander for garnish. Add fresh artichokes if using, mint, remaining parsley and coriander, and cayenne to stew and cook 3 minutes. Taste and adjust seasoning. Put matzo pieces on top, stir gently, cover, and let stand 1 to 2 minutes to soften. Sprinkle with reserved herbs and serve.

Makes 6 servings

STRAWBERRY CREAM PUFFS
FOR PASSOVER

Made from Passover rolls, these elegant puffs are filled with strawberries in a white wine custard and served with Strawberry Sauce. They contain no dairy products and are perfect for a meat or poultry dinner. For dairy meals, you can instead prepare Passover profiteroles by filling the puffs with vanilla ice cream and serving them with warm Chocolate Sauce (page 323).

White Wine Pastry Cream

¾ cup dry white wine
¼ cup water
3 large egg yolks
5 tablespoons sugar

2 tablespoons potato starch
2 tablespoons (¼ stick) unsalted
    nondairy margarine
1 teaspoon vanilla extract

1½ cups strawberries, halved and
    sliced
1 tablespoon plus 1 teaspoon sugar

10 Passover "Rolls" (page 34)
Strawberry Sauce (page 59, optional)

In a small, heavy saucepan bring wine and water to a boil; remove from heat.

Whisk egg yolks and sugar in a bowl until smooth. Gently stir in potato starch, using whisk. Gradually add hot wine mixture, whisking quickly, then return mixture to saucepan. Cook over medium-low heat, whisking constantly, until mixture comes just to a boil, then reduce heat to low and, whisking constantly, cook for 1 minute. Remove from heat and whisk in margarine, then vanilla. Transfer to a bowl and cool to room temperature, stirring often to prevent a skin from forming. Refrigerate at least 1 hour or up to 2 days.

Sprinkle strawberries with sugar and toss well. Let stand a few minutes. Whisk pastry cream until smooth and fold in berries.

Fill puffs just before serving. Cut "rolls" nearly in half and spoon berry mixture inside. Serve with Strawberry Sauce, if desired.

Makes 10 servings

CHOCOLATE MOUSSE FOR PASSOVER

When a Hebrew edition of my book, Chocolate Sensations, *was published in Israel, every recipe that was suitable for Passover was marked with an asterisk. Until then I had not realized that so many of my favorite chocolate desserts are perfect for Passover.*

This chocolate mousse does not contain cream, so it is a great finale for kosher dinners featuring meat. Serve this mousse on its own or accompanied by almond macaroons or Passover meringues. It also makes a good filling for Passover cream puffs.

7 ounces semisweet or bittersweet
   chocolate, chopped
¼ cup sweet red Passover wine or
   concord grape wine, orange juice, or
   water

1 tablespoon unsalted nondairy
   margarine
4 large eggs,* separated
1 tablespoon sugar

In a medium bowl melt chocolate with wine above hot water over low heat. Remove from pan of water and stir until smooth. Stir in margarine, then add egg yolks, one by one, stirring vigorously after each addition.

Beat egg whites until stiff. Beat in sugar and continue beating about 30 seconds or until whites are very shiny. Quickly fold one-fourth of the whites into chocolate mixture. Gently fold in remaining whites. Pour into 4 dessert dishes, ramekins, or stemmed glasses. Cover and chill at least 2 hours or until set. (Mousse can be kept, covered, 2 days in refrigerator.)

Makes 4 servings

*If you are concerned about the safety of using raw eggs in a recipe, you may wish to choose another dessert.

CITRUS-SCENTED ALMOND MACAROONS

Jewish pastry shops in Paris display almond macaroons all year long, but as Passover treats they are the most popular. Be sure to use fresh almonds.

1½ cups (about 6½ ounces) whole
   blanched almonds
1 cup sugar
2 large egg whites

1 teaspoon orange juice
1 teaspoon grated orange rind
1 teaspoon grated lemon rind

Position rack in upper third of oven and preheat to 350°F. Line baking sheet with parchment paper or wax paper; grease paper lightly with margarine.

Grind almonds with 4 tablespoons sugar in food processor by processing continuously until mixture forms fine, even crumbs. Add egg whites, orange juice, and orange and lemon rinds and process until smooth, about 20 seconds. Add remaining sugar in 2 additions and process about 10 seconds after each or until smooth.

With moistened hands, roll about 1 tablespoon of the mixture between your palms into a smooth ball. Put on prepared baking sheet. Continue with remaining mixture, spacing cookies about 1 inch apart.

Press to flatten each macaroon slightly so it is about ½ inch high. Brush entire surface of each cookie with water. Bake until very lightly but evenly browned, 18 to 20 minutes; centers should still be soft. Remove from oven.

Lift one end of paper and pour about 2 tablespoons water under it, onto baking sheet; the water will boil on contact with hot baking sheet. Lift other end of paper and pour about 2 tablespoons water under it. When water stops boiling, remove macaroons carefully from paper. Transfer to a rack to cool. (Macaroons can be kept 1 week in airtight containers.)

Makes about 20 macaroons

2

SHAVUOT: THE CHEESECAKE HOLIDAY

The Jewish festival of Shavuot, which is celebrated in May or June, has many names. Because it comes seven weeks after Passover, in Hebrew it is called *Shavuot*, or "weeks." In English it is Pentecost, which comes from a Greek word meaning "fifty days." Often it is referred to as the Festival of the Torah, because it commemorates Moses' receiving the Ten Commandments and the Torah, or Judaic scriptures. Still another name is Feast of the First Fruits, which was observed in ancient Israel because this was the joyful time of the harvest of grain and early fruits.

One more nickname should be added: the holiday of cheesecake. It is a custom, although not a law, to prepare dairy delicacies for Shavuot. Some say this is because the Hebrews abstained from eating meat the day before they received the Torah. Another explanation is based on economics: a large amount of cheese is produced because cows, goats, and sheep give more milk in the spring. No matter what the reason, this holiday is a good excuse to enjoy cheesecake one day, and cheese blintzes the next, since the festivities last for two days.

In Israel Shavuot is celebrated for only one day, but that one day can become a real feast! In addition to cheesecake, blintzes, and noodle and sour cream kugels prepared by Jews of eastern

53

European origin, there are the bourekas preferred by some of the Sephardic communities. These rich, savory pastries often made with filo dough are known under various names in Greece, Turkey, and much of the Middle East. They can contain many fillings, but for Shavuot a zesty cheese mixture is a favorite.

One of the greatest pleasures of festivals is the traditional dishes that go with them. Many of the foods of Shavuot have become so popular that they can be found in delis year round. But they are even more delicious and enjoyed much more when prepared at home, among family or friends.

Other ideal Shavuot dishes:

Savory Cheese Knishes (page 150)
Romanian Cornmeal Kugel (page 284)
Creamy Noodle Kugel with Almonds (page 331)
Meringue-Topped Cheesecake (page 306)

A SHAVUOT PARTY

Although cheese dishes are a tradition for Shavuot, you would probably not serve several of them at dinner because it would be too rich. For a get-together with quite a few guests, you might like to prepare a selection of dairy specialties, and those who wish can try small portions of each. This menu features mainly Ashkenazic dishes (blintzes and cheesecake), but the filo turnovers are Sephardic. Today in Israel all these dishes are well-loved by most people, and it's not at all unusual to find them together at the same party.

For a dinner for a small number of people, use the same menu but choose either the blintzes or the cheesecake, and prepare a simple baked or broiled fish such as Broiled Salmon with Moroccan Seasonings (page 221) for a main course.

A SHAVUOT PARTY MENU

Cheese Filo Turnovers (Cheese Bourekas)
Israeli Vegetable Salad (page 20)
Cheese-Walnut Challah
Classic Cheese Blintzes with Strawberry Sauce
Salad of Seasonal Fruits
Creamy Cheesecake, or Israeli Cheesecake
with Pine Nuts and Orange

CHEESE FILO TURNOVERS
(CHEESE BOUREKAS)

In Israel these turnovers are known as bourekas *and are considered a specialty of Sephardic Jews, especially those from Turkey and Syria. They have become as popular as pizza and can be found at many cafés throughout the year. Restaurant chefs often make them with filo dough but home cooks sometimes substitute purchased puff pastry, since in Israel it is easier to find.*

Cheese-filled bourekas can be triangular, ring-shaped, or half-moons. For the filling I like to mix a flavorful cheese such as kashkaval, parmesan, or feta with a mild cheese such as cottage cheese or pot cheese. These pastries are great for entertaining, and few parties in Israel are complete without some form of this savory appetizer.

1 pound filo dough (about 20 sheets)

Cheese Filling

¼ cup low-fat cottage cheese
2 large eggs, beaten lightly
2 cups grated cheese, such as Swiss,
  kashkaval, or cheddar (about 10
  ounces)

2 green onions, finely chopped
salt (optional) and pepper to taste

1 cup (2 sticks) butter or margarine,
  melted

about 2 teaspoons sesame seeds, for
  sprinkling

If filo sheets are frozen, thaw them in refrigerator for 8 hours or overnight. Remove sheets from refrigerator 2 hours before using and leave them in their package.

Put cottage cheese in a strainer and press gently to remove excess liquid; do not push cheese through strainer. Leave cheese in strainer for 10 minutes and press gently again. Mix cottage cheese with eggs, grated cheese, and green onions until smooth. Add pepper; taste before adding any salt.

Remove filo sheets from package and unroll them on a dry towel. Using a sharp knife, cut stack in half lengthwise to form 2 stacks of sheets of about 16 × 7 inches each. Cover filo immediately with a piece of wax paper, then with a damp towel. Work with only one sheet at a time and always keep remaining sheets covered with paper and towel so they don't dry out.

Remove a filo sheet from pile. Brush it lightly with melted butter and fold it in half lengthwise so its dimensions are about 16 × 3½ inches. Dab it lightly with butter. Place about 1½ teaspoons cheese filling at one end of strip. Fold end of strip diagonally over filling to form a triangle, and dab it lightly with butter. Continue folding it over and over, keeping it in a triangular shape after each fold, until end of strip is reached. Set triangular pastry on a buttered baking sheet. Brush it lightly with butter. Shape more pastries with remaining filo sheets and filling. (Pastries can be shaped 1 day ahead and refrigerated on baking sheets or on plates. Cover them tightly with plastic wrap.)

Preheat oven to 350°F. Brush pastries again lightly with melted butter and sprinkle with sesame seeds. Bake 20 to 25 minutes or until golden brown. Serve warm (not hot) or at room temperature.

Makes about 32 turnovers; 10 to 12 servings

CHEESE-WALNUT CHALLAH

Cheese-flavored challah is not a traditional recipe, but challah is delicious prepared in this manner and is especially appropriate to make for Shavuot, the holiday of dairy specialties. The cheese is kneaded into the dough, which is then sprinkled with walnuts, rolled up like a jelly roll, and baked in a loaf pan.

Challah dough (page 289), made with
  1 teaspoon sugar
1½ cups (about 5 ounces) grated Swiss
  cheese

1 cup (about 3 ounces) walnut pieces,
  coarsely chopped
1 large egg, beaten with a pinch of
  salt, for glaze

When making dough, sprinkle 1 teaspoon sugar over yeast mixture. Prepare dough by any method and let rise twice.

Grease a 9 × 5-inch loaf pan. After dough has risen for second time, sprinkle about half the cheese over a 5-inch square area on work surface. Put dough on top and pat it out over cheese. Sprinkle remaining cheese over dough. Knead cheese lightly into dough.

Pat dough out into a 9-inch square. Sprinkle evenly with walnuts and press them into dough. Roll up tightly in a cylinder. Put in prepared loaf pan. Cover with a warm, slightly damp cloth and let rise until nearly doubled in size, about 1 hour. Preheat oven to 375°F.

Brush risen loaf gently with beaten egg. Bake until top and bottom of bread are firm and bread sounds hollow when tapped on bottom, about 45 minutes.

Run a thin-bladed flexible knife carefully around bread. Turn out of pan and cool on rack.

Makes 1 medium loaf

CLASSIC CHEESE BLINTZES
WITH STRAWBERRY SAUCE

Blintzes can be served as a main course, a dessert, or a breakfast treat. For dessert, use the larger quantity of sugar in the filling and add 4 to 5 tablespoons raisins if desired. The fresh Strawberry Sauce is a relatively modern partner for the blintzes, but you can instead serve the customary accompaniments of fruit preserves or jam, or a mixture of 1 tablespoon sugar and ½ teaspoon cinnamon. For a main course, omit the sweet accompaniments and serve the blintzes only with sour cream or plain yogurt.

A mixture of cheeses is best for filling blintzes. Farmer cheese is a firm, dry cheese that gives the filling body, so it will not be soft and runny. Cream cheese provides richness. Pot cheese, a rich version of cottage cheese that can be purchased at specialty stores, adds moistness.

**Basic Blintzes, 9 inches in diameter
(page 198)**

Filling

2 cups (about 15 ounces) farmer
   cheese
3 tablespoons cream cheese, softened
5 tablespoons pot cheese (rich cottage
   cheese) or cottage cheese

2 large egg yolks
3 to 4 tablespoons sugar, or to taste
¼ to ½ teaspoon ground cinnamon, or
   to taste

3 to 4 tablespoons (½ stick) butter, for
   frying or baking blintzes

sour cream or yogurt, for serving
Strawberry Sauce (page 59, optional)

Prepare blintzes, stack them, and keep them warm, covered with a kitchen towel.

Mash cheeses. Beat them with egg yolks, sugar, and cinnamon until mixture is smooth and thoroughly blended.

Spoon 2½ to 3 tablespoons filling onto brown side of each blintze near one edge. Fold over edges of blintze to right and left of filling so that each covers about half the filling; roll up, beginning at edge, with filling. (Blintzes can be filled 1 day ahead and refrigerated, covered.)

Blintzes can be baked or fried. To bake them, preheat oven to 425°F. Arrange blintzes in one layer in a shallow buttered baking dish. Dot each blintze with 2 small pieces of butter. Bake for about 15 minutes, or until heated through and lightly browned.

To fry blintzes, heat butter in a skillet. Add blintzes open end down. Fry over low heat for 3 to 5 minutes on each side; be careful not to let them burn.

Serve blintzes hot, with sour cream and Strawberry Sauce.

Makes 12 to 14 blintzes; 4 to 6 main-course servings

Strawberry Sauce

This bright red, fresh-tasting sauce is great with blintzes or cheesecake. If you wish to make it for Passover, sweeten the berries with 1 or 2 tablespoons granulated sugar instead of confectioners' sugar.

2 cups fresh or frozen strawberries,
  thawed
3 tablespoons confectioners' sugar,
  sifted, or more to taste
few drops fresh lemon juice (optional)

Puree the strawberries in a food processor or blender until very smooth. Whisk in confectioners' sugar, taste, and add more sugar if desired. Add lemon juice. Refrigerate until ready to use. (Sauce can be kept, covered, for 2 days in refrigerator.)

Makes 4 to 6 servings

CREAMY CHEESECAKE

This is my favorite cheesecake. I love its pure flavor of sweetened cheese enhanced only with a hint of lemon and vanilla, as well as its creamy texture, which is lighter than most cream cheese cakes. For my taste, the sour cream topping is all the embellishment it needs. If you prefer a colorful dessert, serve it with Strawberry Sauce (page 59) or with fresh strawberries.

Pecan and Crumb Crust

5 ounces graham crackers
¼ cup pecan halves
3 tablespoons sugar

6 tablespoons (¾ stick) unsalted
   butter, melted

Cheese Filling

1 pound cream cheese, cut into pieces
   and softened
½ cup sour cream
¾ cup sugar
3 large eggs

grated rind of 1 large lemon
1 vanilla bean, split lengthwise; or 1
   teaspoon vanilla extract

Sour Cream Topping

1½ cups sour cream
3 tablespoons sugar
1 teaspoon vanilla extract

Prepare the crust. Preheat oven to 350°F. Process graham crackers in a food processor to fine crumbs, or put them in a bag and crush them with a rolling pin. You need 1¼ cups. Chop pecan halves, then mix with crumbs and add sugar. Add melted butter and mix well. Lightly butter a 9-inch springform pan. Press pecan mixture in an even layer on bottom and about 1 inch up sides of pan. Bake 10 minutes, then let cool completely. Leave oven at 350°F.

   For the filling, beat cream cheese with sour cream at low speed until very smooth. Gradually beat in sugar, then beat in eggs, one by one. Beat in lemon rind. If using a vanilla bean, scrape its seeds with the point of a knife into cheese mixture; or stir in vanilla extract. Carefully pour filling into cooled crust and bake about 45 minutes or until firm in center. Remove from oven and cool for 15 minutes. Raise oven temperature to 425°F.

   For the topping, mix sour cream, sugar, and vanilla. Carefully spread topping on cake in an even layer, without letting it drip over crust. Return cake to oven and bake 7 minutes.

Remove cake from oven and cool to room temperature. Refrigerate at least 2 hours before serving. (Cake can be kept 3 days in refrigerator.) Remove sides of springform pan just before serving.

Makes 8 to 10 servings

CHEESECAKE WITH PINE NUTS AND ORANGE

Pine nuts lend an exotic note to the delightful, light-textured streusel topping of this cheesecake and provide an intriguing contrast to the smooth, rich, orange-scented cheese filling. I got the idea for this cake from a course given by WIZO, the Women's International Zionist Organization, in Tel Aviv. During the years I lived in Israel I looked forward eagerly to these classes, which took place on a regular basis in many communities. I found them especially exciting because of the chance to exchange culinary tips with other women. SEE PHOTOGRAPH.

Orange-Scented Pastry Dough

2½ cups all-purpose flour
½ cup sugar
pinch of salt

1 cup (2 sticks) cold unsalted butter,
   cut into small pieces
2 teaspoons grated orange rind
1 large egg, beaten

Cheese Filling

1 pound cottage cheese
1 pound cream cheese, softened
¾ cup sugar
2 large eggs

2 large egg yolks
½ cup heavy cream
5 teaspoons grated orange rind

⅓ cup pine nuts

Lightly butter a 9-inch springform pan. For the pastry dough, combine flour, sugar, and salt in food processor. Process briefly to blend, then scatter butter pieces over mixture. Mix using on/off turns until mixture resembles coarse meal. Sprinkle with grated rind and pour egg evenly over mixture in processor. Process with on/off turns, scraping down occasionally, until dough forms sticky crumbs; do not allow them to come together in a ball.

Sprinkle two-thirds of crumbs (about 3 cups) evenly in pan. Put rest of crumbs in a bowl in freezer. With floured hands press crumbs in pan together and pat them 2 inches up side of pan. Chill pan in freezer while preparing filling. Preheat oven to 350°F.

For cheese filling, push cottage cheese through a strainer. Beat cream cheese with sugar until smooth. Add eggs, one by one, and beat after each addition, then beat in yolks. Stir in cottage cheese, cream, and orange rind.

Pour filling into lined pan. Crumble remaining pastry crumb mixture between your fingers and sprinkle on top of filling. Sprinkle pine nuts over crumbs and pat very gently so topping adheres to filling.

Set springform pan on a baking sheet. Bake 1 hour and 15 minutes or until set. If topping is not brown enough, broil about 30 seconds, checking every few seconds, until golden brown. Cool completely. Refrigerate at least 2 hours before serving. (Cake can be kept 3 days in refrigerator.) Serve cold.

Makes 10 servings

3
ROSH HASHANAH: THE JEWISH NEW YEAR

 The timing of the Jewish holidays is determined by the traditional Jewish calendar, which is lunar. For this reason the holidays occur on different dates of the common (solar) calendar each year, although they are always in the same season. The first month of the Jewish calendar, Tishrei, is in September or October, and the first two days of this month are the Jewish New Year, Rosh Hashanah.

In modern days many of the time-honored culinary traditions gain new value. Food customs for the Jewish New Year are a good example. They somehow are in accord with the latest nutritional guidelines.

Rosh Hashanah menus often begin with fish, an ancient symbol of fertility and abundance. In some families, the fish is served with its head on, to stand for "the head of the year," the literal meaning of the words *Rosh Hashanah*. Today fish is the appetizer of choice for an additional reason—its lean flesh is considered one of the most healthful of foods.

The date of Rosh Hashanah coincides with the beginning of the agricultural year, according to ancient tradition in the Middle East. As tokens of the wish for a plentiful harvest, vegetables and fruits play an important role on the Jewish New Year table. Part of the ritual of the holiday teaches appreciation of the season's bounty, since it involves saying a blessing over a fruit that is tasted for the first time in the year. A first sampling of the new produce is a custom in all ethnic groups, and many people precede dinner with a taste of pomegranate, dates, and figs. Among Jews from Iraq, pomegranate juice is a favorite holiday drink. Today, of course, an abundance of produce on the menu also signifies a concern for healthful eating.

The best-known food custom of Rosh Hashanah seems to have been developed with children in mind. On this holiday, one is supposed to eat sweet foods! The wish for a sweet year is taken literally in menu planning, and seems to have inspired the tone of the dinner. Honey appears in many dishes. In biblical times honey was *the* sweetener. It also represented richness and good living, as in the Bible's many romantic references to Israel as "the land of milk and honey." Today honey-sweetened desserts are considered among the most nutritious of sweets.

Jews throughout the world begin the holiday meal with the traditional apples dipped in honey (and, in some North African families, dipped in toasted sesame seeds as well). Fruit appears in unexpected places—cinnamon-scented quince are featured as an appetizer in Moroccan dinners, and fruits and vegetables are cooked together in a special Ashkenazic stew called *tzimmes,* which includes carrots, prunes, and sometimes sweet potatoes. Tzimmes can be a vegetable side dish or can include beef and become a colorful main course.

Sweet vegetables, especially carrots, winter squash, and sweet potatoes, are favorites on Rosh Hashanah menus. Their sweetness is often accentuated in the kitchen. For example, carrots are glazed with honey in Romanian and Hungarian Jewish cuisine, while winter squash is cooked with sugar and cinnamon in certain Sephardic communities. Other Sephardim prepare these vegetables as savory pancakes.

The Prophet Nehemiah is said to have introduced to the ancient Israelites the Persian custom of eating something sweet to celebrate the new year. So important is this tradition that it also works in the other direction: many people avoid sour ingredients such as vinegar.

Many foods served at the traditional Jewish New Year feast have a special meaning. Carrots, besides being sweet, stand for prosperity because carrot slices resemble gold coins. They provide a lively decoration for the Ashkenazic gefilte fish, which is popular at many holiday meals. Sephardim serve a spinach omelet to illustrate a "green" year with plenty of produce, and accompany the main dish with rice, a symbol of abundance.

Challah, or Jewish egg bread, is made differently for Rosh Hashanah. Raisins and sometimes honey are added, so that the challah is slightly sweeter than usual. Its shape is round to represent a full year—either smooth and dome shaped or braided to form a crown.

Other ideal Rosh Hashanah dishes:

Zesty Pepper-Tomato Salad (page 18)
Chicken Baked with Quince and Almonds (page 232)
Couscous with Lamb and Seven Vegetables (page 244)
Beef Stew with Winter Squash and Raisins (page 86)
Honey-Glazed Carrots (page 109)
Zucchini with Tomatoes and Dill (page 265)
Okra with Tomatoes and Coriander (page 267)
Noodle Kugel with Colorful Vegetables (page 88)
Honey-Glazed Cookies with Walnuts (Tayglach) (page 321)

Following are two menu suggestions for Rosh Hashanah dinners.

AN ASHKENAZIC ROSH HASHANAH

For a traditional holiday menu that requires practically no last-minute work, start with apple wedges and slices of challah, and provide small bowls of honey for dipping. Serve gefilte fish as a first course, as well as a green bean salad garnished with pecans, and follow these with beef tzimmes with sweet potatoes and carrots for the main course. Finish with a cinnamon-scented honey cake or an apple cake with honey frosting for dessert, and have a sweet New Year!

ASHKENAZIC MENU FOR ROSH HASHANAH

Apples and Honey
Round Holiday Challah with Raisins
Gefilte Fish (page 9),
or Chicken Soup with Kreplach
Green Bean Salad with Pecans
Beef and Sweet Potato Tzimmes
Light Honey Cake
with Cinnamon and Walnuts,
or Apple Cake with Honey Frosting

ROUND HOLIDAY CHALLAH WITH RAISINS

Braided challahs are most often made for Sabbath, while round challahs, often sweetened with honey, are the custom for Rosh Hashanah. They can be purchased at Jewish bakeries, but are also fun to make at home. Sometimes they contain raisins, as in this loaf. If some raisins start to come out of the dough when you are shaping these loaves, pinch the dough around them; otherwise the exposed raisins will burn in the oven.

This recipe gives two alternatives for shaping the challah: as a round dome or as a round braid.

4 cups all-purpose flour
½ cup plus 3 tablespoons lukewarm
  water
2 envelopes active dry yeast
½ teaspoon sugar
3 tablespoons honey
⅓ cup vegetable oil

2 large eggs
2 teaspoons salt
½ cup raisins, rinsed, drained, and
  dried on paper towels
1 large egg, beaten with a pinch of
  salt, for glaze
2 teaspoons sesame seeds (optional)

Sift 3¾ cups flour into a large bowl. Make a large well in the center and pour in ½ cup lukewarm water. Sprinkle yeast on top and add sugar. Leave for 10 minutes, until yeast is foamy. Whisk honey with remaining 3 tablespoons water. Add honey mixture, oil, eggs, and salt to well. Mix in flour, first with a spoon and then by hand, until ingredients come together to a dough.

Knead dough vigorously on a work surface, gradually adding remaining 4 tablespoons flour, until dough is very smooth, fairly stiff, and no longer sticky, about 12 minutes. Transfer to a clean oiled bowl, cover with a damp cloth, and let rise in a warm place 1 to 1¼ hours or until nearly doubled in volume.

Remove dough again to a lightly floured surface and knead lightly. Return to bowl, cover, and let rise 30 to 45 minutes or until nearly doubled again.

Pat dough to approximately a 9-inch square on work surface. Sprinkle evenly with raisins. Roll up tightly from one end to other, as in making a jelly roll; lightly flour surface if dough begins to stick.

Cut roll of dough in 2 equal parts. To form a smooth round loaf, roll one part back and forth on a working surface, pressing with your palms, to form a smooth rope about 2 feet long. Twist dough around one end in a spiral; pull other end upward over spiral and press it on center of loaf. Press whole loaf firmly with your hands to adhere end to top and to give loaf an even dome shape. Repeat for second loaf, or follow next paragraph.

To form a braided round loaf, divide remaining dough in 3 equal parts. Roll each back and forth on a work surface, pressing with your palms, to form a smooth rope about 12 inches long and tapered slightly at ends. Put ropes side by side, with one set of ends close to you. Join ends far from you; cover end of rope on your right side with end of center rope, then end of left rope. Press to join. To braid, bring outer ropes alternately over center one; braid tightly, pinch ends to join ropes. Bring ends of braid together, curving braid into a circle, and pinch ends together.

Oil 2 baking sheets. Set loaves carefully on them. Cover with a damp cloth and let rise about 45 minutes or until nearly doubled in volume.

Preheat oven to 350°F. Brush each challah with beaten egg. Sprinkle braided loaf with sesame seeds. Bake about 20 minutes or until beginning to brown. Reduce oven temperature to 325°F. and bake about 25 more minutes or until bottom of bread sounds hollow when tapped. Cool on a rack.

Makes 2 small loaves: 1 round and 1 braid, or 2 of either one

CHICKEN SOUP WITH KREPLACH

Of Russian and Polish origin, kreplach are most often served in soup. Owing to their shape, they are sometimes called ''Jewish tortellini,'' although I have seen them shaped as half-moons, triangles, or squares. Making kreplach used to be a lot of work, but today with the help of a food processor, the dough can be made in a few minutes.

Cooked chicken or meat mixed with sautéed onions is the favorite filling, but others include cheese and potato, chicken liver, potato and fried onion, and kasha (buckwheat). There are even sweet kreplach, with fillings of berries or pitted cherries stewed with sugar or honey, thickened lightly with cornstarch, and served with sour cream or fruit.

The most popular way to enjoy chicken or meat kreplach is in clear chicken soup. Some members of my family prefer their kreplach cooked directly in the soup, since this gives them more flavor, while others like them cooked in water so the starch does not cloud the soup. Kreplach are also good served in other ways: drizzled with oil or melted margarine and heated briefly in the oven, tossed with herb-accented tomato sauce, or added to a pan of fried onions and sautéed lightly.

Noodle Dough

3 large eggs
¾ teaspoon salt

1¾ cups plus 2 tablespoons all-
    purpose flour

Chicken Filling

2 tablespoons vegetable oil, nondairy
    margarine, or chicken fat
1 medium onion, finely chopped
8 ounces boneless, skinless chicken
    thighs or breasts

salt and pepper to taste
1 large egg, beaten
2 tablespoon chopped fresh parsley

Chicken Soup, for serving (page 347)

Make the dough: In a food processor combine eggs, salt, and 1½ cups flour. Process until dough begins to form a ball. Add remaining flour 1 tablespoon at a time and process a few seconds after each addition. Process 30 seconds so dough forms ball; if dough is not very smooth, knead a few seconds by hand on a lightly floured surface. Place dough on a plate, cover with an overturned bowl, and leave 30 minutes at room temperature. (Dough can be refrigerated, covered, for 1 day.)

Make the filling: Heat oil in a small skillet, add onion, and sauté until soft and just beginning to brown, about 10 minutes. Add chicken and sprinkle with salt and pepper. Cover and cook over low heat about 7 minutes. Turn over, cover, and cook about 5 more minutes or until just tender. Be careful not to let onion burn. Remove chicken and let cool. Cut chicken into pieces and grind in food processor until fine. Add egg and puree again until fine. Transfer to a mixing bowl. Mix in sautéed onion and parsley. Taste for seasoning; mixture should be highly seasoned. Leave to cool.

 Set rollers of a pasta machine to widest setting. Cut dough in 2 or 3 pieces. Work with 1 piece at a time and keep others covered. Flour the piece of dough, pat to flatten it slightly, and put it through rollers. Fold in 2 or 3 pieces and put it through again, still at widest setting. Put it through 6 or 7 times, or until very smooth.

 Set rollers at next setting. Lightly flour the dough and put it through without folding. Continue putting dough through machine, once at each setting, until you reach the next-to-finest setting; if dough isn't smooth after putting it through a certain setting, put it through again.

 Place ½-teaspoon mounds of filling about 1½ inches apart on sheet of dough, then cut dough in approximately 2½-inch squares. Brush 2 adjacent sides of each square lightly with water; fold dough over filling into a triangle, pressing moistened sides to unmoistened sides; and press edges firmly to seal. (If desired, join 2 edges to form a ring shape.) If necessary, dampen edges with a little water so they are easier to join. Lay each triangle on a floured sheet of wax paper as it is completed. Repeat rolling and shaping with remaining dough and filling, using 1 piece of dough at a time. (Kreplach can be made ahead to this point, put in one layer on a floured paper or tray, covered, and kept 1 day in refrigerator.)

 To cook kreplach, add half of them to a large pot of boiling salted water. Bring to a boil, reduce heat so water simmers, cover, and cook over low heat 15 minutes. Remove kreplach with a slotted spoon and drain in a colander. Repeat with second batch. (Cooked kreplach can be kept 2 days in refrigerator. They can also be frozen.)

 To serve, simmer kreplach in hot chicken soup or meat soup to heat through for 10 to 15 minutes. Serve in soup, with a few carrot slices and parsley.

Makes about 50 kreplach; 10 servings

GREEN BEAN SALAD WITH PECANS

This simple salad makes a beautiful platter and can be served buffet style as a first course or side dish. The dressing has no lemon juice or vinegar, since some communities avoid sour ingredients for Rosh Hashanah; besides, acid ingredients turn the color of the green beans from bright green to gray. For other occasions, add 2 tablespoons lemon juice to the dressing if you wish, and spoon it over the beans at the last moment.

½ cup pecans

½ cup vegetable or olive oil

2 to 3 tablespoons minced green
  onions

salt and pepper

4 hard-boiled large eggs

3 pounds green beans, ends removed

Preheat oven to 350°F. Toast pecans in a baking dish in oven, shaking pan occasionally, until nuts are aromatic and very lightly browned, about 5 minutes. Transfer to a plate and cool. Chop fine but not to a powder.

Mix oil with green onions, salt, and pepper to taste. Halve hard-boiled eggs and remove yolks. Chop whites and yolks separately.

Boil beans in a large pan of boiling salted water until crisp-tender, about 5 minutes. Rinse under cold water until cool and drain thoroughly. Gently pat dry.

Transfer beans to a large round platter, with all beans pointing to center. Spoon oil mixture evenly over beans.

Sprinkle nuts over center, covering partly where ends of beans meet. Sprinkle chopped egg yolks in a circle around walnuts. Then sprinkle chopped egg whites in a circle around yolks. Allow ends of green beans to show. Serve at room temperature.

Makes 8 servings

BEEF AND SWEET POTATO TZIMMES

Tzimmes is a dish from eastern Europe that usually includes sweet vegetables, dried fruit, or a mixture of both. Sometimes it is simply a sweetened vegetable stew—for example, of carrots simmered with honey. Or it can be a more elaborate casserole including beef, sweet potatoes, carrots, and prunes, as in this main-course version, which is similar to the tzimmes I grew up with. SEE PHOTOGRAPH.

1 tablespoon vegetable oil or chicken
  fat

2 pounds boneless chuck or stew meat,
  cut into 1½-inch cubes

2 large onions, chopped

5 large carrots, peeled and cut into 1-
  inch chunks

½ teaspoon salt

3 to 4 cups water

2 large potatoes

2 yams or sweet potatoes

¼ to ⅓ cup honey

½ teaspoon ground cinnamon

pinch of pepper

½ pound pitted prunes

1 tablespoon all-purpose flour
  (optional)

1 tablespoon chopped parsley
  (optional)

Heat oil in a Dutch oven or heavy casserole over medium heat. Add meat and brown well on all sides; if necessary brown meat in batches to avoid crowding. Remove meat from pan and add onions and sauté until browned. Return meat to pan and add carrots, salt, and enough water to just cover. Bring to a boil, skimming occasionally, then cover and simmer over low heat, skimming once or twice, for 1 hour.

Peel both types of potatoes and cut in large dice. After meat and carrots have cooked 1 hour, add potatoes, sweet potatoes, honey, cinnamon, and pepper to pan and mix gently. Push vegetables into liquid and bring to a boil. Partly cover and simmer 30 minutes. Meanwhile, soak prunes in enough hot water to cover for about 30 minutes.

Gently stir stew once. Remove prunes from their liquid, reserving liquid if later thickening the stew, and add prunes to pan. Uncover and simmer 30 minutes longer or until meat is very tender. Shake pan occasionally to prevent sticking but avoid stirring so as not to break up ingredients.

The stew should be moist but not soupy. If allowed to stand for 1 hour or more before being served, it will absorb enough of the excess liquid. If too much liquid remains, bake uncovered in a 350°F. oven for 15 to 30 minutes. Alternatively, stir flour with 2 tablespoons prune liquid in a bowl, gradually stir in about 1 cup of meat cooking liquid, and return mixture to pan; simmer about 5 minutes. (Stew can be made 1 day ahead and reheated gently in a covered pan over low heat or in a 300°F. oven.) Serve from a deep serving dish. Spinkle with parsley if desired.

Makes 4 to 6 servings

LIGHT HONEY CAKE WITH CINNAMON AND WALNUTS

Honey cake usually contains more than one flavoring and in fact the Alsatian version is called pain d'épices, *or "spice bread." This honey cake has less oil and sugar than many versions and therefore fewer calories, but the coffee, cinnamon, and nuts, as well as the honey, give it plenty of flavor.*

1½ teaspoons instant coffee granules
6 tablespoons hot water
1½ cups all-purpose flour
1 teaspoon baking powder
½ teaspoon baking soda
½ teaspoon ground cinnamon
¼ teaspoon ground ginger

small pinch of ground cloves
2 large eggs
½ cup sugar
½ cup honey
⅓ cup vegetable oil
½ cup walnuts, coarsely chopped

Preheat oven to 325°F. Lightly grease an 8 × 4-inch loaf pan, line it with parchment paper or wax paper, and grease the paper.

In a cup, dissolve the instant coffee in the hot water. Let cool. Sift flour with baking powder, baking soda, cinnamon, ginger, and cloves.

Beat eggs lightly. Add sugar and honey and beat until mixture is very smooth and light in color. Gradually add oil and beat until blended. Stir in flour mixture alternately in 2 batches with coffee. Stir in walnuts.

Pour batter into prepared pan and bake for 50 to 55 minutes or until a cake tester inserted in cake comes out clean. Cool in pan for about 15 minutes. Turn out onto rack and carefully peel off paper. Wrap in foil when completely cool. (If tightly wrapped, cake keeps 1 week at room temperature.) Serve in thin slices.

Makes 8 to 10 servings

APPLE CAKE WITH HONEY FROSTING

I developed this recipe with the Rosh Hashanah apple and honey theme in mind. The easy-to-make cake is moist and delicious on its own, but the honey frosting turns it into a lavish holiday dessert. The cake and frosting can be made with butter for meatless meals.

2¼ pounds sweet apples, such as
    Golden Delicious, peeled, halved,
    cored, and finely diced
1¼ cups sugar
1 cup plus 2 tablespoons (2¼ sticks)
    unsalted nondairy margarine or
    butter, softened

¼ cup honey
3 large eggs
3 cups all-purpose flour
2½ teaspoons baking powder
2 teaspoons finely grated orange rind
1 cup walnuts, coarsely chopped

Honey Frosting (optional)
2 large eggs, at room temperature
½ cup honey
1 cup (2 sticks) unsalted nondairy
    margarine or butter, slightly softened
    but still cool

½ cup walnuts, coarsely chopped, for
    garnish

Preheat oven to 350°F. Lightly grease a 13 × 9-inch cake pan with 2-inch sides. Line base and sides of pan with a sheet of foil and grease foil.

Thoroughly mix apples and ½ cup of sugar. Let stand while preparing batter.

Beat margarine until smooth. Add remaining ¾ cup sugar and beat until fluffy. Beat in honey, then add eggs one by one, beating well after each addition. Sift flour with baking powder and stir into egg mixture. Stir in orange rind. Add apple mixture, which will be syrupy, and nuts.

Spread batter in prepared cake pan and smooth top. Bake for 45 minutes or until cake tests done with toothpick or tester. Cool in pan on a rack about 20 minutes or until just warm. Turn out onto a rack. Cool to room temperature.

To make frosting, beat eggs in a large bowl until smooth and fluffy. Bring honey to a boil in a small saucepan, then gradually pour honey onto eggs, whisking constantly. Whip at high speed of mixer until completely cool and thick, about 5 minutes.

Cream margarine in a large bowl until smooth and fluffy. Beat in honey mixture gradually until thoroughly mixed.

Spread frosting over top and sides of cake. Sprinkle top with chopped walnuts. Refrigerate about 2 hours before serving. Serve cool or at room temperature.

Makes 12 servings

AN ECLECTIC MEAL FOR ROSH HASHANAH

This menu for the Jewish New Year is composed of dishes from a variety of Jewish groups and fits the spirit of a traditional and healthful Rosh Hashanah dinner. Italian-style fish in a tomato and garlic sauce is a zesty Sephardic specialty and will come as a surprise to those who are used to thinking that gefilte fish is the only Jewish way of preparing fish. Roast chicken stuffed with rice and fruit is a favorite in both Israel and America, and is accompanied here by Sephardic pumpkin pancakes. The honey cake comes to us from eastern Europe, while the sweet and spicy quince compote with cinnamon is a North African Jewish treat for beginning the holiday as an appetizer or for a dessert.

ECLECTIC ROSH HASHANAH MENU

Apples and Honey
Round Holiday Challah with Raisins (page 66)
Italian-Style Fish in Tomato-Garlic Sauce
Roast Chicken with Rice and Fruit Stuffing
Sephardic Pumpkin Pancakes
Hazelnut Honey Cake (Lekach),
or Chocolate-Almond Cake
with Chocolate-Honey Frosting
Quince Compote with Cinnamon

ITALIAN-STYLE FISH IN TOMATO-GARLIC SAUCE

For a delicious cold fish appetizer of pure, fresh flavors, try this specialty of the Jews of Italy. The fish is cooked directly in an easy-to-make, quick-cooking tomato sauce, for which a food processor comes in very handy. I usually chop the parsley first in the processor, then the garlic, and finally the onion. Then I wipe the processor bowl and puree the tomatoes. The fish is also very good served hot as a main course, accompanied by rice or pasta.

4 tablespoons olive oil
⅓ cup minced onion
3 medium garlic cloves, minced
1½ pounds ripe tomatoes, peeled,
    seeded, and pureed; or 1 28-ounce
    and 1 14-ounce can plum tomatoes,
    drained and pureed

½ teaspoon dried leaf oregano
salt and pepper
1½ to 1¾ pounds fish fillets, such as
    halibut, about 1 inch thick
3 tablespoons chopped fresh parsley,
    preferably flat-leaf

In a large sauté pan or skillet, heat 3 tablespoons oil with onion and sauté over medium-low heat for 5 to 6 minutes or until onion begins to turn golden. Add garlic and sauté 30 seconds. Add tomatoes, oregano, salt, and pepper and cook over medium-high heat, stirring often, about 8 to 10 minutes or until thick. (Sauce can be kept, covered, for 1 day in refrigerator. Reheat in sauté pan before continuing.)

    Add fish in one layer to hot sauce and sprinkle with 1 tablespoon oil, salt, and pepper. Cover and cook over medium-low heat, spooning sauce over fish from time to time, about 10 minutes or until thickest part of fish has changed color inside when checked with a sharp knife. Taste sauce and adjust seasoning. Stir parsley gently into sauce. Serve fish hot or cold.

Makes 4 servings

ROAST CHICKEN WITH RICE AND FRUIT STUFFING

The light fruity stuffing fits the Rosh Hashanah theme and provides a delicate hint of sweetness. It's also delicious with turkey or goose; double it for a 10- to 12-pound turkey or multiply it by 1½ for an 8- or 9-pound goose.

½ cup pecan halves (optional)
4 tablespoons vegetable oil
1 small onion, minced
½ cup chopped celery
1 cup long-grain white rice
1½ cups hot chicken soup or water
½ cup orange juice

salt and pepper
1 small apple
½ cup raisins
¼ teaspoon ground cinnamon
1 teaspoon finely grated orange rind
3½- to 4-pound roasting chicken

Preheat oven to 400°F. If using pecans, toast lightly in oven for 5 minutes. Cool and cut in half lengthwise.

Heat 3 tablespoons oil in a deep skillet or sauté pan, add onion and celery, and cook over low heat about 5 minutes or until tender. Add rice and sauté over medium heat about 2 minutes. Add hot soup, orange juice, salt, and pepper and bring to a boil. Cover and cook over low heat for 10 minutes. Meanwhile, peel, halve, and core apple and cut it into small dice. Add raisins and apple to rice and stir very lightly with a fork. Cover and cook 5 more minutes or until rice is nearly tender. Stir in cinnamon, orange rind, and pecans and taste for seasoning. Let cool.

Sprinkle chicken with salt and pepper on all sides. Spoon enough stuffing into chicken to fill it, packing it lightly; reserve extra stuffing at room temperature. Set chicken in a roasting pan and roast for about 1 hour; when a skewer or trussing needle is inserted into thickest part of leg, juices should come out clear. If juices are pink, roast a few more minutes. Let stand 5 to 10 minutes before serving.

Heat remaining tablespoon oil in a skillet or sauté pan and add remaining stuffing. Cook 3 minutes over low heat until very hot.

Serve chicken and its stuffing on a platter, and remaining rice mixture in a side dish or next to chicken. If desired, serve roasting juices in a sauceboat.

Makes 4 servings

SEPHARDIC PUMPKIN PANCAKES

Whether these delicately flavored pancakes are made with pumpkin or with orange-fleshed winter squash, they make a colorful addition to festive menus and are ideal for Rosh Hashanah, Succot, or Hanukkah.

1¾ to 2 pounds pumpkin or winter
   squash such as banana squash
½ cup plus 1 tablespoon all-purpose
   flour
2 large eggs

¼ teaspoon sugar
¼ teaspoon salt
pepper to taste
about 5 tablespoons vegetable oil, for
   frying

Cut pumpkin or squash into 6 or 8 pieces. Add to a large saucepan with enough boiling salted water to cover it. Bring to a boil, cover, and simmer over low heat for 15 minutes or until tender. Drain thoroughly and cut off peel. Cut in pieces and mash with a fork. Press gently in a strainer to remove excess liquid. Transfer to a bowl.

In a medium bowl mix flour, eggs, sugar, salt, and pepper to a very thick batter. Add to mashed pumpkin and mix very well. Taste for seasoning.

Heat 4 tablespoons oil in a heavy skillet over medium heat. Fry pumpkin mixture by tablespoonfuls, flattening each after adding it, about 2 minutes or until golden brown on each side. Turn carefully using 2 pancake turners. Transfer to paper towels to drain. Continue making pancakes, adding more oil to skillet if necessary. Serve hot or at room temperature.

Makes 22 to 24 small pancakes; 4 to 6 servings

HAZELNUT HONEY CAKE (LEKACH)

Known in Yiddish as lekach, *honey cake is very easy to prepare and is the traditional treat served by Jews of eastern European extraction on the first night of Rosh Hashanah and during Succot two weeks later. This version is moist, delicately enhanced with fresh lemon rind and sweet spices, and studded with nuts. Another great advantage of honey cake is its keeping qualities; if wrapped in foil, it will stay fresh-tasting for two weeks. In fact, it is best to make this cake one or two days ahead so its flavor matures. If hazelnuts are not available, use almonds instead.*

2¼ cups all-purpose flour
2¼ teaspoons baking powder
¾ teaspoon baking soda
¾ teaspoon ground cinnamon
½ teaspoon ground ginger
pinch of cloves
3 large eggs

¾ cup dark brown sugar
1 cup honey
¾ cup vegetable oil
1½ teaspoons grated lemon rind
½ cup unsweetened applesauce
¾ cup hazelnuts, chopped

Preheat oven to 350°F. Lightly grease a 9-inch square pan, line it with parchment paper or wax paper, and grease the paper. Sift the flour with the baking powder, baking soda, cinnamon, ginger, and cloves.

Beat the eggs lightly. Add the brown sugar and honey and beat until the mixture is smooth and lightened in color. Gradually add the oil and beat until blended. Beat in the lemon rind. On low speed, beat in the flour mixture alternately in 2 batches with the applesauce. Stir in the nuts.

Pour the batter into the prepared pan. Bake for about 55 minutes or until your finger does not leave an indentation when you press lightly on top of cake, and a cake tester inserted in the center comes out clean. Cool in the pan for about 15 minutes.

Turn cake out onto rack and carefully peel off the paper. Cover tightly when completely cool. (If tightly wrapped, cake keeps 2 weeks at room temperature.) Serve at room temperature. Cut into squares or bars.

Makes 9 to 12 servings

CHOCOLATE-ALMOND CAKE WITH CHOCOLATE-HONEY FROSTING

Although honey symbolizes a sweet new year, for some people honey and chocolate say this even better! The frosting is flavored with honey, which marries very well with the taste of chocolate.

1½ cups (about 7 ounces) almonds
6 ounces semisweet chocolate
¾ cup sugar
¼ cup all-purpose flour
½ teaspoon baking powder

¾ cup (1½ sticks) unsalted nondairy margarine or butter
6 large eggs, separated, at room temperature
¼ teaspoon cream of tartar

Chocolate-Honey Frosting

½ cup nondairy creamer or heavy cream
6 ounces semisweet chocolate, finely chopped
6 tablespoons (¾ stick) unsalted nondairy margarine or butter, slightly softened

3 tablespoons plus 1 teaspoon honey
about ¼ cup blanched almonds, chopped, for garnish

Preheat oven to 350°F. Toast almonds in shallow baking dish in oven for 7 minutes. Transfer to plate and cool completely.

Melt chocolate in a double boiler above hot water over low heat. Stir until smooth, then remove from pan of water and let cool.

Lightly grease a 9-inch springform pan with 3-inch sides. Line base of pan with parchment paper or foil and grease paper or foil. Flour side of pan and lined base, tapping to remove excess.

In a food processor, grind ¾ cup almonds with 2 tablespoons sugar as finely as possible.

Transfer to a large bowl. Repeat with remaining almonds and 2 more tablespoons sugar and add to first batch. Sift flour and baking powder onto almond mixture and mix thoroughly.

Cream margarine and 6 tablespoons sugar. Beat in egg yolks, one by one. Stir in melted chocolate.

Whip egg whites with cream of tartar in a large bowl until soft peaks form. Gradually beat in remaining 2 tablespoons sugar and whip at high speed until whites are stiff but not dry. Sprinkle about one-third of almond mixture over chocolate mixture and fold in gently, followed by about one-third of whites. Repeat with remaining almond mixture and whites in 2 batches. Fold lightly but quickly just until batter is blended.

Transfer batter to prepared pan and spread evenly. Bake about 45 minutes or until a cake tester inserted in center of cake comes out clean. Cool in pan on a rack for 10 minutes. Cake will settle slightly in center during cooling.

Run a thin-bladed flexible knife or metal spatula carefully around cake. Invert cake onto rack, release spring, and remove sides and base of pan. Carefully peel off paper. Invert cake onto another rack so its smooth side is against rack; let cool completely. (Cake can be wrapped and kept 2 days in refrigerator.) Turn cake back over so smooth side is up. Transfer to a platter.

For frosting, bring cream to a boil in a small, heavy saucepan. Remove from heat and immediately add chopped chocolate. Using a small whisk, stir quickly until chocolate is completely melted and mixture is smooth. Transfer to a bowl and cool to room temperature. Whip mixture at high speed for about 3 minutes.

Cream margarine until very soft and smooth. Add chocolate mixture in 3 batches, beating constantly until frosting is smooth. Gradually beat in honey.

Spread frosting on top and side of cake. Using spatula, swirl frosting at top, from edge inward, forming small curves. Spoon remaining frosting into pastry bag fitted with small star tip. Pipe a ring of rosettes of frosting about halfway between edge and center of cake. Fill center of ring with chopped almonds. Press gently so they adhere to frosting. Chill at least 1 hour before serving. When frosting is firm, cake can be wrapped. (Cake can be kept, covered, for 3 days in refrigerator.)

Makes 12 servings

QUINCE COMPOTE WITH CINNAMON

This is a prized Rosh Hashanah dish among Jews of different origins—Moroccan, Greek, and Turkish, for example. Along with apple slices and bowls of honey, pomegranate seeds, and other fruits, it is placed on the table before the actual dinner begins. This sweet compote also makes a tasty dessert.

3 large quince (about 1¾ pounds total)
1 cup sugar

¼ cup strained fresh lemon juice
  (optional)
2 teaspoons ground cinnamon

Peel quince, cut them in eighths, and cut out core and seed section from each piece. Put into a heavy saucepan, add water just to cover, and bring to a boil. Cook, uncovered, over medium heat, carefully turning slices from time to time, for about 50 minutes or until they are tender and much of the water is evaporated and slices are about half-covered. (Cooking time varies with size of quinces and their degree of ripeness.)

Add sugar, lemon juice, and cinnamon. Swirl pan and baste quince with the liquid to dissolve the sugar. Cook over medium heat for 5 minutes, then over low heat for 30 minutes, basting from time to time. When quince are ready, they should be very tender, have turned a pink hue, and appear shiny and glazed; syrup should taste concentrated. Spoon them into serving dishes with their syrup. Serve cold.

Makes 4 servings

A NOTE ABOUT YOM KIPPUR

Ten days after Rosh Hashanah is the most solemn holiday of the Jewish calendar, Yom Kippur. This is a day of fasting, but there are food customs for before and after the fast. The dinner prior to the fast takes place in the evening before Yom Kippur day. It is a copious dinner that is less seasoned than usual, so that people won't become too thirsty during the fast. Generally chicken is the main course. Often it is a whole poached chicken that also produces a rich chicken soup. Some Ashkenazic families serve the soup with kreplach.

Following the fast, a fairly light meal is usually prepared. What to serve depends on family traditions. Some families have a dairy supper, such as bagels with lox and cream cheese, or other foods that require little preparation. When I was growing up, a favorite treat in our family for breaking the fast was a slice of Sour Cream Coffee Cake with Walnuts (page 310).

4
SUCCOT: THE HARVEST HOLIDAY

 Succot is a festival to show appreciation for the harvest, and is celebrated in early autumn (for eight days in Israel and nine days outside Israel). Meals are served in a *succah*, a hut with a roof of leafy branches, to commemorate the temporary shelters in which the Hebrews lived when they fled from Egypt. (Although the escape from Egypt is the theme of Passover, this major event in Jewish history is recalled in the customs of other festivals as well.) From the roof of branches, fruit are suspended on pieces of string, as a natural decoration.

The agricultural theme is echoed in the holiday foods—Succot is the time to serve plenty of fruits and vegetables. In Israel stuffed vegetables are frequently prepared for the holiday. Popular choices are stuffed cabbage leaves, eggplant, zucchini, and peppers. As on Rosh Hashanah, tzimmes, a stew with vegetables and fruits, is a favorite item on the menu of Jews of eastern European origin.

Even the holiday ritual involves produce. A special "ceremonial" fruit for Succot is the citron, called an *etrog* in Hebrew and an *esrog* in Yiddish. It plays a part in special Succot prayers. In this country the fruit is rare and expensive and is not used for cooking. In Israel, however, the

81

fruit is sometimes made into preserves. My in-laws have an *etrog* tree in their garden and use the fruit to prepare a wonderful marmalade.

Other ideal Succot dishes:

Zesty Pepper-Tomato Salad (page 18)
Yemenite Tomato Salsa (page 166)
Mushroom-Barley Chicken Soup (page 185)
Baked Sweet Potatoes with Dried Fruit
(page 255)
Sephardic Pumpkin Pancakes (page 76)
Zucchini with Tomatoes and Dill (page 265)
Spicy Meat-Stuffed Peppers (page 259)
Stuffed Eggplant with Meat, Pine Nuts, and Almonds
(page 260)
Okra with Tomatoes and Coriander (page 267)
Beef and Sweet Potato Tzimmes (page 70)
Veal with Olives, Tomatoes, and Fresh Herbs (page 248)
Spiced Apple Blintzes (page 324)
Cinnamon-Scented Apple Noodle Kugel (page 139)

AN ASHKENAZIC SUCCOT

Succot menus are quite individual, with each family selecting its own favorites. The dishes should be easy to carry to the succah, which is located outside the house—a fragile soufflé would definitely not be chosen! The most festive dinners are served during the first and last days of Succot, and on the Sabbath that may fall in the middle of the holiday.

Ashkenazic cooks make lavish use of both vegetables and fruits throughout the meal. Stuffed vegetables, such as stuffed cabbage, might also be featured, or casseroles of vegetables and fruit, such as Baked Sweet Potatoes with Dried Fruit (page 255).

ASHKENAZIC SUCCOT MENU

Beet Salad with Apples
Ashkenazic Chicken Soup with Fresh Dill
and Light Matzo Balls
Beef Stew with Winter Squash and Raisins,
or Roast Duck with Prunes and Red Wine
Noodle Kugel with Colorful Vegetables
Pear Strudel,
or My Mother's Chocolate Applesauce Cake

BEET SALAD WITH APPLES

I learned to prepare this salad of eastern European inspiration at a cooking course I took at the Institute for Nutrition and Home Economics in Tel Aviv. With students of so many different ethnic origins, we enjoyed learning each other's favorite recipes.

The delicately sweet, bright pink salad is good with fresh pumpernickel bread. For meatless dinners, 2 tablespoons sour cream can replace half the mayonnaise.

7 medium beets (1½ inch diameter,
   about ¾ pound, not including
   greens), trimmed
2 tart apples, such as Granny Smith
1 tablespoon plus 1 teaspoon prepared
   mustard

4 tablespoons mayonnaise
1 teaspoon sugar
salt and freshly ground pepper
lettuce leaves (optional)

In a medium saucepan cover beets with water and cook, covered, about 45 minutes to 1 hour or until tender when pierced with a sharp knife. Rinse and peel. Slice beets, then cut them into 1-inch sticks about ¼ inch thick. Coarsely grate the apples and mix with beets. Stir together remaining ingredients. Add to beet mixture and mix. Taste and adjust seasoning. Serve cold, on a bed of lettuce leaves.

Makes 3 or 4 servings

ASHKENAZIC CHICKEN SOUP WITH FRESH DILL AND LIGHT MATZO BALLS

Matzo balls, also known as kneidlach, *are the subject of an ongoing controversy in many families, including ours. Some people like them light and airy, while others prefer them more substantial. A friend of mine calls them ''floaters'' versus ''sinkers.'' My mother taught me that light matzo balls require a very soft batter and gentle shaping. If it is firm enough so the balls can be formed in a neat, perfectly round shape, they will not be fluffy.*

2 pounds chicken wings or drumsticks
9 cups cold water
1 large onion, peeled
1 large carrot, peeled
1 small parsnip, peeled (optional)

2 celery stalks, including leafy tops
5 parsley sprigs
3 dill sprigs
salt and pepper
1 tablespoon snipped fresh dill

Matzo Balls

2 large eggs
2 tablespoons vegetable oil
½ cup matzo meal
½ teaspoon salt

½ teaspoon baking powder
1 to 2 tablespoons water or chicken
  soup

about 2 quarts salted water, for
  simmering

Combine chicken wings, water, onion, carrot, parsnip, celery, parsley and dill sprigs, and pinch of salt in a large saucepan and bring to a boil. Partly cover and simmer 2 hours, skimming occasionally. Skim off excess fat. (Chicken soup can be kept 3 days in refrigerator or can be frozen; reheat before serving.)

Make matzo balls: In a medium bowl, lightly beat eggs with oil. Add matzo meal, salt, and baking powder and stir until smooth. Stir in water, then let mixture stand for 20 minutes so matzo meal absorbs liquid.

Bring salted water to a boil. With wet hands, roll about 1 teaspoon of matzo ball mixture between your palms into a ball; mixture will be very soft. Set balls on a plate. With a rubber spatula, carefully slide balls into boiling water. Cover and simmer over low heat for about 30 minutes or until firm. Cover and keep warm until ready to serve. (Matzo balls can be kept 2 days in their cooking liquid in a covered container in refrigerator; reheat gently in cooking liquid or in soup.)

To serve soup, remove chicken wings, onion, celery, parsnip, and parsley and dill sprigs. Take meat off bones and add to soup; or reserve for other uses. Add pepper to soup, stir in snipped dill and taste soup for seasoning. Slice carrot and add a few slices to each bowl. With a slotted spoon, add a few matzo balls. Serve hot.

Makes 8 servings

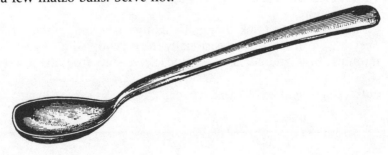

BEEF STEW WITH WINTER SQUASH AND RAISINS

Some say that a fondness for sweet-and-sour dishes accounts for the Jewish taste for Chinese food. This version of the sweet Ashkenazic stew known as tzimmes has a touch of soy sauce and cinnamon, which impart a nice flavor and result in a dish that borrows from both styles of cooking. The Noodle Kugel with Colorful Vegetables in this menu makes a pleasing accompaniment for the beef and its rich sauce, as do plain noodles, rice, or couscous.

3 tablespoons vegetable oil
3½ to 4 pounds boneless lean beef
    chuck, cut into 1¼- to 1½-inch
    pieces, trimmed of fat and patted dry
2 large onions, chopped
2 tablespoons all-purpose flour
1½ cups dry white wine
2½ cups water

2 tablespoons soy sauce
1 cinnamon stick, about 2 inches long;
    or a pinch of ground cinnamon
pinch of freshly ground pepper
3 pounds orange-colored winter
    squash
3 tablespoons mild honey
½ cup dark raisins

Heat oil in a large heavy casserole over medium-high heat. Add beef in batches and brown on all sides. Using slotted spatula, transfer it to a plate. Add onions to casserole and sauté over medium-low heat until softened, about 7 minutes. Return meat to pan, reserving any juices on plate, and sprinkle meat with flour. Toss lightly to coat meat with flour. Cook over low heat, stirring often, for 5 minutes.

Stir in wine, water, juices from plate, and soy sauce, add cinnamon stick and pepper, and bring to a boil, stirring often. Cover and cook over low heat, stirring and turning beef cubes occasionally, until beef is very tender, about 2½ to 2¾ hours; when a cube is pierced and lifted with thin-bladed sharp knife, it should fall from knife. Discard cinnamon stick.

Meanwhile, scrape off any stringy parts from center of squash with spoon. Cut squash into large pieces, cut off peel, and cut squash into 1-inch cubes. When meat is tender, stir in honey. Add squash and raisins, and push squash down into liquid. Cover and simmer 10 minutes. Turn squash pieces over, cover, and simmer until squash is tender, about 15 minutes more.

Sauce should be thick enough to lightly coat a spoon; if it is too thin, uncover and simmer over low heat, stirring occasionally very gently, until lightly thickened, about 10 to 15 minutes. Taste and adjust seasoning. Serve stew from deep serving dish.

Makes 8 servings

ROAST DUCK WITH PRUNES AND RED WINE

Duck with prunes is popular among Jews from central Europe and France, since the sweetness of the fruit is a pleasing balance for the duck's richness. This duck also makes an elegant main course for Rosh Hashanah, accompanied by rice or potatoes and by sugar-snap peas or shelled peas.

16 pitted prunes (about 6 ounces)
¾ cup dry or lightly sweetened red wine
¾ cup water
2 ducks (each about 4½ to 5 pounds), thawed if frozen, patted dry

salt and freshly ground pepper
1½ cups chicken stock or soup
1 teaspoon potato starch or cornstarch dissolved in 2 teaspoons water

Combine prunes, wine, and water in small deep bowl or cup and cover. Soak prunes for 2 hours.

Preheat oven to 450°F. Remove fat from inside ducks near tail and under neck skin. For easier carving, remove wishbone from each duck: Set duck on its back and lift neck skin; the first bone above neck is V-shape wishbone. Outline it carefully with a thin-bladed knife and pull wishbone out.

Sprinkle duck inside and out with salt and pepper. Using skewer, pierce skin all over, especially where fat is thickest, at intervals of about ½ inch; do not pierce meat.

Set ducks on their side on rack in a heavy roasting pan. Roast 10 minutes, then turn ducks onto other side and roast 10 minutes more. Using a bulb baster, remove fat from pan. Set ducks on their breasts and roast 10 minutes. Turn ducks on their backs and roast 10 minutes more.

Reduce oven temperature to 400°F., and roast duck, discarding fat occasionally, about 40 minutes. To check whether duck is done, prick thigh meat in plumpest part: if juices that escape are still red, duck is not done; if they are clear, duck is well done. If browner skin is desired, transfer duck to a broiler pan and broil about 5 inches from heat source until skin is deep brown.

Transfer ducks to a platter, draining juices from inside duck into roasting pan. Cover loosely and keep warm. (Ducks can be kept warm for 30 minutes in oven with heat turned off and door slightly ajar.)

When ducks are nearly done, transfer prunes with their soaking liquid to a saucepan. Add more water, if necessary, to barely cover them and bring to a simmer. Cover and cook over low heat until prunes are just tender, about 10 minutes. Pour liquid into bowl and set prunes aside.

Pour off fat from roasting pan but leave darker duck juices. Reheat juices in a pan over medium-high heat, then add ½ cup stock and bring to boil, stirring and scraping up any browned bits and moving pan back and forth over burner to heat evenly. Strain into medium saucepan. Add prune liquid and remaining 1 cup stock. Boil until sauce is reduced to about 1¼ cups, about 5 minutes. Remove from heat. Skim excess fat from sauce.

Bring sauce to a simmer over medium heat. Whisk potato starch mixture to blend, then gradually whisk into simmering sauce. Return to a boil, whisking, and cook over low heat for 1 minute. Add salt and pepper to taste. Add prunes, cover, and let stand 2 minutes.

Spoon prunes around ducks and spoon a little sauce over prunes. Serve remaining sauce separately.

Makes 6 servings

NOODLE KUGEL WITH COLORFUL VEGETABLES

Serve this savory noodle kugel accented with carrots, zucchini, and sautéed mushrooms as an accompaniment for meat, chicken, or fish. See photograph.

1 pound wide egg noodles
9 tablespoons vegetable oil
2 large onions, minced
¾ pound small mushrooms, sliced
salt and freshly ground pepper to taste
1 teaspoon dried thyme
1 teaspoon paprika

5 large eggs, beaten
2 large carrots, coarsely grated
2 small zucchini, coarsely grated
⅓ cup chopped parsley or chopped
  fresh coriander (cilantro)
cayenne pepper to taste

Preheat oven to 350°F. Cook noodles, uncovered, in a large pot of boiling salted water over high heat, stirring occasionally, for about 4 minutes or until nearly tender but firmer than usual, since they will be baked. Drain, rinse with cold water, and drain again. Transfer to a large bowl.

Heat 6 tablespoons oil in a large skillet over medium-low heat. Add onions and sauté about 15 minutes or until very tender. Add 2 tablespoons oil and heat again. Add mushrooms, salt, pepper, thyme, and paprika and sauté about 15 minutes or until mushrooms are tender and onions are browned. If mixture is watery, increase heat and cook about 5 minutes or until excess liquid evaporates.

Add mushroom mixture, eggs, carrots, zucchini, and parsley to noodles and mix well. Add cayenne. Taste and adjust seasoning. Oil a 3½- to 4-quart baking dish or two 7- to 8-cup baking dishes and add noodle mixture. Sprinkle with remaining tablespoon oil.

Bake 45 to 55 minutes or until set; kugel will bake faster in shallow dishes than in deep ones. Serve hot, from baking dish.

Makes 8 to 10 servings

PEAR STRUDEL

Whether in Paris, New York, or Los Angeles, if you were looking for strudel, your best bet would be to go to a Jewish pastry shop. This eastern European specialty was adopted by Jewish cooks and showcased in Jewish bakeries and delis throughout the West. For home cooks, strudel used to be a lot of work, but now it's easy to make using packaged filo dough, which is sometimes labeled ''strudel dough.'' For dairy meals, prepare the strudel with butter and serve it, if you like, with whipped cream (see Variation) or vanilla ice cream and chocolate sauce.

Pear Filling

⅓ cup finely chopped dried pears or golden raisins
½ cup pecans, chopped
2 large ripe pears (12 to 14 ounces total), peeled, halved, cored, and thinly sliced

¼ cup granulated sugar
2 teaspoons strained fresh lemon juice
1 teaspoon grated lemon rind
1 teaspoon ground cinnamon
2 tablespoons apricot preserves

4 strudel or filo sheets, thawed if frozen
6 tablespoons (¾ stick) unsalted nondairy margarine or butter, melted

4 tablespoons dry cookie crumbs or bread crumbs

confectioners' sugar, for serving

Thoroughly mix dried pears with pecans in a large bowl. Add remaining filling ingredients and mix well.

Preheat oven to 375°F. Lightly grease a baking sheet. Lay 1 filo sheet on a large sheet of wax paper. Brush with melted margarine and sprinkle with 1 tablespoon crumbs. Top with a second sheet of filo. Brush with butter and sprinkle with 1 tablespoon crumbs. Keep remaining filo sheets covered.

Put half the filling near one long end of top sheet, arranging it in a log shape and leaving a 1-inch border. Starting with that end, carefully roll up dough as for a jelly roll, using the paper to help support dough. End the roll with the seam on the bottom. Transfer roll to baking sheet and brush top with margarine. Repeat with remaining filling and remaining dough. Bake 25 minutes or until golden.

Just before serving strudel, sprinkle it with confectioners' sugar. Serve warm if desired.

Makes 6 servings

VARIATION: Whipped Cream

¾ cup heavy cream
1½ teaspoons granulated sugar
½ teaspoon vanilla extract

Chill bowl and beaters. Whip cream with sugar and vanilla in chilled bowl at high speed of mixer until stiff. (Cream can be whipped up to 2 hours ahead and kept in refrigerator but retains its shape best when whipped a short time before serving.)

MY MOTHER'S CHOCOLATE APPLESAUCE CAKE

My mother often bakes this cake for Sabbath, and it has served as many a birthday cake as well. Applesauce gives it moistness, and it is rich, dark, and delicious, although it is enriched with oil rather than butter, has a low proportion of eggs, and contains no dairy products. The chocolate frosting and garnish of chopped nuts are optional, but they do give the cake a festive note. This is one of the quickest and easiest cake recipes I know.

½ cup vegetable oil
1 cup sugar
1 large egg
1½ cups all-purpose flour

⅓ cup unsweetened cocoa
1½ teaspoons ground cinnamon
1 teaspoon baking soda
1 cup unsweetened applesauce

Easy Chocolate Frosting (optional)

3 ounces semisweet chocolate
2 tablespoons (¼ stick) unsalted nondairy
    margarine, cut in 4 pieces, softened
¼ cup diced pecans or walnuts

Preheat oven to 350°F. Grease and flour an 8- or 9-inch square baking pan. Beat oil, sugar, and egg until pale in color and fluffy. Sift flour with cocoa, cinnamon, and baking soda. Stir flour mixture alternately with applesauce into egg mixture and mix well. Bake in greased pan for 25 to 35 minutes, depending on pan size, or until a cake tester inserted in cake comes out clean. Turn out onto a rack or leave in the pan; cool completely.

   Melt chocolate for frosting in a medium saucepan set above hot water over low heat. Remove from heat and stir in margarine. Cool about 2 minutes or until thick enough to spread. Spread over top of cake and sprinkle with nuts. Refrigerate about 1 hour or until set. (Cake can be kept, covered, for 3 days in refrigerator.) Serve at room temperature.

Makes 8 to 10 servings

A SEPHARDIC SUCCOT

A selection of stuffed vegetables is the star on the Succot menu of most Sephardic Jews. Many cooks prepare a large batch of a single stuffing and use it to fill a few different vegetables. In addition to or as alternatives to the recipes here, stuffed peppers or stuffed eggplant might be featured (recipes are in Chapter 14, "Vegetables"). Instead of the first course, many families serve a variety of salads, such as eggplant salad, potato salad, humus, and carrot salad, together with pita bread.

SEPHARDIC SUCCOT MENU

Sautéed Eggplant in Spicy Tomato Sauce,
or Moroccan Sea Bass with Red Peppers
Aromatic Stuffed Onions
Stuffed Zucchini with Lamb,
Almonds, and Raisins
Middle Eastern Stuffed Cabbage Leaves
Fresh Fruit,
or Pine Nut–Almond Filo Fingers

SAUTÉED EGGPLANT IN SPICY TOMATO SAUCE

Eggplant appears in a great variety of recipes in Israel, ranging from salads to fritters to stews to sautés. Jews in the Middle East like their vegetables well seasoned and very tender, as in this Yemenite eggplant recipe. If you like, the sautéed eggplant slices can be simmered in the tomato sauce instead of baked in it. The dish can be served with rice for a vegetarian meal, or as a vegetable accompaniment for chicken or meat.

As with many eggplant dishes, zucchini can also be prepared this way. But I don't think that I'd go as far as my friend Haim Shapiro, the restaurant critic of the Jerusalem Post, *who feels that anything made with eggplant can be made—even better—with zucchini.*

1 large eggplant (about 1¼ pounds)
salt

Spicy Tomato Sauce

3 tablespoons olive or vegetable oil
1 medium onion, minced
1½ teaspoons ground cumin
¾ teaspoon paprika
¼ teaspoon turmeric
1¾ pounds ripe tomatoes, peeled,
   seeded, and chopped; or 2 28-ounce
   cans plum tomatoes, drained and
   chopped

salt and freshly ground pepper
pinch of cayenne pepper
2 teaspoons tomato paste (optional)
3 medium garlic cloves, minced

6 tablespoons olive or vegetable oil, for
   sautéing

Cut peel from eggplant with a knife and discard ends. Cut eggplant into ⅜-inch crosswise slices. Sprinkle lightly but evenly with salt on both sides and put in a colander. Place bowl with a weight on top, pressing against slices, and leave to drain 1 hour, turning slices over after 30 minutes. Pat dry with paper towels.

Heat oil for sauce in large saucepan. Add onion and sauté over medium-low heat for about 7 minutes or until soft and light brown. Add cumin, paprika, and turmeric and cook, stirring, for 30 seconds. Add tomatoes, salt, pepper, and cayenne and stir well. Bring to a boil over medium-high heat. Cook over low heat, uncovered, stirring occasionally, for about

30 minutes or until tomatoes are very soft. Sauce will be chunky. Add tomato paste and taste for seasoning. Stir in garlic. (Sauce can be kept, covered, for 2 days in refrigerator.)

Preheat oven to 350°F. Heat 3 tablespoons oil in a large heavy skillet. Quickly add enough eggplant slices to make one layer. Sauté over medium heat for about 2 minutes on each side; remove to plate. Add 3 tablespoons oil to skillet, heat oil, and sauté second batch of eggplant in same way.

Lightly oil a shallow 5-cup baking dish. Arrange alternate layers of eggplant and sauce, ending with sauce. Bake 30 minutes or until eggplant is very tender, basting occasionally. Serve hot or at room temperature.

Makes 4 servings

MOROCCAN SEA BASS WITH RED PEPPERS

From Moroccan Jews comes this flavorful fish dish, dotted with bright red sautéed peppers, coriander leaves, and sautéed garlic. It is simple to make and is delicious hot or cold, as a first course for Sabbath or a main course on other occasions.

¼ cup vegetable oil
2 fresh pimientos or red bell peppers, diced
20 medium garlic cloves, minced
6 tablespoons minced fresh coriander (cilantro) leaves

1½ pounds small sea bass steaks, about 1 inch thick, or 1¼ pounds sea bass fillets
salt and pepper
1 teaspoon paprika
2 cups water

In a sauté pan large enough to hold fish in one layer, heat oil and add peppers. Sauté lightly over medium heat for 2 minutes. Add garlic and coriander and cook over low heat, stirring, for 1 minute. Add fish and sprinkle with salt, pepper, and paprika. Add water and bring to a simmer, basting fish occasionally. Cover and cook over very low heat about 8 minutes or until fish is just tender; when a thin skewer is inserted into center of fish, it should come out hot to the touch.

Transfer fish to a deep platter, using a slotted spoon. Remove skin from fish.

Boil liquid with peppers, stirring occasionally, until only about ½ cup liquid remains. Taste for seasoning and pour it over fish. Serve hot or cold.

Makes 4 or 5 first-course servings or 2 or 3 main-course servings

AROMATIC STUFFED ONIONS

I learned the technique for preparing stuffed onions from Suzanne Elmaleh of Jerusalem, who cooks in the traditional style of the Jews of Lebanon. For a special touch, she adds a few tablespoons of pomegranate juice to the cooking liquid when the onions are nearly done, for an intriguing hint of sweetness. The juice can be found in Iranian grocery stores, specialty markets, and some supermarkets. If you prefer a tart note, add 2 tablespoons lemon juice instead.

½ cup long-grain white rice
1 cup boiling water
3 large yellow or white onions (about
   2 pounds total), peeled
pinch of ground cinnamon
¼ teaspoon ground allspice
½ teaspoon salt
½ teaspoon pepper

1 tablespoon vegetable oil
¼ pound lean ground beef
1 cup water
3 tablespoons pomegranate juice
   (optional)
Basic Tomato Sauce (page 348,
   optional)

In a bowl combine rice and boiling water. Let stand until mixture is cool.

Slit each onion once halfway to center, cutting from top to bottom. Put onions in a large pan of boiling salted water and boil for about 20 minutes or until it is easy to separate them in layers. Drain and leave until cool enough to handle. Separate carefully in layers.

Drain rice thoroughly. Mix with cinnamon, allspice, salt, pepper, and oil. Taste for seasoning. Add beef. Knead to mix well. Put about 1 teaspoon stuffing at one end of an onion piece and roll it up tightly, following shape of onion. Cut any large onion pieces in half, to make 2 stuffed onion pieces.

Put onions in a sauté pan, arranging them in a tight layer with seam side down. Add enough water to barely cover them. Sprinkle with salt and bring to a simmer. Cover and cook over low heat about 1 hour or until onions are very tender, adding a little water from time to time if pan gets dry; watch them, as onions burn easily. If desired, add pomegranate juice and cook 5 more minutes.

If not adding pomegranate juice, serve stuffed onions with tomato sauce.

Makes about 6 servings

STUFFED ZUCCHINI WITH LAMB, ALMONDS, AND RAISINS

There are several ways to stuff zucchini. You can simply halve them, remove the center, and fill and bake them, as here. Or you can turn them into little tubes and simmer them as in the variation. To hollow out the zucchini for stuffing in this manner, buy a special tool for this purpose or use an apple corer or vegetable peeler. Jews from the Middle East use very small zucchini for stuffing in this manner; the easiest way to prepare larger zucchini is to cut the vegetable in two, so you have two stuffed zucchini from each one.

Lamb and Rice Stuffing

½ cup long-grain white rice, rinsed and drained
3 cups boiling water
2 tablespoons plus 1 teaspoon vegetable oil

2 to 2½ pounds small zucchini
1 tablespoon tomato paste
¼ cup water
salt and pepper

3 tablespoons slivered almonds
1 medium onion, finely chopped
½ pound lean ground lamb
2 tablespoons chopped fresh parsley
3 tablespoons raisins

4 medium garlic cloves, coarsely chopped
2 tablespoons vegetable oil

Add rice to boiling salted water in a medium saucepan and boil for 10 minutes. Rinse with cold running water and drain well.

Heat 1 teaspoon oil in a small skillet over medium-low heat. Add almonds and sauté lightly about 5 minutes. Transfer to a plate and let cool.

Heat 2 tablespoons oil in a skillet, add onion, and sauté over medium-low heat until softened, about 5 minutes. Let cool. Mix all stuffing ingredients and taste for seasoning.

Preheat oven to 425°F. Cut zucchini in half lengthwise. Use a spoon to scoop out centers. Rinse zucchini shells and pat them dry, then put into a baking dish large enough to fit them in 1 layer. Fill each with stuffing.

Mix tomato paste with water and a pinch of salt and pepper. Spoon mixture over zucchini, then add enough water to pan to cover zucchini by one-third. Add garlic and spoon oil over zucchini. Cover and bake 15 minutes. Reduce oven temperature to 350°F. and bake 15 more minutes. Uncover and bake, basting occasionally, for 15 minutes or until zucchini are very tender.

Makes 4 to 6 servings

VARIATION: Stuffed Zucchini Tubes

Cut small zucchini in half crosswise. Carefully scoop out pulp with a special zucchini hollowing gadget, vegetable peeler, or apple corer, leaving a hollow cylinder for stuffing. Stuff zucchini. Heat oil in a skillet and sauté zucchini on all sides, turning carefully. Transfer to a large shallow saucepan and add tomato paste, water, and garlic as above. Cover and simmer 45 minutes to 1 hour or until zucchini are very tender.

For a lemony taste prized by many Sephardic Jews, omit the tomato paste and garlic; add the juice of 1 or 2 lemons to the water about 5 minutes before zucchini are done.

MIDDLE EASTERN STUFFED CABBAGE LEAVES

Stuffed cabbage is typical of the cuisine of Jews of many origins, and is a traditional dish for Succot. This aromatic version of stuffed cabbage is based on my mother-in-law's recipe and includes the favorite Middle Eastern spices of cumin and turmeric. In the Polish sweet-and-sour stuffed cabbage, the stuffing is seasoned with salt and pepper only and the sauce is cooked with raisins, a little sugar, and vinegar or lemon juice.

3-pound head green cabbage, cored

Stuffing

½ cup long-grain white rice
3 cups water
salt
2 tablespoons olive oil
1 medium onion, minced

½ teaspoon ground cumin
¼ teaspoon turmeric
½ pound lean ground beef
2 tablespoons minced fresh parsley
freshly ground pepper

Sauce

3 tablespoons olive oil
1 medium onion, minced
2 medium garlic cloves, minced
½ teaspoon ground cumin
¼ teaspoon turmeric

3 cups chicken soup or stock, beef stock, or Yemenite Beef Soup (page 187)
1 tablespoon tomato paste
salt and freshly ground pepper

Carefully remove 15 large outer cabbage leaves by cutting them from core end of cabbage. In a kettle of boiling salted water, boil leaves for 5 minutes, transfer them carefully to a colander, and rinse gently with cold water. Pat dry with a towel. Coarsely chop remaining cabbage, add to boiling water, and boil for 2 minutes. Drain, rinse with cold water, and drain well.

Sprinkle rice into a medium saucepan with boiling salted water and boil it, stirring occasionally, for 10 minutes. Drain rice, rinse with cold water, and drain well. In a skillet, heat oil, add onion, and cook over medium-low heat for 7 minutes, or until softened. Add cumin and turmeric and cook, stirring, for 1 minute. Transfer mixture to a large bowl and let it cool. Stir in rice, beef, parsley, and salt and pepper to taste. Knead by hand to blend ingredients thoroughly.

Heat oil for sauce in a large casserole, add onion, and cook over low heat, stirring, for 5 minutes or until softened. Stir in garlic and cook 1 minute. Add cumin and turmeric, and cook another minute. Remove from heat.

Trim thick ribs of each cabbage leaf slightly so leaf can be easily bent. Put 2 tablespoons of stuffing near stem end of each leaf and fold stem end over it. Fold sides over stuffing to enclose it. Beginning at stem end, roll up leaf to a neat package. If any leaves are torn, place a piece of another leaf over hole and make cabbage rolls from these, too. Arrange cabbage rolls tightly, with seam end down, side by side in casserole. Chop any remaining leaves and add them to casserole.

Add 2¾ cups soup to casserole. Mix tomato paste with remaining soup until smooth, and add to casserole, with salt and pepper to taste. Bring to a simmer, cover, and simmer over low heat for 1 hour and 15 minutes. Taste cooking liquid for seasoning. To serve, spoon chopped cabbage into shallow bowls, with cabbage rolls on top. Spoon cooking liquid over cabbage rolls.

Makes 6 servings

PINE NUT–ALMOND FILO FINGERS

Unlike some Middle Eastern filo pastries, these are not drenched in syrup, but rather are crisp, light, delicate, and not very sweet. I learned to make them from Suzanne Elmaleh, who lives in Jerusalem.

The filling is quickly made by chopping nuts in the food processor. Many versions of this pastry call for ground nuts, but I prefer them the way Mrs. Elmaleh taught me, with small but distinct pieces so the filling has a more interesting texture. Fresh, good-quality nuts are essential to the fine taste of these pastries. They are convenient to prepare because they can be kept in the freezer, ready to bake.

½ pound (½ package) filo dough
½ cup (1 stick) unsalted nondairy
   margarine, melted

Nut Filling

¾ cup almonds
¾ cup walnuts
¼ cup pine nuts

1 teaspoon ground cinnamon
2 tablespoons confectioners' sugar
   (optional)

confectioners' sugar, for sprinkling

If filo sheets are frozen, thaw them in refrigerator for 8 hours or overnight. Remove filo sheets from refrigerator 2 hours before using and leave them in their package.

In food processor, chop almonds and walnuts together, leaving some pieces; do not grind finely. Transfer to a bowl and stir in pine nuts, cinnamon, and confectioners' sugar.

Line 2 baking sheets with parchment paper or grease them. Remove filo sheets from their package and unroll them on a dry towel. Using a sharp knife, cut stack in half lengthwise, then in half crosswise. Cover filo dough immediately with a piece of wax paper, then with a damp towel. Work with only one sheet at a time and always keep remaining sheets covered with paper and towel, so they don't dry out.

Remove one pastry square from pile. Brush it lightly with melted margarine. Put about 2 teaspoons filling at one end of a filo square so it extends all along the edge. Fold the 2 ends of dough in slightly over filling, then roll up tightly to form a thin finger. Transfer to baking sheet. Make more filo fingers with remaining dough and filling. (Pastries can be shaped 1 day ahead and refrigerated, tightly covered with plastic wrap, on baking sheets or on plates; or they can be frozen.)

Preheat oven to 350°F. Bake pastries 15 to 20 minutes or until very light golden. Cool on a rack. (Pastries can be kept in airtight container in freezer, or 1 day at room temperature.) Before serving, sprinkle generously with confectioners' sugar.

Makes about 30 pastries

5

HANUKKAH: THE FESTIVAL OF LIGHTS AND LATKES

 The feast of Hanukkah has different meanings for different people. To the religious scholar, it is a commemoration of a historic event—the rekindling of the eternal light in the Temple in Jerusalem. To a Jewish child in the United States, it means Hanukkah parties, potato pancakes, and presents. To his cousin in Israel, it is the time to enjoy fluffy doughnuts filled with red jam.

The miracle of the oil, the central theme of Hanukkah, lies behind the holiday's traditions. A little over 2,000 years ago, the Jews defeated the Syrians, who had tried to force them to give up their culture and to worship Greek gods. The Jews drove the foreign army out of Jerusalem, cleansed the Temple, and relit the light in the Temple with pure oil. Legend says that only enough ritually clean oil for one day could be found, but it miraculously lasted for eight days, until more could be prepared. For this reason, Hanukkah is celebrated for eight days and is known as the Festival of Lights. The lights are only a symbol; the real celebration is of religious freedom.

The most important Hanukkah custom is the lighting of colorful candles. These are placed in a menorah, a candelabrum with eight branches of equal size, one for each night of Hanukkah, and one prominent branch that holds the candle used to light the others. On the first night one

101

candle is lit and each succeeding night another is added so that on the last night all eight are alight.

Traditional foods also symbolize the miracle of the oil. Potato pancakes have become a Hanukkah specialty not because of the potato, which did not exist in Israel at the time of the Temple, but because of the oil.

Potato pancakes, called *latkes* in Yiddish and *levivot* in Hebrew, appear to have come to us from Russia. There, the Jews make latkes from a great variety of other ingredients, from cheese to buckwheat flour to noodles. A latke usually is a shallow-fried pancake but it sometimes can be a deep-fried fritter.

Besides potatoes, latkes can be made from other vegetables. Creative Jewish cooks have extended the repertoire, and now many prepare pancakes from zucchini, corn, cauliflower, spinach, and even mixtures of several vegetables. Our zucchini cakes with garlic are of Sephardic origin, while the dill-flavored vegetable pancakes are eastern European. Cumin, one of the favorite spices in Israel, adds a special accent to the corn cakes.

Vegetable pancakes can be served the same way as potato pancakes. They are delicious as appetizers, as vegetarian main courses, or as partners for roasts or braised poultry or meat; of course, any toppings with dairy products would be omitted.

The Israeli doughnuts, or soofganiyot, originated in central Europe and are prepared in a broad area stretching from Romania through Hungary, Austria, and Germany to Alsace in France. They have become so widespread in Israel because many of the pastry chefs there are Austrian and Hungarian Jews. Indeed, the common Hebrew word for pastry shop is *konditoria*, from the German *konditorei*. Soofganiyot are lighter than American doughnuts and do not have holes. Two types are prepared in Israel, the "classic" type made with yeast and a quick version made with baking powder. At Hanukkah, the yeast version is sold fresh by all the bakeries.

The remaining dishes served for the holiday are usually family favorites of the season and vary from one country to another. Brisket or roast chicken, goose, or duck appear on the tables of many homes, either on the first night of Hanukkah or on the Saturday that falls during the holiday week. Apples are popular, both in desserts and as applesauce to accompany the latkes.

Hanukkah is a time for parties and fun. The children play special Hanukkah games and often receive gifts or coins made of chocolate. In both the U.S. and Israel, family and friends get together for relaxed dinners or buffet-style parties. Hanukkah food suits this atmosphere. Crisp latkes and light doughnuts disappear quickly when served at a casual get-together of family or friends and add warmth to the cold winter days.

Other ideal Hanukkah dishes:

Spinach Pancakes (page 257)
Easy Cauliflower Latkes (page 258)
Potato and Walnut Fritters (page 258)
Sephardic Pumpkin Pancakes (page 76)
Potato and Vegetable Kugel (page 22)
Yemenite Tomato Salsa (page 166)
Savory Pastries with Buckwheat Filling (Kasha Knishes)
(page 151)
Roast Goose with Apples (page 237)

HANUKKAH DINNER

The following menu is composed of dishes that are quick and easy to prepare and are ideal for serving as a Hanukkah buffet dinner or party.

HANUKKAH DINNER MENU

Chopped Liver and Eggplant Pâté
Israeli Vegetable Salad (page 20)
Aromatic Cornish Hens with Raisins,
or Brisket, American-Jewish Style
Celery and Potato Pancakes with Dill
Honey-Glazed Carrots
Apple Cake with Pecans and Cinnamon,
or Hanukkah Doughnuts (Soofganiyot),
or Quick Hanukkah Pastry Puffs

CHOPPED LIVER AND EGGPLANT PÂTÉ

Eggplant gives this version of chopped chicken liver a lighter texture. Jaklyn Cohen of Holon, Israel, who was born in Iraq, taught me this specialty of hers. For a colorful, fresh appetizer, the chopped liver can be spread on slices of cucumber instead of the usual bread or crackers.

1 medium eggplant (1 to 1¼ pounds)	2 medium onions, chopped
9 tablespoons vegetable oil	salt and freshly ground pepper
1 pound chicken livers	4 hard-boiled large eggs

Garnish

2 hard-boiled large eggs, quartered
fresh parsley sprigs
fresh bread or crackers, for serving

Peel eggplant, halve it lengthwise, and cut it into thin slices. Heat 2 tablespoons oil in a large skillet, add about ⅓ of the slices, and sauté over medium-high heat about 1 minute on each side or until they begin to brown. Cover and cook over low heat about 5 minutes or until very tender. Remove and repeat with remaining eggplant in 2 batches, adding 2 tablespoons oil to skillet each time.

Preheat broiler with rack about 3 inches from heat source. Rinse livers and pat dry on paper towels; cut off any green spots. Put livers on foil in broiler and sprinkle with salt. Broil 3 minutes or until top is light brown. Turn livers over, sprinkle second side with salt, and broil 3 or 4 more minutes or until cooked through and color is no longer pink; cut to check. Discard juices from foil. Cool livers slightly, then cut in half.

Heat 3 tablespoons oil in a large skillet. Add onions and sauté over medium-low heat about 15 minutes, or until very tender and light brown. Add livers, salt, and pepper and sauté over medium heat, tossing and stirring constantly, for 2 minutes.

Grind half the onions, liver, eggplant, and eggs in a food processor until fairly fine but not completely pureed. Remove and repeat with remaining ingredients. Season to taste with salt and pepper. Refrigerate at least 1 hour before serving, or up to 3 days.

To serve, spoon into a bowl and garnish with hard-boiled eggs and parsley sprigs. Serve cold or at room temperature, accompanied by fresh bread or crackers.

Makes 8 to 10 servings

AROMATIC CORNISH HENS WITH RAISINS

This dish is based on a recipe I learned from my friend and culinary mentor, Ruth Sirkis, the "Julia Child" of Israel. It is typical of the new cuisine that is developing in the Jewish state, featuring a combination of Western techniques, Israeli fruit, and Middle Eastern spices. The Cornish hens are fragrant from the spices but are not hot. Serve them for Hanukkah with potato latkes, and for other occasions with rice.

2 large Cornish hens (1¼ to 1½
   pounds each), thawed if frozen
1½ teaspoons ground cumin
1 teaspoon paprika
½ teaspoon salt
pinch of cayenne pepper
1 medium onion, cut in thin slices
1 small carrot, cut in thin slices
1 celery stalk, cut in thin slices

1 cup fresh orange juice
1 cup dry white wine
2 tablespoons vegetable oil
¼ to ⅓ cup dark raisins
2 oranges, divided into neat segments,
   with juice reserved
2 tablespoons water
2 teaspoons potato starch or cornstarch

Cut each hen into 4 pieces by first cutting off leg-and-thigh pieces at thigh joint, then breast-and-wing pieces. Cut off backs and reserve for soup. Mix cumin, paprika, salt, and cayenne pepper and rub mixture thoroughly into hen pieces. Put them in a large bowl and add onion, carrot, celery, orange juice, and wine. Cover and refrigerate at least 2 hours or overnight.

Preheat oven to 400°F. Pat hen pieces dry, reserving their marinade. Heat oil in a large heavy skillet, add hen pieces in batches, and sauté over medium-high heat until brown on each side. Transfer them to a shallow baking dish.

Discard fat from skillet, and add marinade with vegetables and bring to a boil, stirring. Pour mixture over hen pieces, cover, and bake 30 minutes. Uncover and bake 10 to 15 more minutes or until tender. Remove hen pieces and strain cooking juices into a saucepan. Return hen pieces to baking dish, cover, and keep warm.

Add raisins and juice from orange segments to hen cooking juices and boil until raisins are tender and sauce is concentrated and well flavored. Whisk water into potato starch to form a smooth mixture. Add to simmering sauce, stirring, and bring just back to a boil. Taste for seasoning. Add orange segments, heat over low heat a few seconds, and pour sauce with raisins and oranges over hen pieces.

Makes 4 servings

BRISKET, AMERICAN-JEWISH STYLE

In America brisket has come to symbolize Jewish cooking, perhaps because Jewish cooks have developed tasty recipes for using this cut of meat to best advantage. Brisket is sometimes cubed and used in tzimmes with fruit and vegetables (page 70), or cooked as hamin (page 144). But the image that comes to mind most often is of brisket that is roasted slowly as one succulent piece, either pot-roasted on top of the stove or baked in a covered pan in the oven, as here.

American cooks often flavor the brisket with ketchup, which adds a tangy note, as in this version that I learned to prepare from my aunt, Sylvia Saks. She prefers to serve the brisket with tasty Garlic-Scented Roast Potatoes (page 265), but if you wish to cook everything in the same pan, you can instead roast some potatoes around the brisket.

If you are preparing brisket for Hanukkah, for which it is a favorite, accompany it with potato pancakes.

4 large garlic cloves, minced
¾ teaspoon pepper
1 teaspoon paprika
1 teaspoon salt
1 teaspoon vegetable oil
2 medium onions, sliced

3-pound piece boneless brisket, excess fat trimmed
1 cup ketchup
½ cup water
2 pounds large baking potatoes (optional)

Mix garlic, spices, salt, and oil to a paste and rub into meat. Let stand about 30 minutes. Preheat oven to 400°F.

Put onions in a small roasting pan and top with brisket, fat side up. Cover with foil and roast 15 minutes. Reduce oven temperature to 325°F. Pour ketchup over brisket and spread lightly. Add water to pan, pouring it around, not over, meat. Cover and bake 1½ hours, occasionally adding a few tablespoons water to pan if it becomes dry.

Peel and quarter potatoes. Add them to pan around meat. Baste meat and potatoes with pan juices and sprinkle potatoes lightly with salt. Cover and roast 45 minutes; turn potatoes over and roast 45 minutes longer or until brisket and potatoes are very tender when pierced with a fork.

Remove meat to board, ketchup side up. Remove onions with slotted spoon. Put ½ cup onions in a medium saucepan and add roasting juices from meat. Boil about 5 minutes or until well flavored and slightly thickened. Taste this sauce and adjust seasoning. If desired, heat remaining onions in a separate small saucepan to serve on the side.

With a thin-bladed sharp knife, carve meat in thin slices crosswise. Serve sauce and onions separately.

Makes 5 or 6 servings

CELERY AND POTATO PANCAKES WITH DILL

Celery adds a pleasing accent to the usual potato pancakes, and these make a nice change for Hanukkah. They are good accompaniments for Roast Duck with Prunes and Red Wine (page 87), grilled or roast chicken, or for the brisket in this menu.

4 medium celery stalks (about ½ pound total), trimmed
2 tablespoons all-purpose flour
½ teaspoon baking powder
1¼ pounds baking potatoes

1 large egg
½ teaspoon salt
¼ teaspoon ground white pepper
2 tablespoons minced fresh dill
about ½ cup vegetable oil, for frying

Peel celery with vegetable peeler to remove strings and cut into 1½ × ⅛ × ⅛-inch matchsticks. Mix flour with baking powder. Peel potatoes and grate them, using grating/shredding disc of food processor or large holes of hand grater. (Work quickly once potatoes are grated so they won't discolor.) Transfer potatoes and celery to colander. Squeeze mixture by handfuls to remove as much liquid as possible.

Beat egg with salt and pepper and stir in dill. Add to potato mixture and mix well. Add flour mixture and mix well. Do not let batter stand or it will discolor.

Heat oil in 10- to 12-inch heavy skillet over medium heat. For each pancake, drop about 2 tablespoons of potato mixture into skillet, using large tablespoon or half-filled ¼-cup measure. Flatten pancake with back of spoon, pressing ingredients together, so it is 2½ to 3 inches in diameter. Shape 2 more pancakes. Fry over medium heat until golden brown on bottom, about 4 minutes. Turn carefully using 2 slotted spatulas. Fry until second side is golden brown, about 4 minutes. Drain on paper towels.

Keep pancakes warm if necessary in 400°F. oven while frying rest of mixture. Stir mixture before frying each new batch. If oil becomes too hot, reduce heat slightly. Add more oil to skillet if needed and heat it before making more pancakes. (Pancakes can be kept 4 hours at room temperature and reheated on baking sheet in 400°F. oven, but won't be as crisp as when freshly fried.) Serve pancakes hot.

Makes 14 or 15 pancakes; 3 or 4 servings

VARIATION: If you are serving a dairy meal, dill topping makes a tasty accompaniment.

Dill Topping

1 cup sour cream or plain yogurt
2 tablespoons minced fresh dill

Mix sour cream with dill. Bring to room temperature before serving.

HONEY-GLAZED CARROTS

A popular Rosh Hashanah vegetable dish in the Romanian and Hungarian kitchen, glazed carrots are also a favorite among the Jews in France. A hint of grated lemon adds a fresh touch to balance the delicate sweetness of the dish.

1 pound carrots, peeled and sliced	1 tablespoon honey
1 cup water	2 tablespoons vegetable oil
pinch of salt	½ teaspoon grated lemon rind
1 tablespoon sugar	

Combine carrots, water, and salt in a medium saucepan. Bring to a boil and simmer, uncovered, for 10 minutes. Add sugar, honey, and oil and continue cooking over medium-low heat, stirring occasionally, until carrots are very tender and liquid is absorbed, about 15 minutes. Watch so mixture does not burn. Add grated lemon rind and remove from heat. Serve hot or at room temperature.

Makes 4 servings

APPLE CAKE WITH PECANS AND CINNAMON

When I worked at the Tel Aviv University library, exchanging recipes with my co-workers was my preferred coffee-break pastime. This recipe is based on the cake that my librarian friend baked often for Shabbat. *Diced apples flavor the batter and sliced apples are arranged on top in an attractive pattern and glazed with sugar and cinnamon. Use tart apples like Pippin, or medium-tart ones like McIntosh, Jonathan, or Rome Beauty.*

2 teaspoons ground cinnamon
1 cup sugar
1½ pounds apples, peeled, halved, cored, and diced
¾ cup plus 2 tablespoons (1¾ sticks) unsalted nondairy margarine or butter

2 large eggs
2 cups all-purpose flour
1½ teaspoons baking powder
1 cup pecans, coarsely chopped

Topping

2 large apples (about 1 pound)
2 tablespoons (¼ stick) unsalted nondairy margarine or butter, melted

7 tablespoons sugar
2 teaspoons ground cinnamon

Preheat oven to 400°F. Mix cinnamon and ½ cup sugar in a large bowl. Add apples and mix.

In another bowl beat margarine until smooth. Add remaining ½ cup sugar and beat until fluffy. Add eggs one by one, beating well after each addition. Sift flour with baking powder and stir into egg mixture. Stir in apple mixture and pecans. Spread in a greased 13 × 9-inch baking dish with 2-inch-high sides. Smooth top.

Peel, halve, and core apples and cut them into thin slices. Lay slices in overlapping rows to cover cake completely. Brush slices with melted margarine. Mix sugar and cinnamon and sprinkle evenly over top. Bake for 1 hour or until apples are very tender. Cool in pan on a rack. (Cake can be kept, covered, for 3 to 4 days in refrigerator.)

To serve, cut cake into squares. Serve at room temperature.

Makes 16 to 20 servings

HANUKKAH DOUGHNUTS (SOOFGANIYOT)

Fluffy doughnuts without holes similar to these are known by many names; I've seen them as Bismarck Jelly Doughnuts, krapfen, *and in France as* boules de Berlin *(Berlin balls). Probably Austrian bakers brought them to Israel, and now they rival potato pancakes in popularity as Hanukkah food. Other common flavorings for these doughnuts, besides the brandy used in this recipe, are vanilla, grated lemon rind, cinnamon, and nutmeg.*

Before frying the doughnuts, read "Hints on Deep-Frying" (page 112).

¾ cup lukewarm water
2 envelopes active dry yeast
¼ cup granulated sugar
4 cups all-purpose flour, plus 2
 tablespoons more if necessary
2 large eggs
2 large egg yolks
7 tablespoons unsalted nondairy margarine
 or butter, at room temperature

2 tablespoons brandy
2 teaspoons salt
at least 5 cups vegetable oil, for deep-
 frying
about ¼ cup apricot or strawberry
 preserves
sifted confectioners' sugar, for
 sprinkling

Pour ½ cup lukewarm water into a small bowl. Sprinkle yeast on top and add 1 teaspoon sugar. Let stand 10 minutes.

Spoon flour into mixer bowl or another large bowl. Make a well in center and add remaining sugar, eggs, yolks, margarine, brandy, remaining water, and salt. Mix with mixer dough hook or wooden spoon until ingredients are blended. Add yeast mixture and mix with dough hook at low speed or with spoon until ingredients come together to a dough. Beat at medium speed, scraping down dough occasionally, for 5 minutes; or knead by hand for 5 minutes. If dough is very sticky, add 2 tablespoons flour. Knead 5 to 10 minutes more until very smooth.

Put dough in a clean oiled bowl and turn to coat with oil. Cover with a damp cloth and let rise in a warm place 1 to 1½ hours or until doubled in volume.

On a floured surface roll out half the dough until ¼ inch thick, flouring dough occasionally. Using a 2½- to 3-inch cutter, cut dough in rounds. Put ½ teaspoon apricot or strawberry preserves on center of half the rounds. Brush rim of round lightly with water, then set a plain round on top. With floured fingers, press dough firmly all around to seal it. Transfer this "sandwich" immediately to floured tray. If it has stretched out to an oval, plump it gently back into a round shape. Continue with remaining dough. Cover pastries with a slightly damp cloth and let rise in a warm place about 30 minutes.

Knead the scraps of dough, put them in an oiled bowl, cover with a damp cloth, and let stand for about 30 minutes.

Heat oil to 350°F; if a deep-fat thermometer is not available, heat oil until it bubbles gently around a small piece of dough added to it. Add 4 doughnuts or enough to fill pan without crowding. Fry doughnuts about 3 minutes on each side or until golden brown. Drain on paper towels. Pat tops gently with paper towels to absorb excess oil.

Make more doughnuts with scraps if you like; they won't be as light but will still be good.

Serve warm or at room temperature, sprinkled with confectioners' sugar. Don't serve these immediately because the jam is boiling hot.

Makes 14 large doughnuts (not including the scraps)

HINTS ON DEEP-FRYING

It's important to follow a few simple rules so that deep-frying is a pleasant and safe experience:

✗ Don't fill the pan more than half full of oil.
✗ Hold ingredients near the surface of the oil and slide them in gently. Don't hold ingredients high above oil and drop them in because they'll splash the hot oil.
✗ When food is added to the oil, it bubbles vigorously. Don't crowd the pan because the oil can bubble up to the top and even overflow.
✗ Regulate the heat if necessary to keep the oil at the right temperature.
✗ Give your full attention to the frying; don't leave in the middle to do something else.

QUICK HANUKKAH PASTRY PUFFS

These are made by home cooks in Israel as quick substitutes for the yeast-leavened doughnuts. They are ready in minutes and taste good, but are not as light as the yeast version.

1¼ cups all-purpose flour
1¼ teaspoons baking powder
2 large eggs
3 tablespoons granulated sugar
¼ cup vegetable oil
¼ cup water or milk

¼ teaspoon salt
1 teaspoon vanilla extract
at least 5 cups oil, for deep-frying
sifted confectioners' sugar, for
    sprinkling

Sift flour with baking powder. Combine eggs, sugar, oil, water or milk, salt, and vanilla in a bowl and whisk until smooth. Add flour mixture and mix to a smooth, thick batter.

Heat oil to 350°F; if a deep-fat thermometer is not available, heat oil until it bubbles gently around a small piece of dough added to it. Slide mixture gently into oil by rounded table-spoons for large ones, or by teaspoons for small; if mixture doesn't easily come off spoon, dip another spoon in the oil and use to push it off. Do not drop dough into oil from high above or it might make hot oil splatter. Fry 2 to 3 minutes on each side or until golden brown. Drain on paper towels. Pat tops gently with paper towels to absorb excess oil.

Serve hot or warm, sprinkled with confectioners' sugar.

Makes 8 or 9 large or 16 to 20 small pastries; 4 to 6 servings

A LATKE PARTY

A selection of several types of pancakes of different colors makes great Hanukkah party fare, especially when presented with a choice of toppings, like the mint- and garlic-scented yogurt or the dill sour cream in our recipes here. The addition of an Israeli-style salad of diced tomatoes, peppers, and cucumber and a chocolate-almond layer cake turns the menu into a lovely vegetarian Hanukkah feast.

LATKE PARTY MENU

My Mother's Potato Pancakes (Potato Latkes)
Apple Compote
Zucchini Pancakes with Garlic
and Yogurt Mint Topping,
or Corn Cakes with Cumin
Vegetable Pancakes with Dill Sour Cream
Bright Red Cabbage Salad
Orange-Pecan Torte,
or Chocolate-Almond Cake
with Chocolate-Honey Icing (page 78)

MY MOTHER'S POTATO PANCAKES (POTATO LATKES)

The eight-day festival of Hanukkah is celebrated with parties, candles, games, and gifts but most of all, potato pancakes. The pancakes have become the symbol of the holiday and are a must for any Hanukkah party.

These crisp, lacy pancakes are easy to prepare with the aid of a food processor for grating the vegetables. The usual flavoring is grated onion, but some cooks add shredded carrots or zucchini to the potato mixture as well. For a sweet note, others stir in a grated apple and sometimes a pinch of cinnamon, or a little sugar and lemon juice.

Potato pancakes are sprinkled with sugar or accompanied by applesauce when served on their own. They can also be served with meat or chicken, and in this case the sugar and applesauce are usually omitted. If they are part of a meatless meal, they can be topped with a dollop of sour cream or yogurt. SEE PHOTOGRAPH.

4 large potatoes (about 1¼ pounds), peeled
1 medium onion (about ½ pound)
1 tablespoon chopped fresh parsley (optional)
1 large egg
1 teaspoon salt

¼ teaspoon white pepper
2 tablespoons all-purpose flour
½ teaspoon baking powder
about ½ cup vegetable oil, for frying
applesauce, Apple Compote (page 116), sour cream, or sugar, for serving

Grate potatoes and onion, using grating disc of a food processor or large holes of a grater. Transfer to a colander; squeeze mixture to press out as much liquid as possible. In a large bowl mix potatoes, parsley, egg, salt, pepper, flour, and baking powder.

Heat oil in a deep, heavy 10- to 12-inch skillet. For each pancake, drop about 2 tablespoons of potato mixture into pan. Flatten with back of a spoon so each cake is about 2½ to 3 inches in diameter. Fry over medium heat about 4 to 5 minutes on each side, or until golden brown and crisp. Turn carefully with 2 pancake turners so oil doesn't splatter. Cook until crisp on other side, then drain on paper towels. Stir potato mixture before frying each new batch. If all the oil is absorbed, add a little more to pan. Serve hot, accompanied by applesauce, compote, sour cream, or sugar.

Makes about 15 pancakes; 4 or 5 servings

NOTE: Potato pancakes can be prepared ahead and refrigerated or frozen on a cookie sheet;

when frozen, they can be transferred to a bag. They can be reheated (after being slightly defrosted if they were frozen) on a cookie sheet in a 450°F. oven for a few minutes.

APPLE COMPOTE

Instead of canned applesauce, this freshly made accompaniment for potato pancakes can be served as a chunky topping, or can be pureed in a food processor to turn it into a flavorful applesauce. When the apples are left in pieces, the compote can be served as a dessert on its own; it's especially good served hot, crowned with ice cream, sour cream, or yogurt. SEE PHOTOGRAPH.

2 pounds Golden Delicious apples
3 tablespoons butter or margarine
1 teaspoon lemon juice

¼ to ½ teaspoon ground cinnamon
   (optional)
2 to 3 tablespoons sugar

Peel and halve the apples. Core them and cut into thin wedges or slices.

Melt butter in a large skillet or sauté pan over medium-high heat. Add apples and sauté, turning pieces over from time to time, for about 2 minutes or until they are coated with butter. Add lemon juice and cinnamon, cover, and cook over low heat for 5 minutes, or until liquid begins to come out of apples. Uncover and continue cooking over low heat, gently stirring occasionally, for 15 to 20 minutes or until apples are tender and begin to fall apart.

Add 2 tablespoons sugar and sauté over medium-high heat, turning apple wedges over, about 2 minutes or just until sugar dissolves. Remove from heat. Taste and add more sugar if necessary; heat, tossing apples gently, until sugar dissolves. (Apple compote can be kept, covered, for 2 days in refrigerator.) Serve it warm or at room temperature, to accompany potato pancakes.

Makes about 8 to 10 servings

ZUCCHINI PANCAKES WITH GARLIC AND YOGURT MINT TOPPING

In these pancakes the delicate green color of the zucchini shows through the golden brown crust. The Sephardic-style yogurt and mint topping is a refreshing complement to the light pancakes and is also good with plain sautéed zucchini or eggplant or with cooked green beans. SEE PHOTOGRAPH.

Garlic and Yogurt Mint Topping

½ cup plain yogurt
1½ teaspoons chopped fresh mint

½ small garlic clove, finely minced
salt and freshly ground pepper

Zucchini Pancakes

3 cups coarsely grated zucchini (3 medium zucchini, total about 12 ounces)
1 tablespoon chopped garlic
salt and freshly ground pepper

1 large egg, lightly beaten
3 tablespoons all-purpose flour
¼ cup vegetable oil, for frying
mint sprigs, for garnish

Mix yogurt with mint and garlic. Season to taste with salt and pepper. Set aside at room temperature.

Combine zucchini, garlic, salt, and pepper. Add beaten egg and stir in lightly. Stir in flour.

Heat oil in a deep, heavy, large skillet. For each pancake, drop 1 heaping tablespoon of zucchini mixture into pan. Flatten slightly with back of a spoon and fry over medium heat about 2 to 3 minutes on each side, or until golden brown. Turn very carefully so oil doesn't splatter. Drain on paper towels. Stir mixture before frying each new batch. If all the oil is absorbed, add a little more to pan. Serve hot, with topping. Garnish with mint sprigs.

Makes 12 small cakes; 4 appetizer or side-dish servings

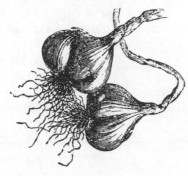

CORN CAKES WITH CUMIN

A combination of whole and pureed corn kernels gives these cakes a great corn flavor. Serve them for Hanukkah instead of or in addition to potato pancakes. Cumin is a common seasoning in Jewish dishes from the Middle East and goes very well with corn. SEE PHOTOGRAPH.

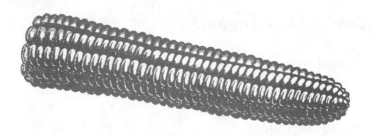

2 cups fresh or frozen corn kernels,
   cooked, drained, and cooled
salt and pepper
1 teaspoon ground cumin

1 large egg
2 tablespoons all-purpose flour
¼ cup vegetable oil, for frying

Topping (optional)

½ cup sour cream or plain yogurt, at
   room temperature

1 tablespoon chopped fresh coriander
   (cilantro) or parsley
¼ cup finely diced ripe tomato

Puree ½ cup cooked corn; a few chunks may remain. Mix pureed corn with salt, pepper, cumin, and egg. Stir in flour, then corn kernels.

Heat oil in a deep, heavy, large skillet. For each pancake, drop 1 heaping tablespoon of corn mixture into pan. Flatten slightly with back of a spoon and fry over medium heat about 2 to 3 minutes on each side, or until golden brown. Turn carefully with 2 pancake turners so oil doesn't splatter. Drain on paper towels. Stir mixture before frying each new batch. If all the oil is absorbed, add a little more to pan. Serve hot.

If desired, top each pancake with ½ to 1 teaspoon sour cream or yogurt, then sprinkle with coriander and diced tomato. Serve remaining sour cream or yogurt separately.

Makes 12 small cakes; 4 appetizer or side-dish servings

BRIGHT RED CABBAGE SALAD

In Israel I was always intrigued by the vibrant color of the red cabbage salad often served in Middle Eastern–style restaurants. Eventually I learned their secret—pouring a small amount of boiling vinegar over the shredded vegetable. This salad is especially good with sausages, cold cuts, and roast poultry and meats.

½ small red cabbage (about 14 ounces)
¼ cup plus 3 tablespoons white wine
   vinegar
1 tablespoon prepared mustard
salt and freshly ground pepper

¾ cup vegetable oil
⅓ cup chopped green onions
1 cup toasted walnut halves or pieces
   (optional)

Cut cabbage half in two and cut out core. Shred cabbage in a food processor or cut into very thin strips with a large knife. Put cabbage in a large bowl.

In a small saucepan bring ¼ cup vinegar to a boil. Pour it over cabbage and toss quickly until mixed well.

In a medium bowl, whisk mustard with remaining 3 tablespoons vinegar, salt, and pepper. Whisk in oil. Add dressing gradually to cabbage, tossing. Taste and adjust seasoning. (Salad can be kept 2 days in refrigerator.)

A short time before serving, add chopped green onions to salad. Serve sprinkled with toasted walnuts.

Makes 6 to 8 servings

VEGETABLE PANCAKES WITH DILL SOUR CREAM

Green peas peak out of these golden brown eastern European–style pancakes, which also contain sautéed mushrooms, onion, and carrot. The pancakes are delicious on their own, but the dill sour cream turns them into a special treat.

Dill Sour Cream

1 cup sour cream or plain yogurt
1 tablespoon snipped fresh dill
salt and pepper

Vegetable Pancakes

¼ pound small mushrooms
½ cup vegetable oil
1 medium onion, finely chopped
¼ cup chopped celery
1 cup coarsely grated carrot (1 large carrot)

½ cup cooked fresh or frozen peas
2 large eggs, lightly beaten
salt and pepper
1 tablespoon snipped fresh dill
2 to 3 tablespoons matzo meal

Mix sour cream or yogurt and dill. Season to taste with salt and pepper. Set aside at room temperature.

Separate mushroom stems from caps; halve both caps and stems lengthwise and cut into thin slices. Heat ¼ cup oil in a large skillet over medium-low heat. Add onion and sauté 5 minutes. Add mushrooms and celery and sauté 8 minutes or until vegetables are tender. Let cool, then transfer to a bowl. Stir in grated carrot. Add cooked peas, eggs, salt and pepper, dill, and 2 tablespoons matzo meal. Mix well; if mixture appears watery, add another tablespoon matzo meal.

Heat remaining ¼ cup oil in a deep, heavy, large skillet. For each pancake, drop 1 heaping tablespoon of vegetable mixture into pan. Flatten slightly with back of a spoon and fry over medium heat for about 2 to 3 minutes on each side, or until golden brown. Turn very carefully using 2 spatulas. Drain on paper towels. Stir mixture before frying each new batch. If all the oil is absorbed, add a little more to pan. Serve hot, accompanied by dill sour cream.

Makes 14 small pancakes; 4 or 5 appetizer or side-dish servings

ORANGE-PECAN TORTE

Moistening a cake with orange juice after it is baked rather than the classic sugar syrup is a trick I learned in Israel. The juice gives the cake a fresh orange flavor. Each slice of this luscious torte has whipped cream on three sides because the cake is baked in a tube pan.

1 cup (about 3½ ounces) pecans
2 tablespoons plus 2 teaspoons
   unflavored bread crumbs
¾ cup sugar

4 large eggs, separated, at room
   temperature
1 teaspoon grated orange rind
¼ teaspoon cream of tartar

¼ cup strained fresh orange juice
1 cup heavy cream

2 teaspoons sugar
6 to 8 pecan halves

Preheat oven to 325°F. Butter a 7¼-inch (8-cup) tube pan with 3-inch sides. Line base with parchment or foil (with hole cut in center for tube) and butter paper or foil. Flour sides of pan and lined base, shaking out excess.

In a food processor grind pecans with bread crumbs and ¼ cup sugar to a fine powder. Transfer mixture to a bowl.

Beat egg yolks in large bowl of mixer until blended. Add 5 tablespoons sugar and beat until pale yellow and thick, about 5 minutes. Beat in orange rind.

Beat egg whites with cream of tartar in another large bowl with clean beater until stiff. Gradually add remaining 3 tablespoons sugar and whip at high speed until whites are stiff but not dry, about ½ minute. Sprinkle one-third of pecan mixture over yolks and fold gently. Spoon one-third of whites on top and fold gently. Repeat until pecan mixture and whites are folded in. Fold as lightly but as quickly as possible.

Spoon batter carefully into pan and smooth top. Bake 30 to 35 minutes or until a cake tester inserted in comes out clean. Without loosening cake, let cool in pan upside down on a rack for 30 minutes.

Run a thin-bladed flexible knife around sides of cake, then around tube. Turn out onto rack set above tray. Using a cake tester, poke 12 holes at equal distances in cake from top nearly to bottom. Slowly pour in orange juice; cake should absorb it. Slide cake carefully onto serving plate. Refrigerate at least 1 hour or up to 2 days.

Whip cream with sugar in chilled bowl until stiff. Spread whipped cream all over cake, including inside edge. Decorate with pecan halves. Refrigerate at least 1 hour before serving. (Cake can be frosted 8 hours ahead.)

Makes about 10 servings

6
PURIM: THE HAMANTASCHEN HOLIDAY

 Purim is a joyous festival celebrated in late February or early March. Most people practice a custom of *mishloah manot*, which literally means "sending of portions" but which could be described as a Jewish "cookie exchange." Friends, relatives, and neighbors send each other boxes of sweets—favorite cookies, slices of cake, and most of all the filled three-cornered cookies called *hamantaschen*, Yiddish for "Haman's pockets."

In Hebrew these traditional Purim treats are called *Oznei Haman* or "Haman's ears," and are meant to recall the story of Esther, in which the Jewish Queen of Persia helped foil the evil intentions of the wicked Prince Haman, who wanted to destroy the Jews. This story is read on Purim in the synagogue, and every time Haman's name comes up, the children in the congregation make lots of noise with special noisemakers they bring for the occasion.

The first time I made hamantaschen, I found it surprising to be instructed to cut the dough in a circle in order to obtain a triangle. I assumed the intriguing triangular shape of hamantaschen was unique to Jewish cooking, and so I was astonished to discover in France a cheese-filled

123

pastry of the same shape known as *talmouses*, which the French claim date from the Middle Ages.

Hamantaschen make a wonderful treat with coffee, tea, or milk. The time-honored filling for these pastries is of poppy seeds, but other fillings are made as well, from a variety of dried fruit. The filling can be enclosed in a tender sour cream dough, a crisp cookie dough, or a rich yeast dough. Since hamantaschen keep well, they are perfect as gifts of homemade goodies to friends. In addition to hamantaschen with several fillings, Purim boxes often include Chocolate Coconut Rum Balls, Strawberry Pecan Squares, and in general, cakes that can be easily cut into bite-size portions.

Other ideal Purim dishes:

Cinnamon-Nut-Raisin Crescents (Rugelach) (page 316)
Citrus-Scented Almond Macaroons (page 52)
Chocolate-Coconut Rum Balls (page 315)
Strawberry Pecan Squares (page 314)

A BOX OF SWEETS FOR PURIM

Hamantaschen with Poppyseed-Raisin Filling
Hamantaschen with Prune Filling
Hamantaschen with Fig Filling
Date-Filled Hamantaschen
Soft Coconut–Chocolate Chip Cookies

HAMANTASCHEN WITH POPPYSEED-RAISIN FILLING

Hamantaschen are triangular filled cookies traditional for Purim. The best-loved filling is made from poppy seeds. You can use a spice grinder for a delicate textured ground seed filling, or you can leave the seeds whole for a more crunchy filling. Both ways are good—which you choose is a matter of personal taste.

Some people simply mix the poppy seeds with the other ingredients, but I much prefer the creamier texture and enhanced flavor achieved by cooking the seeds with milk and honey, a method that is prevalent in Israel.

Poppy seeds are available in gourmet food shops, and in Jewish, Polish, and Iranian grocery stores.

¾ cup (¼ pound) poppy seeds
½ cup milk
⅓ cup sugar
2 tablespoons honey
½ cup raisins

3 tablespoons butter or margarine
1 teaspoon grated lemon rind
Sour Cream Dough (page 126) or One, Two, Three Cookie Dough (recipe follows)

If you like, grind poppy seeds in a spice grinder. In a small saucepan combine poppy seeds, milk, sugar, and honey and bring to a simmer. Cook over low heat, stirring often, about 15 to 20 minutes or until thick. Add raisins and butter and stir over low heat until butter melts. Remove from heat. Stir in grated lemon rind. Chill well before using.

Use one fourth of dough at a time. Roll it out on a lightly floured surface until about ⅛ inch thick. Using a 3-inch cookie cutter, cut dough into circles. Brush edges lightly with water. Put 1 teaspoon filling in center of each circle. Pull up edges of circle in 3 arcs that meet in center above filling. Close them firmly and pinch edges to seal. Put on greased baking sheet and refrigerate. Refrigerate scraps.

Roll remaining dough and scraps and shape more hamantaschen. Refrigerate at least 30 minutes before baking to firm dough. (Unbaked, they can be kept overnight in refrigerator.)

Preheat oven to 375°F. Bake hamantaschen about 14 minutes or until they are light golden at edges. Cool on a rack. (They can be kept for about 4 days in an airtight container.)

Makes about 32 hamantaschen

NOTE: Close hamantaschen well and do not be tempted to use extra filling, or it will come out during baking. If using One, Two, Three Cookie Dough, some dough will be left over; use it to make cookies.

One, Two, Three Cookie Dough

I learned to make this cookie dough at a cooking course I took in Tel Aviv, run by the Israeli Nutrition and Home Economics Institute. The dough is known as "One, Two, Three" for two reasons: (1) preparing it is "as easy as one-two-three," especially in the version I now make, in the food processor; and (2) its basic proportions are 100 grams sugar, 200 grams butter, and 300 grams flour. This Austro-Hungarian pastry is well liked in Israel for hamantaschen and cookies; they come out crisp, sweet, and delicious.

1 large egg
1 large egg yolk
3¾ cups all-purpose flour
1½ cups confectioners' sugar
1½ teaspoons baking powder
¼ teaspoon salt

1 cup (2 sticks) plus 5 tablespoons
   cold unsalted butter or margarine,
   cut in small pieces
2½ teaspoons grated orange rind
1 to 2 tablespoons orange juice
   (optional)

Beat egg with yolk to blend. Combine flour, confectioners' sugar, baking powder, and salt in a food processor fitted with a metal blade. Process briefly to blend. Scatter butter pieces over mixture. Mix using on/off motion until mixture resembles coarse meal. Sprinkle with grated rind and pour egg mixture evenly over mixture in processor. Process with on/off motion, scraping down occasionally, until dough just begins to come together in a ball. If crumbs are dry, sprinkle with 1 tablespoon orange juice and process briefly; repeat if crumbs are still dry.

   Transfer dough to a work surface. Knead lightly to blend. With a rubber spatula, transfer dough to a sheet of plastic wrap, wrap it, and push it together. Shape dough in a flat disc. Refrigerate at least 3 hours or up to 3 days.

Makes about 2¼ pounds dough; enough for 4 dozen hamantaschen (including scraps)

NOTE: If you like, use some of dough to make hamantaschen, and the rest to make Ashkenazic Poppyseed Cookies (page 311). This amount of dough needs about 1½ cups filling.

Sour Cream Dough

This dough is very tender and delicate in flavor. It is only lightly sweetened and is less crisp than One, Two, Three Dough but is easier to work with and can be used for any of the hamantaschen fillings in this chapter.

1 large egg
2 to 3 tablespoons sour cream
2½ cups all-purpose flour
½ cup confectioners' sugar
1 teaspoon baking powder

¼ teaspoon salt
14 tablespoons (1¾ sticks) cold
 unsalted butter or margarine, cut
 into small pieces
1½ teaspoons grated lemon rind

Beat egg with 2 tablespoons sour cream. Combine flour, confectioners' sugar, baking powder, and salt in a food processor. Process briefly to blend. Scatter butter pieces over mixture. Mix using on/off motion, until mixture resembles coarse meal. Sprinkle with grated zest and pour egg mixture evenly over mixture in processor. Process with on/off motion, scraping down occasionally, until dough just begins to come together in a ball. If mixture is dry, add remaining tablespoon sour cream, putting it in teaspoons over mixture, and process briefly again.

Transfer dough to a work surface. Knead lightly to blend. With a rubber spatula, transfer dough to a sheet of plastic wrap, wrap it, and push it together. Shape dough into a flat disc. Refrigerate at least 2 hours or up to 3 days.

Makes about 1½ pounds dough; enough for 32 hamantaschen

NOTE: If you wish to make dough by hand instead of in food processor, follow method in variation of French Sweet Pastry (page 309).

This amount of dough needs about 1 cup filling.

HAMANTASCHEN WITH PRUNE FILLING

When I was a girl, I enjoyed helping my mother shape these hamantaschen, and they have been my favorite version ever since. The prune filling is very simple to prepare. A touch of grated orange gives it a fresh note. These hamantaschen are small and dainty, in contrast to the large ones often found in bakeries.

8 ounces pitted prunes
¼ cup walnuts
6 tablespoons plum jam or jelly or
 strawberry jam
½ cup raisins (optional)

2 teaspoons grated orange rind
One, Two, Three Cookie Dough or
 Sour Cream Dough (page 126)

Cover prunes with cold water and soak 8 hours or overnight; or cover them with boiling water and soak 15 minutes.

Grind walnuts to a fine powder. Drain prunes and chop finely or puree in food processor. Mix prune puree with walnuts, jam, raisins, and orange rind.

Use one-fourth of dough at a time. Roll it out on a lightly floured surface until about ⅛ inch thick. Using a 3-inch cookie cutter, cut in circles. Brush edges lightly with water, then put 1 teaspoon filling in center of each. Pull up edges of circle in 3 arcs that meet in center above filling. Close them firmly and pinch edges to seal. Put on greased baking sheet and refrigerate. Refrigerate scraps.

Roll remaining dough and scraps and shape more hamantaschen. Refrigerate at least 1 hour to firm dough. (They can be kept overnight in refrigerator.)

Preheat oven to 375°F. Bake hamantaschen about 14 minutes or until they are light golden at edges.

Makes about 32 hamantaschen

NOTE: If using One, Two, Three Cookie Dough, some dough will be left over for making cookies. If you wish to use all the dough to make these hamantaschen, prepare the prune filling with the following quantities: 12 ounces prunes, ⅓ cup walnuts, 9 tablespoons jam, ¾ cup raisins, and 1 tablespoon grated orange rind.

HAMANTASCHEN WITH FIG FILLING

The intriguing filling of dark figs gives a delicious Middle Eastern accent to these originally European pastries.

¼ pound small dried figs, stems
  removed, halved
½ cup raisins
¼ cup pecans, chopped

¼ cup plum jam
¼ cup flaked coconut
One, Two, Three Cookie Dough or
  Sour Cream Dough (page 126)

Combine figs and raisins in bowl of food processor. Chop them together, then transfer to a mixing bowl and stir in nuts, jam, and coconut.

Follow shaping and baking instructions for Hamantaschen with Prune Filling (page 127).

Makes about 32 hamantaschen

NOTE: If using One, Two, Three Cookie Dough, some dough will be left over for making cookies. Or if you wish to use all the dough to make these hamantaschen, prepare the filling with the following quantities: 6 ounces figs, ¾ cup raisins, ⅓ cup pecans, ⅓ cup plum jam, and ⅓ cup flaked coconut.

DATE-FILLED HAMANTASCHEN

Cocoa enriches this smooth, easy filling and tempers the natural sweetness of the dates. In Israel dates are sold ground so they can be used in hamantaschen or to fill other cookies, but whole dates can be pureed in no time in the food processor.

One, Two, Three Cookie Dough or Sour Cream Dough (page 126)
¾ pound pitted dates

3 tablespoons unsweetened cocoa
3 tablespoons tangy jam, such as plum jam

Grind dates in food processor. Add cocoa and jam and process to blend.
   Follow shaping and baking instructions for Hamantaschen with Prune Filling (page 127).

Makes about 32 hamantaschen

NOTE: If using One, Two, Three Cookie Dough, some dough will be left over for making cookies. Or if you wish to use all the dough to make hamantaschen, prepare the filling with the following quantities: 1 pound dates, ¼ cup cocoa, and ¼ cup jam.

SOFT COCONUT–CHOCOLATE CHIP COOKIES

For the yearly Purim cookie exchange, American Jewish cooks like to offer American-style cookies, like these moist, rich chocolate chip cookies, alongside the hamantaschen. The cookies are enriched with sour cream and accented with a touch of lemon.

1¼ cups all-purpose flour
1¼ teaspoons baking powder
¼ teaspoon baking soda
¼ teaspoon salt
½ cup (1 stick) unsalted butter, at
  room temperature

¾ cup sugar
1 large egg
2 teaspoons grated lemon zest
¼ cup sour cream
2 cups flaked coconut
1½ cups semisweet chocolate chips

Preheat oven to 350°F. Butter 3 baking sheets. Sift flour, baking powder, baking soda, and salt into a medium bowl.

Cream butter in a mixer bowl, add sugar, and beat until smooth and fluffy. Add egg and beat until smooth. Add lemon zest and beat until blended. Stir in half the flour mixture until blended. Stir in half the sour cream. Repeat with remaining flour mixture and sour cream. Stir in coconut and chocolate chips.

Push batter from a teaspoon with a second teaspoon onto prepared sheets, using about 1 tablespoon batter for each cookie, mounding them high and spacing them about 2 inches apart.

Bake about 12 minutes or until light brown at edges and nearly set but still soft to touch in center. Using a metal spatula, carefully transfer cookies to racks. Cool completely. Cool baking sheets and butter them. Make more cookies with remaining batter. (Cookies can be kept up to 1 week in an airtight container at room temperature; or they can be frozen. They lose their softness after 3 days but still taste good.)

Makes about 42 cookies

7

SABBATH: THE WEEKLY FEAST

The Sabbath, or *Shabbos* in Yiddish or *Shabbat* in Hebrew, is the time when Jewish families enjoy the best meal of the week. The finest flatware, the prettiest tablecloth, and the most delicious food is reserved for this day of rest. Special white *Shabbat* candles add to the atmosphere of festivity.

All the members of the family, and often of the extended family as well, get together for the main meal. Actually there are two *Shabbat* dinners: the first on Friday night after sundown, when the Sabbath begins, and the second on Saturday around noon.

The rhythm of much of the week revolves around preparing for and celebrating *Shabbat*. On Wednesday thoughts turn to planning the menu for the two main Sabbath meals. Cooks who bake their own bread prepare the dough on Thursday, and some might bake cakes, too. The markets in Israel are most crowded on Thursday, when everyone is buying fresh produce, fish, and meat for *Shabbat*. Friday is another busy market day, as there are plenty of last-minute shoppers.

Jews all over the world have created special dishes for the holiday. The food is different from that of the rest of the week also because during the Sabbath itself cooking is not permitted. In

131

observant households everything is cooked ahead, making Friday quite a hectic day. The food is either kept warm or reheated, depending on the custom of the family. Even if the food is reheated, the stove is not turned on during Sabbath, but rather a hot plate or the oven is left on.

These rules have led to the development of such tasty dishes as hamin, a rich stew of meat and beans that is prepared in different versions by both Ashkenazic and Sephardic Jews, and of a variety of appetizers that are suitable for being served cold.

Roast chicken and other poultry are also favorite Jewish choices for main courses for the holiday. Often they are served with roasted potatoes, or might include a stuffing based on bread, rice, or, in the case of Moroccan Jews, couscous. Vegetables are most likely to be served as salads, or as side dishes of the type that taste good when very tender, such as Honey-Glazed Carrots (page 109) or Sautéed Eggplant in Spicy Tomato Sauce (page 93). A festive presentation of vegetables for *Shabbat* is to bake them as a kugel.

A beautiful challah or fresh homemade bread is one of the highlights of the Sabbath table. Baking breads, cakes, and cookies for *Shabbat* is an important activity in many families, including ours. When I lived in Israel, my favorite weekly radio program was called "A Cake for *Shabbat*." It remained one of the most popular radio shows in Israel for many years.

The Sabbath dinner generally includes several courses. When I was growing up, the menu usually began with either chopped liver or gefilte fish as well as a simple tomato and lettuce salad, and was followed by chicken soup with fluffy matzo balls. For the main course we had roast chicken, noodle kugel, and cooked carrots or other seasonal vegetables. Dessert was often a chocolate cake, such as My Mother's Chocolate Applesauce Cake (page 91) or Chocolate-Nut Chiffon Cake. This is still my mother's weekly Sabbath menu, and sometimes is mine as well.

My mother-in-law's *Shabbat* menu features a garlic-pepper chutney, an eggplant salad with olive oil or a fenugreek dip, and an Israeli diced vegetable salad. The main course might be hamin, cumin-accented chicken in the pot, or a savory chicken and meat casserole served with rice and a seasonal cooked vegetable. For dessert, there is luscious fresh seasonal fruit—it might be guavas, mangos, or a variety of citrus fruit.

Other ideal Sabbath dishes:

Piquant Cooked Carrot Salad (page 174)
Yemenite Chicken Soup (page 186)
Chicken Soup with Rice, Tomatoes, and Coriander (page 187)

Chicken Soup with Kreplach (page 68), or with Egg Noodles
Iranian Meatball Soup for Shabbat (page 195)
Sweet and Sour Salmon (page 210)
Fish with Light Lemon and Dill Sauce (page 213)
Moroccan Sea Bass with Peppers and Tomatoes (page 211)
Braised Cod with Chickpeas and Olive Oil (page 216)
Roast Chicken with Noodle-Mushroom-Walnut Stuffing
(page 225)
Chicken with Tomatoes, Peppers, and Coriander (page 234)
Couscous with Lamb and Seven Vegetables (page 244)
Roast Lamb with Garlic, Onions, and Potatoes (page 11)
Veal with Olives, Tomatoes, and Fresh Herbs (page 248)
Cauliflower Kugel with Mushrooms (page 252)
Potato and Vegetable Kugel (page 22)
Potato Kugel with Asparagus and Broccoli (page 250)
Italian-Jewish Cold Noodles with Tomatoes and Parsley
(page 275)
Noodle Kugel with Onions and Mushrooms (page 271)
Challah (Egg Bread) (page 289)
Shabbat Breakfast Bread (Kubaneh) (page 292)
Shabbat Pastry Rolls (Jihnun) (page 302)
Browned Eggs (page 205)
Sour Cream Coffee Cake with Walnuts (page 310)
Chocolate-Orange Marble Cake (page 305)
Pear Strudel (page 89)
Raspberry Almond Tart (page 308)
Crisp Almond Slices (Mandelbrot) (page 312)
Dried Fruit Compote with Wine (page 326)

ASHKENAZIC SHABBAT MENU

Chopped Liver, or Gefilte Fish (page 9)
Challah (purchased or homemade, page 289)
Tomato and Lettuce Salad
Ashkenazic Chicken Soup with Fresh Dill
and Light Matzo Balls (page 84)
Roast Chicken with Pecan and Herb Stuffing
Jerusalem Noodle Kugel,
or Cinnamon-Scented Apple Noodle Kugel
Honey-Glazed Carrots (page 109),
or Other Seasonal Vegetables
Chocolate-Nut Chiffon Cake,
or My Mother's Chocolate Applesauce Cake
(page 91)

CHOPPED LIVER

This may be the favorite Jewish appetizer, and perhaps the best known as well. The proportions of grilled liver, sautéed onions, and hard-boiled eggs vary considerably, according to each family's preference. Traditional recipes call for chicken fat for sautéing the onion, but my mother has always made it with oil; either way, it tastes wonderfully rich.

Chopped liver is often served in a scoop or spoonful on a bed of lettuce, with a garnish of tomato slices, radishes, parsley sprigs, chopped onion, olives, cucumber slices, dill pickles, or pickled sweet and hot peppers. It should be accompanied by or spread on challah, rye bread, crackers, or matzo. At my brother's wedding in Jerusalem, the caterer served it as a filling for swan-shaped cream puffs!

¾ to 1 pound chicken livers
salt
3 tablespoons vegetable oil or chicken
  fat
2 medium onions, chopped

1 or 2 hard-boiled large eggs, coarsely
  grated or chopped
freshly ground pepper
lettuce leaves and tomato slices, for
  serving

Preheat broiler with rack about 3 inches from flame. Rinse livers and pat dry on paper towels; cut off any green spots. Put livers on foil in broiler and sprinkle with salt. Broil 3 minutes or until top is light brown. Turn livers over, sprinkle second side with salt, and broil 3 or 4 more minutes or until cooked through and color is no longer pink; cut to check. Discard juices from foil. Cool livers slightly.

Heat oil or fat in a large heavy skillet over medium-low heat. Add onions and sauté, stirring occasionally, for 15 minutes or until tender and beginning to turn golden.

Chop the liver in a food processor. Add onions and chop with on/off pulses until blended in. Transfer to bowl and lightly mix in eggs. Season well with salt and pepper. (Chopped liver can be kept, covered, for 2 days in refrigerator.) Serve cold, in scoops on lettuce leaves. Garnish with tomato slices.

Makes 4 to 6 appetizer servings

NOTE: If using rendered chicken fat in a jar, stir to blend before using if it is in 2 layers.

ROAST CHICKEN WITH PECAN AND HERB STUFFING

Like most Ashkenazic Jews, my mother frequently serves roast chicken for the Sabbath meal. She often prepares a bread stuffing like this one, enhanced with chopped nuts, sautéed onions, and celery. Occasionally she adds a grated carrot and grated zucchini for a tasty variation, and sometimes a diced red pepper and chopped mushrooms as well.

Since a chicken cannot hold as much stuffing as everyone wishes to eat, this recipe includes extra stuffing for baking in a separate dish.

Pecan and Herb Stuffing

½ cup pecans
about 4 to 5 ounces day-old or stale challah or French or Italian white bread
¼ cup (½ stick) nondairy margarine or vegetable oil
1 medium onion, finely 1hopped
½ cup chopped celery
1 bay leaf
salt and freshly ground pepper
1 medium zucchini, coarsely grated (optional)

1 medium carrot, coarsely grated (optional)
½ teaspoon dried thyme, crumbled
1 teaspoon minced fresh sage, or ½ teaspoon dried, crumbled
¼ cup chopped fresh parsley
1 large egg, beaten (optional)
2 to 4 tablespoons chicken soup or stock
1 to 2 tablespoons (¼ stick) nondairy margarine, for baking

3½- to 4-pound chicken
¼ teaspoon salt
¼ teaspoon pepper
½ teaspoon paprika

2 teaspoons vegetable oil
additional ¼ to ½ cup chicken soup or stock, for basting

Preheat oven to 350°F. Toast nuts on a small baking sheet until lightly browned, about 5 minutes. Cool nuts and coarsely chop.

Reduce oven temperature to 275°F. Cut bread in ½-inch cubes; you will need 4 cups. Put bread cubes on 1 large or 2 small baking sheets. Bake until crisp and dry, stirring frequently, about 20 minutes. Cool and transfer to a large bowl.

Heat 3 tablespoons margarine in a medium skillet over medium heat. Add onion, celery, bay leaf, and a pinch of salt and pepper. Cook, stirring occassionally, until onion is softened, about 10 minutes. Add remaining margarine, zucchini, carrot, thyme, and sage and stir until blended. Remove from heat; discard bay leaf.

Add onion mixture, parsley, egg, and nuts to bread and toss lightly until blended. Gradually add soup, tossing lightly. Mixture may appear dry, but will become much moister from juices in bird. Taste and adjust seasoning. (Stuffing can be refrigerated up to 1 day in covered container. Do not stuff bird in advance.)

Preheat oven to 375°F. Discard excess fat from chicken. Mix salt, pepper, paprika, and oil. Rub chicken all over with mixture. Spoon stuffing lightly into chicken. Fold skin over stuffing; truss or skewer closed, if desired. Set chicken in a roasting pan.

Add a little more soup, if necessary, to extra stuffing so that most of bread is very lightly moistened. Grease a baking dish of same or slightly larger volume than amount of remaining mixture and spoon stuffing into it. Dot with margarine and cover dish.

Roast chicken for 45 minutes. Put extra pan of stuffing in oven and roast both together about 45 minutes more, basting chicken occasionally with pan juices if desired, and basting stuffing occasionally with a few tablespoons soup. To check whether chicken is done, insert a skewer into thickest part of drumstick; it should be tender and juices that run from chicken should be clear. If juices are pink, roast chicken a few more minutes and check it again. Also insert a skewer into stuffing inside chicken; it should come out hot.

Transfer chicken to a carving board or platter and remove any trussing strings. Carve chicken and serve hot, with stuffing.

Makes 4 servings

NOTE: To bake all of stuffing separately, preheat oven to 325°F. Grease a 5- to 6-cup casserole and spoon stuffing into it. Dot stuffing with margarine and cover casserole. Bake 1 hour, basting twice with ¼ cup soup. Uncover for last 10 minutes for crisper top.

To save time, omit toasting the bread cubes; stuffing will be softer.

JERUSALEM NOODLE KUGEL

Although kugel is an Ashkenazic specialty, Jerusalemites of all origins prepare this rather peppery version of the dish. It is flavored with caramelized sugar but is not sweet because the caramel is cooked until it is very dark. The secret to avoiding chunks of caramel is to cook the sugar mixture without stirring and to add it to the still-warm pasta. The traditional way to prepare this kugel of fine noodles is to bake it all night in a very low oven, so that it turns a deep brown throughout. For serving, it is turned out and cut in slices like a cake.

At Jerusalem synagogues this kugel often appears on the table for the light meal that is served after the morning services on Shabbat. *For this purpose the kugel is often purchased the day before from women who make it in large cauldrons in Mea Shearim, the most Orthodox section of the city.*

12 ounces fine egg noodles	1 teaspoon salt
½ cup vegetable oil	1 teaspoon ground pepper
¼ cup sugar	few pinches of cayenne pepper
2 large eggs	

Cook noodles in a large pot of boiling salted water for about 5 minutes or until barely tender. Drain well, return to pot, and toss briefly with ¼ cup oil. Keep on stove so noodles remain warm but do not cover.

Pour remaining ¼ cup oil into a heavy saucepan, then add sugar. Heat over low heat without stirring, but shaking pan gently from time to time. Cook until sugar turns dark brown; this can take between 15 and 25 minutes. Gradually add mixture to noodles, mixing well with tongs.

Beat eggs with salt, pepper, and cayenne. Add to noodles and mix well. Taste and adjust seasoning; mixture should be quite peppery. Transfer to a greased round 7- or 8-cup casserole. Cover with foil and with a lid. (Kugel can be kept a few hours in refrigerator at this point.)

Preheat oven to 180°F. Bake kugel overnight, or about 14 hours. Run a knife around edge and turn out onto a round platter. Serve hot. (To reheat leftovers, you can slice them, wrap in foil, and heat in a toaster oven at about 350°F.)

Makes 8 to 10 servings

NOTE: For a quicker version, bake kugel uncovered at 350°F. for 1 hour. It will not be as deep brown but will still have a golden color and will taste good.

CINNAMON-SCENTED APPLE NOODLE KUGEL

Meltingly tender apples form a layer in the center of this nut- and raisin-studded baked noodle pudding. I like to sauté the apples to give them a rich taste and delicate texture instead of adding them raw, as in most apple-noodle kugels. Serve this as a slightly sweet accompaniment for meat or chicken, or for a supper or brunch dish with yogurt or sour cream. In the unlikely event you have leftovers, they can be cut into portions, wrapped in foil, and reheated in the oven.

14 ounces medium egg noodles
3 Golden Delicious apples (about 1½ pounds total)
6 tablespoons (¾ stick) nondairy margarine
6 tablespoons sugar
1 teaspoon ground cinnamon

½ cup pecans, walnuts, or almonds, coarsely chopped
⅓ cup dark raisins
1 teaspoon grated lemon rind
pinch of salt
4 large eggs, separated
1 teaspoon vanilla extract

Preheat oven to 350°F. Grease a 13 × 9-inch baking dish with 2-inch sides. Cook noodles in a large pot of boiling salted water until barely tender, about 5 minutes. Drain, rinse with cold water, and drain well again. Transfer to a large bowl. Separate noodles with your fingers.

Peel apples, halve, core, and slice them. Heat 2 tablespoons margarine in a large skillet over medium heat. Add half the apples and sauté over medium heat for 5 minutes, turning once. Remove with a slotted spoon, add rest of apples to skillet, and sauté them also. Return all apples to skillet, sprinkle with 2 tablespoons sugar and ½ teaspoon cinnamon, and sauté another minute, tossing apples to coat well. Transfer to a bowl. Add remaining margarine to skillet and melt it over low heat. Add 3 tablespoons melted margarine to noodles and mix well. Stir in nuts, raisins, lemon rind, and salt.

Whip egg whites until soft peaks form. Beat in remaining 4 tablespoons sugar and whip at high speed until whites are stiff but not dry. Stir egg yolks and vanilla into noodles. Stir in one-fourth of whipped whites, then fold in remaining whites.

Add half the noodle mixture to the greased baking dish. Top with sautéed apples in an even layer and sprinkle with any margarine remaining in bowl. Top with remaining noodle mixture and spread gently to cover apples. Sprinkle with remaining ½ teaspoon cinnamon, then with remaining melted margarine. Cover dish and bake 30 minutes. Uncover and bake 15 to 20 minutes or until set. Serve hot.

Makes 8 servings

CHOCOLATE-NUT CHIFFON CAKE

Chiffon cakes like this one are frequently made by Jewish cooks for the Sabbath dinner because they taste rich but do not contain dairy products. And chocolate is a useful ingredient for kosher desserts, since there is no problem in using it for meat meals as long as it's not milk chocolate or white chocolate, which contain milk powder. A generous proportion of chocolate makes this chiffon cake especially rich. For meatless meals it's even richer with the chocolate cream frosting.

3 ounces semisweet chocolate,
  chopped
2 ounces unsweetened chocolate,
  chopped
1 cup pecans
1½ cups sugar
2 cups sifted cake flour
1 teaspoon salt

1 tablespoon baking powder
6 large egg yolks
½ cup vegetable oil
¾ cup cold water
8 large egg whites, at room
  temperature
½ teaspoon cream of tartar

Frosting (optional)

6 ounces semisweet chocolate,
  chopped
3 tablespoons water
2 large egg yolks

1¼ cups heavy cream, well chilled
2 tablespoons sugar
10 to 12 pecan halves, for garnish

Preheat oven to 325°F. Have ready a 10-inch tube pan with 4-inch sides and removable tube; do not butter pan.

Melt chocolates for cake in a medium bowl set above hot water over low heat. Stir until smooth, then remove from pan of water and let cool.

Grind pecans in food processor with ¼ cup sugar, then transfer to a bowl. Sift the flour, salt, and baking powder into a large bowl, add ¾ cup sugar, and stir until blended. In another bowl combine egg yolks, oil, and water and beat until smooth.

Make a large well in the bowl of dry ingredients and pour in yolk mixture. Gently stir dry ingredients into yolk mixture, using a wooden spoon. Add chocolate and stir just until there are no lumps.

Whip egg whites with cream of tartar in a large bowl until soft peaks form. Gradually beat in remaining ½ cup sugar and whip at high speed until whites are stiff but not dry. Fold about one-fourth of the whites into chocolate mixture until nearly incorporated. Gently fold chocolate mixture into remaining whites. Sprinkle ground pecans over batter and fold in lightly but quickly, just until batter is blended. Pour batter into pan. Bake about 1 hour and 10 minutes or until a cake tester inserted in cake comes out clean.

Turn pan upside down and cool cake in pan on a rack for 1½ hours. Run a metal spatula gently around cake. Push up tube to remove sides of pan, then run a thin-bladed knife around tube. Run metal spatula carefully under cake to free it from base and turn out carefully onto a platter. (Cake can be kept, wrapped, for 2 days at room temperature.)

Place chocolate and water for frosting in a medium bowl and set it above a pan of hot water over low heat. Whisk until smooth, then remove from pan of water. Whisk egg yolks, one by one, into chocolate mixture. Set bowl of chocolate mixture back above pan of hot water over low heat and cook, whisking, for 1 minute. Remove from pan of water and let stand about 15 minutes or until cool but not set; mixture will be very thick.

Whip cream with sugar in a large chilled bowl until soft peaks form. Stir about ½ cup cream into chocolate mixture. Return mixture to bowl of cream and fold gently until blended.

Brush any loose crumbs off top of cake. Spread frosting evenly and generously all over cake, including inner surface. Garnish with pecans. Refrigerate at least 1 hour before serving. (Frosted cake can be kept, covered with a tall cake cover, for 3 days in refrigerator.)

Makes 14 to 16 servings

YEMENITE SHABBAT MENU

Hot Pepper–Garlic Chutney (Zehug)
Pita Bread (purchased or homemade, page 295)
Fried Cauliflower with Cumin and Turmeric
Israeli Vegetable Salad (page 20)
Aromatic Beef and White Bean Casserole (Hamin),
or Yemenite Beef and
Chicken Casserole (page 43)
Easy Rice Pilaf (if not serving bean casserole)
Fresh Fruit

HOT PEPPER–GARLIC CHUTNEY (ZEHUG)

The Yemenite condiment known as zehug *is a fiery pepper paste, made basically of equal parts of uncooked fresh hot peppers and garlic, and is a well-known feature of Yemenite cuisine. It tastes somewhat like certain hot fresh Indian chutneys. Zehug is made in two basic variations: green zehug from hot green peppers and red zehug from hot red peppers. Like chutney, it appears on the table from the beginning of the meal, for spreading on bread. It can also be used as a hot seasoning for sauces.*

Zehug is popular among Israelis of many origins, and in Israel is readily available in stores, but many people prefer the fresh taste of homemade zehug. Cooks used to pound the ingredients for zehug in a mortar with a pestle, but since the mixture is very easy to make with a blender or food processor, this is how it's usually made today.

5 medium jalapeño peppers (about 2 ounces total)
½ cup medium garlic cloves, peeled
2 to 3 tablespoons water, if needed
½ cup fresh coriander (cilantro)

½ teaspoon salt
freshly ground black pepper to taste
1 tablespoon cumin, preferably freshly ground

Wear gloves when handling hot peppers. Remove stems from peppers; remove seeds and ribs, if desired (so chutney will be less hot). Put garlic and peppers in food processor and puree until finely chopped and well blended. If necessary, add 2 or 3 tablespoons water, just enough to enable food processor to chop mixture. Add coriander and process until blended. Add salt, pepper, and cumin. Keep in a jar in refrigerator. (It keeps about 1 week.)

Makes ½ to ⅔ cup; about 4 to 6 servings

FRIED CAULIFLOWER WITH CUMIN AND TURMERIC

This is one of the most delicious cauliflower recipes I know. The spiced batter imparts a wonderful aroma and taste to the vegetable, as well as a lovely golden color.

1 medium cauliflower (about 2 pounds)	1 teaspoon ground cumin
½ teaspoon salt	½ cup all-purpose flour
pinch of black pepper	2 large eggs
¼ teaspoon turmeric	2 tablespoons water
	5 cups vegetable oil, for frying

Divide cauliflower into fairly large florets with stems attached. Cook cauliflower, uncovered, in a large pan of boiling salted water for 3 minutes, but do not let it cook completely. Drain and rinse gently until cool.

Mix salt, pepper, turmeric, cumin, and flour in a medium bowl. Sprinkle cauliflower florets lightly with spice mixture. Add eggs and water to remaining spice mixture and stir with whisk until blended to a smooth, thick batter. Dip a floret in batter—it should coat floret lightly; if it sticks to floret in a thick layer, stir in 1 teaspoon water.

Heat oil in a deep, heavy saucepan to 350° to 360°F., or until it bubbles vigorously around a batter-coated floret. Holding floret by its stem, dip flower and part of base in batter and add gently to oil. Dip 5 or 6 more florets. Fry about 2 or 3 minutes or until golden brown. Drain on paper towels. Serve as soon as possible.

Makes 4 servings

NOTE: If you prefer to shallow-fry, heat about ⅓ cup vegetable oil in a large skillet, preferably with a nonstick surface, over medium heat. Fry dipped florets about 5 minutes per side.

AROMATIC BEEF AND WHITE BEAN CASSEROLE (HAMIN)

French books on Jewish cooking refer to hamin as "Jewish cassoulet." Both share the technique of slow, gentle cooking of meat and beans, so the meat gives the beans a rich taste. This stew exists in many versions among Jews of most diverse origins, from Yemen to Morocco to Poland. It has many names—European cooks call it by its Yiddish name, cholent; *North African cooks refer to it as* defina; *and in Hebrew it's called* hamin.

The ingredients vary widely. Some cooks use navy beans or kidney beans, while others use chickpeas; some add kasha, barley, or wheat berries. The meat can be beef, lamb, or chicken. Most cooks flavor the casserole with onions and some add potatoes to the pot. The seasonings can be as basic as salt and pepper, or might include any number of spices, as in this Middle Eastern version accented with garlic, cumin, and turmeric. My sister-in-law from India insists that the secret to a good rich sauce is to add half a teaspoon of jam.

This stew traditionally cooks about eighteen hours; it is put in the oven just before sundown on Friday and is served on Saturday for an early lunch. There is no need to soak the beans because of the long slow cooking. From my Yemenite mother-in-law I learned the trick of putting eggs in their shells on top of the stew; they turn brown inside during the slow cooking, and are a treat.

2 pounds boneless beef chuck, trimmed and cut into 2-inch pieces	1 large onion, sliced
1½ cups Great Northern beans, picked over and rinsed	4 medium garlic cloves, chopped
	2 teaspoons salt
4 medium boiling potatoes (about 1¼ pounds total), peeled and halved	½ teaspoon pepper
	5 teaspoons ground cumin
1 cup wheat berries (available at natural foods shops), rinsed	4 teaspoons turmeric
	7 cups water
	6 large eggs in shells, rinsed

Preheat oven to 200°F. In a large heavy casserole combine meat, beans, potatoes, wheat berries, onion, and garlic. Sprinkle with salt, pepper, cumin, and turmeric and mix thoroughly. Add water and bring to a boil, stirring occasionally. Remove from heat. Set eggs gently on top and push them slightly into liquid.

Cover tightly and bake mixture, without stirring, for 10 to 11 hours, or until most of the liquid is absorbed by the beans. Serve stew from casserole, or carefully spoon it into a heated serving dish. Shell and halve the eggs and set them on top for garnish.

Makes 6 servings

NOTE: For a faster method, bake mixture in a preheated 250°F. oven for 5 hours, then simmer, uncovered, over low heat without stirring for 1 more hour, or until enough liquid evaporates so mixture is moist but no longer soupy.

EASY RICE PILAF

On the menus of Sephardic Jews, rice pilaf appears often as an accompaniment for meats, poultry, and vegetables. Many cooks sauté the onion until golden, in contrast to the way pilaf is prepared in classic French cooking, with onions that are softened but remain white. Next, the rice is sautéed with the onion, to help keep the grains separate. Rice cooked with water will be lighter in color but less flavorful than rice cooked with chicken stock. For a slightly spicy rice, use Yemenite Chicken Soup (page 186) for the cooking liquid.

2 tablespoons vegetable or olive oil
1 medium onion, minced
1½ cups long-grain white rice

3 cups hot chicken soup, broth, or
   boiling water
pinch of pepper
½ teaspoon salt (optional)

Heat oil in a sauté pan or large skillet. Add onion and cook over low heat, stirring occasionally, for about 10 minutes or until golden. Add rice and sauté, stirring, about 2 minutes or until grains turn milky white.

Add soup or water and pepper. Add salt if using unsalted or lightly salted soup or water. Bring to a boil, then stir once with a fork and cover. Cook over low heat, without stirring, for 18 to 20 minutes or until rice is tender and liquid is absorbed. Remove from heat and let stand, covered, for 10 minutes. Taste and adjust seasoning. (Rice will keep hot about 45 minutes. It can be prepared 2 days ahead and kept, covered, in refrigerator. To reheat, heat 1 tablespoon oil in a large skillet, add rice, and heat over low heat, stirring gently with a fork.) Fluff it with a fork just before serving. Serve hot.

Makes 4 to 6 servings

PART II

Everyday Jewish Dishes

8

APPETIZERS

 Festive Jewish meals, whether Ashkenazic or Sephardic, generally begin with several appetizers. One is most likely to be a spread or dip, such as chopped chicken liver, avocado spread, the chickpea spread called *hummus*, or the sesame dip known as *tehina* or tahini sauce. All are accompanied, of course, by good fresh bread and frequently by piquant treats such as olives and pickled vegetables. Fiery Hot Pepper–Garlic Chutney (page 142) and a hot tomato salsa, as well as a tangy dip made from fenugreek seeds, are served on the tables of Yemenite Jews.

For special occasions like weddings there will often be a pastry appetizer, such as Russian piroshki, eastern European knishes, or Sephardic bourekas. All of these may have meat, cheese, or vegetable fillings. Moroccan Jews prepare fried pastries called "cigars," with meat or potato fillings.

Perhaps the most famous Israeli appetizer is falafel, or chickpea croquettes. Falafel is most commonly served in a pita, with tahini and Israeli salad, as a quick meal or satisfying snack. In recent years falafel restaurants have expanded on the theme and serve falafel with a selection of sauces each person can add, which include tomato sauce, hot pepper sauce, fenugreek sauce, and a sort of curry sauce, as well as an assortment of pickles and fried eggplant slices. Falafel balls also make a delicious hors d'oeuvre or cocktail snack, served with tahini sauce for dipping. As a restaurant appetizer, falafel is sometimes served on a platter with a variety of colorful salads (see "Salads," Chapter 9).

Fish is a popular appetizer as well. It might be smoked or pickled fish or lox purchased from a deli, served on its own or made into salads; or a home-cooked fresh fish, served cold or at room temperature.

In Israel an assortment of appetizers might be the basis of a light meal or party menu. They might be accompanied by cut vegetables and perhaps some cheeses or sliced cold meats. The breads are chosen according to the type of appetizer—pita is the natural choice for serving with humus, tahini sauce, or marinated eggplant slices, while challah or rye bread is a favorite with chopped liver.

SAVORY CHEESE KNISHES

Appetizer pastries known as knishes symbolize the Ashkenazic kitchen almost as much as gefilte fish. Besides cheese, fillings vary from buckwheat groats to chopped meat to liver to potatoes. Sometimes the dough is potato-based as well.

Knishes do have a reputation for being heavy, perhaps because in some delis they are made quite large. These knishes, although rich and satisfying, are fairly small and thus leave room for the rest of the meal. They make delightful appetizers and are much easier to prepare than most other knishes. The dough is made in seconds in a food processor. The quick cheese filling is spread over the dough, which is then rolled up like a jelly roll, sliced, and baked.

Sour Cream Dough

1½ cups all-purpose flour
1 teaspoon baking powder
½ teaspoon salt

½ cup (1 stick) unsalted butter or
   margarine
⅓ cup sour cream
1 teaspoon water, if needed

Four-Cheese Filling

4 ounces farmer cheese
2 tablespoons cream cheese, softened
¾ cup grated Swiss cheese

2 ounces feta cheese, finely crumbled
   (scant ½ cup)
1 large egg
pepper to taste

In a food processor combine flour, baking powder, salt, and butter and process with on/off motion until mixture resembles coarse meal. Spoon sour cream fairly evenly over mixture. Process with on/off motion until dough just holds together and forms sticky crumbs, adding 1 teaspoon water if necessary. Knead lightly on work surface. Wrap dough and flatten to a square. Refrigerate for 2 hours.

Mix all ingredients for filling with fork. Season with pepper to taste.

Lightly grease a baking sheet. Divide dough into 2 pieces. Roll one to an 8 × 10-inch rectangle, slightly under ⅛ inch thick. Spread with half the filling, leaving a ½-inch border. Beginning at a long side, roll up tightly like a jelly roll. Cut in slices 1 inch thick. Put them on baking sheet with cut side (the less open side) facing down. Refrigerate slices. Repeat with remaining dough and filling. Refrigerate slices at least 30 minutes or up to overnight.

Preheat oven to 400°F. Bake knishes for 15 to 18 minutes or until lightly browned. Serve hot or warm.

Makes 16 to 18 pastries

SAVORY PASTRIES WITH BUCKWHEAT FILLING (KASHA KNISHES)

Roasted buckwheat kernels, also known as kasha, are a frequently used ingredient in the Russian Jewish community. Besides playing the role of a filling for knishes, kasha can be served on its own as a side dish for chicken or meat; simply omit the second egg and the almonds in the recipe below. Another time-honored Ashkenazic recipe for serving the kasha, after flavoring it with sautéed onions, is to toss it with cooked bowtie pasta. Kasha is heated with an egg to keep it fluffy.

Pastry Dough

¾ cup (1½ sticks) unsalted margarine
  or butter, well chilled
2½ cups all-purpose flour

scant ¾ teaspoon salt
5 to 7 tablespoons ice water

Kasha Filling

2 large eggs
salt and pepper
½ cup kasha (buckwheat groats or
   kernels)
1 cup boiling water

3 tablespoons vegetable oil
1 medium onion, chopped
4 ounces mushrooms, chopped
salt and pepper
2 tablespoons chopped almonds

1 large egg, beaten with pinch of salt,
   for glaze

Cut margarine into small pieces. Combine flour and salt in food processor and blend briefly. Add margarine and process with on-off motions until mixture resembles small crumbs. With blades turning, add ice water gradually, until dough begins to clump together. Wrap dough, press together to form a ball, and flatten to a disc. Refrigerate dough at least 1 hour or up to 2 days before using it.

Beat 1 egg for filling with a pinch of salt. Combine kasha with beaten egg in a wide bowl and stir with a fork until grains are thoroughly coated. Add to a heavy skillet and warm it over medium heat for about 3 minutes, stirring to keep grains separate. Add boiling water and stir. Cover and cook over low heat for 15 minutes or until all water is absorbed. Stir with a fork to fluff.

Heat oil in a skillet, add onion, and sauté over medium-low heat until soft and beginning to brown. Add mushrooms, sprinkle with salt and pepper, and sauté over medium-high heat for 2 minutes. Stir into kasha with a fork and add chopped almonds. Transfer to a bowl. Cool slightly. Beat second egg and stir into mixture. Taste for seasoning; mixture should be generously seasoned with salt and pepper. Cool completely.

Roll out half the dough on a lightly floured surface until as thin as possible, at most ⅛ inch thick. Using a 3-inch cutter, cut dough into circles. Put about 1½ teaspoons filling in center of each. Moisten edges about halfway around circle and fold in half, bringing un-moistened side over to moistened side. Pinch edges together to seal. Put pastries on a greased baking sheet. Continue making knishes from remaining dough and from scraps left from cutting. Chill knishes 30 minutes or up to overnight.

Preheat oven to 375°F. Brush knishes with beaten egg. Make 2 or 3 slits in pastry with a small sharp knife so steam can escape, then bake knishes for 20 to 25 minutes or until light brown. Knishes can be baked ahead and reheated in a low oven. Serve warm.

Makes about 40 small knishes

PIROSHKI WITH SALMON AND CABBAGE

With the influx of Russian immigrants in recent years, piroshki have become popular in Israel. Other fillings include cabbage on its own, meat, chicken, buckwheat, and liver. Piroshki are served as an appetizer or as an accompaniment for soup. These piroshki are baked, but some versions are fried.

¼ ounce (about 2 tablespoons) dried
   cèpes, porcini, or Polish mushrooms
½ green cabbage (1 pound), cored,
   rinsed, and finely chopped
3 tablespoons unsalted butter
salt and pepper

¼ pound salmon fillet, cut in tiny dice
5 teaspoons sour cream
Piroshki Dough (recipe follows),
   prepared a day before baking

1 large egg, beaten with a pinch of
   salt, for glaze

Soak mushrooms in a bowl of hot water for 30 minutes. Drain and chop. In a large pan of boiling salted water, boil cabbage for 3 minutes or until tender. Drain, rinse with cold water, and drain thoroughly. Squeeze out excess liquid. Melt butter in a large skillet and add cabbage with salt and pepper to taste. Cover and cook over low heat for 10 minutes or until tender. Add salmon and cook another ½ minute, until barely tender. Stir in cèpes. Transfer mixture to a bowl and cool to room temperature. Stir in sour cream and taste for seasoning. Refrigerate 15 minutes.

Lightly butter 2 or 3 baking sheets. Cut dough into 4 equal parts and return 3 parts to refrigerator. Shape fourth part into a round. Roll it about ⅛ inch thick and stamp out 3-inch rounds with a cutter, reserving scraps. Brush each round lightly with egg glaze. Place 1½ teaspoons filling in center of each round and shape filling in an oval across center of round to about ⅜ inch from each edge. Bring up 2 long opposite edges around filling and mold dough around it to a boat shape, joining 2 edges at top over filling. Pinch edges together along top, fluting them neatly. Arrange piroshki 1½ inches apart on baking sheets, cover with a towel, and let rise in a warm place for 15 minutes. Continue with remaining dough and filling.

Preheat oven to 400°F. Brush risen piroshki with egg glaze and bake 15 minutes or until golden brown.

Knead dough scraps together and refrigerate 2 hours. Refrigerate remaining filling. Shape and bake more piroshki. (Piroshki can be baked up to 8 hours ahead and reheated for serving; refrigerate them, covered. They can also be frozen.) Serve them warm.

Makes about 40 piroshki

Piroshki Dough

Although some people prepare piroshki from a pie dough, I prefer this rich, traditional yeast-risen dough.

2½ teaspoons active dry yeast
1 tablespoon sugar
¼ cup lukewarm water
3¼ cups all-purpose flour
1¾ teaspoons salt

⅔ cup lukewarm milk
7 tablespoons unsalted butter, melted and cooled
2 large eggs

In a small bowl proof yeast with sugar in lukewarm water for 10 minutes, or until foamy. In a large bowl combine 3 cups flour with salt; make a well in center and add yeast mixture, milk, butter, eggs, and remaining sugar. Combine mixture until a soft dough is formed and knead dough on a lightly floured surface, adding more of remaining flour as necessary to keep it from sticking, for 10 to 15 minutes, or until smooth. Form dough into a ball, put it in an oiled bowl, and turn to coat with oil. Cover and let rise in a warm place for 1 to 1½ hours or until it is doubled in bulk. Punch it down, cover, and refrigerate overnight.

Makes enough for 40 piroshki

SEPHARDIC SPINACH-STUFFED FILO TURNOVERS (SPINACH BOUREKAS)

Spinach rivals cheese as the filling of choice for the savory Sephardic pastry known as bourekas. Some cooks simply use strips of raw spinach leaves, but I like to cook the spinach first and squeeze out its water, so more filling will fit in each turnover. Often warm Browned Eggs (page 205) are served as an accompaniment.

1 pound filo sheets (about 20 sheets)

Spinach Filling

2 pounds fresh spinach, stems
   discarded, leaves rinsed well; or 1
   16-ounce package frozen leaf spinach
3 tablespoons olive oil
1 medium onion, finely chopped

2 large eggs
1 cup grated Swiss cheese
salt and pepper to taste
freshly grated nutmeg to taste

1 cup (2 sticks) butter or margarine,
   melted

about 2 teaspoons sesame seeds, for
   sprinkling

If filo sheets are frozen, defrost them in refrigerator 8 hours or overnight. Remove sheets from refrigerator 2 hours before using and leave them in their package.

Place spinach leaves in a large skillet with water clinging to them or put frozen spinach in skillet with amount of water specified on package. Cover and cook over medium-high heat, stirring occasionally, about 4 minutes or until wilted. Drain, rinse, and squeeze to remove as much liquid as possible. Chop spinach finely with a knife. Heat oil in a skillet, add onion, and cook over low heat, stirring, about 10 minutes or until tender. Remove from heat, transfer to a bowl, and let cool slightly. Mix with spinach, eggs, and cheese and season to taste with salt, pepper, and nutmeg; filling should be highly seasoned.

Remove filo sheets from their package and spread them out on a dry towel. Using a sharp knife, cut stack in half lengthwise, to form 2 stacks of sheets of about 16 × 7 inches. Cover filo immediately with a piece of wax paper, then with a damp towel. Work with only 1 sheet at a time and always keep remaining sheets covered with paper and towel, so they don't dry out.

Remove 1 pastry sheet from pile. Brush it lightly with melted butter and fold it in half lengthwise, so its dimensions are about 16 × 3½ inches. Dab it lightly with butter. Place about 1½ teaspoons spinach at one end of strip. Fold end of strip diagonally over filling to form a triangle, and dab it lightly with butter. Continue folding it over and over, keeping it in a triangular shape after each fold, until end of strip is reached. Set pastry on a lightly buttered baking sheet. Brush it lightly with melted butter. Continue making pastries with remaining filo sheets and filling. (Pastries can be shaped 1 day ahead and refrigerated on a baking sheet or on plates. Cover them tightly with plastic wrap.)

Preheat oven to 350°F. Brush pastries again with melted butter and sprinkle with sesame seeds. Bake for 20 to 25 minutes or until golden brown. Serve warm (not hot) or at room temperature.

Makes about 32 turnovers; 10 to 12 servings

MUSHROOM TURNOVERS

Lately cooks have been preparing bourekas with fillings other than the traditional spinach and cheese. Mushroom filling is now fashionable, and so is potato, with or without cheese. Instead of using filo dough, many home cooks use puff pastry, as in this version.

These turnovers are good as hors d'oeuvre, but they can be made larger and served as a first course.

Mushroom Filling

1 tablespoon butter or margarine
2 shallots or white part of 2 green
  onions, finely chopped
½ pound button mushrooms, chopped
salt and freshly ground pepper

¼ cup heavy cream or chicken soup
2 tablespoons minced fresh parsley
1 tablespoon bread crumbs
1 large egg yolk

2 pounds good-quality puff pastry,
  well chilled
1 large egg, beaten with a pinch of
  salt, for glaze

about 2 teaspoons sesame seeds
  (optional)

Melt butter in a medium skillet over low heat. Add shallots and cook 1 minute. Add mushrooms and a small pinch of salt and pepper. Cook over medium-high heat, stirring often, for 7 minutes or until liquid that comes out of mushrooms evaporates. Stir in cream or soup and bring to a boil. Simmer, stirring often, about 2 minutes or until mixture is thick and liquid is absorbed.

Transfer mixture to a bowl. Stir in parsley and bread crumbs. Cool to lukewarm, then add egg yolk and beat until blended. Taste and adjust seasoning. Cover and refrigerate 30 minutes. (Filling can be kept 1 day in refrigerator.)

Sprinkle 2 baking sheets with water. Roll out half the dough on a cool, lightly floured surface until about ⅛ inch thick. Using a 3-inch round cutter, cut rounds of dough. Separate rounds from rest of dough, reserving scraps. Roll each round to elongate it slightly to an oval. Put 1 teaspoon filling in center of each oval. Brush half of oval, around a narrow end, with beaten egg. Fold oval in half to enclose filling, joining second side to egg-brushed side. Press to seal well. Set turnovers on a prepared baking sheet. Refrigerate at least 30 minutes, or wrap and keep pastries in freezer until ready to bake. Shape turnovers from remaining pastry and filling. Refrigerate scraps at least 30 minutes and make turnovers from them also.

Preheat oven to 425°F. Brush turnovers with beaten egg. Sprinkle with sesame seeds, if desired.

Bake pastries about 10 minutes. Reduce oven temperature to 375°F. and bake about 12 minutes or until puffed and brown. (Pastries can be kept for 2 days in an airtight container or they can be frozen.) Serve warm or at room temperature.

Makes about 40 pastries

NOTE: As with all filled pastries, avoid the temptation to put too generous an amount of filling in the turnovers or they will burst open.

CRISP MEAT-FILLED PASTRIES (KUBEH)

These football-shaped pastries of a brown, delicately crunchy bulgur wheat shell enclosing a meat and pine nut filling are absolutely irresistible. To many Jews of Middle Eastern origin, kubeh rival chicken soup as the ideal comfort food. An Israeli friend of mine who lived in Paris when we did used to return from visits to his family in Israel with a bag full of kubeh that his mother made for him "so he'd have something good to eat in Europe."

Kubeh do require practice to give them a perfect shape so that the shell is fine and even, but in the note following the recipe there is an easier method. I was delighted to have a chance to learn to make them from Suzanne Elmaleh, one of the best hostesses in Jerusalem, who is known for these tasty treats.

Kubeh are made in much of the Middle East, and the pastry and seasonings vary from place to place. Besides bulgur wheat, the shell might be made from rice, semolina, or mashed potatoes, and the kubeh might be poached instead of fried. For Passover, kubeh are made with a matzo meal shell instead of one of bulgur wheat. Friends of ours from Iraq generally shape their kubeh in flat cakes and flavor the dough with turmeric, which gives it a currylike aroma when it is fried. One of my in-laws from India prepares a filling spiced with dill, paprika, cumin, and turmeric. Kurdish Jews sometimes serve their lamb-filled kubeh in a tomato sauce with chickpeas. Other popular fillings are made of chicken, or of equal parts chicken and beef.

The finest grind of bulgur wheat is required for these; it is available in natural food stores and in specialty shops that carry Middle Eastern or Mediterranean products. Often the pastries are accompanied by tahini sauce for dipping, and are served with a glass of beer.

Meat and Pine Nut Filling

2 tablespoons vegetable oil
1 medium onion, chopped
5 ounces (about ¾ cup) extra-lean
  ground beef

2 tablespoons water
salt and freshly ground pepper
2 tablespoons pine nuts

Bulgur Wheat Dough

1 cup bulgur wheat, finest grind,
  soaked in 3 cups cold water for 1
  hour or until softened
2 tablespoons fine dry unseasoned
  bread crumbs

3 tablespoons all-purpose flour
1 teaspoon salt
½ teaspoon paprika
3 to 4 tablespoons water

about 1 cup vegetable oil for frying
Tahini Sauce with Parsley (page 164),
  as an accompaniment

Heat oil for filling in a heavy medium skillet over medium heat. Add onion and sauté about 10 minutes or until golden brown. Add beef, water, salt, and pepper and sauté, stirring often, until meat is thoroughly cooked, about 10 minutes. Transfer mixture to a strainer to thoroughly drain excess fat. Transfer to a bowl. Add pine nuts.

Drain bulgur wheat thoroughly in a strainer. Squeeze out excess liquid then return to bowl. Add dry ingredients for dough and mix well. Gradually add water, kneading mixture with your hands, until it is just moist enough to form a stiff dough; it will be sticky.

Taste both dough and filling and adjust seasoning. Both should be well seasoned.

Take about 2 tablespoons dough and squeeze together into a patty shape between both hands about 15 times to knead further, pressing to make dough compact. Then roll between your palms to a smooth ball. Put balls on a plate.

Prepare a bowl of water. Line a baking sheet with wax paper. Moisten the palm of your left hand and the index finger of your right hand. Put a ball of dough in your left palm. With your right index finger, make a hole in ball of dough and gradually push it to elongate it and to form a cavity in it, at the same time squeezing and turning the dough around your finger with your left hand. Try to form a thin, even shell without any cracks. If cracks form, make a ball of the piece of dough and start again. Put in enough filling to come nearly to top. Wet your right thumb and index finger and pinch open end of dough closed, completely enclosing filling. (Try not to use too much water when working because kubeh then become wet and sticky, and will make frying oil splatter.) Shape each end into a point, so pastry is shaped like a long football. Set aside on prepared baking sheet. Continue with remaining dough and remaining filling. Refrigerate, uncovered, for 1 hour. (Kubeh can be prepared to this point and refrigerated overnight.)

Heat oil in a large, deep heavy skillet over medium-high heat; when oil is hot enough, it should sizzle when the end of a kubeh is touched to it. Fry kubeh in batches, without crowding, about 4 minutes per side or until deep golden brown; reduce heat if they brown too fast. Stand back while frying, as oil tends to splatter. Use 2 slotted spatulas to turn them carefully. Drain well on several layers of paper towels. Serve hot, warm, or at room temperature, accompanied by Tahini Sauce with Parsley.

Makes about 14 pieces; 6 or 7 portions

NOTE: An easier, if less traditional, way to shape kubeh is as flat cakes. Prepare balls of dough as above. With moistened hands, flatten dough to a disc, then press to flatten further in your palm. Cup your palm so there is a hollow in middle of dough. Place about 1½ teaspoons filling in the hollow. Bring dough around it and press to join edges to completely enclose filling. Pat again to a disc. Fry as above.

ARTICHOKES WITH LEMON DRESSING

Jews from Mediterranean countries frequently prepare this appetizer for Passover, when artichokes are in season.

8 fairly small artichokes
2 tablespoons strained fresh lemon
   juice
salt and pepper

6 tablespoons olive oil
2 teaspoons chopped fresh thyme, or ¾
   teaspoon dried thyme, crumbled
1 tablespoon chopped fresh parsley

Break off stem of each artichoke. With scissors cut off sharp point of each leaf. Add artichokes to a large saucepan of boiling salted water, cover with a slightly smaller lid to keep them submerged, and cook over medium heat about 45 minutes or until a leaf can be pulled out easily. Remove them and drain thoroughly, upside down.

For dressing, whisk lemon juice with salt and pepper. Whisk in oil and thyme and taste for seasoning. Whisk dressing again before using and add parsley.

Serve artichokes warm or at room temperature, accompanied by dressing.

Makes 8 servings

MARINATED EGGPLANT SLICES

Marinated eggplant slices are loved throughout the Mediterranean basin and are an important part of Sephardic cooking. In this recipe, which is inspired by a dish I enjoyed at a small restaurant in Tel Aviv, the zesty spiced vinegar penetrates the sauteed eggplant and balances its richness. Herbs such as cilantro can be used to flavor the marinade instead of spices. Generally the marinated slices are served as an appetizer or a side dish, but they are also wonderful in a sandwich with cold meats or with sliced cheese. SEE PHOTOGRAPH.

2 medium eggplants (2 pounds)
2 teaspoons salt
¾ cup olive oil

Garlic-Chili Marinade

6 medium garlic cloves
2 tablespoons olive oil
1 fresh serrano chili, halved
   lengthwise, cored, and seeded

1 teaspoon sweet paprika
1 teaspoon ground cumin
salt
3 tablespoons mild white wine vinegar

freshly ground black pepper
1 medium red bell pepper, roasted and
   peeled (page 346)

quartered pita or sliced French or
   Italian bread, for accompaniment

Cut eggplants in ½-inch slices crosswise, discarding ends. Arrange slices in 1 layer on a rack set over a tray. Sprinkle each side evenly with about 1 teaspoon salt. Let slices drain for 1 hour, turning them over after 30 minutes. Pat them dry very thoroughly with several changes of paper towels.

In a large heavy skillet heat 3 tablespoons oil over medium heat. Quickly add enough eggplant slices to make 1 layer. Sauté eggplant about 2½ minutes on each side, or until tender when pierced with a fork. Transfer slices to a plate. Add 3 tablespoons oil to skillet, heat oil, and sauté remaining eggplant in batches, adding remaining oil between batches as necessary. Transfer eggplant to a large shallow serving dish or baking dish, such as a 15-inch oval gratin dish.

Peel 2 garlic cloves without crushing them. Cut them into very thin slices lengthwise, then peel and mince remaining garlic cloves. Heat oil in a small saucepan, add chopped garlic and halved chili, and cook over low heat for 2 minutes. Stir in paprika, cumin, and a small pinch of salt. Add vinegar and sliced garlic, bring to a boil, and cook over low heat for 1 minute. Remove marinade from heat and discard chili.

Pour marinade evenly over eggplant slices and sprinkle them with black pepper to taste.

Turn slices over so that all come in contact with marinade. Halve the roasted pepper crosswise and cut halves lengthwise in ½-inch-wide strips. Put pepper strips on top of eggplant. Let stand at room temperature for 30 minutes before serving. (Slices can be kept, covered, for 3 days in refrigerator.)

When serving, set a pepper strip on each eggplant slice, with skinned side of pepper facing up, and top strip with a garlic slice. Serve eggplant cold or at room temperature, accompanied by fresh pita or bread.

Makes 4 to 6 servings

NOTE: If you are sensitive to chilies, wear rubber gloves when handling them. If you do not wear gloves, wash your hands immediately after handling chilies.

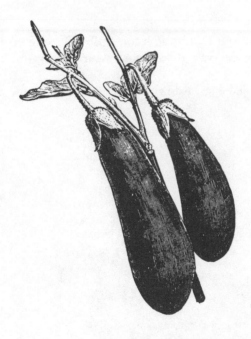

AVOCADO AND EGG SALAD

It was during my college years in Israel that I tasted avocado for the first time. In this avocado-rich country many people prepare the fruit by simply mashing its pulp with salt and pepper and perhaps a squeeze of lemon juice and spreading it on bread. I loved this simple spread; it reminded me of butter!

In this variation of the basic spread, the avocado is mixed with grated hard-boiled egg. Garnished with a few black olives or radish slices and served with fresh bread, this is a delicious first course.

The proportions of avocado and egg can change as you like; if you add more eggs, you will have a new version of egg salad. Egg salad is a favorite at Jewish delis, either in the familiar form in which the grated eggs are mixed with mayonnaise, or as eggs and onions, for which the eggs are combined with sautéed chopped onions and plenty of black pepper.

1 large or 2 small ripe avocados
1 teaspoon lemon juice, or to taste
salt and freshly ground pepper or
    cayenne pepper

1 or 2 hard-boiled large eggs
2 tablespoons chopped green onions or
    red onion (optional)

Halve the avocado and remove pit by hitting it forcefully with the heel of a heavy knife, so knife sticks in pit. Remove avocado flesh and mash with a fork. Add lemon juice, salt, and pepper.

Coarsely grate the hard-boiled eggs. Add eggs and onion to avocado and mix lightly. Taste and adjust seasoning.

Makes 2 servings

HUMMUS (CHICKPEA DIP)

Hummus is a golden chickpea puree flavored with tahini (sesame paste), garlic, and lemon juice and served as an appetizer, spread, or dip. Generally it is served on a flat plate and garnished with olive oil or more tahini sauce, then with paprika and chopped parsley. It is an inexpensive, easy to make party dish.

In Jerusalem you can buy two other types of hummus: a country-style hummus of whole chickpeas mixed into tahini with red pepper flakes and parsley or coriander; and "Jerusalem hummus," the smooth type sprinkled with pine nuts, olive oil, and paprika.

½ pound (1¼ cups) dried chickpeas (garbanzo beans), or 2 15- to 16-ounce cans, rinsed
5½ cups plus 2 tablespoons water
3 medium garlic cloves, minced

¼ cup strained fresh lemon juice
¼ cup tahini (stirred before measuring)
salt to taste
cayenne pepper

Garnish

4 to 6 tablespoons extra-virgin olive oil or Tahini Sauce (page 164)
paprika or cayenne pepper

1 tablespoon chopped fresh parsley
pita, for serving

Pick over dried chickpeas, discarding pebbles and broken or discolored peas. Soak chickpeas for 8 hours or overnight in water to cover generously; or quick-soak by putting them in a medium saucepan with 1 quart water, bringing to a boil, and boiling uncovered for 2 minutes; remove from heat, cover, and let stand 1 hour.

Drain chickpeas and rinse. Put in a medium saucepan and add 5 cups water. Bring to a simmer, cover, and cook over low heat for about 2 hours or until very tender. Drain well. Cool slightly.

Set aside about ⅓ cup whole cooked or canned chickpeas. Mince garlic in a food processor. Add remaining chickpeas and process coarsely. Add lemon juice, tahini, and ¼ cup water and puree until finely blended. Transfer to a bowl. Stir in enough additional water so that mixture has consistency of a smooth spread. Season with salt and cayenne to taste. (Spread can be kept 4 or 5 days in refrigerator.)

To serve, spread hummus about ¼ inch thick on a platter or serving plates. Make a hollow in center with back of a spoon and fill with olive oil or tahini. Sprinkle hummus with paprika or a little cayenne, then sprinkle parsley on hummus or on tahini for garnish (but not on olive oil). Garnish with reserved chickpeas, and serve with fresh or warmed pita.

Makes 4 to 6 servings

TAHINI SAUCE (SESAME DIP)

Tahini, or sesame paste, is used in Israel and in much of the eastern Mediterranean as the basis for a sauce, a dip, and a flavoring. Tahini Sauce is rich with a slight touch of bitterness. Some people use it as an all-purpose sauce instead of mayonnaise, and spoon it over fish or meat. It is sometimes mixed with diced tomato and cucumber or simply with plenty of parsley and served as a salad. But most often it is served on its own, accompanied by pita for dipping.

The proportions of water used for Tahini Sauce vary; add water to the paste gradually to obtain the thickness you want. Tahini Sauce is made thinner if used as a pouring sauce to serve over food than if served as a dip to be scooped up with pita. SEE PHOTOGRAPH.

½ cup tahini (sesame paste)
½ cup water
¼ teaspoon salt, or to taste
2 tablespoons strained fresh lemon
  juice

3 large garlic cloves, minced
pinch of cayenne (optional)

Garnish

2 to 3 tablespoons olive oil (optional)
paprika or cayenne, for sprinkling

3 tablespoons chopped fresh parsley
pita, for serving

In a medium bowl, stir tahini to blend in its oil. Stir in ½ cup water. Add salt, lemon juice, garlic, and cayenne. If sauce is too thick, gradually stir in more water. Taste, and add more salt or lemon juice if desired. (Tahini Sauce can be kept 2 days in refrigerator; it thickens on standing, and may need a little water when served.)

To serve as a dip, spread tahini on a serving plate. If desired, make a small hollow in center and spoon in a little olive oil. Sprinkle Tahini Sauce lightly with paprika or cayenne and with chopped parsley. Serve with fresh or warmed pita.

Makes 1 cup; 4 to 6 servings

VARIATION: Tahini Sauce with Parsley
  Stir ¼ to ⅓ cup chopped flat-leaf (Italian) or curly parsley into Tahini Sauce before serving, instead of sprinkling parsley on top. This version is popular as a sauce, especially for accompanying the meat-filled pastries known as kubeh (see recipe page 157).

FALAFEL (CHICKPEA CROQUETTES)

With its humble ingredients of chickpeas, garlic, and spices, it might be surprising that falafel has become the number one snack in Israel. It is for Israel what the hamburger is for America—fast, inexpensive, and adored as a snack or quick meal. And it is available everywhere, from restaurants to markets to central bus stations. There is even a popular song in Hebrew about ''falafel, the national dish.''

Actually, falafel is loved throughout the Middle East. The chickpea version in Israel is similar to that made in Lebanon, while in Egypt falafel is made of fava beans. Falafel is rising in popularity in America, partly because it is vegetarian and thus in tune with today's food preferences.

I learned to make falafel from my mother-in-law, Rachel Levy, who prepared falafel at her restaurant near Tel Aviv every day. She served them the way they are preferred in Israel: in a pita with tahini sauce and Israeli salad of diced cucumber and tomato and shredded green or red cabbage. For those who wanted, she added a pickled hot pepper or hot sauce, which she made by mixing Zehug (page 142) with a little water.

Professionals use a gadget known as a falafel maker for shaping the balls evenly, but they are easy to shape by hand, too. Note that the chickpeas are soaked but are not boiled—the frying cooks them enough. SEE PHOTOGRAPH.

12 ounces (2 cups) dried chickpeas
  (garbanzo beans)
2 medium heads garlic (22 to 24
  medium cloves), peeled
1 medium onion
¼ cup small parsley sprigs (optional)
2 tablespoons small sprigs fresh
  coriander (cilantro) (optional)

1 slice stale white bread, crusts
  removed
2 tablespoons ground coriander
2 tablespoons ground cumin
2½ teaspoons salt
2 teaspoons ground black pepper
3 tablespoons all-purpose flour
1 teaspoon baking powder
6 cups vegetable oil, for frying

For Sandwich

pita
Israeli Vegetable Salad (page 20)

Tahini Sauce (page 164)
hot sauce

Soak chickpeas overnight or for 12 hours in water to generously cover; drain in colander and rinse.

Mince garlic in a food processor; remove. Mince onion in processor; remove. Dry processor. Mince parsley and coriander; remove. Sprinkle bread with about 1 tablespoon water, then squeeze dry. Grind chickpeas and bread in processor in batches. Add onion, garlic, parsley, fresh coriander, ground coriander, cumin, salt, pepper, flour, and baking powder.

Knead thoroughly with hands to mix very well. (Mixture can be kept in refrigerator 2 days.)

To shape falafel, squeeze 1 tablespoon of mixture to compact it, then press into a ball. Roll lightly between your palms to give it a smooth round shape.

Heat oil to about 350°F. Add about one-fourth to one-third of the falafel balls. Slide them into hot oil near surface; do not drop them into oil from high or the oil will splash. Fry about 2 minutes until falafel balls are deep golden brown and coating is crisp. Drain briefly on paper towels. Serve hot.

To serve falafel in sandwiches, use either a half or whole pita for each serving. If using a whole pita, cut off a thin strip near one edge to make a pocket. Put in a few falafel balls, top with salad, and spoon in a little Tahini Sauce. Serve more Tahini Sauce and hot sauce separately.

Makes 47 falafel balls; about 8 to 10 servings

YEMENITE TOMATO SALSA

Yemenite women often make this dip by adding cut-up tomatoes to the food processor after making Zehug (page 142). Otherwise, an amount of Zehug to taste is stirred into fresh tomato puree. There is no need to peel the tomatoes, since the peel is ground up finely in the food processor.

The salsa is served as a dip or appetizer with pita or other bread, or for Sabbath breakfast, with Browned Eggs (page 205) and rich breads or pastries like Shabbat Breakfast Bread (page 292) or Shabbat Pastry Rolls (page 302). It can also play the role of chutney or ketchup, and has the advantage over the latter in being fresh and free of preservatives and sugar. For example, it's great with hamburgers or with Aromatic Meat Patties (page 241). SEE PHOTOGRAPH.

¼ pound ripe tomatoes
2 to 3 teaspoons Hot Pepper–Garlic
   Chutney (page 142), or to taste
salt to taste

Puree the tomatoes in a food processor. Stir in chutney and salt to taste. Serve cold.

Makes ⅔ cup; about 4 servings

9

SALADS

Living in Israel introduced me to new ideas for light, healthful Mediterranean eating. One is that a meal is not complete unless it includes *salat*, or Israeli salad. But this salad is quite specific: it is nothing like our green salad or restaurant-style dinner salads. Rather, it consists of a colorful mixture of diced tomatoes, sweet peppers, and cucumbers. Israelis insist that these cubes be very small, and they often kid Americans like me, saying the longer the time since our last visit to Israel, the larger our dice become!

Usually served as an accompaniment, this quick-to-make salad adds a lively note to any menu. It can be served as is, or can be embellished with parsley or other herbs; my Israeli mother-in-law likes to stir in chopped fresh coriander and green onions, for example. A dash of extra-virgin olive oil gives a nice touch, and because it is so flavorful, a little goes a long way.

Of course, there are many other salads in the Jewish repertoire. Some are of raw vegetables like the Cucumber Salad with Yogurt and Mint or Fresh and Tangy Carrot Salad in this chapter. Others are based on steamed or boiled vegetables, like Beet Salad with Apples (page 84). There is a wealth of potato salads—both creamy Ashkenazic and tangy Sephardic styles. For some

Middle Eastern–style salads the vegetables are grilled, as in Eggplant Salad with Tahini or Grilled Pepper and Tomato Salad.

Salads are served as appetizers or accompaniments, and at least one salad appears at every meal, sometimes even for breakfast. For a sumptuous dinner in the Mediterranean style, a great assortment of colorful salads, along with olives and pickles, plays the role of an enticing beginning to the feast.

CREAMY POTATO SALAD WITH DILL PICKLES

Pickles are an important staple of the Jewish table. Although those made from cucumbers are the most common, at a typical Jerusalem market you can also find pickled green tomatoes, small eggplants, beets, baby onions, lemon slices, and mixed vegetables. Most often they are served as accompaniments but they also add zest to salads like this one.

2 pounds red-skinned potatoes of uniform size, scrubbed but not peeled
salt
2 tablespoons dry white wine
1 tablespoon mild white wine vinegar
1 tablespoon vegetable oil
freshly ground pepper

¼ cup finely chopped red onion
2 tablespoons plus 1 teaspoon Dijon mustard, or to taste
1¼ cups mayonnaise
3 hard-boiled large eggs
1 medium dill pickle, cut into tiny dice (about ⅓ cup)
3 tablespoons chopped fresh parsley

Put potatoes in a large saucepan, cover with water by about ½ inch, and add salt. Bring to boil. Cover and simmer over low heat about 25 minutes, or until a knife can pierce the center of largest potato easily and potato falls from knife when lifted. Meanwhile, combine wine, vinegar, oil, salt, and pepper in a small bowl and whisk until blended.

Drain potatoes and peel while hot. Cut into fairly small dice, then put potatoes in a large bowl. Rewhisk wine mixture until blended and pour over potatoes. Toss or fold gently to mix thoroughly. Fold in onion. Cool to room temperature.

Whisk mustard into mayonnaise and fold into potatoes. Chop 2 eggs; cut third egg in 6 wedges. Add chopped eggs, pickle, and 2 tablespoons parsley to salad and fold in gently. Taste and adjust seasoning. (Salad can be kept, covered, overnight in refrigerator.) Garnish with remaining parsley and egg wedges. Serve at cool room temperature.

Makes 6 servings

POTATO AND LOX SALAD

If you are fond of that "all-American" Jewish sandwich of bagel with lox and cream cheese, you will like this colorful salad. It is a great way to use small, less expensive pieces of lox.

2 pounds red-skinned potatoes of uniform size, scrubbed but not peeled	1 tablespoon vegetable oil
salt	freshly ground pepper
2 tablespoons dry white wine	½ to ⅔ cup Mustard Vinaigrette (recipe follows)
1 tablespoon mild white wine vinegar	3 ounces thinly sliced lox
	2 tablespoons sliced or snipped chives

Put potatoes in a large saucepan, cover with water by about ½ inch, and add salt. Bring to boil, cover, and simmer over low heat about 25 minutes, or until a knife can pierce center of largest potato easily and potato falls from knife when lifted. Meanwhile, combine wine, vinegar, oil, salt, and pepper in a small bowl and whisk until blended.

Drain potatoes and peel while hot. Cut into fairly small dice, then put potatoes in a large bowl. Rewhisk wine mixture until blended and pour it over potatoes. Toss or fold gently to mix thoroughly. Cool to room temperature.

Whisk vinaigrette until blended. Add about ½ cup vinaigrette to salad and fold it in gently using a rubber spatula. (Salad tastes best on day it is made but it can be prepared 1 day ahead, covered, and refrigerated.)

Bring salad to cool room temperature. Cut lox lengthwise in 2 × ½-inch strips, using thin-bladed knife. Reserve 6 strips for garnish. Fold chives and remaining lox into salad. Taste and adjust seasoning, adding 1 or 2 tablespoons more vinaigrette if desired. Transfer to serving dish. Garnish with reserved lox strips.

Makes 4 servings

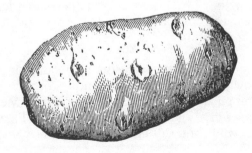

MUSTARD VINAIGRETTE

This dressing is good for potato salads, other salads of cooked vegetables, and green salads. Use your favorite mustard; I like to use the smooth Dijon type.

3 tablespoons white wine vinegar
salt and freshly ground pepper
1½ teaspoons mustard, or more to taste

½ cup plus 1 tablespoon vegetable or
  olive oil

Whisk vinegar with salt, pepper, and mustard in a small heavy bowl until well blended. Gradually whisk in oil. Taste and adjust seasoning. (Can be prepared 1 week ahead, covered and refrigerated.) Bring to room temperature and whisk before using.

Makes about ¾ cup

POTATO SALAD WITH SMOKED TURKEY

Smoked turkey has long been a favorite of the kosher cold cuts, and today its lean meat makes it a frequent choice for sandwiches. It is also good in salads, and can turn a potato salad like this one into a main course.

2 pounds red-skinned potatoes of
  uniform size, scrubbed but not
  peeled
salt
2 tablespoons dry white wine
1 tablespoon mild white wine vinegar
1 tablespoon vegetable or olive oil

freshly ground pepper
3 ounces thinly sliced smoked turkey
3 tablespoons snipped fresh dill or
  minced parsley
2 tablespoons minced green onions
1¼ cups mayonnaise

Put potatoes in a large saucepan, cover with water by about ½ inch, and add salt. Bring to boil, cover, and simmer over low heat about 25 minutes, or until a knife can pierce center of largest potato easily and potato falls from knife when lifted. Meanwhile, combine wine, vinegar, oil, salt, and pepper in a small bowl and whisk until blended.

Drain potatoes and peel while hot. Cut into fairly small dice, then put potatoes in a large bowl. Rewhisk wine mixture until blended and pour it over potatoes. Toss or fold gently to mix thoroughly. Cool to room temperature.

Cut turkey slices in half crosswise, then lengthwise into 2 × ⅜-inch strips. Add turkey, dill or parsley, green onions, and mayonnaise to potatoes and fold gently. Taste and adjust seasoning. (Salad tastes best on day it is made but it can be prepared 1 day ahead, covered and refrigerated.) Serve at cool room temperature.

Makes 4 servings

EGGPLANT SALAD WITH TAHINI

For this Middle Eastern salad, the eggplant is grilled so that it acquires a smoky taste. This is the preferred way of preparing eggplant salad in Israel. In addition to the tahini, garlic, and lemon juice, some cooks flavor this salad with ½ to 1 teaspoon ground cumin.

If you want to cook the eggplants in the broiler, choose long, fairly slender ones so they will fit.

1 medium eggplant (about 1¼ pounds)
3 medium garlic cloves, minced
3 tablespoons strained fresh lemon
   juice
1 tablespoon water

4 tablespoons tahini (sesame paste),
   stirred before measuring
salt and freshly ground black pepper
2 tablespoons chopped fresh parsley,
   for garnish (optional)

Prick eggplant a few times with fork. Grill eggplant above medium-hot coals about 1 hour or broil it about 40 minutes, turning often, until skin blackens, flesh is tender, and eggplant looks collapsed. Remove eggplant peel and cut off stem. Drain off any liquid from inside eggplant. Chop flesh very fine with knife; there should still be small chunks. Transfer to a bowl and add garlic.

Stir lemon juice and water into tahini until smooth. Add to eggplant and mix well. Add salt and pepper to taste. To serve, spread on a plate and sprinkle with parsley.

Makes 4 servings

BULGARIAN EGGPLANT SALAD WITH GRILLED PEPPERS

When I lived in Bat Yam, a suburb of Tel Aviv, a neighbor gave me the recipe for this hot, delicious salad, a specialty of Bulgarian Jews. Bulgarian cuisine is part of the Balkan style and bears a certain similarity to that of Greece and Turkey. Some people omit the hot peppers in the salad, but in my family we love it this way.

2 long, fairly slender eggplants (about 1 pound each)
1 medium green bell pepper
1 medium red bell pepper
2 jalapeño peppers
2 medium garlic cloves, minced
2 tablespoons chopped fresh parsley
1 tablespoon vinegar
1 tablespoon olive oil
salt to taste

Prick eggplant a few times with fork. Broil eggplant about 40 minutes or grill it above medium-hot coals about 1 hour, turning often, until skin blackens and flesh is tender. Remove eggplant peel and cut off stem. Drain off any liquid from inside eggplant. Chop flesh very fine with knife; there should still be small chunks. Transfer to a bowl.

Broil bell and jalapeño peppers about 2 inches from heat source, turning them often, until skins are blistery all over, about 5 minutes for jalapeño peppers and 15 to 20 minutes for bell peppers. Transfer them to plastic bags and close bags. Let stand 10 minutes. Peel peppers using paring knife, handling jalapeños with rubber gloves if you are sensitive. Remove seeds from peppers. Dice bell peppers. Mince jalapeño peppers.

Add jalapeño peppers, garlic, and parsley to eggplant and mix well. Add vinegar, oil, and salt to taste. Stir in bell peppers. Taste and adjust seasoning. (Salad can be kept, covered, for 2 days in refrigerator.) Serve cold or at room temperature.

Makes 6 servings

CREAMY EGGPLANT SALAD

This easy to make version of eggplant salad, a favorite delicatessen item in Israel, combines Middle Eastern and European influences with the addition of mayonnaise to the salad. To give it a more "Mediterranean" flavor, grill the eggplant as in the previous recipe instead of baking it.

4 medium eggplants (about 4½ pounds total)
2 medium garlic cloves, minced (1½ teaspoons)
2 tablespoons minced onion
¾ cup mayonnaise

2 teaspoons strained fresh lemon juice
salt and pepper to taste
parsley sprigs, for garnish
black olives, for garnish
quartered pita or sliced French or Italian bread, for accompaniment

Preheat oven to 400°F. Pierce each eggplant a few times with a fork to prevent it from bursting. Bake whole eggplants on a large baking sheet lined with foil for 30 minutes. Turn eggplants over and bake them 30 to 40 minutes, or until they are very tender. Leave eggplants until cool enough to handle. Holding cap, peel off skin of each eggplant. Drain eggplants in a colander for 1 hour.

Cut off caps. Chop eggplant flesh, using a knife, until it is a chunky puree. In a large bowl combine eggplant, garlic, onion, mayonnaise, lemon juice, and salt and pepper to taste and mix well; salad should be highly seasoned. Refrigerate at least 30 minutes before serving. (Salad can be kept for 3 days in refrigerator.)

Spoon salad into a shallow bowl or plate, garnish it with parsley sprigs and olives, and serve it with fresh pita or bread.

Makes 8 to 10 servings

FRESH AND TANGY CARROT SALAD

Here is proof that a salad of grated carrots can be exciting, as the lemony dressing provides a delightful balance to the sweetness of the vegetable. This Moroccan salad is often featured on menus of Middle Eastern restaurants in Tel Aviv. It makes a pretty addition to a selection of salads for a colorful first course, or a good accompaniment for cold meats.

1 pound carrots (about 6 medium)
1 medium garlic clove, minced
½ teaspoon Tabasco or other hot
   pepper sauce, or freshly ground
   black pepper to taste
2 tablespoons chopped fresh coriander
   (cilantro) or parsley

¼ cup strained fresh lemon juice
¼ cup extra-virgin olive oil
pinch of salt
coriander or parsley sprigs, for garnish

Peel carrots and coarsely grate them. Mix with garlic, hot pepper sauce, coriander, lemon juice, oil, and salt. Taste and adjust seasoning; be generous with pepper. Serve on a flat plate. Garnish with coriander sprigs around edges.

Makes 4 servings

PIQUANT COOKED CARROT SALAD

My friend Hannah, who lives near Tel Aviv, prepares wonderful North African dishes like this spicy salad, for which she sometimes cooks pieces of pumpkin with the carrots. In the authentic version the carrots are mashed before being seasoned, but I leave the slices whole so they retain an attractive shape and a more interesting texture.

1 pound (about 5) medium carrots,
   sliced
pinch of salt
3 tablespoons vegetable oil
3 medium garlic cloves, finely chopped
3 tablespoons red or white wine
   vinegar

¼ cup water
½ teaspoon Tabasco or other hot
   pepper sauce
¼ teaspoon caraway seeds
¼ teaspoon paprika

In a saucepan cover carrots with water and add salt. Bring to a boil and simmer over medium heat 20 to 25 minutes or until tender.

Heat oil in a skillet over medium heat. Stir in garlic and sauté just a few seconds. Add vinegar, water, hot pepper sauce, caraway seeds, paprika, and a pinch of salt. Bring to a boil, stirring. Reduce heat to low.

When carrots are tender, drain them thoroughly. Add them to vinegar mixture. Simmer, uncovered, for 5 minutes or until sauce is reduced and coats carrots thoroughly. Taste and add more salt if necessary. Serve hot or cold.

Makes 4 servings

CUCUMBER SALAD WITH YOGURT AND MINT

Garlic-scented cucumber salad with yogurt is prepared in many Mediterranean countries, such as Turkey and Lebanon, and is a favorite among Sephardic Jews in general. It is similar to some versions of an Indian salad called raita. *Sometimes the yogurt quantity is increased, and then the dish is served as a cold soup.*

If you wish to serve this salad to accompany the rice and lentil stew called Majadrah (page 278) in a traditional manner, finely dice the cucumbers and substitute 1 or 2 teaspoons dried mint for the fresh.

1 small clove garlic, crushed and minced
1 teaspoon salt
2½ tablespoons coarsely chopped mint
1 quart plain yogurt
1 large (European) cucumber (about 1 pound)
small sprigs of mint, for garnish

Mash garlic with salt and mint in a bowl, using back of a spoon. Add yogurt and blend well. Be sure to mix garlic mixture from bottom of bowl into yogurt.

Peel cucumber and halve it lengthwise. Cut it into thin slices and add to yogurt mixture. Fold in gently. Taste for seasoning. Refrigerate at least 15 minutes or up to 4 hours before serving. Serve garnished with small sprigs of mint.

Makes 6 servings

GRILLED PEPPER AND TOMATO SALAD

When you are barbecuing, it is convenient to put a few peppers and tomatoes on the grill to prepare this easy salad, a specialty of Jews from North Africa. At other times, use the broiler.

4 ripe fairly small tomatoes	1½ tablespoons lemon juice
4 medium garlic cloves, unpeeled	1½ tablespoons extra-virgin olive oil
2 medium green bell peppers	salt and pepper

Preheat broiler. Put tomatoes, garlic cloves, and peppers on broiler rack and broil, turning them often. Broil tomatoes for 4 or 5 minutes or until their skin begins to wrinkle; broil garlic for about 12 minutes; broil peppers for about 15 to 20 minutes or until their skin turns blistery all over and is black in spots.

Core tomatoes and peel with aid of a small knife. Put peppers in a plastic bag, close bag, and leave for 10 minutes. Peel peppers and remove their cores and seeds.

Peel garlic cloves and chop the pulp until very fine and practically a puree. Put garlic in a small bowl. Stir in lemon juice, oil, and salt and pepper to taste.

Quarter the tomatoes and cut the peppers into wide lengthwise strips. Arrange them on a serving plate. Pour sauce over them and leave for 1 hour for flavors to blend. Serve cold or at room temperature.

Makes 4 servings

NOTE: The vegetables can be grilled on a barbecue instead of in broiler. Put garlic on a fine-meshed barbecue screen so it won't fall into coals.

SEPHARDIC BEET SALAD WITH CORIANDER

My sister-in-law from India often prepares a beet salad like this as a first course for Shabbat *dinner. It's easy to make and delicious.*

2 bunches or 10 small beets (about 1½ inches in diameter)
2 tablespoons lemon juice or vinegar
salt and freshly ground pepper

5 to 6 tablespoons vegetable oil
2 tablespoons chopped fresh coriander (cilantro)
lettuce leaves (optional)

Rinse beets, taking care not to pierce skin. Put 1 inch of water in a steamer and bring to a boil. Place beets on steamer rack or on another rack or in a colander above boiling water. Cover tightly and steam 50 to 60 minutes or until tender, adding boiling water occasionally if water evaporates. Let cool. Rinse beets with cold water and slip off skins.

In a small bowl whisk lemon juice with salt and pepper. Whisk in 5 tablespoons oil. Taste and adjust seasoning. Stir in 1 tablespoon coriander.

Dice the beets. Put in a bowl and add enough dressing to moisten. Toss gently. Taste and adjust seasoning; add remaining tablespoon oil if needed. Serve salad on a bed of lettuce. Sprinkle with remaining coriander just before serving.

Makes 6 servings

CHICKEN SALAD WITH AVOCADO AND ALMONDS

Chicken salad makes frequent appearances on the tables of traditional Jewish cooks, since the essential ingredient is a natural by-product of making chicken soup. This recipe is inspired by a chicken salad I enjoyed at the home of Betty Solomon, a popular hostess in Jerusalem. She garnished the edge of the salad with a row of sliced peaches, but you can use orange segments as a substitute in winter; or if you prefer a vegetable garnish, surround the salad with lightly cooked broccoli florets or cherry tomatoes.

⅓ cup slivered almonds
1 hard-boiled large egg, chopped
  (optional)
3 cups diced cooked chicken
1 tablespoon chopped fresh tarragon or
  snipped chives
2 tablespoons chopped fresh parsley

2 to 3 teaspoons prepared mustard
  (optional)
6 to 8 tablespoons mayonnaise, or
  more to taste
1 ripe avocado
about 16 leaves tender lettuce

Preheat oven to 350°F. Toast almonds on a small baking sheet until light brown, about 4 minutes. Transfer to a plate and cool.

In a medium bowl combine egg, chicken, tarragon, and parsley. Mix mustard with 6 tablespoons mayonnaise and add to salad. (Salad can be kept, covered, for 1 day in refrigerator.)

A short time before serving, halve the avocado and remove pit. Scoop out flesh and dice it. Reserve a few avocado dice and about half the almonds for a garnish. Fold remaining avocado and almonds into salad. Taste, and add more mayonnaise, salt, and pepper if desired.

Make a bed of lettuce on each of 4 plates or on a platter. Spoon salad onto lettuce. Garnish with avocado dice and sprinkle top with remaining toasted almonds.

Makes 4 servings

NOTE: ⅓ cup diced oil-packed sun-dried tomatoes are a nice addition to this salad.

CAULIFLOWER AND GREEN BEAN SALAD WITH LOX VINAIGRETTE

This pretty, easy-to-prepare salad is perfect for summer, and is a good way to make use of a tiny amount of lox. In America lox is associated with Jewish cooking, and indeed the word lox *came into English from Yiddish.*

1 small cauliflower, cut into medium
   florets
salt
¼ pound green beans, trimmed and
   cut in half
1 tablespoon white wine vinegar

3 tablespoons vegetable oil
freshly ground pepper
2 teaspoons snipped fresh dill
1 to 2 tablespoons (about ½ ounce)
   finely diced lox or smoked salmon

Boil cauliflower, uncovered, in a large saucepan of boiling salted water for about 7 minutes or until just tender. Drain, rinse gently with cold water, and drain well. Boil green beans, uncovered, in a medium saucepan of boiling salted water for about 5 minutes or until just tender. Drain and rinse in same manner.

To make vinaigrette, whisk vinegar with oil, salt, and pepper until blended.

Arrange cauliflower in center of a platter, with florets facing up and outward, reforming the shape of a cauliflower. Arrange green beans around it. Spoon 1 tablespoon vinaigrette over green beans. Add dill and lox to remaining vinaigrette and spoon over cauliflower. Serve at room temperature.

Makes 2 or 3 servings

BULGUR WHEAT AND PARSLEY SALAD WITH MINT AND TOMATOES (TABBOULEH)

This is a great party dish. I received the recipe from Ronnie Venezia, a talented cook who lives in Jerusalem and was born in Lebanon. There are many versions of this Middle Eastern salad but I find hers is the best: colorful, tangy, and with generous quantities of herbs. It is vibrant with the fresh flavors of the market, and should be made with the best ingredients—fresh herbs, ripe tomatoes, freshly squeezed lemon juice, and extra-virgin olive oil.

1½ cups fine bulgur wheat
5 cups cold water
5 plum tomatoes
4 small pickling cucumbers or ½ long
  (European) cucumber
1 bunch parsley

2 bunches mint
1 bunch green onions
juice of 2½ to 3 lemons
¾ cup extra-virgin olive oil
salt and freshly ground black pepper

Soak bulgur wheat in cold water overnight or for about 8 hours or until tender; taste it to check. (If you are in a hurry, pour hot water over the bulgur wheat instead, and soak it until it is completely cool and tender.) Transfer bulgur to a colander and drain off excess water. Squeeze wheat dry and transfer to a large bowl.

   Dice tomatoes and cucumbers until very small. Chop parsley and mint leaves. Cut green onions into thin slices. Mix diced vegetables with herbs and wheat. Add lemon juice to taste and olive oil; salad should be fairly tart. Season to taste with salt and pepper. (Salad can be kept, covered, for 1 day in refrigerator.) Serve cold or at cool room temperature.

Makes 12 cups; about 8 appetizer or 4 to 6 main-course servings

COUNTRY-STYLE HUMMUS WITH TAHINI

Unlike the usual hummus, which is served as a spread, this is a salad of whole chickpeas in a rich, white tahini dressing. It is quick and easy to make. Serve it as a first course, accompanied by pita, and, if you wish, by plum tomato slices.

⅔ cup tahini (sesame paste), stirred before measuring
½ cup water, or more as needed
¼ teaspoon salt, or to taste
¼ teaspoon hot red pepper flakes
2 tablespoons strained fresh lemon juice

1 medium garlic clove, minced
1 15- or 16-ounce can chickpeas (garbanzo beans), drained and rinsed
2 tablespoons chopped fresh coriander (cilantro) or parsley

In a medium bowl, stir tahini with ½ cup water. Add salt, pepper flakes, lemon juice, and garlic. Dressing should be thick enough to flow from spoon, but should not run from spoon. If it is too thick, gradually stir in another tablespoon water.

Drain chickpeas in a strainer, rinse thoroughly with cold water, and drain well. Reserve a few chickpeas and a pinch of coriander for garnish. Add remaining chickpeas and coriander to tahini dressing. Taste, and add more salt or lemon juice if desired. Spoon into a fairly shallow bowl. Garnish with reserved chickpeas and coriander and serve.

Makes 4 to 6 servings

NOTE: If you wish, soak and cook ⅔ cup dried chickpeas as for Hummus (page 163) instead of using canned ones; or, if you happen to have cooked chickpeas, use 1½ cups for this recipe.

10
SOUPS

Chicken soup is so thoroughly identified with Jewish cooking that food writers and chefs occasionally try to prove that other cuisines have it, too! A bowl of steaming chicken soup has long been known as "Jewish mothers' penicillin" and as the ultimate comfort food with which Jewish women pamper their families. When I was growing up in Washington, D.C., my mother made chicken soup with matzo balls every Friday, a tradition she still cherishes in her home in Jerusalem.

Most versions of chicken soup are fairly delicate in seasoning and uncomplicated. My mother adds onions, carrots, and dill; my mother-in-law adds cumin, turmeric, and tomato; my Moroccan cousin adds onion, rice, and Italian parsley or coriander. But for all of them the most important thing is to use plenty of chicken for the amount of water and to simmer it until the soup is well flavored.

Hearty soups are part of the culinary repertoire of Jewish cooks from all over the world, from the robust Polish mushroom-barley soups to the aromatic lentil soups of Indian Jews to the spicy Yemenite meat soups. For dairy meals, lighter soups are generally the rule. Most of these are vegetable soups, which are made in countless versions. They might be based on a single vegetable,

183

as in Fresh Mushroom Soup with Dill Dumplings, or on a selection of what's available at the market, as in Vegetable Soup with Matzo Balls and Fresh Herbs.

Often, chicken or meat soup is prepared for *Shabbat* in generous quantities, and some is left for later in the week. This proves to be an efficient way of cooking, since the soup can be quickly reheated, making it easy to put a tasty, home-cooked meal on the table in a very short time.

Besides matzo balls, the most common soup additions are noodles and rice; and some cooks serve chicken soup with both matzo balls and fine noodles. For festive occasions, meat- or chicken-filled kreplach are prepared by Ashkenazic cooks, and served in clear chicken or meat broth. But it's rare that home cooks present deli-style chicken soup with "the works"—kreplach, matzo balls, and noodles!

For Passover, there are matzos for crumbling into the soup, or packaged matzo farfel, which is matzo cut in small squares. During the rest of the year, the standard accompaniment for soups is fine-quality bread. In Israel a favorite addition to clear soups is "soup nuts," a tasty sort of tiny fried dumpling, which is available in grocery stores.

MAIN-COURSE CHICKEN SOUP WITH VEGETABLES

This is a dish my husband and I prepare often at home—it's convenient to reheat, easy to make, light, and low in fat. We call a few days of menus built around this soup our "chicken soup diet." It is inspired by the custom of many Jewish families from Yemen of serving the main meal of soup containing meat or chicken pieces, accompanied by pita or other bread, at midday.

We have expanded this idea by adding a large amount of vegetables, for good flavor and nutrition. Instead of bread, we sometimes serve the soup with separately cooked white, brown, or wild rice, fine noodles, or couscous. Sometimes we briefly cook fresh or frozen vegetables, such as corn, peas, zucchini, and carrots, in a separate pan to keep their color, taste, and texture, and spoon a generous helping of these vegetables into each bowl before adding the soup.

We usually prepare the soup in one of two versions: either as here, in the Middle Eastern fashion with cumin and turmeric, or in the Ashkenazic style, delicately seasoned with bay leaves and fresh dill. The latter is presented here as a variation.

The soup can be prepared with a whole chicken, which is cut in pieces before being served, or with chicken pieces.

1 whole chicken (about 3½ pounds), or 2½ to 3 pounds chicken pieces	**salt and freshly ground pepper** **2 tablespoons ground cumin**

1 teaspoon turmeric
1 large onion, whole or sliced
4 medium carrots (¾ pound total),
   peeled and cut in 2-inch lengths
about 2 quarts water
4 to 6 medium boiling potatoes (about
   1¼ pounds)

6 garlic cloves, coarsely chopped
4 medium zucchini (about 1 pound),
   cut in 2-inch lengths
8 ounces button mushrooms, quartered
2 tablespoons chopped fresh parsley or
   coriander (cilantro)

Remove fat from chicken. Put chicken in a large casserole or pot. If chicken giblets are available, add neck and other giblets, except liver. Sprinkle with salt, pepper, and spices on both sides. Let stand while preparing vegetables.

Add onion and carrots to casserole and cover ingredients generously with water. Bring to a boil, skim excess foam from surface, cover, and cook over low heat 1 hour.

Peel potatoes. Add potatoes and garlic to casserole, cover, and cook over low heat 45 minutes. Add zucchini and mushrooms, sprinkle with salt and bring to a simmer. Cover and cook over low heat 30 minutes.

Skim off fat. (This is easier to do when soup is cold.) Taste and adjust seasoning. If desired, remove skin from chicken and cut meat from bones; return chicken to soup. (Soup can be kept, covered, for 3 days in refrigerator.) Serve soup in fairly shallow bowls with chicken and vegetables. If desired, add parsley or coriander to each bowl when serving.

Makes about 6 main-course servings

VARIATION: Ashkenazic-Style Chicken Soup with Dill
   Omit cumin, turmeric, and coriander. Add 2 bay leaves with water. At serving time, stir in 4 or 5 tablespoons chopped fresh dill or 1 tablespoon dried dill. Parsley can be added also.

MUSHROOM-BARLEY CHICKEN SOUP

This chicken-based version of mushroom-barley soup, which eastern European Jews have popularized in both America and Israel, is substantial enough to be a main course. For a first course the soup can be made with vegetables alone or with strained meat or chicken stock or soup but without the pieces of chicken. The seasoning is delicate so the taste of the mushrooms comes through. In Hungary the soup is flavored generously with both hot and sweet paprika. We sometimes add spicy beef sausages to the soup to make it a hearty main-course soup.

1 ounce dried porcini or Polish
    mushrooms
1 cup hot water
1½ pounds chicken wings
½ pound (about 3 medium) carrots,
    diced
1 parsnip or parsley root, diced
1 medium onion, diced
2 quarts water

½ cup pearl barley
1 large leek, with 2 inches green tops,
    split, cleaned, and sliced
3 celery stalks, diced
salt and freshly ground pepper
4 to 8 ounces fresh button mushrooms,
    halved and sliced (optional)
2 to 3 tablespoons chopped fresh
    parsley, dill, or mixture of both

Rinse mushrooms and soak 20 minutes in hot water. Remove mushrooms, reserving liquid. Dice any large ones.

In a large casserole combine chicken, carrots, parsnip, onion, and 2 quarts water and bring to boil. Skim foam from surface and reduce heat to low. Add barley, leek, celery, salt, and pepper. Add fresh and dried mushrooms. Pour mushroom soaking water into another bowl, leaving behind and discarding the last few tablespoons of liquid, which may be sandy, then add mushroom liquid to soup. Cover and cook about 1½ hours or until chicken is tender and soup is well flavored. Skim off excess fat. Taste and adjust seasoning.

Remove chicken meat from bones, and add it to soup. (Soup can be kept, covered, for 2 days in refrigerator. When reheating, add a little water if soup is too thick.) When serving, sprinkle each bowl with chopped herbs.

Makes 4 main-course or 6 first-course servings

YEMENITE CHICKEN SOUP

This aromatic chicken soup is quite a change from the usual "Jewish" chicken soup familiar in this country. I learned how to make it from my husband's aunt, who is an expert in old-fashioned Yemenite cooking. To make sure the soup has its fresh, authentic taste, we grind the cumin seeds in a spice grinder. The spices give the soup a golden hue and seem to intensify the natural chicken soup color.

This soup has become so popular in Israel that now it often appears on menus of "Israeli" restaurants, even those that do not specialize in Yemenite food. Yemenite beef soup is equally well loved and is made the same way, with meaty beef bones instead of chicken.

In both versions an onion is added whole so it can be easily removed, because some people dislike onion in their soup. My father-in-law is an example, and he has a good reason—he told us that during his week-long journey by boat from Yemen to Israel there was nothing to eat but raw onions!

2 tablespoons ground cumin
2 teaspoons turmeric
¼ teaspoon ground black pepper
2½ to 3 pounds chicken pieces, or 1
  medium chicken, cut into pieces
salt to taste

1 large onion
2 ripe, medium tomatoes, or 4 plum
  tomatoes
about 2 quarts boiling water
4 to 6 fairly small boiling potatoes,
  peeled (optional)

Mix cumin, turmeric, and black pepper. Put chicken in a large heavy casserole and heat over low heat. Sprinkle with salt and spice mixture and heat over low heat about 7 minutes, turning pieces occasionally so they are well coated with spices.

Cut a deep *X* in the onion and in each tomato and add whole to casserole. Add boiling water to cover, pouring it in along side of casserole so spices are not washed off chicken. Add potatoes, push them into liquid, and add more water if necessary so they are covered. Bring to a boil, then skim foam from surface. Cover and cook over low heat 2 hours or until soup is well flavored. (Soup can be kept, covered, for 3 days in refrigerator.) Skim excess fat. Taste and adjust seasoning. Serve hot, in shallow bowls.

Makes 8 first-course or 4 to 6 main-course servings

VARIATION: Yemenite Beef Soup
  Use 2 ½ to 3 pounds meaty beef bones, such as shank bones, instead of chicken.
  Cook soup for 3 or 4 hours.

CHICKEN SOUP WITH RICE, TOMATOES, AND CORIANDER

In this zesty North African version of Jewish chicken soup, the chicken can be served in the soup or reserved for other uses.

2 tablespoons olive or vegetable oil
1 medium onion, chopped
2½ pounds chicken pieces (legs,
  thighs, or wings)
salt and freshly ground black pepper
½ pound ripe plum tomatoes, peeled
  and diced

3 quarts water
1 celery stalk, cut in thin strips
2 medium garlic cloves, chopped
¾ cup long-grain white rice
½ cup coarsely chopped fresh
  coriander (cilantro)

Heat oil in a large, heavy casserole. Add onion and sauté over medium heat until golden, about 7 minutes. Add chicken, sprinkle with salt and pepper, and sauté 7 minutes. Add tomatoes and sauté lightly. Add water, celery, and garlic and bring to a simmer. Skim foam from surface. Cover and simmer 45 minutes, skimming fat occasionally.

Rinse rice with cold water, drain, and add to soup. Stir once, cover, and cook over low heat for 20 minutes or until rice is tender. (Soup can be kept, covered, for 2 days in refrigerator; since it thickens on standing, add a little water when reheating it.) Add coriander. Either serve as is, adding chicken pieces to soup bowls; or remove chicken meat from bones and return meat to pot; or reserve chicken meat for other uses. Taste soup and adjust seasoning. Serve hot.

Makes 4 to 6 main-course or 8 first-course servings

VEGETABLE SOUP WITH MATZO BALLS AND FRESH HERBS

Kneidlach, or matzo balls, are a treat not only in chicken soup but also in milchig *(dairy) vegetable soups like this one. My mother began making this quick, light, colorful soup with small matzo balls when our family moved to Jerusalem from Washington, D.C. The lavish use of fresh dill and parsley are characteristic of the style of cooking she learned from her Israeli friends.*

2 tablespoons (¼ stick) butter, margarine, or vegetable oil	1 pound zucchini, coarsely grated
1 medium onion, chopped	1 ripe, medium tomato, diced
1 large carrot, grated	1 quart water
	salt and freshly ground pepper

Matzo Balls

¼ cup matzo meal	¼ teaspoon baking powder
¼ teaspoon salt	1 large egg
pinch of pepper	
1 cup milk	2 tablespoons snipped or chopped
3 tablespoons chopped fresh parsley	fresh dill, or 2 teaspoon dried

Melt butter in a medium saucepan over medium-low heat. Add onion and sauté 7 minutes. Add carrot, zucchini, tomato, water, salt, and pepper. Bring to boil, then simmer 10 minutes.

Meanwhile make small matzo balls. Stir together the matzo meal, salt, pepper, and baking power in a small bowl. Add egg and stir until blended. Take 1 teaspoon of mixture, roll gently between your palms to a ball, and transfer to a plate. Repeat with remaining mixture.

Add matzo balls to soup after it has simmered 10 minutes. Cover and cook 10 minutes. Stir in milk and heat briefly; do not boil. Just before serving, add chopped parsley and dill. Taste and adjust seasoning.

Makes 4 first-course servings

HERBED BEAN AND PASTA SOUP

Jews from Italy prepare this thick chunky soup, which is similar to the well-known dish, pasta e fagioli. *It is flavored with rosemary, sage, garlic, and vegetables and makes a warming first course or light main course for winter.*

1½ cups (about 10 ounces) small dried
   white beans
1 quart plus 6 cups water
1 large sprig fresh rosemary, or 2
   teaspoons dried, crumbled
2 cups chicken soup or stock
2 tablespoons olive oil
1 medium onion, minced
1 celery stalk, diced
⅓ cup finely diced carrot
1 pound fresh tomatoes, peeled,
   seeded, chopped; or 1 28-ounce can
   plum tomatoes, drained and
   chopped

2 large garlic cloves, minced
1 cup small pasta shapes—shells,
   bowties, squares, wheels, or elbow
   macaroni
3 tablespoons chopped fresh parsley
   leaves
2 tablespoons chopped fresh sage or
   basil, or 2 teaspoons dried, crumbled

Pick over beans, discarding any pebbles and broken or discolored beans. Rinse beans, drain, and place in a large bowl; add 6 cups water. Cover and let stand at least 8 hours or overnight. Or, for quicker soaking, place beans in a large saucepan with 6 cups water, bring to a boil, and boil briskly, uncovered, for 2 minutes. Remove from heat, cover, and let stand 1 hour.

Drain beans, discarding soaking liquid. Combine beans, rosemary, chicken soup, and 1 quart water in a large saucepan. Bring to a boil, then regulate heat at medium or medium-low so soup simmers and cook, uncovered, adding hot water occasionally so beans remain covered, for 1¼ hours or until beans are tender. Drain beans, reserving cooking liquid. Measure liquid; add enough water to make 4 cups. Discard rosemary.

Heat oil in a heavy medium saucepan over medium-low heat. Add onion, celery, and carrot and sauté, stirring often, about 10 minutes or until onion is soft. Add tomatoes and bring to a boil. Cook, uncovered, over medium heat for about 15 minutes or until vegetables are tender. Add cooked beans and measured liquid. (Soup can be kept, covered, for 2 days in refrigerator.)

Bring soup to a boil. Add garlic and pasta and cook uncovered over medium-high heat, stirring occasionally, for 5 to 8 minutes or until pasta is tender but firm to the bite. Stir in parsley and sage or basil. Taste and adjust seasoning. Serve hot.

Makes 4 or 5 first-course servings

FRESH MUSHROOM SOUP WITH DILL DUMPLINGS

This winter treat features a Hungarian touch—hearty dumplings that cook directly in the soup. A two-way soup, it can be made with chicken stock to begin meals with meat, or with vegetable stock, milk, and cream for a meatless menu.

Dill Dumplings

1 large egg
⅛ teaspoon salt
pinch of cayenne

¼ teaspoon paprika
½ teaspoon dried dill
¼ cup all-purpose flour

3 tablespoons nondairy margarine
½ cup minced onion
¾ pound small white mushrooms,
  halved and thinly sliced
1 teaspoon paprika

salt and freshly ground pepper
2 tablespoons all-purpose flour
3 cups chicken soup or stock
2 tablespoons snipped fresh dill, or 2
  teaspoons dried

Whisk egg with salt, cayenne, paprika, and dill. Gradually stir in flour with whisk until mixture forms a smooth thick batter. Do not beat it.

Melt margarine in medium, heavy saucepan over medium heat. Add onion and cook 10 minutes, stirring often. Stir in mushrooms and add paprika and a small pinch of salt and pepper. Cover and cook, shaking pan occasionally, for 10 minutes. Uncover and cook over medium heat, stirring, about 5 minutes or until liquid produced by mushrooms evaporates.

Reduce heat to low. Add flour and cook, stirring constantly, about 3 minutes or until mixture is well blended and bubbly. Remove from heat. Pour in chicken soup, stirring and scraping bottom of saucepan thoroughly. Bring to a boil over medium-high heat, stirring constantly. Reduce heat to low so soup simmers.

Add bits of dumpling batter to simmering soup, about ¼ teaspoon at a time. Simmer, uncovered, occasionally shaking pan, about 5 minutes or until dumplings no longer taste floury; taste one to check. (Soup can be kept, covered, up to 2 days in refrigerator. Reheat, uncovered, over low heat.)

Stir in 1 tablespoon fresh or 2 teaspoons dried dill. Taste, and add salt and pepper if needed. Serve hot, sprinkled with remaining fresh dill.

Makes 4 servings

VARIATION: Creamy Mushroom Soup

Substitute butter for margarine, if desired. Replace chicken stock with 1 cup water and 2 cups milk, stirring in water first. Just before serving, remove hot soup from heat and gradually stir in 6 tablespoons heavy cream. Bring just to simmer, then add dill.

AROMATIC LENTIL SOUP

As might be expected, rice and lentils are used to good advantage in the kitchens of Jews from India, as in this hearty, thick soup flavored with dill and cumin. My sister-in-law, Mati Kahn, who was born in India, prepares it often for her family as the centerpiece for a winter vegetarian meal. Indian Jews accompany the soup with lemon wedges and like to squeeze lemon juice over their portion.

1½ cups (about ½ pound) lentils
2 tablespoons vegetable oil
1 large onion, chopped
½ pound ripe tomatoes, finely diced
4 medium garlic cloves, chopped
1 teaspoon ground cumin
6 cups water

2 bay leaves
3 tablespoons snipped or chopped
 fresh dill
salt and freshly ground pepper
1 to 1¼ cups long-grain white rice
lemon wedges, for accompaniment

Spread lentils on a plate, pick through them carefully to remove pebbles, rinse, and drain them.

Heat oil in a medium saucepan, add onion, and sauté over medium-low heat 7 minutes. Add lentils and sauté together 1 minute. Add tomatoes, garlic, and cumin and sauté 1 minute. Add 3 cups water and bay leaves. Bring to a boil, cover, and simmer over low heat for 45 minutes or until lentils are tender, adding 2 cups water in 3 or 4 portions during the course of the cooking time. If soup is too thick, add remaining cup water and bring to a boil. Discard bay leaves. (Soup can be kept, covered, for 2 days in refrigerator. Reheat before serving.) Add dill and salt to taste; season generously with pepper.

Add rice to a large saucepan with 5 to 6 cups boiling salted water. Boil, uncovered for 14 minutes or until tender. Drain well.

To serve, spoon a generous portion of rice into each bowl and ladle soup over it. Serve with lemon wedges.

Makes 4 main-course servings

SPICY WINTER BEAN SOUP

Beef and bean soup is popular in most Jewish ethnic groups. Ashkenazic versions are flavored with onion, carrot, and parsley rather than the garlic and tomatoes in this North African version. In some Sephardic families, the soup is made with saffron instead of turmeric, and chopped fresh coriander is sprinkled over each serving.

1 pound (about 2½ cups) dried white
  beans, such as Great Northern
3 tablespoons vegetable oil
2 large onions, sliced
1½ pounds beef with bones, such as
  beef shank
4 medium garlic cloves, chopped
1 tablespoon tomato paste
2 teaspoons paprika

1 teaspoon turmeric
2 quarts water
1½ pounds white boiling potatoes
salt to taste
4 large eggs in shell, rinsed (optional)
¼ teaspoon cayenne pepper
¼ cup chopped fresh parsley or
  coriander (cilantro)

Sort beans, discarding any broken ones and any stones. In a large bowl soak beans overnight in cold water to generously cover. Or, for a quicker method, cover beans with 2 quarts water in a large saucepan, bring to a boil, and boil 2 minutes; cover and let stand off heat for 1 hour.

Rinse beans and drain. Heat oil in a large saucepan over medium heat, add onions, and sauté about 10 minutes. Add beef, beans, garlic, tomato paste, paprika, turmeric, and water and bring to a boil. Cover and cook over low heat 1 hour.

Peel and halve potatoes and add to saucepan. Add salt and eggs in their shells and continue to cook 1 hour or until meat is very tender. (Soup can be kept, covered, for 2 days in rcfrigerator.)

To serve, remove meat. Dice any meat from bone and add to soup. Serve any marrow bones, if desired. Shell eggs and halve them lengthwise. Stir cayenne pepper and parsley into soup. Garnish with eggs.

Makes 6 to 8 main-course servings

HEARTY MEAT SOUP WITH GREEN BEANS

This is a spicy meat soup like my Yemen-born mother-in-law makes, with chunks of beef, chickpeas, and green beans. It is seasoned with a curry-like spice mixture that gives it a wonderful aroma and intriguing flavor. For a touch of heat, the fiery pepper chutney called Zehug (page 142) can be served on the side.

1 veal or beef soup bone (optional)
about 6 cups water
1 pound boneless beef chuck roast or
   stew meat, excess fat removed
2 tablespoons vegetable oil
2 medium onions, chopped
1 tablespoon ground cumin
½ teaspoon turmeric
salt and freshly ground pepper to taste

4 ounces green beans, ends removed,
   broken into 1-inch pieces
4 large garlic cloves, minced
1½ cups small pasta shapes, such as
   wheels, medium shells, or elbow
   macaroni
pinch of cayenne pepper
3 tablespoons chopped fresh coriander
   (cilantro) or parsley

If using a soup bone, put it in a large saucepan, add water, and bring to a boil. Skim foam from surface. Simmer uncovered over low heat for 2 hours. Remove bone and reserve. Measure broth and add enough water to make 6 cups.

Cut beef into 1-inch cubes. Heat oil in a large saucepan. Add onions, and sauté over medium heat for 5 minutes. Add beef cubes, cumin, turmeric, and a pinch of salt and pepper. Sauté 5 minutes, stirring. Add bone and measured liquid and bring to a boil. Cover and simmer over low heat for 1½ to 2 hours or until beef is very tender. (Soup can be kept, covered, for 2 days in refrigerator. Reheat over medium-low heat, covered.)

Add green beans to soup and simmer, uncovered, for 7 minutes. Remove soup bone and add any meat from it to soup. Add garlic, sprinkle in pasta, and stir to submerge it. Simmer, uncovered, over medium-low heat, stirring occasionally, for 7 to 9 minutes or until pasta and beans are tender. Stir in cayenne pepper and coriander or parsley. Taste and adjust seasoning. Serve hot.

Makes 6 to 8 first-course servings

BEET BORSCHT WITH POTATOES AND SOUR CREAM

This refreshing soup of Polish origin is a great favorite among Jews from eastern Europe. Traditional recipes call for thickening the soup with eggs or egg yolks, but this is a lighter version that is good warm or cold. I like to serve garnishes of snipped dill, sour cream, diced hard-boiled egg, diced cucumber, and warm potatoes so that the soup makes a colorful first course, and each person can choose what to add to his or her bowl.

9 beets, each 1½ to 2 inches in
 diameter (1½ pounds total,
 including 2 to 3 inches of beet tops)
1 medium onion, halved
6 cups water

½ teaspoon salt
1 tablespoon sugar
2 tablespoons strained fresh lemon
 juice

Accompaniments

6 small boiled potatoes, hot or at room
 temperature
sour cream

diced cucumber
snipped fresh dill
diced or sliced hard-boiled eggs

Scrub beets clean with a stiff brush under cold water. Leave 2 to 3 inches of tops on. Combine beets, onion, and water in a medium saucepan and bring to a boil. Cover and simmer over low heat for about 1 hour or until beets are tender. Discard onion. Remove beets and slip off their skins. Pour soup into a bowl. Rinse saucepan. Slowly pour beet cooking liquid back into pan, leaving last few tablespoons soup, which may be sandy, behind in bowl; discard this liquid.

Grate beets coarsely in food processor or with grater. Return to soup and add salt and sugar. Cook 2 minutes, stirring, over low heat. Remove from heat and add lemon juice. Taste and adjust seasoning; soup should be slightly sweet and sour.

Serve hot or cold. If serving hot, garnish with potato and sour cream. If serving cold, taste again before serving; serve plain, or with any or all of the accompaniments in separate bowls.

Makes 5 or 6 first-course servings

IRANIAN MEATBALL SOUP FOR SHABBAT (GUNDI)

In recent years southern California has become one of the world's largest centers of Jews from Iran. In fact, during the last few years several Iranian kosher grocery stores have opened in my hometown of Santa Monica. For Shabbat a traditional Iranian dish is gundi, a spicy chicken soup containing meatballs made with chickpeas, accompanied by rice. Iranians use chickpea flour, but this recipe uses the more available canned chickpeas. The meatball mixture can also be sautéed in small cakes, as in the variation, and served as an appetizer.

1½ pounds chicken wings or legs
1 medium onion

salt and freshly ground pepper
7 cups water

Meatballs

¼ cup parsley sprigs
1 8- or 9-ounce can chickpeas
   (garbanzo beans), drained and
   rinsed

2 large boiling potatoes (about ¾
   pound), peeled and cut in large dice
2 large carrots, diced
1 tablespoon tomato paste
1 teaspoon ground cumin
¼ teaspoon turmeric

½ large onion, cut in chunks
½ pound lean ground beef
¼ teaspoon salt
¼ teaspoon black pepper

½ teaspoon red pepper flakes, or
   cayenne pepper to taste
1 to 1½ cups long-grain white rice,
   preferably basmati
2 tablespoons chopped fresh parsley

Cook chicken with onion, salt, and pepper in water for 1 hour, partly covered. Discard onion and remove chicken; reserve meat for other dishes.

Mince parsley in a food processor and remove. Add chickpeas to food processor and chop them, then remove them. Mince onion in processor. Mix beef, chickpeas, onion, salt, pepper, and parsley. Shape tablespoons of mixture into small meatballs. Squeeze each well so it will be compact, then roll it between your palms to a smooth ball. Put on a plate and refrigerate.

Add potatoes to soup along with carrots and cook, covered, for 20 minutes. Add tomato paste, cumin, turmeric, and pepper flakes. Stir to blend. Add meatballs, cover, and simmer over low heat for 30 minutes. (Soup can be kept, covered, for 2 days in refrigerator.)

Add rice to a large saucepan of 2 quarts boiling salted water. Boil, uncovered, for 14 minutes or until tender. Drain well.

Add parsley to hot soup. Taste and adjust seasoning. To serve, spoon a generous amount of rice into each bowl and top with soup and meatballs.

Makes 4 main-course to 6 first-course servings

NOTE: Instead of canned chickpeas, you can use ⅓ cup dried chickpeas, soaked 8 hours or overnight and drained.

VARIATION:

The meatball mixture can instead be fried as patties. Flatten each ball, heat 3 tablespoons vegetable oil in large skillet over medium heat, and fry meat patties in batches, 4 minutes per side. Drain on paper towels. Add more oil to skillet if necessary to cook remaining patties. Serve as an appetizer with Hot Pepper–Garlic Chutney (page 142) or bottled hot sauce. These patties also taste good heated in the soup.

11

BLINTZES, PANCAKES, AND EGG DISHES

 Blintzes are the most famous type of pancake in Jewish cooking, and in Israel are often the highlight of restaurants specializing in dairy foods.

Cheese blintzes filled with soft cheeses like cottage cheese and farmer cheese are the best known and are especially popular for the holiday of Shavuot, but there are many other fillings. Dessert blintzes contain apples, blueberries, cherries, or other fruit, while savory blintzes are wrapped around fillings of mushrooms, cabbage, potatoes, or meat.

The batter for making blintzes resembles that of French crepes, except that for meat blintzes water replaces the milk in the batter. The cooking technique for blintzes is different from that of crepes, however. Blintzes are sautéed on only one side before being filled. After the filling is added, the blintzes are folded so the uncooked side faces outward, and then are baked or sautéed, thus heating the filling and lightly browning the second side of each blintze. The folding technique is different also. Two opposite sides of the blintze are folded lightly over the filling, and then the blintze is rolled up in a cylindrical shape with both ends closed so the filling will not come out.

Jews from Yemen prepare a special type of pancake known as *melawah*. Unlike other pancakes,

197

they are made from a pastry somewhat resembling puff pastry rather than a batter and are sautéed until crisp outside and tender inside. These pancakes are served for breakfast or supper, sometimes accompanied by browned eggs (see below), but I find them wonderful for brunch. They have become à la mode in Israeli cafés as a rich, savory snack.

Eggs play an important role on the Jewish menu, since they are pareve, or neutral, and can thus be combined in a meal with either *milkchig* (dairy) or *fleishig* (meat) ingredients. A typical supper in Israel is an omelet with Mediterranean diced vegetable salad and a pita. The omelet is most frequently prepared in the Sephardic style—flat and resembling an Italian *frittata*. Also popular among Jewish cooks are scrambled eggs, either with lox in the American-Ashkenazic style, with tomatoes and onions in the Moroccan fashion, or with sautéed mushrooms, which are well liked by everyone.

A special type of egg dish, known simply as Browned Eggs, is a favorite among Sephardic Jews and is made for *Shabbat*, Passover, and other festive occasions. Basically these are eggs cooked in their shells for a long time until the shells turn deep brown, the whites become light brown, and the yolks acquire a rich, creamy texture. There are several ways to prepare them. Often a few eggs are simply added to a meat soup or stew dish and simmered with the meat. Yemenite cooks sometimes place eggs in their shells on top of a special bread called *Shabbat Breakfast Bread* (page 292) that is baked in a covered pot. When cooks wish to prepare browned eggs without making stew or bread, they simply cook the eggs with onion skins, as on page 205.

BASIC BLINTZES

The word blintze *comes from Yiddish, and blintzes are one of the great specialties of the Ashkenazic kitchen that have become staples of American-Jewish deli menus. Like crepes, blintzes can be wrapped around a mixture that is sweet or savory, and they can play the role of appetizer, main course, or dessert. Cheese filling is the favorite, but other well-liked sweet fillings are apple, cherry, and blueberry. Frequent savory filling choices are meat, chicken, mushroom, and potato-onion.*

3 large eggs
1¼ cups milk or water, or more as
   needed
¾ cup all-purpose flour
½ teaspoon salt

2 tablespoons (¼ stick) butter or
   margarine
1 to 3 teaspoons vegetable oil, for
   brushing pan

To prepare batter in food processor: Combine eggs, ¼ cup milk, flour, and salt in work bowl and mix using several on/off turns; batter will be lumpy. Scrape down sides and bottom of work bowl. With machine running, pour 1 cup milk through feed tube and process batter about 15 seconds. Scrape down sides and bottom of container thoroughly. Blend batter for about 15 seconds.

To prepare batter in blender: Combine eggs, 1¼ cups milk, flour, and salt in blender. Mix on high speed about 1 minute or until batter is smooth.

To prepare batter in bowl: Sift flour into medium bowl. Push flour to sides of bowl, leaving large well in center of flour. Add eggs, salt, and ¼ cup milk to well and whisk ingredients in well briefly until blended. Using a whisk, stir flour gently and gradually into egg mixture until mixture is smooth. Gradually whisk in 1 cup milk.

Strain batter if it is lumpy. Cover and refrigerate about 1 hour. (Batter can be refrigerated, covered, up to 1 day.)

Melt butter in small saucepan over low heat. Stir batter well. Gradually whisk melted butter into batter. (Batter should have consistency of whipping cream. If it is too thick, gradually whisk in more milk, about 1 teaspoon at a time.)

Heat a 6- to 6½-inch crepe pan or skillet (for small blintzes) or an 8- to 9-inch skillet (for larger blintzes) over medium-high heat. Sprinkle with a few drops of water. If water immediately sizzles, pan is hot enough. Brush pan lightly with oil; if using a nonstick pan, no oil is needed. Remove pan from heat and hold it near bowl of batter. Working quickly, add 2 tablespoons batter to small pan, or 3 tablespoons to large pan, adding batter to edge and tilting and swirling pan until its base is covered with thin layer of batter. Immediately pour any excess batter back into bowl.

Return pan to medium-high heat. Loosen edges of blintze with metal spatula, discarding any pieces clinging to sides of pan. Cook blintze until its bottom browns lightly. Slide blintze out onto plate, with uncooked side facing up. Top with sheet of wax paper or foil if making them a few days ahead or if freezing them. Reheat pan a few seconds. Continue making blintzes, stirring batter occasionally with whisk. Adjust heat and brush pan with more oil if necessary. If batter thickens on standing, very gradually whisk in a little more milk, about 1 teaspoon at a time. Pile blintzes on plate, each separated with paper or foil, as they are done. (Blintzes can be kept, wrapped tightly, up to 3 days in refrigerator; or they can be frozen. Bring them to room temperature before using, to avoid tearing them.)

Makes 12 to 15 blintzes

VARIATION: Chive Blintzes

Prepare batter, using ¾ teaspoon salt and adding a pinch of white pepper and 2 teaspoons snipped fresh chives. This version can be used for appetizer or main-course blintzes.

NOTES: To easily measure batter, use a ¼ cup measure. Fill it half-full of batter to measure 2 tablespoons or three-quarters full to measure 3 tablespoons.

If your first blintzes are too thick, whisk a teaspoon of milk or water into batter.

If batter is too runny and blintzes are too thin and fragile, sift 2 or 3 tablespoons all-purpose flour into another bowl and gradually stir batter into it.

CHIVE BLINTZES WITH CABBAGE AND SOUR CREAM

In this luscious Polish-style dish, sour cream enriches the filling of sautéed cabbage and onions, and is also served as a topping. Chives add a modern, fresh touch to the blintz batter. Serve these blintzes as a main course for lunch.

Cabbage Filling

½ large green cabbage (1½ pounds), cored and rinsed
salt and freshly ground pepper
3 tablespoons butter

½ large onion, minced
1 hard-boiled large egg, chopped
½ cup sour cream, at room temperature

12 Chive Blintzes, each about 9 inches in diameter (page 199)
3 tablespoons butter, cut in small cubes

½ cup sour cream
4 teaspoons snipped fresh chives
salt and freshly ground pepper

Chop cabbage as fine as possible, preferably in a food processor in batches. In a large pan of boiling salted water, boil cabbage for 3 minutes. Drain, rinse under cold water, and drain thoroughly. Squeeze out excess liquid. Melt butter in a large skillet, add onion, and cook over low heat for 7 minutes or until soft but not browned. Stir in cabbage and sprinkle with salt and pepper. Cover and cook over low heat, stirring occasionally, for 15 minutes or until tender. Transfer mixture to a bowl and cool to room temperature. Stir in egg and sour cream and taste for seasoning.

Spoon about 2 tablespoons filling onto the cooked side near one edge of each blintze. Fold sides over so that each covers about half the filling; roll up, beginning at filling edge. Arrange rolls in one layer in a shallow buttered baking dish. Dot blintzes with cubes of butter.

Preheat oven to 425°F. Bake blintzes for 15 minutes, or until heated through and lightly browned. Mix sour cream with 1 tablespoon chives and salt and pepper to taste. Spoon a dollop of sour cream mixture over center of each blintze. Sprinkle with chives.

Makes 6 servings

MUSHROOM BLINTZES

Creamy mushroom-filled blintzes originated in Europe and now are relished by Jews of all origins. In Tel Aviv you can order them at a special blintze restaurant, the Jewish counterpart of the French creperie.

Mushroom Filling

3 tablespoons butter
8 ounces small mushrooms, halved and
  sliced
salt and freshly ground white pepper
½ teaspoon paprika
2 tablespoons all-purpose flour

1¼ cups milk
freshly grated nutmeg
⅓ cup heavy cream
pinch of cayenne pepper
2 tablespoons chopped fresh parsley

10 to 12 small Basic Blintzes (page
  198) or Chive Blintzes (page 199)
2 tablespoons (¼ stick) butter, for
  dotting blintzes

sour cream, for serving (optional)
snipped fresh dill or chives or chopped
  parsley, for garnish (optional)

Melt 1 tablespoon butter in a large skillet over medium heat. Add mushrooms, salt, pepper, and paprika and sauté 5 minutes or until tender.

Melt remaining 2 tablespoons butter in a heavy medium saucepan over low heat. Whisk in flour and cook, whisking constantly, about 2 minutes or until foaming but not browned. Remove from heat and whisk in milk. Bring to a boil over medium-high heat, whisking, then add a small pinch of salt, white pepper, and nutmeg. Cook over low heat 3 minutes, then whisk in cream and bring to a boil. Cook over low heat, whisking often, about 5 minutes or until thick. Add cayenne, stir in mushrooms and parsley, taste, and adjust seasoning.

Preheat oven to 425°F. Butter a large shallow baking dish or two 8-inch gratin dishes or other shallow baking dishes. Spoon 3 tablespoons filling onto cooked side of each blintze, across lower third. Fold sides over so that each covers part of filling, then roll up in cigar shape, beginning at edge with filling. Arrange blintzes in single layer in dish. Cut butter into small cubes and dot blintzes with butter. (Blintzes can be prepared to this point and kept, covered, for 1 day in refrigerator. Bring blintzes to room temperature and preheat oven before continuing.)

Bake blintzes about 15 minutes or until heated through and lightly browned. Serve immediately. If desired, top each with a small spoonful of sour cream and a pinch of chopped herbs.

Makes 10 to 12 blintzes; 5 or 6 servings

RICH YEMENITE PANCAKES (MELAWAH)

My mother-in-law taught me to prepare these pancakes, which are made from a pastry dough, rather than from a pourable batter. The pancakes are composed of thin layers of dough and are very rich; they are served at breakfast, brunch, or supper, either plain or with honey. They are a delicious treat, and are well known in Israel as a unique specialty of the Jews from Yemen. Imagine my surprise when I found a nearly identical pastry on the other side of the globe—Chinese scallion pancakes, which I tasted in Taiwan! When I saw them demonstrated in a cooking course in Taipei, the chef made the dough using a very similar technique to my mother-in-law's, but sprinkled the dough with chopped scallions before rolling it.

3¾ cups all-purpose flour
1 teaspoon baking powder
1½ teaspoons salt
1 large egg

1¼ cups water
¾ cup (1½ sticks) margarine, cut in 6
    pieces, plus 2 additional tablespoons
    (¼ stick), for frying

Combine flour, baking powder, and salt in food processor and process to blend. Add egg and 1 cup water and process with on/off turns to mix. With motor running, gradually add enough remaining water so mixture comes together to a smooth, fairly stiff dough. It will be sticky.

Remove dough from processor and knead well by slapping it vigorously on a work surface. Divide into 6 pieces and knead each with a slapping motion until smooth. Roll each in your palm to a ball. Put on an oiled plate or tray, cover, and refrigerate at least 4 hours or overnight.

Oil a work surface and rolling pin. Let the ¾ cup margarine stand at room temperature until very soft. Roll out 1 ball of dough as thin as possible, so you can almost see through dough, to about a 12-inch square. If dough tears, simply press it together. Spread dough with about one-sixth of the soft margarine. Roll up as for a jelly roll. Tap the roll with your knuckles to flatten it and roll it up in a spiral. Put on a plate, cover, and refrigerate overnight or up to 2 days. (Dough can also be frozen; thaw overnight in refrigerator before using.)

Set a ball of dough on a lightly oiled plate and flatten it with your lightly oiled hands to a round as large as the skillet. Heat 1 teaspoon margarine in a heavy 9-inch skillet and add the round of dough. Cover and fry over medium-high heat for 30 seconds, then over medium-low heat for about 5 minutes per side or until brown on both sides and cooked through. Repeat for remaining balls of dough, adding margarine to pan as needed. Serve hot.

Makes 6 generous servings

LOX AND EGGS WITH SAUTÉED ONIONS

A choice menu item at Jewish delis, this deluxe version of scrambled eggs is easy and much less expensive to prepare at home. At some fish markets you can purchase small pieces of lox that are perfect for this dish and make it more economical. If you prefer larger pieces of lox with the eggs, cut it into strips instead of dicing it.

3 tablespoons butter or margarine
¾ cup chopped onion
10 large eggs
¼ teaspoon salt

pinch of freshly ground white pepper
¾ cup diced lox
parsley sprigs, for garnish

Melt butter in a large skillet. Add onion and sauté over medium-low heat, stirring often, about 7 minutes or until tender and light golden.

Whisk eggs with salt and pepper in a large bowl until well blended. Add to skillet and scramble over low heat, stirring often, until eggs are set to taste. Remove from heat and gently stir in lox. Taste and adjust seasoning. Serve immediately, garnished with parsley sprigs.

Makes 4 or 5 servings

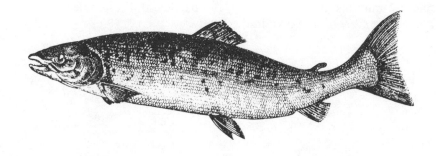

EGGS WITH PEPPERS AND TOMATOES (SHAKSHUKA)

Shakshuka is the name of a whole class of egg and vegetable dishes typical of the North African Jewish kitchen. Potatoes, cauliflower, zucchini, or other cooked vegetables might be used. The technique can vary, too. Some people cook the mixture over low heat without stirring, and the result is similar to a flat omelet or an Italian frittata. *Others add the eggs whole and poach them in the vegetable mixture.*

The most popular version is of eggs scrambled with tomatoes, peppers, and onions and is rather similar to the French Basque recipe, piperade, *except in the seasoning. This recipe is from Mazal Cohen, my husband's aunt from Yemen, who flavors the eggs with cumin and turmeric. It is fairly delicate, but you can add chopped hot pepper and garlic with the tomatoes if you like. In Israel Shakshuka is a supper dish, but it's good for brunch, too. Serve it with fresh or toasted pita or sesame bread.*

2 to 3 tablespoons vegetable oil
1 small onion, chopped (about ½ cup)
½ medium green bell pepper, diced
3 ripe, medium tomatoes (¾ pound total), diced
salt and freshly ground black pepper

½ teaspoon ground cumin
¼ teaspoon turmeric
cayenne pepper to taste (optional)
3 large eggs, beaten
2 tablespoons chopped fresh parsley (optional)

Heat oil in a medium skillet over medium heat. Add onion and sauté about 5 minutes or until golden brown. Add green pepper and sauté 2 minutes. Add tomatoes, salt, and spices and cook about 2 minutes. Add beaten eggs and parsley and scramble over low heat until set. Taste and adjust seasoning. Serve immediately.

Makes 2 servings

BROWNED EGGS (HUEVOS HAMINADOS)

A Sephardic treat for Shabbat *and Passover, these eggs cook gently over a very low fire until they are light brown, creamy textured, and rich in flavor, in a technique somewhat similar to preparing Chinese tea eggs. They are enjoyed during the rest of the year, too, especially to accompany Spinach or Cheese Bourekas (pages 154 and 55). Browned Eggs are often made as part of meaty soups or stews like Hamin (page 144), but this is the way to prepare them on their own.*

If you think onion peels have no use, here's proof that they do! To make this dish, you'll need to save the peels when you're using several onions. The onions impart a bright Burgundy color to the egg shells; some cooks add coffee to the cooking liquid to give them a dark brown hue. For people who leave a low oven or a hot plate on all night for Shabbat *to keep other dishes warm, these eggs are convenient to prepare.*

skins of 6 brown or yellow onions
   (about 3 to 4 cups)
8 large eggs, with no cracks
1 teaspoon salt

2 quarts water
2 tablespoons olive or vegetable oil
½ teaspoon black pepper

Put half the onion peels in a medium saucepan in which the eggs will fit in a single layer. Set eggs on top. Add remaining ingredients and bring to a boil. Cover and cook over very low heat for 6 hours or overnight. Serve eggs hot or warm.

Makes 8 servings

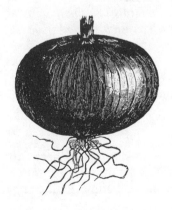

SALAMI WITH VEGETABLES AND EGGS

I prefer this Mediterranean-style version of the deli standard, salami and eggs, because it is lighter, and the diced eggplant, zucchini, and tomatoes provide a pleasing counterpoint to the salami's salty taste. The dish is very easy to make, since the eggs poach directly in the vegetable mixture.

2 slices salami, finely diced
1 small eggplant, finely diced
3 small zucchini, finely diced
1 medium tomato, finely diced

2 tablespoons chopped green onions
salt and pepper
½ teaspoon dried oregano
4 large eggs

Heat salami in a large skillet until the fat renders. Add eggplant, cover, and cook 8 to 10 minutes. Add zucchini and cook 5 minutes. Add tomato, green onions, salt and pepper, and oregano and cook 5 minutes or until vegetables are tender. Taste and adjust seasoning. Make 4 hollows in mixture. Add 1 whole egg to each hollow and sprinkle lightly with salt and pepper. Cover and cook 4 to 5 minutes or until eggs are done to taste. Serve at once.

Makes 2 to 4 servings

SCRAMBLED EGGS
WITH SPICED MUSHROOMS

A zesty change from the usual scrambled eggs, this dish is great for brunch, lunch, or supper, accompanied by fresh pita and Israeli Vegetable Salad (page 20).

2 tablespoons olive oil, butter, or a
   mixture of both
8 ounces small mushrooms, quartered
salt and pepper
½ teaspoon ground cumin

4 large eggs
cayenne pepper to taste
1 tablespoon chopped fresh parsley
   (optional)

Heat oil in a medium skillet over medium-high heat. Add mushrooms, salt, pepper, and cumin. Sauté, stirring often, for 7 to 10 minutes or until tender and lightly browned.
   Beat eggs with a pinch of salt and cayenne. Reduce heat under skillet to low. Add eggs

and scramble them, stirring often, until they are set to taste. Remove from heat and stir in parsley. Taste, adjust seasoning, and serve.

Makes 2 servings

ZUCCHINI FRITTATA WITH GARLIC

An omelet in Israel is called a havitah *and is generally flat like an Italian* frittata. *Sephardic Jews often prepare* frittatas *for a light supper, and some experts believe they might have originated this tasty style of cooking eggs.*

This omelet has a distinct garlic flavor because the garlic is not precooked. Finishing the omelet in the broiler is the easiest method, as in the recipe below, but if you prefer, you can turn it over according to one of the methods in the note following the recipe.

3 tablespoons olive oil
8 ounces (2 small) zucchini, cut into
  ¼-inch slices

salt and pepper
4 large eggs
1 large garlic clove, finely chopped

Heat 2 tablespoons oil in a heavy 9- or 10-inch skillet, if possible with an ovenproof handle. Add zucchini and sauté over medium-high heat, turning occasionally, about 5 minutes or until just tender. Season to taste with salt and pepper.

Thoroughly beat eggs with garlic, salt, and pepper. With a slotted spoon, transfer zucchini to eggs and mix gently.

Dry the skillet, then add remaining oil and heat over medium heat. Swirl pan slightly so oil coats sides as well. Add egg mixture and cook without stirring; occasionally lift edge of omelet and tip pan so uncooked part of egg mixture runs to edge of pan. When top of omelet is nearly set, place pan in broiler. Broil until top is set and lightly browned. Serve from pan.

Makes 2 servings

NOTE: If skillet doesn't have an ovenproof handle, turn the omelet in the pan, thus: When top is nearly set, carefully slide a wide utensil such as a pancake turner under omelet to free it from pan. Cut omelet in half and turn it over. Cook about ½ minute over low heat to brown second side, then transfer to a platter or to plates and serve. (If you wish to keep the *frittata* whole, slide it onto a plate, then turn it over onto another plate, and slide it back into pan to cook second side.)

NORTH AFRICAN BAKED EGGS WITH TOMATOES AND ONIONS

This baked version of the North African egg dish, Shakshuka (page 204), bears a certain resemblance to the French oeufs au plat. *In Israel the eggs are usually cooked thoroughly rather than being left soft, as in the French style.*

2 tablespoons vegetable or olive oil
1 medium onion, halved and sliced
1 small garlic clove, minced
2½ pounds ripe tomatoes, peeled, seeded, and chopped; or 2 28-ounce cans plum tomatoes, drained and chopped
¼ teaspoon dried thyme
1 bay leaf

salt and freshly ground pepper
pinch of cayenne pepper or hot sauce to taste
2 or 3 tablespoons chopped fresh coriander (cilantro) (optional)
4 large eggs
2 tablespoons vegetable oil or melted butter or margarine

Preheat oven to 425°F. Heat oil in a heavy large skillet over medium heat. Add onion and sauté about 10 minutes or until soft and beginning to brown; remove with slotted spoon. Add garlic to skillet and cook over low heat, stirring, about ½ minute. Add tomatoes, thyme, bay leaf, salt, and pepper. Bring to a boil, then cook over medium heat, stirring often, until tomatoes are soft and mixture is thick and smooth, about 20 minutes. Discard bay leaf. Stir in onion. Add cayenne or hot sauce and coriander, reserving a little for garnish. Taste and adjust seasoning. (Mixture can be kept, covered, for 2 days in refrigerator.)

Reheat the tomato mixture if necessary. Grease 4 individual 6-inch shallow baking dishes or one 5-cup shallow dish of about 8½-inch diameter. Spread tomato mixture in dishes. With a spoon make a hollow in center of mixture in each small dish, or make 4 hollows in large dish, each large enough to contain 1 egg. Break egg carefully into each hollow. Sprinkle a little oil or melted butter over each egg.

Bake about 10 minutes or until eggs are done to taste. Set individual baking dishes on plates, sprinkle eggs lightly with coriander, and serve immediately.

Makes 4 servings

12
FISH

Fish is a traditional first course for *Shabbat* and holiday dinners, and therefore Jewish cooks all over the world have developed festive fish dishes. Often these appetizer dishes are served cold, because of the prohibition of cooking food on *Shabbat*.

Although fish is pareve, or suitable for dairy or meat meals, many Jewish fish specialties do not contain dairy products because the fish usually begins a menu that features a meat or poultry main course. As a main course, however, fish is a frequent choice for dairy meals, and in these cases the recipe might contain butter or cream, as in Sole with Mushrooms in Paprika Cream.

In this country the most famous Jewish fish dish is Polish-style gefilte fish served with a dab of spicy red horseradish. When I was growing up, my mother worked for hours to prepare it every week, chopping the fish in a wooden bowl with a round-bladed knife. Today gefilte fish is easy to make in a food processor. Even though we had such wonderful, delicately flavored gefilte fish at home, my little brother was a great fan of the cocktail-size gefilte fish balls served

209

at our temple's weekly bar mitzvah buffet. This fish came in jars, and I would not touch it, since I was a rather picky eater and I much preferred the taste of my mother's version.

The seasonings popular among Jews from Mediterranean and Middle Eastern lands also result in delicious fish dishes. Sephardic fish with lemon, and hot and spicy Moroccan fish with garlic and peppers, for example, are time-honored appetizers that appear regularly on the *Shabbat* table. For weekday meals, fish shows up as a main course. It will often be sprinkled with cumin and either turmeric or thyme, then grilled, broiled, or fried; or it might be served in a zesty sauce, as in Yemenite-style haddock in a coriander–green onion tomato sauce.

Most classic Ashkenazic fish recipes feature freshwater fish because these were the varieties found in the rivers and lakes of eastern and central Europe. Traditional Sephardic dishes make use of Mediterranean fish. Of course, good cooks always take advantage of the best fish available, and now in Israel both fresh- and saltwater fish can be found in the skillets of Jews of all origins.

Do try to go to the best fish market so you can buy the freshest and best quality fish. It makes an enormous difference in the taste of whatever recipe you choose.

SWEET AND SOUR SALMON

Salmon with currants, walnuts, and parsley makes a colorful, low-fat appetizer or a refreshing summer main course. The fish is served cold, and its sweet-and-sour taste is delicate.

Sweet-and-sour fish is traditionally prepared with carp and is popular among Jews from Poland, Germany, and much of eastern Europe. The carp recipe has even become part of classic French cuisine, in which it is known as carpe à la juive *(Jewish-style carp). It appears in four versions in Escoffier's authoritative* Guide Culinaire*—carp with white wine, garlic, and shallots; with wine, shallots, garlic, and lots of fresh parsley; with saffron and almonds; and with sugar, vinegar, raisins, and currants.*

Many old-fashioned versions of the recipe specify adding crumbled gingersnaps or a pinch of dried ginger to the cooking liquid, but I like the zing of fresh ginger. SEE PHOTOGRAPH.

2 salmon steaks, 1 inch thick (about
   1½ pounds total)
salt and freshly ground pepper
1 medium onion, sliced
2 medium carrots, sliced in rounds
2 bay leaves
2 slices fresh ginger (½-inch cube)
2 whole cloves
2 cups water

½ cup dry white wine
2 tablespoons vegetable oil
2 teaspoons white wine vinegar
1 teaspoon sugar
3 tablespoons dried currants
2 tablespoons chopped fresh parsley
¼ cup walnut halves or pieces
lemon wedges, for garnish

Sprinkle salmon lightly with salt and pepper and set aside.

Combine onion, carrots, bay leaves, ginger, cloves, salt and pepper to taste, and water in a sauté pan or deep skillet in which salmon can just fit. Bring to a boil, cover, and simmer 15 minutes. Add wine and oil and bring to a simmer. Add salmon, cover, and cook over low heat for 10 to 12 minutes or until fish is tender; check near bone—flesh should have turned a lighter shade of pink. Transfer fish carefully to a deep serving dish.

Boil the cooking liquid for 5 minutes or until it is reduced to 2 cups. Strain, reserving a few carrot slices for garnish, and return strained liquid to pan. Add vinegar, sugar, and currants and simmer 1 minute. Add parsley, taste, and adjust seasoning. Add walnuts and pour or spoon mixture over fish.

Serve fish cold. When serving, spoon a little of the liquid over fish. Garnish with a few carrot slices and lemon wedges.

Makes 4 first-course servings or 2 main-course servings

MOROCCAN SEA BASS WITH PEPPERS AND TOMATOES

Moroccan-Jewish cooks are talented in cooking fish, and this easy dish of exuberant flavors is one of their best known. The fish is arranged in layers with sliced tomatoes and both hot and sweet peppers, and sprinkled with fine olive oil.

2 pounds fish steaks or fillets, such as sea bass, cod, ling cod, or halibut, 1 inch thick

2 jalapeño peppers, seeded and chopped

1 red bell pepper, fresh pimiento, or green bell pepper, cut into thin strips

3 large ripe tomatoes (about 1¼ pounds), sliced ¼ inch thick

salt and freshly ground pepper

6 medium garlic cloves, chopped

⅓ cup chopped fresh coriander (cilantro) or Italian parsley

⅓ cup olive oil, preferably extra-virgin

cayenne pepper (optional)

Rinse fish and pat dry. Put both types peppers in a sauté pan. Cut any large tomato slices in half, then top peppers with tomatoes in one layer. Sprinkle with salt, pepper, 1 tablespoon garlic, and 2 tablespoons coriander. Top with fish in one layer. Sprinkle fish with salt and pepper. Pour oil evenly over fish, then sprinle with remaining garlic and 2 tablespoons coriander.

Cover and cook over low heat for 30 minutes or until fish can be easily flaked with a fork. Remove fish and vegetables with a slotted spatula. Boil liquid to reduce it until slightly thickened. Taste liquid and adjust seasoning. Add cayenne pepper if desired. To serve, spoon sauce over fish and sprinkle with remaining coriander. Serve hot or cold.

Makes 3 or 4 main-course or 6 first-course servings

SPICY SAUTÉED SOLE

Sautéed fish with a crisp coating is a delicious dish, but with the typical Yemenite-Jewish spice mixture of cumin and turmeric, it is irresistible. In fact, this Yemenite-Jewish spice mixture, known as hawaij marak *(soup spice) and which sometimes also includes cardamom seeds, has become so much in demand in Israel that it is now sold at the markets.*

1½ pounds sole fillets
½ teaspoon salt
¼ teaspoon ground black pepper
1½ teaspoons ground cumin

½ teaspoon turmeric
¼ cup all-purpose flour
5 tablespoons vegetable or olive oil

Run your fingers over the fillets to check for bones. Gently remove any bones using tweezers, pastry crimper, or small sharp knife. Cut each fillet in 2 pieces crosswise. Arrange them in one layer on plate.

Mix salt, pepper, cumin, and turmeric. Sprinkle 1¼ teaspoons spice mixture as evenly as possible over top of fish. Rub spices thoroughly into fish. Turn fish over. Sprinkle remaining spice mixture over fish and rub thoroughly into it. Let stand 10 minutes. Preheat oven to 300°F.

Spread flour on a plate. Lightly coat fish with flour on both sides. Tap and shake to remove excess flour. Transfer fish to a large plate and arrange side by side.

Heat oil in heavy large skillet over medium-high heat. Add enough fillet pieces to make one layer. Sauté until coating is golden brown and flesh is opaque, about 1 minute on each side; turn fish carefully using 2 wide slotted metal spatulas. If oil in skillet begins to brown, reduce heat to medium. Transfer fish pieces to ovenproof platter, arrange side by side, and keep them warm in oven while you sauté remaining pieces. Serve immediately.

Makes 4 main-course servings

FISH WITH LIGHT LEMON AND DILL SAUCE

Cold fish in lemon sauce is a favorite first course among Jews from Greece and Turkey. Most versions of the dish use an egg-based sauce, but this eggless recipe is lighter and simpler to prepare. I like it because the fresh taste of the dill balances the lemon flavor. The fish can be either poached, as here, or sautéed.

2 tablespoons lemon juice
3 tablespoons olive oil
¾ cup water

salt and pepper
1½ pounds halibut fillet, ½ to 1 inch
  thick

Lemon-Dill Sauce

2 tablespoons lemon juice
6 tablespoons olive oil, preferably
  extra-virgin
1 medium garlic clove, very finely
  minced

2 tablespoons snipped fresh dill
salt and cayenne pepper to taste
¼ teaspoon paprika

lettuce leaves and lemon wedges, for
  serving

Combine lemon juice, oil, water, and a pinch of salt and pepper in a sauté pan or deep skillet. Bring to a simmer. If fish is ½ inch thick or less, fold it in half. Add fish to simmering liquid and sprinkle with salt and pepper. Cover and cook over low heat for 10 minutes or until fish changes color throughout. Cool slightly in the liquid, then transfer carefully to a platter to cool.

Combine sauce ingredients in a bowl and whisk until blended. Arrange lettuce leaves on a platter or plates and set fish on top. Whisk sauce again and spoon a little over fish. Garnish with lemon wedges. Serve any remaining sauce separately.

Makes 3 or 4 main-course or 6 first-course servings

HADDOCK IN CORIANDER–GREEN ONION TOMATO SAUCE

This aromatic dish features an easy-to-make sauce based on pureed fresh tomatoes. In Israel the dish is made with mullet or tilapia, which are commonly available fresh, but here in the United States I use haddock, sea bass, halibut, cod, or sometimes salmon. Simply cooked rice is a good accompaniment for the flavorful sauce.

1 pound ripe tomatoes, cored and cut in large chunks
2 tablespoons vegetable oil
½ large onion, diced
6 large garlic cloves, chopped
2 tablespoons tomato paste
about 2¼ teaspoons ground cumin
½ teaspoon turmeric
¼ teaspoon paprika
pinch of cayenne pepper
½ cup chopped fresh coriander (cilantro)
1¾ pounds haddock, cod, or other fish fillets, about 1 inch thick
salt and pepper
3 tablespoons chopped green onions

Puree the tomatoes in a food processor or blender. Heat oil in a large sauté pan, add onion, and sauté over medium heat until golden brown. Add tomato puree, garlic, tomato paste, ¼ teaspoon cumin, turmeric, paprika, cayenne, and ¼ cup coriander. Bring to a boil, cover, and simmer 10 minutes.

Sprinkle fish lightly on both sides with salt, pepper, and remaining cumin. Add fish to sauce and sprinkle with 2 tablespoons chopped green onions. Cover and cook over low heat 15 minutes. Turn over and cook 10 to 15 more minutes or until it can flake easily.

Sprinkle fish with remaining ¼ cup coriander and remaining green onions. Serve hot or at room temperature.

Makes 4 main-course servings

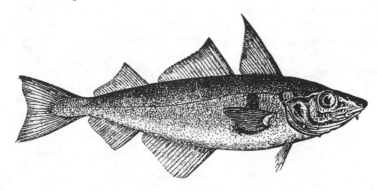

COLD OVEN-POACHED TROUT WITH HORSERADISH SAUCE

In the Jewish kitchen, horseradish is a favorite with fish. Here it flavors an easy, mayonnaise-based sauce to slightly tone down its sharpness, making it a fitting, but still very zesty, partner for the delicate trout. The dish will be prettiest if pink salmon trout are used.

   This recipe features a mayonnaise and yogurt or sour cream sauce, but you can omit the yogurt or sour cream for a fleishig *meal. A refreshing accompaniment for the fish is thinly sliced cucumbers.*

1 medium carrot, sliced
1 medium onion, sliced
1 bay leaf
½ teaspoon dried thyme
1 teaspoon salt

¼ teaspoon black peppercorns
5 cups water
½ cup dry white wine
4 small trout (8 ounces each)

Horseradish Sauce

⅔ cup mayonnaise
½ cup plain yogurt or sour cream
¼ teaspoon strained fresh lemon juice
2 tablespoons prepared horseradish, or
   to taste

1 tablespoon chopped fresh parsley
   (optional)
salt and white pepper
2 to 3 teaspoons water (optional)

Combine carrot, onion, bay leaf, thyme, salt, peppercorns, and water in a large saucepan. Cover and bring to a boil. Simmer over low heat 20 minutes, then strain into a bowl and add wine. Let cool slightly.

   Preheat oven to 400°F. Snip fins off fish and trim tails straight, using sturdy scissors. Rinse fish inside and out, removing any scales, and pat dry. Leave on heads and tails. Season fish inside and out with salt and pepper.

   Set fish in one layer in a large, heavy, flameproof baking dish. Pour enough of wine mixture over fish to cover them and bring to a simmer. Cover with foil, transfer to oven, and bake until a cake tester or thin skewer inserted into thickest part of fish comes out hot to touch, about 12 minutes. Uncover fish and let cool in liquid until lukewarm.

   Whisk mayonnaise with yogurt in a bowl until smooth. Whisk in lemon juice, then stir in horseradish and parsley. Taste, and add salt and pepper if needed. If sauce is too thick, gradually whisk in 2 or 3 teaspoons water.

   Transfer fish carefully to a plate lined with paper towels, using 2 slotted spatulas. Remove skin of each fish by scraping gently with paring knife; leave skin on head and tail. Let fish cool to room temperature. (Fish can be kept, covered, up to 1 day in refrigerator; refrigerate sauce in separate dish, covered.)

Serve fish with horseradish sauce.

Makes 4 main-course servings

BRAISED COD WITH CHICKPEAS AND OLIVE OIL

I first tasted this dish in Florence, Italy. Later I learned that it is also characteristic of the cuisine of Moroccan Jews. Dried hot peppers and garlic cook with the chickpeas, and these cooking juices then flavor the fish but do not make it excessively hot. It's a simple and delicious dish, especially when made with superior quality olive oil. Some cooks add fresh coriander, paprika, cumin, and turmeric to the fish.

3 to 3½ cups cooked chickpeas (garbanzo beans), or 2 15- or 16-ounce cans
5 large garlic cloves, sliced
4 dried hot red peppers, such as *chiles japones*
salt
5 or 6 tablespoons extra-virgin olive oil

freshly ground pepper
¼ cup chickpea cooking liquid or water
2 pounds cod or scrod steaks or fillets, about 1 inch thick
coriander (cilantro) or parsley sprigs, for garnish
lemon wedges, for garnish (optional)

Preheat oven to 400°F. If using canned chickpeas, rinse and drain them. Combine chickpeas with garlic, peppers, pinch of salt, and 3 or 4 tablespoons oil in a medium saucepan. Add ¼ cup cooking liquid from chickpeas, or ¼ cup water if using canned ones. Push peppers to bottom of pan and bring liquid to a simmer. Cover tightly and cook over medium-low heat for 20 minutes.

Transfer half the chickpea mixture to a 9-inch square baking dish. Set fish on top and sprinkle with salt and pepper. Top fish with remaining chickpea mixture. Sprinkle with remaining 2 tablespoons oil. Cover and bake 30 to 35 minutes or until fish can just be flaked but is not falling apart.

Discard the peppers. Serve fish hot or lukewarm. Spoon a few tablespoons of juices over fish and chickpeas when serving. Garnish with coriander or parsley sprigs and lemon wedges.

Makes 4 main-course servings

NOTE: If using dried chickpeas, use ½ pound (1¼ cups). Soak overnight or quick-soak (see the recipe for Hummus, page 163), drain, rinse, and cook in water to generously cover for 1¼ to 1½ hours.

SEPHARDIC FISH STEAKS WITH CUMIN AND GARLIC

Jews from Morocco and other North African countries often marinate fish in this savory cumin-garlic–olive oil marinade, called tchermela, *before cooking. The fish can be cooked directly in the marinade, as here, or can be drained and then baked, broiled, grilled, or fried.*

4 steaks of halibut or other firm lean
   fish, about 1 inch thick (about 1½
   pounds)

Marinade

1 tablespoon chopped fresh coriander
   (cilantro)
1 medium garlic clove, minced
1 teaspoon ground cumin

1 teaspoon paprika
pinch of cayenne pepper
2 tablespoons olive oil
pinch of salt

Sauce

1 teaspoon paprika
½ teaspoon ground cumin
⅓ cup water
1 teaspoon tomato paste

1 tablespoon fresh lemon juice
2 tablespoons vegetable oil
2 medium garlic cloves, minced

pinch of salt

Put fish steaks in a tray in one layer. Mix the marinade ingredients and rub them over both sides of fish steaks. Cover and marinate in refrigerator for 1 to 3 hours, turning steaks occasionally.

   Mix paprika and cumin in a small dish. In a cup, stir water into tomato paste until smooth. Add lemon juice. Heat oil in a large deep skillet and add garlic and spice mixture. Sauté for 30 seconds over medium heat, stirring, then remove from heat and add tomato paste mixture. Bring to a simmer, stirring.

Add fish steaks to sauce with their marinade and a pinch of salt. Reduce heat to low, cover, and simmer, basting fish occasionally, about 10 minutes or until fish can be flaked with a fork.

With a slotted spoon, transfer fish to a platter; keep it warm. Boil sauce, stirring constantly, until it measures about ¼ cup. Taste sauce for seasoning, spoon it over fish, and serve immediately.

Makes 4 main-course servings

SOLE WITH MUSHROOMS IN PAPRIKA CREAM

This rich Hungarian-style dish is a festive main course for a milchig *dinner—that is, one featuring dairy products. Spaetzle (page 277), fresh noodles, or steamed potatoes are the perfect accompaniment.*

¼ pound small mushrooms
2 tablespoons (¼ stick) butter
salt and freshly ground pepper
1½ pounds sole fillets
about ¼ cup all-purpose flour
2 tablespoons vegetable oil
2 tablespoons chopped green onions
    (mostly white part)

½ cup heavy cream
1 teaspoon paprika
½ cup sour cream, at room temperature
pinch of hot paprika or cayenne
    pepper (optional)
2 tablespoons chopped fresh parsley
    (optional)

Quarter the mushrooms. Melt 1 tablespoon butter in a medium skillet, add mushrooms, salt, and pepper and sauté over medium-high heat about 5 minutes or until tender and lightly browned. Set aside.

Check fillets and remove any bones. Sprinkle fillets with salt and pepper on both sides. Dredge them lightly with flour and tap them to remove excess.

Heat oil and remaining 1 tablespoon butter in a large skillet over medium-high heat. Add fillets and sauté about 2 minutes per side, or until they can be pierced easily with a skewer. Transfer them to a platter and keep them warm.

Add green onions to skillet and sauté 2 minutes. Stir in cream, paprika, and a little salt and pepper. Simmer over medium heat, stirring, until sauce is thick enough to coat a spoon. Add mushrooms and sour cream, and heat gently without boiling. Add hot paprika or cayenne. Taste and adjust seasoning, then remove from heat. Pour sauce and mushrooms over fillets, sprinkle with parsley, and serve immediately.

Makes 4 main-course servings

SAFFRON FISH BALLS IN TOMATO SAUCE

I received this recipe from Paule Tourdjman, a Jewish woman from Morocco who worked with me at La Varenne Cooking School in Paris. The fish balls in their aromatic tomato sauce are good as an appetizer, or a light main course with white rice. Some cooks use cumin instead of the saffron, or a combination of dried ginger and grated orange peel.

⅛ teaspoon saffron threads
3 tablespoons extra-virgin olive oil

Sauce

2 pounds ripe tomatoes, or 2 28-ounce
 cans plum tomatoes
2 tablespoons olive oil
1 medium onion, chopped
½ cup diced red bell pepper (optional)

3 sprigs fresh thyme, or ½ teaspoon
 dried
1 bay leaf
salt and freshly ground pepper

Fish Balls

1 medium onion, quartered
1 pound cod or scrod fillet, any bones
 removed, cut into pieces
1 teaspoon salt
¼ teaspoon ground white pepper

1 slice white bread, crust removed,
 torn into pieces
1 large egg
1 large egg white
½ cup chopped fresh parsley

Slightly crush the saffron with your fingers and soak in oil about 30 minutes.

Peel and seed the fresh tomatoes, reserving juice; if using canned tomatoes, drain and reserve juice. Coarsely chop the tomatoes. In a medium saucepan, heat oil, add onion and red pepper, and sauté over medium-low heat for 7 minutes. Add tomatoes, thyme, bay leaf, salt, and pepper. Bring to a boil, cover, and cook over low heat for 20 minutes. Remove bay leaf and thyme sprigs. Set aside.

In a food processor, mince onion and remove. Chop fish in processor. Add salt, pepper, bread, egg, egg white, and 1 tablespoon of saffron oil. Transfer to a bowl. Stir in chopped parsley and onion. Form mixture into small balls, using 1 tablespoon mixture for each, and roll them between your palms until smooth. Put on a plate.

Measure the reserved tomato juice, adding water if necessary to make 1 cup. Add measured juice and remaining saffron oil to sauce. Transfer sauce to a sauté pan or deep skillet. Put half the fish balls in sauce, cover, and cook, without stirring, for 20 minutes. Carefully remove them with a slotted spoon. Cook remaining fish balls in sauce. Return all fish balls to sauce. Taste sauce and adjust seasoning. Serve hot or cold.

Makes 4 main-course or 6 or 7 first-course servings

HALIBUT WITH GARLIC SAUCE AND AVOCADO

Garlic sauce of this type, resembling the southern French aïoli *and the* alioli *of Spain, is relished in Mediterranean Jewish cooking as an accompaniment for fish or vegetables or as a dip. It is rich and creamy but does not contain dairy products, and so is pareve, or neutral—perfect for dairy or meat meals. For a quicker version of the sauce without uncooked egg yolks, see the variation.*

Garlic Sauce

4 medium garlic cloves
2 large egg yolks, at room temperature
1 tablespoon plus 1-2 teaspoons
    strained fresh lemon juice

1 cup fine quality olive oil, preferably
    extra-virgin, at room temperature
1 or 2 tablespoons warm water
salt and freshly ground pepper

1 small ripe avocado
1½ pounds halibut fillet, about 1 inch
    thick, cut into 4 pieces

salt and freshly ground pepper
4 teaspoons olive oil

Drop garlic cloves through feed tube of food processor with motor running, and process until finely chopped. Add egg yolks, 1 tablespoon lemon juice, 1 tablespoon oil, and a pinch of salt and pepper. Process until thoroughly blended. With motor running, gradually pour in more oil in a thin trickle. After adding ¼ cup of oil, remaining oil can be poured in a little faster, in a fine stream. With motor still running, gradually pour in remaining lemon juice. Gradually add lukewarm water to make sauce slightly thinner. Taste and adjust seasoning. (Sauce can be kept, covered, for 2 days in refrigerator.)

A short time before serving, peel avocado and cut into thin slices. Position broiler rack 4 inches from heat source and preheat broiler.

Season fish with salt and pepper on both sides. Brush with oil and put on broiler rack, oiled side down. Broil about 4 minutes per side or until a skewer inserted into center of fish piece comes out hot to touch and fish can just be flaked with fork. Transfer fish to plates and spoon a little sauce over each. Garnish each fish with a few avocado slices. Serve remaining sauce separately.

Makes 4 main-course servings

VARIATION: Quick Garlic Sauce
   Finely chop 4 medium garlic cloves. Blend with 1 cup mayonnaise, 1 tablespoon lemon juice, and 1 tablespoon fine olive oil. Taste for seasoning, and add more lemon juice if desired.

BROILED SALMON
WITH MOROCCAN SEASONINGS

Although Moroccan-Jewish cooking has a reputation in Israel for being rather hot, each cook adds only the amount of seasoning liked by his or her family. And there are plenty of delicate dishes too, because of the French influence. This is an example of such a dish, subtly spiced with the popular combination of cumin, paprika, and olive oil. It's very quick and easy, and is wonderful with rice or couscous.

2 salmon steaks, 1 inch thick (about
   1¼ pounds total)
½ teaspoon ground cumin
¼ teaspoon paprika
½ teaspoon dried leaf thyme, crumbled

salt and freshly ground pepper
1 to 2 tablespoons olive oil
cucumber slices
tomato slices

Line broiler rack with foil if desired. Preheat broiler with rack about 4 inches from heat source. Lightly oil broiler rack or foil.
   Remove any scales from salmon steaks. Mix cumin, paprika, and thyme in a small bowl. Sprinkle about half the mixture on one side of salmon, then sprinkle with salt and pepper. Drizzle with half the oil. Set salmon on broiler rack and broil 4 minutes. Turn over, sprinkle with remaining spice mixture, a pinch more of salt and pepper, and remaining oil. Broil 4 to 5 more minutes. To check whether salmon is done, make a small cut with a sharp knife near bone; color of flesh should have become lighter pink all the way through, or nearly all the way through if you like fish a bit less done.
   Serve hot, with cucumber and tomato slices.

Makes 2 main-course servings

GRILLED SEA BASS WITH CAPER VINAIGRETTE

Caper plants grow in the area around Jerusalem, and the pickled buds are a great partner for grilled fish. In this area of the world, grilling rivals frying as the most popular technique for cooking fish.

2 tablespoons fresh lemon juice or
  white wine vinegar
salt and freshly ground pepper
cayenne pepper to taste
6 tablespoons olive oil
1 tablespoon drained capers, rinsed
  and chopped

1 tablespoon chopped fresh parsley
1½ to 2 pounds sea bass or halibut
  fillets, about 1 inch thick
2 to 3 teaspoons vegetable oil
1 hard-boiled large egg, chopped

Whisk lemon juice with salt, pepper, and cayenne pepper in a small bowl. Whisk in oil, capers, and parsley. (Dressing can be kept up to 2 days in refrigerator.)

Prepare grill, or preheat broiler with rack about 2 inches from heat source. Sprinkle fish lightly with salt and pepper. Brush or spread gently with oil on both sides. Arrange on broiler pan or grill. Broil or grill until fish are just opaque and tender, or until a skewer inserted into fish comes out hot to touch, about 4 minutes per side.

Whisk dressing, then stir in chopped egg. Taste and adjust seasoning.

Serve fish hot or at room temperature. Spoon dressing over fish when serving.

Makes 4 main-course servings

13
POULTRY AND MEAT

Roast chicken, quickly sautéed turkey schnitzel, and aromatic meat patties are frequently prepared by Jewish cooks. Yet it is for gently simmered stews and braised dishes that Jewish cuisine is best known.

There are several reasons for this. First, the rules for *Shabbat*, for which the most festive dinner of the week is prepared, prohibit cooking during the day on Saturday. Everything must be cooked before sundown on Friday and kept hot for the main meal on Saturday, which is served around noon.

The types of dishes most suited to this cooking schedule are braised or stewed meats. Jewish communities all over the world have developed delicious stews; some have surprising similarities, even though they originate in places far away from each other. The most celebrated example is the flavorful meat and bean stew called *hamin*, which is prepared in different versions by Ashkenazic and Sephardic Jews from many localities. The dried beans used differ from place to place, and so do the meats and seasonings, but the method is the same—the ingredients are combined in a covered casserole, which is then left over the lowest heat or baked slowly all night.

Stews are especially popular among Jews of Mediterranean and Middle Eastern origin. "The secret to good cooking," a Sephardic chef once told me, "is very slowly simmering the ingredients together for a long time, so the seasonings penetrate the meat as much as possible. If you treat the ingredients gently, you will get the most out of them, but if you heat them violently over a high flame, you will ruin them." The technique of long cooking over low heat promotes an exchange of flavors among the meat, the sauce, and the vegetables. The result is a wonderful aroma and a rich harmony of tastes, which intensify if the dish is reheated the next day, because the ingredients have been in contact for a longer time. In addition, stewing is especially suitable to many of the kosher cuts of meat, which come from the front of the animal and many of which require long, gentle simmering to tenderize them.

Many Sephardic stews contain a relatively large quantity of vegetables for a small amount of meat. This practice, which began for reasons of economy, also makes sense from the point of view of nutrition and produces dishes that are colorful and not heavy. Aromatic vegetables, such as onions and carrots, are often put in the pot from the beginning, while tender vegetables may be added later. In addition to the Mediterranean favorites of tomatoes, onions, and peppers, numerous green vegetables enliven the stews. A perfect example is Msouki (page 48), the Tunisian Passover stew, which includes spinach, artichokes, zucchini, leeks, carrots, and many other vegetables.

Flavorings for stews and other meat dishes vary tremendously, according to the cook's country of origin. A variety of herbs such as mint, dill, flat-leaf parsley, and fresh coriander, and spices such as saffron, cumin, turmeric, and cinnamon, give Sephardic stews their liveliness. Because they are enhanced by so many flavors, most of these stews do not usually require stock.

For Rosh Hashanah and other occasions, many Jews prepare dishes with a sweet touch, combining meat and fruit. There are the meat and dried fruit tzimmes of Ashkenazic Jews, the Moroccan sweet tajines, and Iranian dishes such as Chicken Baked with Quince and Almonds.

Many of the traditional Jewish stews thicken naturally by reduction during the long, slow cooking and are not usually thickened with flour. These stews vary in consistency and in many cases there is no need for the sauce to be so thick that it clings to the meat. Often there is a generous amount of sauce. Some are designed to moisten the rice, potatoes, noodles, or couscous served as an accompaniment.

These savory stews have withstood the test of time and have remained the basis of home cooking of many Jewish cooks. Because they can be more or less left alone, can be prepared ahead, and require little or no last-minute work, they are often the most convenient choice for both everyday meals and for entertaining.

ROAST CHICKEN WITH NOODLE-MUSHROOM-WALNUT STUFFING

Instead of serving chicken with a noodle kugel, you can roast the bird with a stuffing that includes kugel ingredients but does not contain egg. For the tasty stuffing used here, the mushrooms are made into a French preparation known as duxelles—*they are finely chopped and then sautéed to intensify their flavor.*

¾ cup (about 2½ ounces) walnut halves

Duxelles and Pasta Stuffing

4 tablespoons (½ stick) nondairy
 margarine, at room temperature
2 small shallots, minced
4 ounces button mushrooms, finely
 chopped

salt and freshly ground pepper to taste
4 ounces fresh or 3 ounces dried egg
 noodles or fettuccine
2 tablespoons minced fresh parsley
 leaves

4-pound roasting chicken
6 tablespoons (¾ stick) nondairy
 margarine, softened
salt and freshly ground pepper to taste
4 ounces mushrooms, halved and
 sliced

8 ounces fresh or 6 ounces dried egg
 noodles or fettuccine
2 tablespoons minced fresh parsley

Preheat oven to 400°F. Toast walnuts in a baking dish in oven, shaking it occasionally, about 7 minutes or until lightly browned. Transfer to a bowl and cool. Break 6 tablespoons of toasted walnut halves in pieces and reserve for stuffing.

Melt 2 tablespoons margarine for stuffing in a medium skillet over low heat. Add shallots and cook 2 minutes or until soft but not browned. Add chopped mushrooms, salt, and pepper and cook over high heat, stirring often, about 5 minutes or until mixture is thick and dry.

Cook noodles uncovered in a medium saucepan of boiling salted water over high heat about 1 to 2 minutes for fresh or 2 to 5 minutes for dried, or until tender but firm to the bite. Drain, rinse with cold water, and drain again. Transfer to a large bowl. Add chopped mushroom mixture, remaining 2 tablespoons margarine, reserved walnut pieces, and parsley and toss mixture. Taste and adjust seasoning. Let stuffing cool completely.

Preheat oven to 400°F. Discard excess fat from chicken. Rub chicken with 1 tablespoon soft margarine and sprinkle it lightly with salt and pepper. Spoon stuffing into chicken, packing it in gently. Set chicken in a roasting pan or shallow baking dish just large enough to contain it. Roast chicken, basting it occasionally, about 1 hour and 10 minutes or until thickest part of drumstick is tender when pierced with a skewer and juices that run from chicken are clear; if juices are pink, roast chicken a few more minutes and check again.

Melt 2 tablespoons margarine in a large skillet over medium-high heat. Add sliced mushrooms, salt, and pepper and sauté about 3 minutes or until lightly browned.

Cook noodles in boiling salted water as above. Drain them well and transfer to pan of mushrooms. Add remaining 3 tablespoons margarine, 3 tablespoons toasted walnut halves, and parsley and toss mixture. Season to taste with salt and pepper.

To serve, set chicken on a heated platter and spoon noodle and sliced mushroom mixture around it. Sprinkle pasta with remaining toasted walnut halves. Carve chicken at the table and serve with stuffing.

Makes 4 servings

EXOTIC ROAST CHICKEN

This unusual recipe for chicken with a stuffing studded with almonds and pine nuts and flavored with fresh coriander and cinnamon is inspired by a recipe called Jewish partridge, from a thirteenth-century book on the cooking of Spain and the Maghreb area of North Africa. Culinary historian Charles Perry gave me the Jewish recipes from the book, known simply as "Anonymous Manuscript," which was written in Arabic and published in translation in Madrid.*

Almond–Pine Nut Stuffing

⅓ cup almonds
¼ cup pine nuts
about 4 to 5 ounces day-old or stale white bread, preferably challah or French or Italian bread (enough to make 2 cups crumbs)
¼ cup vegetable oil
1 medium onion, finely chopped
salt and freshly ground pepper

½ pound (1 cup) ground chicken or turkey
¼ teaspoon ground cinnamon
¼ cup chopped fresh coriander (cilantro)
¼ cup chopped fresh parsley
¼ to ½ cup chicken soup or stock
1 to 2 tablespoons (¼ stick) nondairy margarine

3½- to 4-pound chicken
¼ teaspoon salt
¼ teaspoon pepper
2 teaspoons vegetable oil
¼ to ½ cup chicken soup or stock, for basting

about ⅓ cup mixed toasted nuts (pistachios, almonds, and pine nuts), for garnish
cilantro or parsley sprigs, for garnish

*The translated version is *Traduccion Espanola de un Manuscrito Anonimo del Siglo XIII sobre la Cocina Hispano-Magaribi*.

Preheat oven to 350°F. Toast almonds and pine nuts in small baking dish in oven until lightly browned, about 4 minutes. Cool nuts and coarsely chop.

If using challah, remove crust. Slice bread. Grind it, a few slices at a time, in food processor to make crumbs. You will need 2 cups crumbs. Transfer to a large bowl.

Heat 3 tablespoons oil in medium skillet over medium heat. Add onion, salt, and pepper. Sauté until onion is soft and light brown, about 10 minutes. Remove onion with slotted spoon and add remaining oil to skillet. Heat briefly, then add ground chicken, cinnamon, and a small pinch of salt and pepper. Cook over medium-high heat, breaking up meat with wooden spoon, for about 5 minutes. Return onion to skillet and mix well with chicken.

Add onion-chicken mixture and toasted nuts to bread crumbs and toss lightly until blended. Add coriander and parsley and toss. Gradually add ¼ cup soup, tossing lightly. Mixture may appear dry, but juices in bird will moisten it. Taste and adjust seasoning. (Stuffing can be refrigerated up to 1 day in covered container. Do not stuff bird in advance.)

Preheat oven to 375°F. Discard excess fat from chicken. Mix salt, pepper, and oil. Rub chicken all over with seasoning mixture. Spoon stuffing lightly into chicken; do not pack it tightly. Fold skin over stuffing; truss or skewer closed, if desired. Set chicken in a roasting pan.

Add a little more soup, if necessary, to extra stuffing so that most of bread is very lightly moistened. Grease a 3–4-cup casserole and spoon stuffing into it. Dot with margarine. Cover and refrigerate.

Roast chicken for 45 minutes, then put pan of extra stuffing in oven, cover it, and roast both together about 45 minutes, basting chicken occasionally with pan juices if desired, and basting stuffing occasionally with a few tablespoons stock. To check whether chicken is done, insert a skewer into thickest part of drumstick; it should be tender and juices that run from chicken should be clear. If juices are pink, roast chicken a few more minutes and check it again. Insert a skewer into stuffing inside chicken; it should come out hot.

Carve the chicken. Spoon stuffing onto platter with chicken pieces and garnish with toasted nuts and with coriander or parsley sprigs.

Makes 4 servings

ISRAELI GRILLED CHICKEN

Grilled meats and poultry are as popular in Israel as in America, and are often the star of Israeli Independence Day barbecue menus. (I wonder what there is about celebrating national freedom that drives people to cook outside!)

The meats are typically seasoned as in this recipe, which is our favorite way to flavor chicken, beef, and lamb for barbecuing. As accompaniments we serve aromatic mushrooms, Eggplant Salad with Tahini (page 171), or Zucchini with Tomatoes and Dill (page 265), Easy Rice Pilaf (page 145) or cooked basmati rice, Israeli Vegetable Salad (page 20), good bread, and for dessert, either fresh fruit salad or My Mother's Chocolate Applesauce Cake (page 91).

4½ to 5 pounds chicken pieces
2 tablespoons olive oil
pinch of salt (optional)
2 tablespoons cumin, preferably freshly
   ground

2 teaspoons turmeric
about ¼ teaspoon freshly ground black
   pepper

Rub chicken with oil and sprinkle lightly with salt. Mix cumin, turmeric, and pepper and sprinkle on both sides of chicken. Let stand while coals are heating.

Set chicken on rack about 4 to 6 inches above glowing coals. Grill breast pieces about 10 minutes per side, and leg and thigh pieces about 15 to 18 minutes per side or until thickest part of meat near bone is no longer pink when cut. Serve immediately.

Makes 6 to 8 servings

NOTE: If you are using koshered chicken (that has been salted), salt is not needed for this recipe.

STUFFED CHICKEN WITH COUSCOUS, RAISINS, AND PECANS

Moroccan Jews make a delicious couscous stuffing for chicken. I love the taste of fresh ginger and toasted pecans in the saffron-scented stuffing in this recipe, but if you wish to prepare a more authentic Moroccan version, use 1 teaspoon dried ginger instead of fresh and substitute almonds for the pecans.

Couscous Stuffing

2 pinches of saffron threads (about ¼ teaspoon)
1¼ cups boiling water
2 teaspoons olive oil
½ cup pecan halves, broken in pieces
salt
2 tablespoons plus 1 teaspoon peeled and minced fresh ginger

4 tablespoons (½ stick) unsalted nondairy margarine, at room temperature
1¼ cups couscous
freshly ground pepper
¼ cup dark raisins
2 tablespoons minced fresh parsley leaves

4-pound roasting chicken
¼ teaspoon salt
¼ teaspoon pepper

½ teaspoon ground ginger
½ teaspoon paprika
1 tablespoon olive oil

Crush saffron between your fingers. In a small saucepan add saffron to boiling water; cover and let stand 20 minutes.

In a small heavy skillet, heat oil, add pecan pieces with a pinch of salt, and sauté over medium heat, stirring, for 2 minutes, or until lightly browned. Transfer nuts to a plate and let cool.

In a large skillet melt 2 tablespoons margarine, add ginger, and sauté over medium heat, stirring, for 1 minute. Add couscous with salt and pepper and stir mixture with a fork until blended. Scatter raisins on top. Remove skillet from heat and shake it to spread couscous in an even layer. Bring saffron-flavored water to a boil, pour it evenly over couscous, immediately cover skillet tightly, and let mixture stand 3 minutes. Fluff couscous with a fork. Cut remaining margarine in small pieces and add them. Add pecans and parsley and toss mixture to combine it. Taste and adjust seasoning. Let stuffing cool completely.

Preheat oven to 400°F. Discard excess fat from chicken. In a small bowl mix salt, pepper, ginger, paprika, and oil. Rub chicken all over with mixture. Spoon 1½ cups stuffing into chicken, packing it in gently. Keep remaining couscous mixture at room temperature. Set chicken in a roasting pan or shallow baking dish just large enough to contain it. Roast chicken, basting it occasionally, for 1¼ hours, or until thickest part of drumstick is tender when pierced with a skewer and juices that run from chicken are clear. If juices are pink, roast chicken a few more minutes and check it again.

To serve, spoon stuffing from chicken onto a platter. Carve chicken and arrange pieces over stuffing. Add 2 tablespoons of pan juices to remaining couscous mixture and reheat it gently, stirring with a fork, for 2 minutes. Fluff couscous mixture with a fork. Serve couscous in a separate dish.

Makes 4 servings

SPICY ROAST CHICKEN WITH MATZO-ONION STUFFING

"East meets West," or combination cuisine, is a theme that is very much in vogue in America today, but this dish, like many others, was created in this fashion in Israel years ago as a natural result of neighbors' exchanging recipes. It has a typical Ashkenazic onion-flavored matzo stuffing served inside an aromatic, Middle Eastern spiced chicken. Serve the chicken with colorful vegetables, such as asparagus, broccoli, or carrots, and with Garlic-Scented Roast Potatoes (page 265).

The chicken is also delicious without stuffing, and we prepare it this way when we want plain roast chicken.

Matzo and Onion Stuffing

2 matzos
½ cup hot chicken soup or broth
2 tablespoons vegetable oil
1 large onion, chopped

salt and pepper
½ teaspoon ground cumin
¼ teaspoon turmeric
1 large egg, beaten

3½-pound chicken
¼ teaspoon salt
¼ teaspoon pepper

1 teaspoon ground cumin
¼ teaspoon turmeric
1 tablespoon vegetable oil

Crumble matzos into a bowl and pour chicken soup over them. Heat oil in a skillet and add onion, salt, pepper, cumin, and turmeric. Sauté over medium heat, stirring often, until tender and golden brown. Add onion to matzo mixture and let cool. Stir in egg and taste for seasoning.

Preheat oven to 400°F. Discard excess fat from chicken. Mix salt, pepper, cumin, turmeric, and oil. Rub chicken all over with mixture.

Spoon stuffing into chicken. Set in a roasting pan and roast about 1¼ hours, basting occasionally if desired. Chicken is done when juices that run from thickest part of leg are clear when meat is pierced, and a skewer inserted into stuffing comes out hot. Spoon stuffing into a serving dish. Transfer chicken to a carving board or platter. Serve hot, with stuffing.

Makes 4 servings

CHICKEN WITH PEPPERS AND RICE

Jewish cooks in both Latin America and the Middle East prepare this colorful, ''all-in-one-pan'' main course, a distant cousin of paella.

3½-pound fryer, cut into 8 serving
    pieces
salt and freshly ground pepper
1½ teaspoons ground cumin
1 tablespoon vegetable oil
1 medium onion, thinly sliced
1 medium green bell pepper, cut into
    thin strips

1 medium red bell pepper, cut into
    thin strips
1 large garlic clove, minced
1 cup long-grain white rice
2 ripe medium tomatoes, peeled,
    seeded, and chopped
1½ cups hot chicken soup, stock, or
    water

Sprinkle chicken pieces with salt, pepper, and ½ teaspoon cumin. Rub seasonings into chicken. Turn pieces over and sprinkle again with salt, pepper, and ½ teaspoon cumin. Rub again into chicken.

Heat oil in a very large, heavy skillet, at least 12 inches in diameter. Add chicken leg and thigh pieces and brown them on all sides over medium-low heat for about 15 minutes. Remove them and brown remaining chicken pieces for 5 minutes; remove.

Add onion to skillet and cook over low heat until soft but not browned. Stir in peppers and garlic and cook, stirring often, about 5 minutes. Add rice and remaining cumin to skillet and sauté over low heat, stirring, for 2 minutes. Stir in tomatoes. Set chicken pieces on top, putting in leg and thigh pieces first to be sure they are close to base of pan.

Pour hot stock over all and add another pinch of salt and pepper. Reduce heat to very low and cook, covered tightly, for 45 to 50 minutes or until chicken and rice are tender and liquid is absorbed. If all of liquid is absorbed but rice is not yet tender, add a few more tablespoons stock or water and simmer a few more minutes.

Makes 4 servings

NOTE: All drumsticks or all breast pieces with bone can be substituted for the cut chicken. For a lovely orange hue and a Middle Eastern flavor, rub chicken with ½ teaspoon turmeric along with other seasonings.

CHICKEN BAKED WITH QUINCE AND ALMONDS

Chicken with quince is prepared by many Sephardic communities. I learned to prepare this Persian version of the dish at a cooking course in Israel. Like many dishes prepared by Jews from Iran, it combines meat with fruit, but it is not really sweet. The chicken and quince are lightly seasoned with cinnamon and ginger. White rice pilaf and a simply cooked green vegetable are perfect accompaniments.

3 pounds chicken pieces, patted dry
1½ teaspoons paprika
¾ teaspoon ground ginger
about ¼ teaspoon salt
freshly ground pepper to taste
4 tablespoons vegetable oil
2 large quince (1 pound total)

½ teaspoon ground cinnamon
1 medium onion, halved and sliced
 thin
2 tablespoons dark raisins, rinsed with
 hot water
¼ cup whole or coarsely chopped
 almonds

Preheat oven to 400°F. Choose 1 large or 2 smaller shallow baking dishes that can hold chicken pieces in one layer. Set chicken on a plate. Mix paprika, ginger, salt, pepper, and 1 tablespoon oil and spoon evenly over chicken. Rub spices thoroughly into chicken on both sides.

  Cut quince into eighths and cut out core from center of each segment. Heat 2 tablespoons oil in a heavy skillet over medium heat. Add half the quince pieces and sauté to brown lightly on all sides, including side where peel was, for a total of about 7 or 8 minutes. Remove with tongs. Sauté remaining slices. Return all quince slices to pan set over low heat and sprinkle with ¼ teaspoon cinnamon. Turn slices over and sprinkle with remaining cinnamon. Toss to coat. Transfer to prepared baking dishes.

Add remaining 1 tablespoon oil to skillet and heat. Add onion and cook over medium-low heat about 7 minutes or until softened. Spoon onion over quince and sprinkle with raisins. Set chicken on top. Cover tightly and bake about 30 minutes. Sprinkle chicken with chopped almonds; if using whole almonds, scatter them among quince and sprinkle a few over chicken. Bake, uncovered, for 20 minutes or until juices that run from thickest part of chicken drumstick pieces when pierced are clear. Serve hot.

Makes 4 servings

NOTE: If quince are unavailable, substitute 2 large tart apples.

EASY LEMON CHICKEN

From a Moroccan-Jewish friend in Paris I learned this simple version of a traditional North African recipe. The slowly cooked onions give the sauce a wonderfully rich flavor, while the slight tartness of the lemon slices impart a refreshing quality. In its homeland the recipe is made with preserved lemons, and if you find some in a Middle Eastern shop, you can chop a few slices and add them to the dish after browning the chicken, rather than using fresh lemons. Some people add black or green olives to the dish during the last five minutes of cooking.

3-pound chicken, cut into pieces, or
   2½ to 3 pounds chicken pieces
2 tablespoons vegetable oil
salt and freshly ground pepper
2 large onions, halved and thinly
   sliced
1 large garlic clove, chopped

¾ cup homemade chicken stock or
   soup (page 347), or ½ cup canned
   broth and ¼ cup water
1 lemon, unpeeled, rinsed and sliced
   thin
1 tablespoon chopped fresh parsley or
   coriander (cilantro)

Pat chicken dry. Heat oil in large deep skillet or sauté pan over medium-high heat. Sprinkle chicken pieces with salt and pepper and brown them in 2 batches in oil, about 3 minutes per side. Remove with tongs to a plate. Add onions and cook over medium-low heat until softened and golden, 10 to 15 minutes. Return chicken to pan and add any juices from plate. Sprinkle garlic over chicken and pour stock into pan. Cover and simmer 30 minutes. Remove breast pieces. Cover and simmer remaining pieces 5 minutes.

Remove any pits from lemon slices with point of sharp knife. Discard end slices of lemon. Put lemon slices in a saucepan and cover with cold water. Bring to a simmer, cover, and cook over medium-low heat for 5 minutes. Drain slices; don't worry that some will not remain whole.

Remove chicken pieces from pan but leave in onion. Boil juices for 3 to 5 minutes to thicken. Return chicken to pan. Top with lemon slices, cover, and warm over low heat for 5 minutes. (Chicken can be kept, covered, 1 day in refrigerator. Reheat in covered pan over low heat.)

Taste sauce and adjust seasoning. Sprinkle with parsley and serve.

Makes 4 servings

CHICKEN WITH TOMATOES, PEPPERS, AND CORIANDER

Most Orthodox Jews do not reheat food for the midday meal on Saturday, and therefore some serve a dish hot on Friday night and cold on Saturday. This aromatic chicken dish of North African inspiration is the perfect choice, since it is delicious hot or cold. Serve it hot with couscous or rice, or cold with fresh bread or potato salad. SEE PHOTOGRAPH.

Pepper Sauce

2 medium green bell peppers
1 medium red bell pepper
1 tablespoon olive oil
1 pound ripe tomatoes, peeled, seeded, and coarsely chopped; or 1 28-ounce can plum tomatoes, drained and chopped
2 medium garlic cloves, minced

3 tablespoons minced fresh coriander (cilantro)
3 tablespoons minced fresh parsley
2 teaspoons paprika
pinch of cayenne pepper
¼ teaspoon ground cumin
¼ teaspoon salt

2 tablespoons olive oil
3½-pound chicken, cut into 4 serving pieces and patted dry
1 large onion, sliced
1 medium garlic clove, chopped

3 tablespoons minced fresh coriander (cilantro)
salt and pepper
1 cup water

Broil peppers and peel them (see page 346). Cut into ½-inch dice. In a large skillet, heat oil over medium heat. Add tomatoes, peppers, garlic, coriander, parsley, paprika, cayenne pepper, cumin, and salt. Cook uncovered, stirring often, for 20 to 25 minutes or until sauce is very thick.

In a heavy casserole heat oil over low heat. Add chicken, onion, garlic, coriander, and a pinch of salt and pepper. Cook, stirring, for 3 minutes. Add water and bring to a boil. Cover and simmer over low heat, turning pieces over occasionally, for 30 minutes, or until just tender. Transfer chicken pieces with tongs to a plate. Boil onion mixture, uncovered, until it is thick and liquid is reduced to about ⅓ cup.

Return chicken to casserole and add pepper sauce. Cover and heat over very low heat, turning chicken pieces occasionally, for 30 minutes, or until sauce is well flavored. Taste for seasoning. (Chicken can be kept, covered, for 2 days in refrigerator. Reheat chicken in sauce over low heat, covered; or serve it cold.)

To serve hot, spoon most of pepper dice onto a heated platter with a slotted spoon. Set chicken pieces on top. Spoon a little sauce over chicken pieces and garnish each piece with a few pepper dice. Serve remaining sauce and vegetables in a separate dish. To serve cold, serve chicken in its jelled sauce.

Makes 4 servings

NOTE: If you prefer browned chicken, brown the pieces first in the oil on all sides, then add remaining ingredients.

CRISP TURKEY SCHNITZEL

One of the most frequently prepared dishes in Israel, whether for fancy weddings or for a quick lunch for the kids, is schnitzel. On an army camping trip to Eilat, a resort town in a beautiful setting on the Red Sea, during my husband's military service, we spent one morning breading schnitzels for about a hundred people—and we still love it!

Unlike the Austrian wiener schnitzel made with veal, in Israel schnitzel is made with turkey or chicken breast and the meat is spiced before being coated. This is my favorite way to prepare turkey breasts, because the lean meat remains juicy and the coating is crisp. For Passover, matzo meal is used instead of the flour and bread crumbs.

As a variation, a friend of mine from Tunisia leaves a little oil in the pan after sautéing the schnitzel, then sautés two chopped garlic cloves and a tablespoon of chopped fresh parsley for a few seconds and pours this sauce over the schnitzels.

1¼ pounds turkey breast slices (about 8 slices), about ¼ inch thick
1½ teaspoons ground cumin
½ teaspoon paprika
½ teaspoon turmeric
½ teaspoon salt
¼ teaspoon ground black pepper
pinch of cayenne pepper
¾ cup unseasoned dry bread crumbs
2 large eggs
⅓ cup vegetable oil
lemon wedges, for serving

If any of the turkey slices is thicker than ¼ inch, pound it between 2 pieces of plastic wrap to an even thickness of ¼ inch, using a flat meat pounder or rolling pin.

Arrange turkey in one layer on plate. Mix cumin, paprika, turmeric, salt, black pepper, and cayenne in a small bowl. Sprinkle 1½ teaspoons spice mixture as evenly as possible over one side of turkey pieces and rub into turkey. Turn pieces over; sprinkle and rub second side with remaining spice mixture.

Preheat oven to 275°F. Spread flour in plate. Spread bread crumbs in second plate. Beat eggs in shallow bowl. Lightly coat a turkey slice with flour on both sides. Tap and shake to remove excess flour. Dip slice in egg. Last dip both sides in bread crumbs so turkey is completely coated; pat and press lightly so crumbs adhere. Repeat with remaining slices. Set pieces side by side on large plate. Handle turkey lightly at all stages so coating does not come off.

Heat oil in heavy large skillet over medium-high heat. Add enough turkey to make one layer and sauté until golden brown on both sides, about 1 minute per side. Turn carefully using 2 wide spatulas. If oil begins to brown, reduce heat to medium. Set turkey slices side by side on an ovenproof platter and keep them warm in oven while sautéing remaining slices. Garnish with lemon wedges and serve hot.

Makes 4 servings

ROAST GOOSE WITH APPLES

Goose is an important bird in Alsace, and Jews there pair it with fruit, as in this recipe, or with sauerkraut. A roast goose makes a festive main course for Hanukkah and for this holiday the best accompaniment is, of course, potato pancakes. Goose fat is prized by Alsatian Jews and can be saved from the roasted bird. Like chicken fat, it is delicious for sautéing, and imparts a wonderful flavor to onions and potatoes.

1 young goose (about 8 to 9 pounds),
   thawed if frozen
salt and freshly ground pepper
5 large tart apples, such as Granny
   Smith
1 medium onion, quartered

3 tablespoons nondairy margarine
¼ cup dry white wine
1½ cups chicken soup or stock,
   preferably homemade (page 347)
1 tablespoon potato starch
3 tablespoons apple juice or water

Preheat oven to 450°F. Remove excess fat from goose. Cut off fatty flap of skin near tail. Prick goose skin a few times with a fork or skewer; do not pierce meat. Season goose inside and outside with salt and pepper. Peel 1 apple and put it and quartered onion inside goose. Put goose on its back on a rack in a roasting pan.

Roast goose for 30 minutes or until it begins to brown. Baste occasionally. Remove fat from pan as it accumulates.

Reduce oven temperature to 350°F. Turn goose over onto its breast and roast 1½ hours. If pan becomes dry, add a little water. Cover goose with foil and continue roasting, removing fat from pan occasionally and basting goose once or twice, about 1 to 1½ more hours. To check whether it is done, pierce thickest part of drumstick deeply with thin knife; juices that run from goose should be pale yellow, and meat should be tender and should no longer look pink.

Meanwhile, peel remaining apples. Core and cut them into eighths. Melt margarine in a large skillet over medium heat. Add apples in batches, and sauté about 5 minutes on each side, or until lightly browned and tender.

When goose is cooked, discard fat from pan. Add wine and ½ cup soup to pan. Bring to a boil, stirring and scraping. (If roasting pan is large, place it over 2 burners.) Strain mixture into a medium saucepan. Add remaining soup and bring to a boil. Season it lightly with salt and pepper, then reduce heat to low. Whisk potato starch with apple juice until smooth, and gradually whisk juice mixture into simmering stock mixture. Remove sauce from heat and taste for seasoning.

Discard onion and apple from inside goose. Carve goose. Reheat sautéed apples and serve with goose. Serve sauce separately.

Makes 6 to 8 servings

SAUTÉED CHICKEN LIVERS WITH RED PEPPERS

Chicken livers with onions are enjoyed by Jews of most origins. According to the Ashkenazic custom, livers must be broiled until done in order to be kosher. Thus after broiling here, the livers should be only briefly sautéed for this dish, just until heated through. In addition to onions, the livers might be sautéed with peppers as in this recipe, or with mushrooms. Serve them on a bed of rice, or serve pasta alongside them.

Like the French, the Jews prize foie gras, or the rich livers of fattened geese or ducks. Israel is now a major exporter of foie gras to France. Israeli chefs have developed a unique foie gras specialty—grilled on skewers, which is very rich, tender, and melts in your mouth. I'm not going to give a recipe for this expensive luxury meat, because if you grill it too long, it falls right into the fire! Instead I suggest you try it at restaurants that specialize in this delicacy; they are located in the Hatikvah section of Tel Aviv, near the large Hatikvah market.

1 pound chicken livers
salt
5 tablespoons vegetable oil
1 large onion, halved and cut into thin slices
1 large red bell pepper, cut into about 2 × ½-inch strips

freshly ground black pepper to taste
pinch of cayenne pepper
½ teaspoon ground cumin
1 tablespoon chopped fresh parsley (optional)
hot cooked rice, for serving (optional)

Preheat broiler with rack about 3 inches from flame. Rinse livers and pat dry on paper towels; cut off any green spots. Put livers on foil in broiler and sprinkle with salt. Broil 3 minutes or until top is light brown. Turn livers over, sprinkle second side with salt, and broil 3 or 4 more minutes or until cooked. Discard juices from foil. Cut livers in half.

Heat 3 tablespoons oil in a large heavy skillet over medium heat. Add onion, bell pepper, salt, and pepper and cook, stirring occasionally, about 15 minutes or until vegetables are very tender and onion is lightly browned. Leave in skillet for reheating.

In another skillet heat remaining 2 tablespoons oil over medium-high heat. Add livers and sprinkle with black pepper, cayenne, and cumin. Toss over heat about 1 minute or until heated through.

Reheat onion mixture. Taste and adjust seasoning. Add livers and heat briefly together. Sprinkle with parsley and serve on heated plates; for a main course, serve on a bed of cooked rice.

Makes 4 main-course or 6 first-course servings

MEDITERRANEAN BEEF STEW WITH CHILIES AND GREEN BEANS

With its selection of jalapeño peppers and Anaheim chilies, this might sound like a Mexican recipe; but hot and mild chilies are often used by Jews from Morocco and other southern Mediterranean countries to flavor beef stews. This version includes potatoes and green and yellow beans to make a complete main course, but you can use either potatoes or beans. Some cooks add turmeric or saffron with the tomatoes to this spicy stew.

Anaheim chilies are long, mild green chilies; if they are not available, substitute a green bell pepper.

2 tablespoons vegetable oil
1 medium onion, halved and sliced thin
2 pounds boneless beef shoulder, excess fat removed, cut into 1-inch cubes
2 green or red Anaheim chilies (also called green chilies), cut into ½-inch dice
2 jalapeño peppers, chopped
1½ teaspoons ground cumin
4 medium garlic cloves, chopped

salt and freshly ground pepper
2 ripe plum tomatoes, diced (optional)
2 tablespoons tomato paste
1 cup water, plus additional as needed
1 pound small or medium boiling potatoes
1 pound green or yellow snap beans, or ½ pound of each
cayenne pepper (optional)
2 tablespoons chopped fresh parsley or coriander (cilantro) (optional)

Heat oil in a large casserole, add onion, and sauté about 7 minutes over medium-low heat. Add beef, both types peppers and cumin, and sauté about 7 minutes, stirring often. Add garlic, salt, pepper, tomatoes, tomato paste, and water. Stir and bring to a boil. Cover and cook over low heat for 1½ hours.

Peel potatoes and cut into chunks about 1 inch thick. Add to stew. If stew appears dry, add about ¼ cup water. Cover and cook 40 minutes or until potatoes are tender.

Meanwhile, remove ends from beans and break them in half. Cook beans in boiling salted water for about 7 minutes or until tender. Rinse with cold water.

When potatoes are tender, add beans to stew and heat gently 2 to 3 minutes to blend flavors. Taste for seasoning, and add cayenne if desired. (Stew can be kept for 2 days in refrigerator. Reheat in covered pan.) Sprinkle with parsley and serve.

Makes 4 servings

JEWISH GOULASH

Although goulash is actually a soup in Hungarian cooking, Jewish cooks prepare goulash as a paprika-flavored beef stew. This became the most common way of making goulash in the United States and Israel. Like many simple recipes, it can be one of the very best. Goulash can be surprisingly spicy, since both sweet and hot paprika are used. If light-green Hungarian peppers, which resemble bell peppers but are slightly longer are available at your market, you can substitute them for the bell peppers in this recipe. Serve the goulash with boiled potatoes, Spaetzle (page 277), noodles, or with plain or toasted egg barley.

3 tablespoons vegetable oil
2 large onions, halved and thinly
  sliced
3 pounds boneless beef chuck, excess
  fat removed, cut into 1-inch cubes
4 teaspoons paprika, preferably good-
  quality Hungarian sweet paprika
salt

½ cup water
5 medium garlic cloves, chopped
¼ teaspoon caraway seeds
freshly ground black pepper
2 medium green bell peppers, diced
2 ripe medium tomatoes (¾ pound to
  1 pound total), peeled and diced
hot paprika or cayenne pepper to taste

Heat oil in a wide saucepan or casserole. Add onions and cook over medium-low heat about 12 minutes or until softened and lightly browned. Remove with slotted spoon. Add meat in batches and sauté over medium heat for about 10 minutes or until meat is lightly browned; remove each batch after browning it.

Return onions and meat to pan. Add paprika, sprinkle lightly with salt, and sauté, stirring, for 5 minutes. Add water, garlic, caraway seeds, and black pepper. Cover and simmer over low heat, stirring occasionally, for 1 hour, adding water in small amounts (about ¼ cup at a time) if pan becomes dry. Add green pepper and tomatoes and simmer 1 hour or until meat is tender when pierced with knife. Add hot paprika or cayenne. Taste and adjust seasoning. Serve hot.

Makes 6 servings

AROMATIC MEAT PATTIES

If you like hamburgers, wait till you try these flavorful patties! Seasoned with thyme, oregano, coriander, and garlic, as well as a hint of cinnamon, they make a good and easy main course. Jews from Tunisia serve them as one of several accompaniments for a couscous feast. The meat mixture is also used as a filling for vegetables.

2 medium onions, minced
1¼ teaspoons salt
4 slices stale white bread
1 pound lean ground beef
2 tablespoons chopped celery leaves
2 tablespoons chopped fresh parsley
3 tablespoons chopped fresh coriander
  (cilantro)
1 teaspoon dried leaf thyme, crumbled

1 teaspoon dried leaf oregano,
  crumbled
½ teaspoon ground cinnamon
½ teaspoon cayenne pepper
1 teaspoon paprika
pinch of freshly ground pepper
3 medium garlic cloves, chopped
2 large eggs
about ¼ cup vegetable oil, for frying

Put onions in a strainer and sprinkle with ½ teaspoon salt. Let stand about 5 minutes, then rinse onions in strainer. Dip each bread slice in a bowl of water to moisten. Add soaked bread to onions and squeeze both dry.

Mix beef with onions, bread, celery leaves, herbs, spices, garlic, and ¾ teaspoon salt. Add eggs. Mix very well with your hands to be sure mixture is evenly combined. Shape mixture in patties, using about ⅓ cup mixture for each. Compact the patties between your hands and flatten them.

Heat vegetable oil in a large heavy skillet over medium-low heat. Add enough patties to make 1 layer and sauté about 5 minutes per side or until cooked through. Fry remaining patties in same way, adding oil to skillet if necessary and heating it before adding more patties. Drain patties on paper towels before serving.

Makes 15 or 16 patties; 6 to 8 servings

NOTE: The technique of salting the onions and rinsing off the salt gives them a more delicate flavor.

SPICY LAMB STEW WITH POTATOES

In the Mediterranean style of cooking, stews simmer very slowly for hours, so the spices penetrate the meat and potatoes and give the sauce a rich flavor. Like many stews, this dish benefits from being prepared a day ahead. Serve a selection of salads before it, such as Fresh and Tangy Carrot Salad (page 174) and any version of eggplant salad.

2 pounds boneless lamb shoulder (see Note)
4 tablespoons vegetable oil
4 medium onions, sliced
2 medium garlic cloves, minced
½ teaspoon paprika

2½ teaspoons ground cumin
1 teaspoon turmeric
salt and freshly ground pepper
about 3 cups water
2 pounds large, firm white-skinned potatoes

Cut off any skin and as much fat as possible from lamb. Cut meat into about 1½-inch cubes. Heat 2 tablespoons oil in a Dutch oven or heavy casserole. Add half the lamb and brown on all sides over medium-high heat. Remove with a slotted spoon. Brown remaining lamb and remove.

Add remaining oil to pan and heat it. Add onions and cook over low heat about 10 minutes or until soft and lightly browned. Add garlic, paprika, 2 teaspoons cumin, and ½ teaspoon turmeric and continue cooking 2 minutes, stirring. Return meat to pan and sprinkle with salt and pepper. Cover and heat 10 minutes, stirring occasionally so meat is coated with onions and spices.

Add enough water to just cover meat and stir. Bring to a boil, cover, and simmer over low heat 1 hour, occasionally skimming fat from surface.

Peel potatoes; keep them in a bowl of cold water until ready to use.

Cut potatoes in 1½-inch chunks and add to stew after 1 hour. Push them down into liquid. They should be barely covered with liquid; if necessary, add a few tablespoons hot water. Add remaining cumin and turmeric and another pinch of salt and pepper. Cover and cook over very low heat for 30 minutes more, stirring occasionally.

Uncover and simmer, skimming occasionally, about 1½ hours more or until meat and potatoes are tender; in spite of the long cooking time, potatoes should not be falling apart. Taste and adjust seasoning. (Stew can be kept, covered, for 2 days in refrigerator; reheat in a covered pan.) Serve in deep dishes.

Makes 6 servings

NOTE: If buying lamb with bone in, buy about 4 pounds; cut meat from bones in large pieces before cutting it into cubes. Add bones to stew with water; remove them before adding potatoes.

BAKED LAMB WITH ORZO

Orzo was once nicknamed for Israel's leader, ''Ben Gurion rice,'' during a recession in the country because this rice-shaped pasta was supplied instead of regular rice, which was scarce. But today orzo is a well-liked accompaniment for lamb, as in this Sephardic-style dish delicately perfumed with cinnamon, oregano, and white wine.

2 to 2½ pounds lamb shoulder chops
   (1 to 1¼ inches thick), trimmed of
   skin and excess fat
3 tablespoons olive oil
1 tablespoon strained fresh lemon juice
salt and freshly ground pepper to taste
¼ teaspoon hot red pepper flakes
   (optional)
1 cup dry white wine
1 small cinnamon stick

1 large onion, halved and sliced thin
2 large garlic cloves, minced
1 cup smooth Basic Tomato Sauce
   (page 348), or from jar
2 teaspoons dried leaf oregano,
   crumbled
2 cups boiling water
1 pound orzo (rice-shaped pasta)
1 tablespoon chopped fresh parsley

Preheat oven to 450°F. Put chops in a 10-cup gratin dish or other large baking dish. Sprinkle lamb with oil, lemon juice, salt, pepper, and red pepper flakes and turn to coat evenly with flavorings. Bake 10 minutes, turning once. Reduce heat to 350°F. Add wine, cinnamon stick, onion, and garlic to pan. Bake about 15 minutes or until meat is still pink, but not red, inside when cut; it will be returned to oven to cook further.

Remove chops and cut meat from bones, keeping meat in large pieces and reserving bones. Reserve meat on plate and cover. Return bones to pan, stir, and return to oven. Bake 25 minutes or until onion is tender. Discard cinnamon stick and bones.

Add tomato sauce, oregano, and boiling water to pan. Season well with salt and pepper. Add pasta and stir. Bake 20 minutes without stirring. Set meat pieces on top in 1 layer and press gently into mixture. Return to oven and bake 10 minutes or until orzo is tender but firm to the bite and meat is done to taste. Sprinkle with parsley. Serve immediately from the dish.

Makes 6 servings

COUSCOUS WITH LAMB AND SEVEN VEGETABLES

This is the time-honored way to prepare couscous, by steaming it several times in a special couscous cooker called a couscoussier, *in which the stew simmers in the pot at the bottom and the couscous cooks in the steamer above it. If you don't have one, you can substitute a vegetable steamer that sits snugly in or above a deep pot, such as the vegetable steamer baskets that come with many pasta pots.*

Steaming is necessary to cook the raw couscous that comes in bulk and that can be purchased at some Middle Eastern stores. Most of the packaged couscous in this country, however, is precooked. It can be steamed as in this recipe but to save time, it can be cooked according to the quick method in Stuffed Chicken with Couscous, Raisins, and Pecans (page 229).

Raisins impart a hint of sweetness to this sumptuous main course, a Moroccan tradition for the Jewish New Year. In some families, a platter with a few of each of the seven "vegetables"— chickpeas, turnips, carrots, onions, zucchini, winter squash, and raisins, all sprinkled with sugar and cinnamon, is set out to begin the Rosh Hashanah meal.

This dish is also prepared with beef. Sometimes chicken pieces are substituted for the meat; in this case the cooking time should be reduced by 30 minutes.

⅔ cup dried chickpeas (garbanzo
   beans), or 1⅓ to 1½ cups canned
3 cups cold water (for dried chickpeas)

salt
1 pound (2½ cups) couscous

Meat Broth

1½ to 2 pounds boneless lamb or beef
   shoulder, excess fat removed
a few lamb or beef bones
2 medium onions, sliced
2 tablespoons vegetable oil

½ cup water
1 teaspoon salt

¼ teaspoon saffron threads
salt and pepper
7 cups water
1 fresh hot pepper, chopped, or 1
   whole dried hot pepper

Seven "Vegetables"

½ pound winter squash, peeled and
   cut into 2-inch chunks
½ pound carrots, halved lengthwise
   and cut into 2-inch pieces
2 medium tomatoes, quartered
1 small turnip, peeled
1 medium onion, quartered

2 celery stalks, cut into 2-inch lengths
½ pound zucchini, cut into 2-inch
   pieces
2 medium garlic cloves, peeled
2 tablespoons chopped fresh coriander
   (cilantro)
⅔ cup dark raisins

¼ to ½ cup vegetable oil or margarine
cinnamon, for garnish

hot pepper sauce, for accompaniment
   (optional)

To prepare dried chickpeas, sort through them, discarding any pebbles or other foreign material; rinse well. Either soak overnight in water to cover generously, or use this quicker method: Put them in a saucepan with 2 cups water and bring to a boil, boil 2 minutes, cover and leave for 1 hour.

Drain soaked chickpeas and place in saucepan. Add 3 cups cold water and bring to a boil. Cover and simmer about 1½ hours, adding hot water occasionally to keep them covered with water. Add a pinch of salt and continue simmering 30 to 45 minutes more or until tender.

Rinse couscous in a bowl and drain in a fine strainer. Transfer to a shallow bowl and rub grains to be sure they are separate. Let dry while preparing meat.

Cut meat into 1½-inch cubes. Put meat and bones in pot of couscous cooker or pot of vegetable steamer and add onions, oil, saffron, salt, and pepper. Cover and heat 5 minutes over low heat, stirring. Add water and hot pepper and bring to a boil.

Put couscous in steamer part of couscous cooker or in a cheesecloth-lined vegetable steamer. Tie a damp towel around base of steamer part of couscous pot so steam won't escape from sides. Steam couscous uncovered above simmering stew for 30 minutes. (If using a vegetable steamer, cover couscous during steaming.)

Remove couscous, put it in a large bowl and let cool. Mix water and salt; then sprinkle couscous lightly with salted water, rubbing and tossing it between your fingers to prevent grains from sticking together.

After meat has simmered 1½ hours, add winter squash, carrots, tomatoes, turnip, onion, celery, zucchini, cooked or canned chickpeas, garlic, and half the coriander. Bring to a boil, then simmer 30 minutes or until meat and vegetables are tender. Simmer raisins separately in about 1 cup broth from the meat for 10 minutes or until tender. Cover and keep them warm.

About 30 minutes before serving (or after meat has simmered 2 hours), put couscous in steamer and set it above simmering broth. Steam uncovered (but cover if using vegetable steamer) about 30 minutes or until steam comes through couscous. Transfer to a large bowl.

Taste meat broth for seasoning. Discard dried hot pepper.

Sprinkle oil over couscous in bowl. Slowly add ¼ cup of meat broth. Mix lightly with a fork or with your fingers.

To serve, pile couscous in a cone shape on a large platter. Decorate by sprinkling cinnamon in a few lines going from top to bottom of cone of couscous, or by spooning raisins on top of and around couscous. Place meat and vegetables on a platter and sprinkle them with remaining coriander. Serve broth from a tureen. Serve in shallow bowls. Accompany with hot pepper sauce.

Makes 5 or 6 servings

VEAL STEW WITH SAFFRON AND CAULIFLOWER

This light, aromatic veal dish is made in the style of Moroccan Jews. Serve it with its traditional accompaniment of couscous, or with rice. A salad of grilled tomatoes and peppers makes a good starter, in keeping with the Mediterranean character of the main course.

large pinch of saffron threads (about ⅛ teaspoon)
¼ cup hot water
3 tablespoons olive oil
2 medium onions, sliced
3 medium garlic cloves, chopped
2 pounds boneless veal shoulder or veal stew meat, cut into 1½-inch pieces
½ teaspoon salt
¼ teaspoon ground pepper
¾ teaspoon ground ginger

2½ to 3 cups water
1 large or 2 small cauliflowers (about 2 pounds), divided into medium florets
2 teaspoons paprika
½ teaspoon ground cumin
1 tablespoon chopped fresh coriander (cilantro)
1 tablespoon chopped fresh parsley
steamed rice or couscous, for accompaniment

Add saffron to hot water and leave to soften for 20 minutes.

Heat oil in a large heavy casserole, add onions and garlic, and cook over low heat, stirring, for 2 minutes. Add veal, salt, pepper, ginger, and saffron in its liquid and mix well. Pour in enough water to barely cover veal, about 2½ to 3 cups. Bring to a boil, cover, and simmer over low heat, stirring occasionally, for 1 hour. (Veal can be kept, covered, for 1 day in refrigerator. Reheat it over low heat, covered.)

In a large saucepan of boiling salted water cook cauliflower, uncovered, for 2 minutes. Drain immediately in a colander.

Stir paprika, cumin, and coriander into stew. Add cauliflower and stir gently; be sure cauliflower stems are immersed in liquid. Cover and simmer over low heat without stirring for 30 minutes, or until veal and cauliflower are tender but cauliflower is not falling apart. Transfer veal and cauliflower with a slotted spoon to a heated plate, leaving most of the onions in casserole. Cover plate and keep veal and cauliflower warm.

Boil cooking liquid, including onions, stirring occasionally, until mixture is reduced to about 1½ cups. Taste for seasoning.

Remove onions from sauce with a slotted spoon and spoon them onto a serving platter. Set veal on top and cauliflower around it, with florets pointing outward. Spoon sauce over veal and cauliflower. Sprinkle with parsley and serve with steamed rice or couscous.

Makes 4 servings

VEAL WITH OLIVES, TOMATOES, AND FRESH HERBS

Olive trees have been prized in Israel since biblical times, and their fruit and its oil are treasured today also. Both enter this flavorful stew, an ideal main course for Succot, when tomatoes are in their prime. SEE PHOTOGRAPH.

2 pounds boneless veal shoulder
2 tablespoons olive oil
1 medium onion, finely chopped
4 large garlic cloves, minced
salt and freshly ground pepper
2 pounds ripe tomatoes, peeled,
   seeded, and chopped; or 2 28-ounce
   cans plum tomatoes,
   drained and chopped

1 tablespoon minced fresh marjoram,
   or 1 teaspoon dried, crumbled
2 teaspoons fresh thyme leaves, or ¾
   teaspoon dried, crumbled
1 cup water
1 bay leaf
1 cup pitted brine-cured black olives,
   drained
2 tablespoons minced fresh parsley
   leaves

Cut veal into 1- to 1¼-inch pieces and pat dry. In a heavy casserole or Dutch oven heat oil over medium-high heat. Add veal in batches and brown lightly on all sides. Transfer veal pieces as they brown to a plate. Add onion to casserole and cook over low heat, stirring often, for 5 minutes or until softened.

Return veal to casserole, reserving any juices on plate. Add garlic and pinch of salt and pepper and cook over low heat, stirring, ½ minute. Stir in tomatoes, marjoram, and thyme and bring to a boil. Add juices from plate, water, and bay leaf and bring again to a boil, stirring. Cover and cook about 1 hour, or until veal is just tender when pierced with a knife.

Remove veal from casserole with a slotted spoon. Boil cooking liquid, stirring, until it is reduced to 2 cups. Drain liquid from meat a few times and add to casserole as liquid reduces. Discard bay leaf.

Return meat to sauce, add olives, and heat over low heat 1 to 2 minutes. (Stew can be kept, covered, for 2 days in refrigerator. Reheat it over low heat, covered.) Remove casserole from heat and sprinkle with parsley. Taste and adjust seasoning. Serve stew from enameled casserole or from a heated deep serving dish.

Makes 4 servings

14

VEGETABLES

 In the area of vegetable cookery, Jewish cooks have made notable contributions in several categories—kugels, latkes, and stuffed vegetables.

For as long as I can remember, kugel has been one of my favorite types of dishes. Kugels are made from vegetables, rice, noodles, or matzo and come in many shapes, colors, and textures. They can be sweet or savory, and can play the role of side dish or dessert. Nearly all are baked. Some kugels are smooth and creamy, almost like a pudding, while others are firm and rather cakelike. Some are served with a spoon; others are cut in squares or slices for serving. Most are served from their baking dish, but some are unmolded like a cake.

Kugels are sometimes translated as soufflés, but they are firmer than the French specialty. Vegetable kugels are often made from single vegetables like carrots or zucchini, or from a mixture of vegetables, as in Cauliflower Kugel with Mushrooms. The most common vegetable kugel is made of potatoes, either grated, as in Passover Potato and Vegetable Kugel (page 22), or mashed, as in Potato Kugel with Asparagus and Broccoli.

Latkes, or pancakes, are also best known when made of potatoes but can be prepared from many other vegetables as well. In fact, my mother taught me to use the same mixtures to either bake as a kugel or to sauté as latkes. Latkes are popular Hanukkah fare; for more information on these delicious pancakes, see Chapter 5, on Hanukkah.

When I lived in Israel, I loved learning to prepare vegetable recipes in the Mediterranean style. Jews from this region brought with them a repertoire of delightful dishes for making good use of zucchini, peppers, leeks, and eggplant, all of which were exotic vegetables to me twenty years ago.

Stuffed vegetables, the most popular of these Sephardic vegetable dishes, are festive fare. Eating the vegetable, stuffing, and sauce together is a gratifying taste sensation. But stuffed vegetables have other advantages as well: they are economical, they can be prepared with easily available ingredients, and they lend themselves to many variations.

Fillings for vegetables, whether for eggplants, zucchini, onions, peppers, celery stalks, or grape leaves, consist generally of rice as the main ingredient, usually combined with beef or lamb. Cooks in Israel add fragrant herbs—always flat-leaved parsley, and sometimes coriander or mint. Spices, especially cinnamon, cumin, turmeric, and plenty of pepper, might also be mixed into the stuffing. For a pleasant flavor and texture contrast, some people throw in a few raisins or sautéed pine nuts, walnuts, or almonds.

Stuffed vegetables are versatile enough to play the role of first course, side dish, or main course, depending on the filling. Most home cooks prepare a generous amount to serve hot one day and cold the next. These vegetables can also be reheated, since they taste best when very tender.

POTATO KUGEL WITH ASPARAGUS AND BROCCOLI

When our good friend, Gregory Dinner, invited us to Thanksgiving dinner one year, I did not expect to eat the best potato kugel I had ever tasted. He gave me the recipe, which he received from his grandmother, Rose Miller. She was born in Denver and still lives there, but her family originally came from Poland. The kugel has become one of the Dinner family's traditional dishes; for them, neither a Passover nor a Thanksgiving would be complete without it. In London, where Gregory now resides, it's not so easy to get schmaltz (rendered chicken fat) for making this kugel, and so he uses a ''vegetarian schmaltz'' made from vegetable fat. Another possibility is preparing your own schmaltz; see page 347.

6 large boiling potatoes (about 2¼ pounds)
salt
¾ pound asparagus, peeled and cut into 1- to 1½-inch pieces
¾ pound broccoli, divided in fairly small florets

7 tablespoons schmaltz (rendered chicken fat), margarine, or butter
3 medium onions, chopped
freshly ground pepper
1 large egg, beaten
½ teaspoon paprika

Put potatoes in a large saucepan with water to cover and a pinch of salt and bring to a boil. Cover and simmer over low heat for 35 to 40 minutes or until very tender. Drain and leave until cool enough to handle.

Boil asparagus in a medium saucepan of boiling salted water to cover for 3 minutes or until tender. Remove asparagus with slotted spoon, rinse with cold water, and drain. Add broccoli to the boiling water and boil, uncovered, for about 4 minutes or until just tender. Rinse with cold water and drain.

In a large skillet heat 4 tablespoons schmaltz, add onions, and sauté over medium heat until golden brown, about 20 minutes. Remove ½ cup sautéed onions for mixing with potatoes. To remaining onions in skillet, add asparagus and broccoli, sprinkle with salt and pepper, and toss over low heat for 2 minutes.

Peel potatoes while still fairly hot. Mash them with a potato masher or food mill, not in a food processor. Add remaining 3 tablespoons schmaltz and stir until melted in. Add beaten egg and reserved ½ cup of fried onion. Add salt and pepper to taste; mixture should be seasoned generously.

In a greased 2-quart casserole, layer half the potato mixture (about 2½ cups), top with all of the asparagus and broccoli mixture, then with remaining potatoes. Smooth top. (Casserole can be covered and refrigerated overnight.)

Preheat oven to 350° F. Sprinkle casserole with paprika and bake, uncovered, for about 50 minutes or until top is firm and light golden at edges. Let stand about 10 minutes before serving. Use a spoon to serve.

Makes 6 servings

CAULIFLOWER KUGEL WITH MUSHROOMS

Vegetables for kugel can be grated, as in Sweet Carrot Kugel (page 253) or Potato and Vegetable Kugel (page 22). Or they can be cooked and pureed, as in this savory cauliflower version, which bears a certain resemblance to a French vegetable timbale mixture but does not contain cream.

The flavoring mixture for this kugel, of sautéed onions and mushrooms seasoned with paprika, is a favorite in the eastern European Jewish kitchen, and is also a delicious addition to cooked rice or pasta or to chicken or meat stews.

1 large cauliflower (2¼ pounds)
salt
4 tablespoons vegetable oil
1 medium onion, chopped
¼ pound medium or small
  mushrooms, quartered

2 large eggs
1 tablespoon matzo meal, or 2
  tablespoons bread crumbs
freshly ground pepper
½ teaspoon paprika
⅓ cup coarsely chopped walnuts
  (optional)

Preheat oven to 375° F. Divide cauliflower into medium florets. Cut peel from large stalk and slice stalk. Boil cauliflower in a large saucepan of boiling salted water for 8 to 10 minutes or until stalks are very tender. Drain well and cool. Puree in food processor, leaving a few chunks. Transfer to a bowl.

Heat 3 tablespoons oil in medium skillet, add onion, and sauté 5 minutes. Add mushrooms and sauté together over medium heat about 5 minutes or until mushrooms and onions are light brown.

Add eggs and matzo meal to cauliflower mixture. Season well with salt and pepper. Lightly stir in mushroom mixture and any oil in pan.

Oil a shallow 8-inch square baking dish. Add cauliflower mixture. Sprinkle 1 tablespoon oil over top and sprinkle with paprika, then with walnuts. Bake 30 minutes or until set. To serve, cut carefully in squares and run knife around edges. Use spoon to remove portions.

Makes 4 to 6 servings

SWEET CARROT KUGEL

Carrots symbolize prosperity because of their golden color and are a favorite for the Rosh Hashanah table, but baked puddings like this are served on a variety of festive occasions. For this kugel the carrots are combined with ground almonds and sweet wine.

3 extra-large eggs, separated
5 tablespoons sugar
4 medium carrots (about 9 ounces total), peeled and grated (about 1⅔ cups)
¼ cup blanched ground almonds
4 tablespoons matzo meal

3 tablespoons all-purpose flour
pinch of salt
1 tablespoon plus 1 teaspoon sweet red wine
2 teaspoons lemon juice
1¾ teaspoons grated lemon rind

Preheat oven to 350° F. Oil a 4- to 5-cup baking dish. Beat egg yolks with 3 tablespoons sugar in a large bowl for about 2 minutes or until thick and light. Stir in grated carrots, almonds, matzo meal, flour, and salt. Add wine, lemon juice, and lemon rind and mix well.

Beat egg whites until stiff but not dry. Add remaining 2 tablespoons sugar and whip at high speed for 30 seconds or until glossy. Fold one-quarter of whites quickly into carrot mixture. Spoon this mixture over remaining whites and fold together quickly but lightly. Transfer to baking dish.

Bake for 35 to 40 minutes or until firm and golden brown. Serve hot or warm.

Makes 4 to 6 servings

BAKED EGGPLANT WITH TOMATOES, CHEESE, AND SESAME SEEDS

Kashkaval cheese, which originated in the Balkans, is a popular partner for eggplant in Israel. In America this cheese is less available, but the dish is also delicious when made with Swiss or gouda cheese.

For this dish the eggplant is layered with sliced tomatoes. The tomatoes are first baked briefly to remove excess juice, which would otherwise make the dish too wet.

1 large eggplant (about 1¼ pounds)
salt
7 tablespoons plus 2 teaspoons mild
  olive oil
1 large onion (about ½ pound), halved
  and thinly sliced
¼ teaspoon dried thyme, crumbled

¼ teaspoon dried oregano, crumbled
freshly ground pepper
¾ pound small ripe tomatoes (about 3
  tomatoes), peeled
1 tablespoon sesame seeds
2 cups (about ½ pound) coarsely
  grated Swiss or kashkaval cheese

Cut peel from eggplant. Cut into ⅜-inch slices crosswise. Sprinkle slices lightly with salt on both sides and put in a colander. Put a bowl with a weight on top and let drain 1 hour, turning slices after 30 minutes. Pat dry with paper towels.

Preheat oven to 425° F. Heat 1 tablespoon oil in a heavy medium skillet over low heat. Add onion, thyme, oregano, and pinch of salt and pepper and cook, stirring often, until very tender and light brown, about 20 minutes.

Cut tomatoes into ¼-inch slices horizontally. Arrange slices in one layer on rack. Carefully poke out seeds, using point of sharp knife. Set rack on a foil-lined baking dish. Sprinkle tomatoes lightly with salt. Bake 10 minutes. Reserve at room temperature. Reduce oven temperature to 400° F.

Toast sesame seeds in a small heavy skillet over medium-low heat, stirring, until light brown, about 2 minutes. Transfer to a small bowl.

Heat 2 tablespoons olive oil in a large heavy skillet over medium heat. Quickly add enough eggplant slices to make 1 layer. (If slices are added too slowly, first ones soak up all of oil.) Sauté until just tender when pierced with fork, about 2 minutes on each side, then remove to plate. Sauté remaining eggplant in 2 batches, heating 2 tablespoons oil in skillet before each batch. (Ingredients can be prepared up to 4 hours ahead up to this point and kept at room temperature.)

Lightly oil a 5-cup gratin dish or other shallow baking dish. Arrange a layer of half the eggplant slices in dish, cutting large ones in half so they fit, and sprinkle with pepper. Spread cooked onion evenly over eggplant. Sprinkle with ½ cup grated cheese. Arrange remaining eggplant on top in 1 layer and sprinkle with pepper. Top with tomatoes in 1 layer. Sprinkle tomatoes with 2 teaspoons olive oil, then with remaining cheese, last with sesame seeds.

Bake until cheese melts, about 15 minutes. Broil until topping browns lightly. Let stand 5 minutes before serving. Serve hot, from baking dish.

Makes 3 main-course or 4 to 6 first-course or side-dish servings

BAKED SWEET POTATOES WITH DRIED FRUIT

This type of colorful dish combining fruit and vegetables is popular for Succot, the festival for giving thanks for an abundance of produce. The dish is garnished with sautéed almonds, but you can substitute toasted almonds or omit them if you prefer. Serve the sweet potato casserole with roast or braised beef or lamb, roast duck, or grilled or roast chicken.

¾ cup pitted prunes
⅔ cup dried apricots
3 tablespoons nondairy margarine, melted
1 large sweet potato (about 1½ pounds)

salt and freshly ground pepper
3 long white boiling potatoes (about 1 pound total)

Honey Glaze

¼ cup honey
2 tablespoons (¼ stick) margarine
½ cup strained fresh orange juice

1 tablespoon strained fresh lemon juice
½ teaspoon ground cinnamon
pinch of ground cloves

2 teaspoons vegetable oil (optional)
¼ cup whole blanched almonds (optional)

Put prunes and apricots in separate bowls and pour boiling water over each. Let soak until nearly tender, prunes about 35 minutes and apricots about 30 minutes.

Preheat oven to 400°F. Pour melted margarine into a 2-quart baking dish. Peel sweet potato, halve lengthwise, and cut into ½-inch slices. Put slices in baking dish, add small pinch of salt and pepper, and toss to coat slices with margarine. Bake, stirring occasionally, until barely tender, about 25 minutes.

Peel white potatoes and cut into ½-inch slices crosswise. Put in medium saucepan with water to cover and pinch of salt. Bring to a boil, cover, and simmer over low heat until barely tender, about 15 minutes. Drain thoroughly.

Combine honey, margarine, orange and lemon juices, cinnamon, and cloves in small saucepan.

Drain prunes and apricots. Add white potatoes, prunes, and apricots to sweet potatoes and mix very gently. Bring glaze to a simmer, stirring, and pour evenly over fruit mixture. Bake, basting twice, for 15 minutes. Remove from oven. Using rubber spatula, stir as gently as possible so ingredients on top go to bottom. Bake, basting 3 times, until most of liquid is absorbed, about 15 minutes. (Dish can be prepared up to 4 hours ahead and kept covered at room temperature. Reheat, covered, in 300°F. oven.)

Heat oil in a heavy medium skillet over medium-low heat. Add almonds and pinch of salt and sauté, tossing them often with slotted spoon, until lightly browned, about 4 minutes. Transfer to plate and reserve at room temperature.

Serve casserole from baking dish. Garnish with almonds.

Makes 4 servings

LEEK FRITTERS

In the Sephardic kitchen, leeks play a major role in a variety of dishes. They are used to flavor soups and frittatas, and are made into fritters, in which the vegetable's taste is intensified from the frying. More substantial fritters are also made in this manner with a combination of leeks and ground beef.

4 pounds leeks, cleaned (page 347)
salt
2 large eggs
¼ cup matzo meal, or more as needed
½ teaspoon dried leaf thyme, crumbled

freshly ground pepper
freshly grated nutmeg to taste
about 5 cups vegetable oil, for frying
lemon wedges, for serving

Cut leeks into about 4-inch pieces. Cook in a large pan of boiling salted water about 10 minutes or until tender. Drain well. Finely chop with a knife; you will have about 4 cups leeks. Drain again in a strainer and squeeze firmly by handfuls to remove excess liquid. Transfer to a bowl. Add eggs, matzo meal, thyme, and salt, pepper, and nutmeg to taste.

Shape mixture into flat cakes, using about 2 tablespoons mixture for each; if mixture won't hold together in cakes, stir in a little more matzo meal, by teaspoons. Put cakes on a plate.

Heat oil in a deep-fat fryer or heavy medium saucepan to 350–360°F. on a deep-fat thermometer, or until oil sizzles vigorously when a small piece of leek mixture is added. Fry leek patties in batches until light golden brown, about 1 to 1½ minutes. Drain on paper towels. Keep fritters warm in a 300°F. oven while frying remaining ones and until ready to serve. Serve with lemon wedges.

Makes 8 servings

SPINACH PANCAKES

These are pretty topped with a dollop of sour cream or yogurt and sprinkled with diced tomato or chives. They can also be served with yogurt-mint topping (see Zucchini Pancakes with Garlic, page 117), or, for a spicy note, with Hot Pepper–Garlic Chutney (page 142).

2¼ pounds fresh spinach, stems removed, leaves rinsed well, or 2 10-ounce packages frozen, thawed
2 tablespoons (¼ stick) butter or margarine
salt and pepper

freshly grated nutmeg to taste
½ cup all-purpose flour
2 large eggs
¼ teaspoon salt
¼ cup vegetable oil, for frying

Cook fresh spinach in a large pan of boiling salted water for 3 minutes or until tender. Rinse with cold water. Squeeze fresh or thawed frozen spinach to remove excess liquid. Chop finely.

Melt butter in a medium skillet over medium heat. Add spinach and cook about 2 minutes, stirring. Season with a pinch of salt, pepper, and nutmeg. Transfer to a large bowl.

In a medium bowl mix flour, eggs, ¼ teaspoon salt, and a pinch of pepper and nutmeg to a very thick batter. Add batter to spinach and mix very well. Taste for seasoning.

Heat oil in a heavy skillet over medium heat. Fry spinach mixture by tablespoonfuls, flattening each after adding it, about 2 minutes or until golden brown on each side. Transfer to paper towels to drain. Serve hot.

Makes 22 to 24 small pancakes; 4 to 6 servings

EASY CAULIFLOWER LATKES

These are good as an appetizer topped with sour cream or Yemenite Tomato Salsa (page 166). I also like them plain as an accompaniment for roast chicken.

1 large cauliflower (about 2 pounds)
salt
6 to 7 tablespoons vegetable oil
1 medium onion, finely chopped

6 tablespoons unseasoned bread crumbs
2 large eggs
freshly ground pepper

Cook cauliflower in a large pan of boiling salted water, uncovered, over high heat for about 12 minutes or until very tender. Meanwhile, heat 2 tablespoons oil in a large heavy skillet, add onion, and cook over medium-low heat about 10 minutes or until soft and golden brown.

Drain cauliflower thoroughly and mash with a fork or chop in a food processor. There should still be pieces but not large ones. Add bread crumbs, eggs, fried onion, and salt and pepper to taste and mix well with a wooden spoon.

Wipe pan used to fry onion, add 4 tablespoons oil, and heat it. Take 1 heaping tablespoon cauliflower mixture in your hand and press to make it compact. Flatten it to a cake about ½ inch thick and add to pan. Make 4 or 5 more cakes and add them. Fry over medium heat about 3 minutes on each side or until brown. Turn carefully using a wide pancake turner. Drain on paper towels. Keep warm by placing in a 300°F. oven with door ajar while frying rest. Add more oil to pan if it becomes dry. Serve plain or with sour cream.

Makes 6 servings

POTATO AND WALNUT FRITTERS

In keeping with the tradition of serving foods fried in oil for Hanukkah, these mashed potato fritters make good appetizers for Hanukkah parties, or crunchy accompaniments for roast or broiled chicken or meat. They can also be served like falafel, with a variety of salads.

2 boiling potatoes (about 9 ounces total)
salt
2 large eggs

½ cup chopped walnuts
freshly ground pepper
5 to 6 cups vegetable oil, for deep-frying

Put potatoes in a saucepan, cover with water, and add salt. Bring to a boil, cover, and simmer about 25 minutes or until tender. Drain, peel, and mash. Mix with eggs and walnuts and season with salt and pepper to taste.

Heat oil for deep frying to 360°F.; if a deep-fat thermometer is not available, test by adding a small piece of potato mixture to oil—it should bubble energetically.

Take a round teaspoonful of potato mixture. Dip another teaspoon into hot oil and use it to push mixture off other spoon into oil. Do not push it from high up or oil will splash. Continue make more fritters from remaining mixture but do not crowd them in oil. Fry 2 to 3 minutes or until golden brown on all sides. Transfer to a tray lined with paper towels. Keep warm by placing in a 300°F. oven with door ajar while frying rest. Serve hot.

Makes about 4 servings

SPICY MEAT-STUFFED PEPPERS

Peppers are the easiest vegetable to stuff because they have a natural cavity for stuffing. Choose peppers that are straight and can stand up easily, since these are baked upright. Although the stuffing uses a familiar base of meat and rice, this Yemenite-style version has a distinctive taste because it is flavored with fresh hot pepper, cumin, and turmeric.

Spicy Meat Stuffing

½ cup long-grain white rice, rinsed and drained
3 cups boiling salted water
2 tablespoons olive or vegetable oil
1 medium onion, finely chopped
½ pound lean ground beef
1 or 2 jalapeño peppers, seeds removed, minced

1 medium garlic clove, minced
2 tablespoons chopped fresh coriander (cilantro) or parsley
½ teaspoon ground cumin
½ teaspoon turmeric
½ teaspoon salt
¼ teaspoon ground pepper

5 or 6 medium red or green bell peppers
1 tablespoon tomato paste

¼ cup water
2 tablespoons olive or vegetable oil

Cook rice in a saucepan of boiling salted water for 10 minutes. Rinse with cold water and drain well.

Heat oil in a skillet, add onion, and cook over low heat until soft but not brown, about 7 minutes. Let cool. Mix with remaining stuffing ingredients and taste for seasoning.

Preheat oven to 350°F. Cut a slice off stem end of peppers. Reserve slice; remove stem, core, and seeds. Spoon stuffing into whole peppers and cover with reserved slices. Stand them in a baking dish in which they just fit. Mix tomato paste with water and spoon mixture over peppers. Sprinkle with oil and bake, uncovered, about 1 hour or until very tender.

Makes 5 or 6 servings

STUFFED EGGPLANT WITH MEAT, PINE NUTS, AND ALMONDS

In Mediterranean countries, eggplant, zucchini, and peppers are the most frequently chosen vegetables for stuffing. A favorite type of stuffing among Jews of the eastern Mediterranean, from Greece to Lebanon, is this one, made with the sautéed flesh of the eggplant, rice, nuts, and meat. In these countries the meat used is likely to be lamb; in Israel it will usually be beef.

2 to 2½ pounds small or 2 medium
   eggplants
salt

Meat Stuffing

½ cup long-grain white rice, rinsed
   and drained
3 cups boiling salted water
2 teaspoons vegetable oil
3 tablespoons pine nuts
3 tablespoons slivered almonds

3 tablespoons olive or vegetable oil
1 to 2 tablespoons tomato paste

3 tablespoons olive oil
1 medium onion, finely chopped
½ pound lean ground beef
2 tablespoons chopped fresh parsley
½ teaspoon salt
½ teaspoon ground pepper

¼ cup water
4 medium garlic cloves, halved

Cut stem ends from eggplants. Halve eggplants lengthwise. Peel if desired; if eggplant is fresh, there is no need to peel it. When they get a bit old, the peel gets tough. Use a spoon to scoop out centers, leaving boat-shaped shells. Set aside centers for use in stuffing. Sprinkle eggplant shells with salt. Put them in a colander upside down and leave to drain for 30 minutes. Preheat oven to 425°F.

Cook rice for stuffing in a saucepan of boiling salted water for 10 minutes. Rinse with cold water and drain well. Transfer to a large bowl.

Heat vegetable oil in a medium skillet, add pine nuts and almonds, and sauté over medium heat about 3 minutes or until lightly browned. Remove with slotted spoon. Add 1 tablespoon olive oil to pan and heat it. Add onion and cook over low heat until soft but not brown. Let cool. Mix with beef, rice, parsley, salt, pepper, and sautéed nuts.

Chop flesh removed from eggplant. Heat 2 tablespoons oil, add chopped eggplant, and sprinkle with salt. Sauté over medium-low heat, stirring often, until tender, about 10 minutes. Leave to cool and mix with stuffing. Taste for seasoning.

Rinse eggplant shells, pat them dry, and put them in a baking dish. Fill them with stuffing. Mix tomato paste with water and spoon mixture over eggplant. Add enough water to dish to cover eggplant by one-third. Add garlic to dish. Spoon remaining tablespoon oil over eggplant, cover, and bake 15 minutes. Reduce oven temperature to 350°F and bake 15 more minutes. Uncover and bake, basting occasionally, 30 minutes or until eggplant is very tender. Serve hot or warm.

Makes 4 to 6 servings

STUFFED EGGPLANT WITH CHICKPEAS AND RICE

Chickpeas, or garbanzo beans, are frequently used by Jews of many different origins because they are satisfying like meat but, of course, they are pareve and thus can be paired with either dairy or meat ingredients. Here they are the basis of a vegetarian stuffing for eggplant. Be sure to choose fairly long, narrow eggplants for this Middle Eastern summer dish, which is served cold. If Japanese eggplants are available, you can use them and shorten the cooking time to a total of 1 hour.

The question of how to cut an eggplant to make room for the stuffing is a subject for debate among cooks. French and Italian cooks halve it lengthwise and scoop out the pulp, leaving boat-shaped shells. In Israel and other parts of the Middle East, another technique is even more popular: hollow out the whole vegetable, to obtain a cylindrical shape, as in this recipe.

2½ pounds small or 2 medium
  eggplants
salt
2 tablespoons olive oil
1 large onion, chopped
pepper
1 medium tomato, peeled, seeded, and
  chopped

½ cup canned chickpeas (garbanzo
  beans)
1 tablespoon chopped fresh parsley
½ teaspoon ground cinnamon
  (optional)
⅓ cup long-grain white rice
2 medium tomatoes, sliced

Leave eggplant peel on or remove it, as desired. Cut a slice from eggplant at stem end and reserve it. With aid of a knife and a spoon, hollow out center, leaving a cylindrical shell and preserving the insides. Sprinkle shell generously with salt. Turn upside down and leave to drain for 30 minutes.

Heat 1 tablespoon oil in a skillet, add onion, and cook over low heat until softened, about 7 minutes. Chop pulp removed from eggplant. Add it to softened onion and season with salt and pepper. Cook, stirring, 5 minutes. Add chopped tomato and cook, stirring, for 5 minutes. Remove from heat and stir in chickpeas, parsley, and cinnamon. Taste for seasoning; mixture should be highly seasoned. Stir in uncooked rice.

Rinse eggplants and pat them dry. Pour remaining 1 tablespoon oil into a saucepan or shallow flameproof casserole in which eggplant can just fit lying down in 1 layer. Add half the tomato slices. Spoon stuffing into eggplants; do not pack it in tightly, as rice needs room to expand. Set eggplants carefully in pan on top of tomato slices; use reserved eggplant slices to block their openings, so stuffing does not come out. Add remaining tomato slices around and on top of eggplants.

Pour in enough boiling water to cover eggplants by about two-thirds. Add salt and cover pan. Simmer eggplant over low heat for 45 minutes. Turn them over as carefully as possible, using 2 wooden spoons. Uncover and simmer another 45 minutes or until very tender.

If sauce is very thin, drain it carefully from pan into a saucepan and boil until reduced by about half. Add salt and pepper to taste. Cool completely. Serve eggplant cold, with a little sauce spooned over each portion.

Makes 4 servings

STUFFED CELERY IN QUICK TOMATO SAUCE

Celery stalks are easy to stuff and, because of their small size, are convenient for serving as either an appetizer or a main course. The sauce is popular among Sephardic Jews and is very flavorful considering how simple it is—it consists of sautéed onion, garlic, tomato paste, and water.

Aromatic Meat Stuffing

1 medium onion, minced
2 slices white bread
½ pound lean ground beef
1 tablespoon chopped celery leaves
1 tablespoon chopped fresh parsley
2 tablespoons chopped fresh coriander
   (cilantro) (optional)
½ teaspoon dried thyme

½ teaspoon dried oregano
¼ teaspoon cayenne pepper
½ teaspoon paprika
freshly ground pepper to taste
1 medium garlic clove, chopped
½ teaspoon salt
1 large egg

6 celery stalks
2 or 3 tablespoons vegetable oil
1 cup chopped onion
4 small garlic cloves, minced

4 teaspoons tomato paste
1½ cups water
salt and freshly ground pepper

Put onion in a strainer and sprinkle lightly with salt. Let stand about 5 minutes. Dip each bread slice in a bowl of water to moisten. Rinse onion in strainer, then add soaked bread to onion and squeeze both dry.

Mix beef with onion, bread, celery leaves, herbs, spices, garlic, and salt. Add egg. Mix very well with your hands to be sure mixture is evenly combined.

Peel celery to remove strings. Cut celery into 3-inch lengths and pat dry. Put meat mixture inside celery pieces, mounding it slightly, and press to adhere well.

Heat oil in a large deep skillet over medium heat. Add stuffed celery, filling side down, and fry 3 minutes. Remove with slotted spatula. Remove all but about 2 tablespoons fat from pan. Add onion and sauté 7 minutes or until beginning to brown. Add garlic and sauté a few seconds. Whisk tomato paste with water and add. Add a little salt and pepper and bring to a simmer. Carefully add celery, stuffing side up. Cover and cook over low heat 30 to 40 minutes, until celery is very tender; add a little water occasionally if sauce becomes too thick. Taste sauce and adjust seasoning. Serve hot or at room temperature.

Makes 4 servings

ASPARAGUS WITH ZEHUG VINAIGRETTE

Israel, like America, is a meeting ground for people from all over the world, and is often the stage for combination, or cross-cultural, cuisine. Here is a typical example: a simple but tasty recipe that I make by flavoring a Provençal-style dressing with the Yemenite pepper-garlic chutney known as Zehug. The asparagus makes a good first course for a Passover meal, and is a reminder that Passover is also a celebration of spring.

1 pound medium asparagus
salt
2 tablespoons olive oil

2 teaspoons Hot Pepper–Garlic
Chutney (page 142)
2 teaspoons strained fresh lemon juice

Peel asparagus by putting it on a board, holding it at the base, and peeling it toward you, turning it after each strip is peeled. Cut off thick bases and rinse asparagus. Put in a medium sauté pan or deep skillet of boiling salted water and cook until just tender, about 5 or 6 minutes.

Meanwhile make dressing. Combine oil, chutney, lemon juice, and a pinch of salt in a small bowl and beat with a fork until blended.

Transfer asparagus carefully to a paper towel-lined plate or tray to drain briefly. Transfer to plates and serve warm, accompanied by dressing.

Makes 2 or 3 servings

ZUCCHINI WITH TOMATOES AND DILL

I like to serve this flavorful, easy-to-make side dish from the Sephardic kitchen for Rosh Hashanah or Succot, when zucchini and tomatoes are at their peak. It tastes good hot or at room temperature and makes a delightful partner for roast or grilled chicken and steamed rice. SEE PHOTOGRAPH.

3 tablespoons olive or vegetable oil
2 medium onions, finely chopped
1½ pounds ripe tomatoes, peeled,
   seeded, and chopped
½ teaspoon sugar
salt and freshly ground pepper

1½ teaspoons paprika
⅓ cup chopped fresh parsley
⅓ cup chopped fresh dill, or 1
   tablespoon dried
2 pounds medium zucchini, sliced
   about ¾ inch thick

Heat oil in a deep skillet or casserole. Add onions and sauté over medium-low heat about 7 minutes or until just beginning to turn golden. Add tomatoes, sugar, salt, pepper, and 1 teaspoon paprika. Reserve 1 tablespoon parsley and 1 tablespoon fresh dill for sprinkling, and add rest of herbs to tomato sauce. Cook, stirring often, over medium-high heat for 7 minutes or until thick.

   Add zucchini to tomato sauce and sprinkle with salt and remaining paprika. Cover and cook over low heat, stirring occasionally, for 30 minutes or until very tender. If pan becomes dry, add a few tablespoons water during cooking. Serve warm, room temperature, or cold, sprinkled with reserved herbs.

Makes 6 servings

NOTE: If you prefer bright-colored zucchini, cook them for only 10 minutes.

GARLIC-SCENTED ROAST POTATOES

This is my aunt's recipe for the perfect accompaniment for brisket, but these tasty crisp-crusted potatoes are wonderful with any roast meat or poultry.

6 tablespoons vegetable oil
2 pounds baking potatoes, peeled and
   quartered
¾ teaspoon salt

3 medium garlic cloves, minced
paprika
2 tablespoons chopped fresh parsley
   (optional)

Preheat oven to 325°F. Pour oil in a baking dish that can hold potatoes in 1 layer. Add potatoes and toss to coat them with oil. Sprinkle evenly with salt and garlic and toss again. Lightly sprinkle with paprika.

Bake potatoes, uncovered, turning them over from time to time, 1¼ to 1½ hours or until they are tender and have a light golden crust. Add oil if pan appears to be getting dry. Sprinkle potatoes with parsley just before serving.

Makes 6 servings

TWO-WAY SWEET AND SOUR CABBAGE

Cabbage is an important ingredient in the Jewish kitchen. I feel that this versatile vegetable has been somewhat overlooked in recent years, and since I like it, I chose it as the subject for my first article for Gourmet *magazine.*

Either red or green cabbage can be used in this dish, a favorite of Russian and central European Jews. Although the cabbage is braised until tender, it cooks for less time than in traditional recipes and thus is in keeping with modern taste. Serve the cabbage with any meats or with roast poultry.

½ large red or green cabbage (about 1¼ pounds), cored and rinsed
1 teaspoon salt
2 tablespoons vegetable oil
½ large or 1 small onion, chopped

¼ cup dark raisins
1 teaspoon sugar
½ cup water
2 to 3 teaspoons lemon juice
freshly ground pepper

Slice cabbage and cut it into strips. In a large bowl, sprinkle cabbage evenly with salt and toss. Let stand for 45 minutes. Squeeze cabbage hard by handfuls to remove excess liquid.

Heat oil in a large casserole, add onion, and cook over low heat, stirring occasionally, for 5 minutes, or until soft and lightly browned. Add cabbage and cook, stirring, for 1 minute. Add raisins, sugar, and water. If using red cabbage, add 3 teaspoons lemon juice now. Bring to a simmer, stirring. Cover and cook over low heat, stirring occasionally, for 20 minutes for green cabbage or 30 minutes for red cabbage, or until very tender.

Uncover and cook cabbage over medium heat, stirring, until liquid evaporates. If using green cabbage, stir in 2 teaspoons lemon juice now or to taste. Add a pinch of pepper and taste for seasoning. Serve hot or cold.

Makes 3 or 4 servings

OKRA WITH TOMATOES AND CORIANDER

This is a typical way of cooking okra in Israel among Jews from Middle Eastern countries, and is my favorite recipe for the vegetable. If you leave the okra pods whole and do not overcook them, they will not be sticky.

2 pounds okra
5 tablespoons olive oil, preferably
  extra-virgin
1 large onion, chopped
5 medium garlic cloves, minced

½ cup chopped fresh coriander
  (cilantro)
2 pounds ripe tomatoes, diced
salt and pepper
cayenne pepper to taste (optional)

Cut off okra stems. In a large, deep skillet or sauté pan, heat 3 tablespoons oil over medium heat and add onion, garlic, and ¼ cup coriander. Sauté, stirring often, until onion begins to turn golden. Add okra and sauté, stirring, 2 minutes.

Add tomatoes, salt, and pepper. Bring to a boil. Cook over medium-low heat for 20 to 30 minutes or until tender. Stir in remaining 2 tablespoons oil and remaining ¼ cup coriander and remove from heat. Add cayenne pepper if desired. Taste and adjust seasoning. Serve hot, lukewarm or cold.

Makes 4 servings

SAUTÉED SPINACH WITH GARLIC

This simple Mediterranean spinach dish can be served hot or at room temperature, and is a good accompaniment for turkey schnitzel or roast chicken.

2½ pounds spinach (about 4 bunches)
salt and freshly ground pepper

¼ cup light olive oil
2 medium garlic cloves, minced

Discard stems from spinach and rinse leaves thoroughly several times by putting them in a sinkful of cold water, lifting them out of water and changing water.

Put spinach in a large saucepan with a pinch of salt and water that clings to leaves. Cover and cook over medium-high heat about 5 minutes or until just tender. Drain thoroughly in a colander.

Combine oil, garlic, and a pinch of salt and pepper in a skillet. Heat over medium heat, stirring often, until garlic is tender and fragrant but not brown. Add spinach and cook, stirring often, until most of liquid evaporates. Taste for seasoning and serve.

Makes 4 servings

EASY CURRIED EGGPLANT

Although this eggplant stew is cooked in the same manner as ratatouille and its other Mediterranean relatives, fresh ginger, coriander, and other Indian spices give it a unique flavor. It is based on a dish I tasted at the home of my relatives from India. Serve it with simple foods such as roast chicken or grilled lamb chops. It is easy to prepare and is good hot or cold.

1 medium eggplant (1 pound 2 ounces)
3 tablespoons vegetable oil
1 medium onion, chopped
1 tablespoon minced, peeled fresh ginger
5 medium garlic cloves, minced
2 teaspoons ground coriander
2 teaspoons ground cumin
½ teaspoon turmeric

⅛ teaspoon cayenne pepper
2 tablespoons chopped fresh coriander (cilantro)
salt to taste
1 pound ripe tomatoes, peeled, seeded, and coarsely chopped; or 1 28-ounce can plum tomatoes, drained and chopped
2 teaspoons tomato paste
2 tablespoons water

Cut eggplant into 1 × 1 × ¾-inch dice. In a heavy 4- or 4 ½-quart casserole, heat oil, add onion and ginger, and cook over low heat for 7 minutes, or until they are soft but not brown. Add garlic, ground coriander, cumin, turmeric, cayenne, and 1 tablespoon fresh coriander. Cook mixture, stirring, for 1 minute.

Add eggplant and salt and mix well over low heat until eggplant is coated with spices. Add tomatoes and cook mixture over high heat, stirring, until juice flows from tomatoes and begins to boil. Mix tomato paste with water, add to eggplant mixture, and bring to a boil, stirring. Cover and simmer over low heat, stirring often, for 40 minutes, or until eggplant is very tender and mixture is thick. Taste for seasoning. (Stew can be kept, covered, for 3 days in refrigerator.) Serve hot or cold, sprinkled with remaining tablespoon of fresh coriander.

Makes 4 servings

15

NOODLES, RICE, AND OTHER GRAINS

A golden kugel, or casserole, of baked noodles was the dish I looked forward to most every Friday night ever since I was a child. As an accompaniment for the Sabbath roast chicken, my mother's recipe calls for egg noodles of medium width mixed with either sautéed mushrooms and onions for a savory kugel, or with sliced apples and cinnamon for a slightly sweet version. For dairy meals she makes kugel by a similar method, but generally stirs in sour cream and occasionally cottage cheese.

Noodle kugels are very easy to prepare, since the pasta is simply mixed with eggs, seasonings, and other ingredients and then baked. They can be made with cooked broccoli, peppers, or mixed vegetables; or for the sweet version, with a variety of fresh or dried fruits, such as pears, apricots, and raisins.

In the Jewish kitchen, pasta is also prepared in other ways besides kugel. It is served with sauce, as in Pasta Shells with Tunisian Artichoke Meat Sauce, or as an accompaniment for stews like Hungarian goulash. Egg barley, sometimes called farfel, is a very small type of pasta that is usually tossed with fried onions and served as a side dish with roast chicken or stewed meats.

269

Couscous is the "pasta" of Jews from Morocco, Algeria, and Tunisia and is often the focus of the Friday night family dinner. Although couscous comes in tiny particles and looks like a grain, it is made of semolina and water, like pasta. Ninette Bachar from Tunisia, who is the next-door neighbor of my in-laws in the Tel Aviv suburb of Givatayim, taught me how to steam it the traditional way. She showed me how to moisten the couscous, then to steam it several times above a simmering lamb stew in the top part of a special small-holed steamer called a *couscoussier*. After each steaming she removed the couscous and rubbed it between her fingers to ensure that the grains remained separate.

When prepared this way, the light golden couscous is the center for a grand dinner, also called a "couscous," in which the grain is accompanied by lamb stew, by Aromatic Meat Patties (page 241), or by a lavish assortment of stuffed vegetables. When served like this, couscous is truly a feast, but it can be enjoyed for casual meals as well, because it is widely available in quick-cooking versions.

Rice is at least as important in the Jewish diet as pasta, especially among Sephardim. A stroll in the central Jerusalem market of Mahane Yehuda reveals the grain's importance for the Israeli menu. There are enormous sacks of various types of rice from different parts of the world—basmati rice from India and Persian rice from Isfahan, for example.

As a simple accompaniment, rice is most often cooked in Israel in one of three basic ways: white rice, yellow rice, and red rice. All three are usually versions of pilaf, for which the rice is lightly sautéed before the liquid is added. Yellow rice is flavored with cumin and turmeric (or occasionally saffron), and the red version contains tomato. For special occasions, rice might be garnished with nuts and raisins. Rice accompanies chicken, meats, and fish, whether these are grilled, roasted, or stewed. Even vegetables are served with rice for a vegetarian meal, especially if these are "saucy" vegetables such as Sautéed Eggplant in Spicy Tomato Sauce (page 93).

Bulgur wheat, also called cracked wheat, is another popular grain among Middle Eastern Jews. Like rice, it is cooked as pilaf to accompany meats, but also is the basis for other specialties, like the meat-filled pastry known as Kubeh (page 157) and the tangy salad called Tabbouleh (page 180).

Buckwheat, or kasha, is a favorite among Russian and Polish Jews as an accompaniment for meat and as a filling for pastries, especially knishes. Barley is used most often in soups, and whole wheat berries are a frequent addition to the slowly simmered stew known as Hamin (page 144).

NOODLE KUGEL WITH ONIONS AND MUSHROOMS

Our family has always loved noodle kugels with mushrooms, and so my mother prepares them in several versions. This rich kugel, which is flavored with cottage cheese and sour cream, is best as a main course for a vegetarian or dairy supper; a supper menu we like combines this kugel with side dishes of steamed asparagus and Israeli diced vegetable salad. For serving with poultry or meat, simply omit the dairy products and use oil or margarine for sautéing the onions and mushrooms. Actually, for meat meals, chicken fat would have been the traditional choice for sautéing among Ashkenazic Jews, but today in Israel many time-honored dishes like this one are made in lighter versions.

7 or 8 ounces medium egg noodles
5 tablespoons butter, margarine, or
   vegetable oil
1 large onion, chopped
1 pound small button mushrooms,
   quartered
salt and freshly ground pepper to taste
2 medium garlic cloves, minced

1½ teaspoons paprika
2 large eggs, beaten
1 cup cream-style cottage cheese
½ cup sour cream
¼ cup snipped fresh dill, or 1
   tablespoon dried
¼ teaspoon cayenne pepper, or to taste

Preheat oven to 350°F. Cook noodles, uncovered, in a large pot of boiling salted water over high heat for about 4 minutes or until nearly tender but firmer than usual. Drain, rinse with cold water, and drain again. Transfer to a large bowl.

Heat 4 tablespoons butter or oil in a large skillet over medium-low heat. Add onion and sauté about 12 minutes or until very tender. Add mushrooms, salt, pepper, garlic, and 1 teaspoon paprika and sauté about 12 minutes or until mushrooms are tender and onion is browned. If liquid remains in pan, cook over high heat, stirring, a few minutes until it evaporates. Cool slightly.

Add eggs, cottage cheese, sour cream, dill, and cayenne to noodles and mix well. Stir in mushroom mixture. Taste and adjust seasoning; mixture should be seasoned generously. Butter or oil a 2-quart baking dish and add noodle mixture. Sprinkle with remaining tablespoon oil or dot with butter, then dust with remaining paprika. Bake, uncovered, for 1 hour or until set. Serve from baking dish.

Makes 4 or 5 main-course or 6 to 8 side-dish servings

MACARONI AND VEGETABLE KUGEL WITH CHEESE

This light-textured macaroni casserole with red bell peppers, zucchini, and onions is a good choice for Shavuot or for any occasion when you would like a meatless main course.

2 medium red bell peppers or fresh
    pimientos, or 1 red and 1 green bell
    pepper
¼ cup (½ stick) butter
1 medium onion, minced
2 celery stalks, cut in thin slices
2 medium zucchini, coarsely grated
salt and freshly ground pepper to taste
2 cups (about 8 ounces) small elbow
    macaroni

3 large eggs
⅔ cup cream-style cottage cheese
¼ cup sour cream
1 teaspoon dried leaf thyme, crumbled
¾ teaspoon paprika
¼ teaspoon Tabasco or other hot sauce
2 tablespoons grated parmesan, or ¼
    cup grated Swiss cheese (optional)

Preheat oven to 400°F. Cut peppers or pimiento in small dice. Melt butter in a large skillet over medium heat. Add onion and sauté 5 minutes. Add celery and sauté 5 minutes. Add peppers and sauté 3 minutes. Add zucchini, salt, and pepper, stir, and sauté over high heat about 3 minutes or until all vegetables are just tender.

Cook macaroni, uncovered, in a large pot of boiling salted water over high heat, stirring occasionally, about 5 minutes or until nearly tender but firmer than usual. Drain, rinse with cold water, and drain well. Transfer to a large bowl.

Whisk eggs until just blended. Whisk in cottage cheese and sour cream. Stir in thyme, ¼ teaspoon paprika, and hot sauce. Add mixture to macaroni and toss. Add vegetables and toss. Taste and adjust seasoning; mixture should be generously seasoned.

Transfer to a buttered shallow 6-cup baking dish. Sprinkle with grated cheese and remaining ½ teaspoon paprika. Bake 25 minutes or until firm. Let stand 5 minutes before serving. Serve from baking dish.

Makes 4 main-course or 6 side-dish servings

PASTA SHELLS WITH TUNISIAN ARTICHOKE MEAT SAUCE

Jews from North Africa often make use of artichokes. They might be baked with a meat stuffing, added to a stew like Msouki (page 48), or simmered in a sauce for pasta like this one. Here artichoke hearts are combined with mushrooms, capers, and a generous amount of garlic, to give this "spaghetti sauce" its Mediterranean character. Shells are a wonderful pasta shape for serving with ground meat sauces because the meat lodges inside them.

5 tablespoons olive oil
12 medium garlic cloves, minced
1 pound lean ground beef
1½ pounds ripe tomatoes, peeled, seeded, chopped; or 1 28-ounce and 1 14-ounce can plum tomatoes, drained
1 bay leaf
salt and freshly ground pepper to taste
¼ cup tomato paste
¼ cup water

8 ounces small button mushrooms, quartered
1 3¼-ounce jar capers, lightly rinsed (5 tablespoons)
4 fresh artichokes or 16 frozen artichoke heart pieces
1 lemon
1 pound medium pasta shells
2 tablespoons chopped fresh parsley leaves

Heat 3 tablespoons oil in a heavy casserole over low heat. Add 1 tablespoon garlic and cook over low heat ½ minute, stirring. Add beef and sauté over medium heat, crumbling with a wooden spoon, until it changes color. Add tomatoes, bay leaf, salt, and pepper and bring to a boil, stirring (and crushing canned tomatoes, if using). Add tomato paste and water, stir, and bring to a boil. Simmer, uncovered, over low heat, stirring occasionally, for 30 minutes. Add mushrooms and 3 tablespoons capers. Cover and simmer about 15 minutes or until mushrooms are tender and sauce is thick.

If using fresh artichokes, squeeze juice of ½ lemon into a medium bowl of cold water. Prepare artichoke hearts, cook them, and remove chokes (see page 346). If using frozen artichokes, cook them in a medium saucepan of boiling salted water with 1 teaspoon lemon juice for about 7 minutes. Cut each fresh artichoke into 8 pieces. If frozen artichoke pieces are large, cut them in half.

Discard bay leaf from beef sauce. Add remaining garlic and cook over low heat for 2 minutes. Add artichokes and reheat. Taste and adjust seasoning; sauce should be quite highly seasoned to balance sharpness of capers. (Sauce can be kept, covered, up to 2 days in refrigerator. Reheat it over low heat, covered.)

Cook pasta, uncovered, in a large pot of boiling salted water over high heat, stirring occasionally, for 5 to 8 minutes or until tender but firm to the bite. Drain well and transfer to a large heated bowl. Toss with remaining 2 tablespoons oil. Add sauce and 1 tablespoon capers and toss. Taste and adjust seasoning. Sprinkle with parsley and remaining tablespoon capers.

Makes 6 main-course servings

NOODLES WITH SAUTÉED CABBAGE AND ONIONS (CABBAGE PLETZLACH)

In this Hungarian-Jewish recipe, the cabbage takes on a slightly sweet taste from slow cooking with fried onions. A combination of oil and margarine is a frequent choice for sautéing today, both for reasons of nutrition and so the dish can be served with either dairy foods or meat. Occasionally chicken or goose fat is used, when the noodles will be served with meats or poultry. Butter is preferred by some cooks when they are serving the dish with fish or in a dairy meal.

½ large green cabbage (1½ pounds),
  cored and rinsed
1 teaspoon salt
4 tablespoons vegetable oil and 2
  tablespoons (¼ stick) margarine; or
  6 tablespoons (¾ stick) butter or
  chicken fat

½ large onion, minced (about ¾ cup)
½ teaspoon sugar
freshly ground pepper
1⅓ cups broad egg noodles

Shred cabbage with a knife. In a large bowl, sprinkle cabbage evenly with salt and toss. Let stand for 45 minutes. Squeeze cabbage by handfuls to remove excess liquid.

Heat 4 tablespoons oil in a large skillet, add onion, and sauté over medium heat for 5 minutes, or until beginning to soften. Add cabbage, sugar, and pepper to taste and mix well. Cover and cook over low heat, stirring often, for 30 minutes or until very tender. Uncover and cook over medium-high heat, stirring, until lightly browned.

In a large pan of boiling salted water cook noodles for 7 minutes, or until just tender. Drain thoroughly and add to cabbage. Add 2 tablespoons margarine. Toss over low heat just until mixed. Taste for seasoning. Transfer to a heated serving dish.

Makes 4 side-dish servings

ITALIAN-JEWISH COLD NOODLES WITH TOMATOES AND PARSLEY

This recipe is based on a dish I read about in La cucina nella tradizione ebraica, *a Jewish cookbook from Italy. There the pasta was combined with a cooked tomato sauce and served cold; for this version, I have used an uncooked sauce instead. Because of the prohibition against cooking during the Sabbath, it makes sense that the pasta would be cooked ahead and served cold. Who knows? This may have been the origin of the pasta salad!* SEE PHOTOGRAPH.

8 ounces small ripe plum tomatoes, cut into small dice

3 to 4 tablespoons virgin or extra-virgin olive oil

1 jalapeño pepper, seeds and ribs removed, minced; or ¼ teaspoon hot pepper sauce

1 small garlic clove, minced

2 tablespoons chopped fresh Italian or curly parsley

salt and freshly ground pepper to taste

½ teaspoon dried leaf oregano, crumbled

8 ounces medium noodles or bowtie pasta

parsley sprigs, for garnish

In a large bowl combine tomatoes, 3 tablespoons oil, jalapeño pepper, garlic, parsley, salt, pepper, and oregano. If possible, let stand 1 or 2 hours at room temperature.

Cook pasta, uncovered, in a large pot of boiling salted water over high heat, stirring occasionally, for 5 to 8 minutes or until tender but firm to bite. Drain well and add to tomato mixture. Mix well, taste, and adjust seasoning; add more olive oil if desired. Garnish with parsley sprigs. Serve at cool room temperature.

Makes 4 first-course servings

EGG NOODLES FOR SOUP

Clear chicken soup (page 347) with homemade noodles is a treasured specialty. In some eastern European Jewish communities, a young woman's ability to roll noodle dough very thin was a sign that she was fit to be a good wife. Thanks to pasta machines, today it's easy for everyone to roll the dough and so people have to use new standards of suitability for marriage!

1½ cups all-purpose flour
2 large eggs
¼ teaspoon salt

1 to 5 teaspoons water, if needed
a little flour, if needed

Combine flour, eggs, and salt in food processor. Process until ingredients are well blended and dough holds together in sticky crumbs that can be easily pressed together, about 10 seconds. If crumbs are dry, sprinkle with water, about 1 teaspoon at a time, processing about 5 seconds after each addition, adding enough to obtain moist crumbs. Press dough together to a ball. Transfer to a work surface and knead a few seconds, flouring lightly if dough sticks to surface, until it is fairly smooth.

Wrap dough in plastic wrap or set it on a plate and cover with an inverted bowl. Let stand 30 minutes. (Dough can be kept up to 4 hours in refrigerator; let stand about 30 minutes to come back to room temperature before using.)

Generously flour 2 or 3 baking sheets. Turn smooth rollers of a pasta machine to widest setting.

Cut dough into 4 pieces; leave 3 pieces wrapped or covered. Flatten 1 piece of dough in a 4-inch square and lightly flour it. Run it through rollers of machine at widest setting. Fold in thirds so ends meet in center, press seams together, and flatten slightly. Run dough through rollers again. Repeat folding and rolling, lightly flouring only when necessary to prevent sticking, until dough is smooth, about 7 more times. Turn dial of machine 1 notch to next setting. Without folding piece of dough, run it through machine. Continue to feed dough through rollers without folding, turning dial 1 notch lower each time; dust with flour as necessary and cut dough in half crosswise if it gets too long to handle. Stop when dough is 1/16 inch thick (generally this is on next to narrowest setting).

Hang dough sheet to dry on a pasta rack or on back of a towel-lined chair. Repeat with remaining dough. Dry dough sheets about 10 minutes or until they are firmer and have a leathery texture but not until they are brittle.

To cut noodles, move the adjustment of pasta machine to narrow noodle setting. Put each sheet of pasta through machine, holding it with 1 hand and catching pasta with other hand. If strands stick together while being cut, dough is too wet; dry remaining dough sheets a bit longer before cutting them. Separate the strands.

Let noodles dry on a pasta rack or on a floured baking sheet for at least 10 minutes, if using immediately, or up to several hours. Gently toss the noodles that are on baking sheets occasionally to prevent sticking. (Noodles can be refrigerated, covered loosely, on tray; or can be gently put in plastic bags. They will keep up to 5 days in refrigerator; they can also be frozen.)

For serving in a clear soup, the noodles are usually cooked in boiling salted water, then are drained and added to the soup. Instead of being served in soup, they can be tossed with olive oil, melted butter, sautéed onions, or sautéed onions with mushrooms and served as a side dish. Or they can be used in any recipe that calls for noodles.

Makes about 9 or 10 ounces fresh noodles

NOTE: To make dough by hand instead of in a food processor, mound flour on work surface or in a large bowl. Make a well in center. Add eggs and salt to well and blend with fork.

Gradually draw flour from inner edge of well into center, first with fork, then with your fingers, until all the flour is incorporated. Add water by teaspoons if flour cannot be incorporated; dough will be very stiff and dry but will soften during kneading. Knead dough on a clean work surface, flouring only if dough is sticky, for about 5 minutes or until fairly smooth and pliable. Let stand 1 hour before using.

SPAETZLE

Whether served in soup or tossed with sautéed onions as a side dish, spaetzle, a cross between a dumpling and a noodle, are a favorite dish among Jews from Alsace, Germany, and Hungary. If you like, instead of adding these to a pan of melted butter or margarine, add them to a sautéed mushroom mixture, as in Noodle Kugel with Onions and Mushrooms (page 271).

1½ cups all-purpose flour
½ teaspoon salt
2 large eggs
¼ cup water

¼ cup milk or additional water
4 tablespoons (½ stick) butter or
    margarine, melted
freshly ground white pepper (optional)

Mix flour and salt in a large bowl and make a well in center. Add eggs, water, and milk to well and whisk to combine. Draw in flour with a wooden spoon and beat just until smooth; batter will be quite thick. Let rest 15 minutes. Put melted butter in an ovenproof serving dish.

Bring a medium saucepan of salted water to a simmer. Use a colander or flat grater to make spaetzle; if using grater, set it on pan so it is easier to handle. Using a rubber spatula, push 2 to 3 tablespoons dough through holes of colander or large holes of grater so that dough falls in small pieces into water; move spatula back and forth to push dough through holes. Move colander or grater so all of dough does not fall in same place. Continue to make spaetzle until about one-fourth of the dough is used.

After spaetzle float to top of pan, cook them over medium heat about 2 minutes or until no longer doughy; taste to check. Remove with slotted spoon, drain well, and transfer to dish of melted butter. Keep warm in 200°F. oven while cooking remaining spaetzle, in batches. If desired, sprinkle spaetzle lightly with salt and white pepper before serving. (Spaetzle can be refrigerated after being tossed with butter. Reheat, covered, at 350°F; gently stir 2 or 3 times.)

Makes 4 side-dish servings

AROMATIC YELLOW RICE

Turmeric and cumin give this rice dish its bright color and zesty flavor. It is frequently prepared in Israel by Jews of Kurdish, Yemenite, and other Middle Eastern origins and by Jews from India, and is a perfect accompaniment for broiled fish, meat, or poultry. SEE PHOTOGRAPH.

1 tablespoon vegetable oil	1 cup long-grain white rice
1 medium onion, thinly sliced	2 cups hot water
1 teaspoon ground cumin	salt and freshly ground pepper
½ teaspoon turmeric	

Heat oil in a medium saucepan. Add onion and cook over low heat, stirring occasionally, until soft but not brown. Stir in cumin and turmeric and cook another minute, stirring. Add rice and sauté 2 minutes, stirring.

Add water, salt, and pepper and bring to a boil. Stir once with a fork and cover. Cook over low heat, without stirring, for 18 to 20 minutes or until rice is tender and liquid is absorbed. Remove from heat and let stand, covered, for 10 minutes. Taste and adjust seasoning. (Rice will keep hot about 45 minutes. It can be prepared 2 days ahead and kept, covered, in refrigerator. To reheat, heat 1 tablespoon oil in a large skillet, add rice and heat over low heat, stirring gently with a fork.) Fluff it with a fork just before serving. Serve hot.

Makes 3 or 4 side-dish servings

SAVORY LENTILS WITH RICE (MAJADRAH)

Lentils have been served in the Middle East ever since Esau sold his birthright to Jacob for a bowl of lentil stew. Majadrah, or lentil and rice stew, used to be considered part of poor people's cuisine among the Jews of Lebanon, said Suzanne Elmaleh of Jerusalem, who taught me how to prepare it. Today in Israel the dish has become very fashionable, not only because it tastes good but also for nutritional considerations, since it makes a healthful vegetarian dish. Its flavor depends on thoroughly sautéed, deeply browned onions. Some cooks add a teaspoon of cumin to the onions.

The classic way to prepare the stew is to use twice as much rice as lentils and to garnish it with crisp, deep-fried chopped onions, but today many people prefer to use equal portions of lentils and rice, as below. The favorite partner to serve alongside the hot lentil stew is a refreshing Cucumber Salad with Yogurt and Mint (see page 175).

1 cup lentils
2 cups water
⅓ cup vegetable oil

2 large onions, chopped
1 cup long-grain white rice
salt and freshly ground pepper

Combine lentils and water in a medium saucepan. Bring to a boil, cover, and cook over medium heat about 20 minutes or until lentils are just tender. Drain liquid into a measuring cup and add enough water to make 2 cups; reserve.

In a heavy skillet heat oil over medium heat. Add onions and sauté, stirring occasionally, until they are well browned, about 15 minutes. Add onions and their oil to pan of lentils. Add measured liquid and bring to a boil. Add salt and rice and return to a boil. Cover, reduce heat to low, and cook, without stirring, until rice is tender, about 20 minutes. Taste and adjust seasoning, adding pepper to taste. Serve hot.

Makes 2 or 3 main-course or 4 or 5 side-dish servings

NOTE: If you wish to double the rice, as in the classic version, add enough water to lentil cooking liquid to make 4 cups.

AVOCADO-ALMOND RICE

Rice with a garnish of toasted nuts is a Sephardic dish for festive occasions. This colorful version also features roasted red bell peppers as well as avocado cubes, and can play the double role of hot dish or salad. A major crop in Israel, avocado from the Jewish state is exported in large quantities to Europe. SEE PHOTOGRAPH.

2 tablespoons (¼ stick) unsalted
  butter, margarine, olive oil, or
  avocado oil
½ cup minced onion
1 cup long-grain white rice
2 cups hot water
1 bay leaf
¼ teaspoon salt
freshly ground pepper

1 medium red bell pepper, roasted and
  peeled (page 346)
1 large ripe avocado (10 or 11 ounces),
  preferably Haas
1½ teaspoons fresh thyme leaves, or ½
  teaspoon crumbled dried
2 tablespoons plus 2 teaspoons olive
  oil
⅓ cup whole or chopped toasted
  almonds

In a heavy medium saucepan, melt butter over low heat. Add onion and cook, stirring, for 7 minutes, or until softened. Add rice and sauté over medium heat, stirring, for 2 minutes. Add hot water and stir once. Add bay leaf, salt, and a pinch of ground pepper. Bring to a boil, cover, and simmer rice over low heat, without stirring, for 18 to 20 minutes or until it is tender and liquid is absorbed.

Discard bay leaf. Dice bell pepper. A short time before serving, peel, pit, and dice avocado. Add thyme, red pepper, oil, and avocado to rice and stir gently with a fork. Gently stir in about half the toasted almonds. Taste rice, adjust seasoning, and transfer rice gently to a serving dish. Sprinkle with remaining almonds.

Makes 4 side-dish servings

SPICY COUSCOUS WITH GARLIC

Among Jews from Tunisia, this dish is sometimes called "Sunday couscous" because it is the way families makes good use of leftover steamed couscous from Shabbat. The recipe is a terrific way to turn instant couscous into a zesty side dish in just a few minutes. The Tunisians use ground caraway seeds, but I have substituted whole ones since they are much easier to find in the United States. This dish is good with either regular or whole wheat couscous.

2 tablespoons Hot Pepper–Garlic
   Chutney (page 142), or 1½
   teaspoons bottled hot pepper sauce,
   or to taste
3 to 4 tablespoons olive oil, preferably
   extra-virgin
½ teaspoon caraway seeds

3 or 4 medium cloves garlic, very
   finely minced
1 teaspoon paprika
salt and freshly ground pepper
2 tablespoons water
1 cup precooked couscous

In a bowl, whisk together chutney, 3 tablespoons olive oil, caraway seeds, garlic, paprika, salt, pepper, and water.

Cook couscous according to package directions. Add sauce to couscous and mix gently. Taste, adjust seasoning, and add remaining tablespoon oil if desired. Serve hot.

Makes 2 or 3 side-dish servings

COLORFUL VEGETABLE COUSCOUS

For this North African Jewish dish, which can be a side dish or a vegetarian main course, the vegetables can be varied according to the seasons. Use as many or as few varieties of vegetables as you like.

⅔ cup dried chickpeas (garbanzo beans), or a 15- to 16-ounce can
5 cups water (for dried chickpeas)
salt
3 tablespoons olive oil
2 large onions, sliced
1 teaspoon ground cumin

2 garlic cloves, chopped
freshly ground pepper
2 medium carrots, peeled and sliced
2 small tomatoes, cored and quartered
½ pound zucchini, cut into thick slices
1 or 2 teaspoons tomato paste

Quick Couscous

⅓ cup olive oil or butter
2 cups precooked couscous
½ teaspoon salt
pinch of pepper

pinch of nutmeg
pinch of ground cloves
1½ cups broth from vegetables
hot pepper sauce, for serving

To prepare dried chickpeas, sort through them, discarding any pebbles or other foreign material; rinse thoroughly. Put them in a saucepan with 2 cups water and bring to a boil. Boil 2 minutes; cover and let stand 1 hour. Drain thoroughly. Return to saucepan. Add 3 cups cold water and bring to a boil. Cover and simmer about 1½ hours, adding hot water occasionally to keep them covered with water. Add a pinch of salt and continue simmering 30 to 45 minutes or until tender. If using canned chickpeas, discard liquid, rinse chickpeas, and drain.

Heat oil in a very large skillet over low heat. Add onions and cook, stirring, until soft but not browned. Add cumin and garlic and sauté ½ minute. Add chickpea liquid or water, salt, and pepper and bring to a boil. Cover and simmer 15 minutes. Add carrots and simmer 15 minutes. Add tomatoes, zucchini, and chickpeas. Cover and simmer 15 minutes. Uncover and simmer 5 minutes more.

Remove vegetables with a slotted spoon and reserve. Reserve 1½ cups vegetable broth for cooking couscous and keep it warm. Boil remaining vegetable broth, stirring often, for about 5 minutes to concentrate its flavor. Whisk in tomato paste and taste for seasoning.

In a medium saucepan combine reserved vegetable broth and 2 tablespoons olive oil or butter. Bring to a boil. Stir in couscous, salt, pepper, nutmeg, and cloves. Cover pan immediately and let stand, off heat, for 5 minutes. Pour remaining olive oil over couscous or cut remaining butter in small pieces and scatter over couscous. Cover and let stand 1 minute.

Fluff couscous with a fork to break up any lumps, tossing it until oil or butter is absorbed. Taste and adjust seasoning. Cover to keep it warm.

To serve, pile couscous in a cone shape on a large platter. Spoon some of the vegetables around sides and serve remaining vegetables and broth from a bowl or tureen. Serve in shallow bowls, so that each person can moisten his or her couscous with broth to taste. Accompany with hot pepper sauce.

Makes 4 main-course or 6 side-dish servings

COUSCOUS WITH RAISINS AND DATES

This buttery version of couscous is a great dairy dish for the holiday of Shavuot. After I tasted this specialty at a couscous restaurant in Paris, I kept coming back and ordering it. It makes a delicious brunch treat, and is also good for breakfast or dessert.

The method given in the recipe is for raw couscous, which can be purchased in bulk at some Middle Eastern stores. If you are using packaged precooked couscous, cook the couscous according to the package instructions, adding the dates after the water.

1 pound (2½ cups) couscous	1 cup dark raisins
½ cup water	⅔ cup butter, at room temperature, cut
½ teaspoon salt	into pieces
1½ cups dates	2 cups hot milk

Fill a couscous pot or base of a steamer about two-thirds full of water and bring to a boil. Meanwhile, rinse couscous in a bowl and drain in a fine strainer. Transfer to a shallow bowl and rub grains to be sure they are separate. Leave to dry about 10 minutes.

Put couscous in steamer part of couscous pot. Tie a damp towel around base of steamer part so steam won't escape from sides. Steam couscous uncovered above boiling water for 30 minutes.

Remove couscous, put it in a large bowl, and let cool. Mix water and salt. Sprinkle couscous lightly with salted water, rubbing and tossing it between your fingers to prevent grains from sticking together.

Return couscous to steamer and set it again above boiling water. Steam uncovered about 15 minutes. Put dates on top and steam 5 minutes longer or until steam comes through couscous.

Meanwhile, in a separate pan simmer raisins in hot water to cover for about 10 minutes or until tender. Drain thoroughly.

Put dates on a plate. Transfer couscous to a large bowl and add butter. Mix lightly with a fork or with your fingers. To serve, mound couscous on a platter and arrange dates and raisins on top. Serve in bowls. Serve hot milk separately in a pitcher, for pouring over couscous.

Makes 4 or 5 main-course servings

BULGUR WHEAT PILAF WITH MUSHROOMS, PEAS, AND PINE NUTS

At the Israel Museum, I attended an exhibition of the customs of the Kurdish Jews and was glad to see that cuisine was highlighted as a prominent element. There was a dinner of typical dishes, and one of these was a delicious peppery bulgur wheat pilaf, which served as a bed for an aromatic meat stew.

Bulgur wheat, sometimes known as cracked wheat, is a staple of Jews from Middle Eastern countries. It is a wonderful ingredient with great flexibility. It can be simply marinated without being cooked to make Tabbouleh (page 180) or it can be made into a dough for a crunchy, meat-filled appetizer known as Kubeh (page 157). A simple way to turn it into a savory side dish that beautifully complements meat, fish, or poultry is to prepare it as a pilaf by the same technique as rice pilaf.

4 tablespoons vegetable or olive oil, or butter
½ medium onion, minced
2 medium garlic cloves, minced
¾ cup medium bulgur wheat
1½ cups water
salt and freshly ground pepper

¼ pound button mushrooms, halved and thinly sliced
1 cup cooked peas
2 tablespoons chopped fresh Italian parsley or curly parsley
2 tablespoons toasted pine nuts

Heat 2 tablespoons oil in a heavy medium saucepan over medium heat. Add onion and cook, stirring often, about 5 minutes or until softened. Add garlic and cook 1 minute. Add bulgur and sauté, stirring, for 2 minutes. Add water, salt, and pepper and bring to boil. Reduce heat to low, cover, and cook about 15 minutes or until water is absorbed. (Pilaf can be kept warm, covered, for 15 minutes.)

Heat the remaining 2 tablespoons oil in large skillet over medium heat. Add mushrooms, salt, and pepper. Sauté about 4 minutes or until golden brown. Add peas and heat gently.

Gently stir mushroom mixture into bulgur pilaf using a fork. Stir in parsley, taste, and adjust seasoning. Transfer to a serving dish, sprinkle with pine nuts, and serve immediately.

Makes 4 side-dish servings

ROMANIAN CORNMEAL KUGEL

This tastes somewhat like cornbread but is moist like bread pudding and slightly tangy. I learned how to make it from a woman from Romania who worked with me at the Tel Aviv University library. She prepares the kugel using a combination of sour cream and eshel, *an Israeli dairy product resembling a delicate yogurt. This kugel makes a good brunch dish, with fruit for accompaniment, as well as the customary sour cream.*

1 cup yellow cornmeal
1 cup all-purpose flour
1 teaspoon baking powder
½ teaspoon salt
½ cup cream-style cottage cheese
1½ cups plain yogurt

1½ cups sour cream
5 tablespoons butter or margarine, softened
¾ cup sugar
3 large eggs, separated
sour cream, for serving

Preheat oven to 350°F. Grease an 8-inch square baking dish. Mix cornmeal, flour, baking powder, and salt. In another bowl mix cottage cheese, yogurt, and sour cream.

Cream butter with ½ cup sugar. Add egg yolks and beat until smooth. Stir in cheese mixture alternately with dry ingredients. Whip whites until they form soft peaks. Beat in remaining ¼ cup sugar and beat until whites are stiff and shiny but not dry. Fold whites gently into cheese mixture. Transfer to baking dish.

Bake about 45 minutes or until a cake tester inserted in center comes out dry. Serve warm with sour cream.

Makes 8 or 9 brunch servings

16
BREADS

I grew up in America eating delicious bread, without even realizing that much of the bread in the country was characterless and cotton textured. The reason for my good fortune was that all the bread in my parents' home came from Jewish bakeries. I still like to buy Jewish rye bread with caraway seeds, pumpernickel, bialys, and onion pletzlach. I also purchase challah and bagels, but I make these at home whenever I can. I also bake pita, or pocket bread, which I often enjoyed in Israel with falafel and other treats. Fresh, good-quality pita and challah are hard to find in many areas of the United States and so the best solution is to bake your own.

CHALLAH

Challah (sometimes spelled *hallah*), a rich loaf with a deep brown crust and soft white crumb, is America's most popular egg bread. A festive bread traditionally prepared for the Sabbath and other Jewish holidays, it is usually a braided free-form loaf but it can also be shaped in spirals or wreaths or baked in a loaf pan.

The tantalizing aroma of challah baking always brings back memories from nearly twenty years ago, of a small bakery in a Tel Aviv suburb. Just before midnight every Thursday, when the streets were quiet and everyone was asleep, the bakers started preparing challahs for the Friday morning shoppers. My husband and I would walk to the neighborhood bakery and would buy one of the beautiful, hot, just-out-of-the-oven, golden-crusted challahs for a midnight snack. By the time we arrived home not much of the loaf was left for eating with butter.

Challah combines the advantages of the richest of egg breads, French brioche, and of homemade white bread. While white bread uses water or milk as its moistening liquid and brioche uses mainly egg, challah uses some of each and achieves some of the lightness of white bread and some of the richness of brioche. Unlike brioche, which contains a generous amount of butter, challah is usually enriched with oil and the dough is much easier to handle.

Like most yeast-leavened doughs, challah dough is kneaded in order to distribute the yeast evenly and ensure that the bread has a uniform texture. Although kneading the dough by hand takes only a few minutes and is a pleasant task, it can also be done in a mixer or in a food processor and then is effortless. Rising times can be flexible, and it is therefore possible to fit breadmaking into busy schedules. (See the first tip, page 288.)

To impart a tender, somewhat cakelike texture to the bread rather than a dense, chewy one, the dough should be soft. Because the absorption power of flour varies with humidity and the flour itself varies from place to place and with the seasons, adding just the right amount of flour to make the dough perfect requires a little experience. The best texture and flavor result when the minimum amount of flour to prevent sticking is added. If a little too much flour is added during kneading, however, the bread will still taste good.

Challah has a delicate flavor, which makes it a good accompaniment for a meal. For a different twist, a variety of sweet or savory flavorings, such as dried fruits, nuts, herbs, cheeses, and even vegetables, can be added to the dough.

Bread is a joy to make. In contrast to many pastries and other baked goods, with bread there is no need to hurry and little to worry about. The dough is easy to prepare and fun to work with. The result is delicious, aromatic bread that turns snacks into special treats and helps transform meals into feasts.

BAGELS

Fresh hot bagels with sweet butter, or with the traditional accompaniments of lox and cream cheese, are one of the attractions of a deli meal or Bar Mitzvah celebration. In New York and Los Angeles there are twenty-four-hour bagel bakeries, with hot bagels ready at any hour of the day or night.

Yet there is no need to wait for special occasions or to travel far in order to enjoy these delicious ring-shaped rolls. Indeed, homemade bagels may taste even better. They fill the kitchen with a wonderful aroma, and have the advantage of being one of the quickest breads to make.

A special technique gives bagels their unique texture, and enables us to "cheat" a little on the rising time: bagels are boiled before they are baked. Boiling gives them a quick push so they puff in the water, complete their rising, and begin to cook. A little sugar added to the water helps give the bagels a crisp crust. Before they are baked, the drained bagels are brushed with beaten egg so the finished bagels have a shiny glaze.

One of two methods can be used to make the hole: the dough can be shaped in balls and the center pushed out with your finger; or it can be formed into thin ropes, and the ends pressed together. The ball technique is more practical, because bagels formed by the rope method may open in the water. Both methods use up all the dough. For this reason "bagel holes," unlike doughnut holes, are not sold in bakeries.

Although basic bagels came to us with the Jews from eastern Europe, flavored bagels appear to be distinctly American. Like other breads, bagels can be varied by the addition of cheese, herbs, garlic, or nuts, or with sweet ingredients like honey and raisins.

Bagels are simple to make, though some recipes are quite strange. In a Jewish story about Chelm, the legendary town of fools, the baker of a neighboring town agreed to give Chelm's representatives his bagel recipe—start with holes, put dough around them, cook them in boiling water, then bake them in the oven. It has been reported that there are no bagels in Chelm to this very day.

TIPS ON BREAD MAKING

✕ To easily fit bread making into a busy schedule, you can refrigerate the dough. The best time to do this is before its second rise, so that this rise takes place in the refrigerator. If this is not convenient, the dough can be refrigerated after it has just begun its first rise or after shaping. Cover it tightly so it does not dry and try not to keep it longer than twelve hours. In the refrigerator the dough continues to expand slowly and stops once it is thoroughly chilled. Before baking, it should be brought to room temperature and left to finish rising to the desired volume.

✕ Use dry yeast before the expiration date on the label; after that date, the yeast loses some of its leavening power. A cake of fresh yeast, which weighs ⅗ ounce, is equivalent to an envelope of dried yeast (¼ ounce or 2½ teaspoons).

✕ Braided loaves keep their shape best when made of a stiff dough but are somewhat dry when baked if the dough is too stiff. Add just enough flour to the dough so it can be rolled into ropes for braiding without sticking to the surface. If too much flour is added or if the surface is floured too much during braiding, the ropes become flat instead of round.

✕ Letting the dough rise twice in the bowl helps ensure a bread with an even texture.

✕ If you let dough rise by setting it on top of stove, be sure to take it off when preheating the oven.

✕ If it is difficult to judge whether a batch of dough (but not a shaped bread) has risen enough, a common test is to quickly poke it with 2 fingers. If the finger imprints remain, the rising has been sufficient.

✕ When brushing a loaf with glaze, avoid letting glaze drip onto the pan, especially when using a loaf pan, because it can make the bread stick. Wipe excess glaze off the brush against the side of the bowl before brushing glaze on a loaf. To glaze a braided loaf, brush each section separately.

✕ Liquid ingredients such as honey are added to the dough from the beginning and provide part of the liquid content. Nuts or large amounts of cheese are generally added to the dough after it has risen so that they will not slow down the rising process.

✕ If you will not be eating the loaf within a day, a convenient way to store it is to slice it, wrap it, and freeze it; briefly warm each slice before serving.

✕ Slices of challah are also delicious when lightly toasted.

KNEADING EGG BREAD DOUGH BY HAND

Egg bread dough can be kneaded by either of the following methods:

Slapping method: For soft dough, this kneading technique is preferable. Using fingertips of both hands, lightly scoop up dough and slap it vigorously onto work surface. Grasp dough again, at about a 90-degree angle from first time (which has the effect of turning the dough), and repeat. Continue slapping dough, adding flour by tablespoons if necessary to prevent excessive sticking, until it is smooth and elastic and holds together in 1 piece; it may still be slightly sticky but will be much less sticky than it was before kneading. The trick in this method is to touch dough lightly and quickly so it does not have a chance to stick much to fingers.

Conventional method: If you prefer, knead the dough by this method, but it will require a little more flour. Push the dough away from you against the work surface with the palm of your hand. Turn it, fold the top third down toward you, and repeat. Continue kneading dough, adding flour by tablespoons if necessary to prevent excessive sticking, until it is smooth and elastic.

CHALLAH (EGG BREAD)

The well-known Jewish egg bread originated in eastern Europe but now is enjoyed by Jews of all origins. Making it at home is most satisfying and those who have never baked bread before will find it surprisingly easy. It can be made with very little sugar, or with a fairly generous amount for a more cakelike loaf. For an article on challah that I wrote for Bon Appétit *magazine, I explored various techniques for making and shaping the dough, and these are presented here.*

½ cup plus 2 tablespoons warm water (105 to 115°F.)
1 envelope active dry yeast
1 tablespoon plus 1½ teaspoons sugar
about 2¾ to 3 cups unbleached all-purpose flour
¼ cup plus 2 tablespoons vegetable oil

2 large eggs, at room temperature
1½ teaspoons salt
1 large egg, beaten with pinch of salt, for glaze
2 to 4 teaspoons sesame seeds, or 1 to 3 teaspoons poppy seeds (optional)

Pour ¼ cup of the warm water into small bowl. Sprinkle yeast over water, then sprinkle 1 teaspoon of sugar over yeast. Let stand until foamy, about 10 minutes. Stir if not smooth.

Oil or grease large bowl. Follow instructions for making dough either by hand, in mixer or in food processor.

To make dough by hand: Sift 2¾ cups flour into a large bowl. Make large deep well in center and add yeast mixture, remaining sugar, oil, eggs, remaining water, and salt. Mix ingredients in well with wooden spoon until blended. Mix in flour, first with a spoon, then by hand, until ingredients come together to a dough. Dough should be soft and sticky. Knead dough vigorously on work surface until very smooth and elastic, about 7 minutes; during kneading, add more flour 1 tablespoon at a time if dough sticks, adding just enough to make dough manageable. (For hints on kneading, see page 289.)

To make dough in mixer with dough hook: Sift 2¾ cups of flour into bowl of mixer fitted with dough hook. Make large deep well in center and add yeast mixture, remaining sugar, oil, eggs, remaining water, and salt. Mix at medium-low speed, pushing flour in often at first and scraping dough down occasionally from bowl and hook, until ingredients come together to a dough that just begins to cling to hook, about 7 minutes. Dough should be soft and sticky. Knead by mixing at medium speed, scraping down twice, until dough is smooth, partly clings to hook, and almost cleans sides of bowl, about 5 minutes. Pinch dough quickly; if it sticks to your fingers, beat in more flour 1 tablespoon at a time until dough is no longer very sticky. If you have added flour, knead dough again by mixing at medium speed about 2 minutes. Dough should be soft, smooth, and elastic.

To make dough in food processor: Combine 2¾ cups of flour, remaining sugar, and salt in food processor fitted with dough blade and process briefly to mix them. Add yeast mixture, oil, and eggs. With blades of processor turning, pour in remaining water. Process until ingredients come together to a soft dough. It will not form a ball. Process for about 30 seconds to knead dough. Pinch dough quickly; if it sticks to your fingers, add more flour 1 tablespoon at a time until dough is no longer very sticky. Knead again by processing about 30 seconds or until smooth. Remove dough and shape in rough ball in your hands.

Put dough in oiled bowl and turn dough over to oil all surfaces. Cover with warm, slightly damp towel or plastic wrap and let rise in warm draft-free area until doubled in volume, about 1¼ hours.

Remove dough with rubber spatula to work surface. Knead dough lightly again to knock out air. Clean bowl if necessary. Return dough to bowl, cover, and let rise again until doubled, about 1 hour.

Knead dough lightly on work surface, flouring lightly only if dough sticks. Shape as desired (see shapes, page 291).

Cover shaped loaf with warm, slightly damp towel and let rise until nearly doubled in size, about 1 hour. Meanwhile, position rack in center of oven and preheat to 375°F.

Brush risen loaf gently with beaten egg and sprinkle with seeds. Bake until top and bottom of bread are firm and bread sounds hollow when tapped on bottom; for approximate baking times, see instructions with each shape, page 291.

Carefully transfer bread to rack and cool. Bread is best on day it is made. (Bread can be kept, wrapped, for 1 day at room temperature; or it can be frozen.)

Makes 1 medium loaf

CHALLAH SHAPES

Simple loaf: Oil or grease an 8 × 4-inch loaf pan (for tall loaf) or 9 × 5-inch pan (for shorter loaf). Pat dough to rough rectangle about 8 × 4 (for smaller pan) or 10 × 5 inches (for larger). Roll up from longer side, jelly roll fashion, to obtain cylinder, pressing firmly. Pinch ends and seam tightly. Then roll cylinder again on work surface to press seam further. Place in pan seam side down and bake as follows: 50 minutes for 8 × 4-inch pan, 40 minutes for 9 × 5-inch. Run thin-bladed knife around bread to unmold only if it sticks.

Free-form braid: Lightly oil baking sheet. Shape dough in rough cylinder and cut dough into 3 equal parts. Knead 1 part briefly and shape in cylinder. Roll back and forth firmly on working surface, pressing with your hands held flat and elongating cylinder from center to edges as you roll, to form smooth rope about 20 inches long and about ¾ inch wide and, if desired, tapered slightly at ends. Repeat with other two parts.

To braid dough, put ropes side by side with one end of each closer to you. Join ends far from you, covering end of rope on your right side with end of center rope, then end of left rope. Press to join. Bring left rope over center one. Continue bringing outer ropes alternately over center one, braiding tightly. Pinch each end and tuck them underneath. Set braided bread carefully on prepared baking sheet and bake for approximately 40 minutes.

Braided crown or wreath: Prepare braid as for free-form braided loaf, but make each rope about 25 inches long and about ⅝ inch wide and tapered slightly at ends. Set braided dough carefully on oiled baking sheet. Bring ends of braid together, curving braid into wreath, and pinch ends tightly together. Bake for approximately 35 minutes.

Braid in loaf pan: This technique gives a rectangular loaf with a slight braided pattern on top. Oil or grease an 8 × 4-inch loaf pan. Prepare braid as for free-form braided loaf, but make each rope about 10 inches long. Braid tightly, pinch ends, and tuck them under. Slip loaf into prepared pan. Bake for approximately 50 minutes. Run thin-bladed knife around bread to unmold it if it sticks.

Spiral loaf: This loaf rises to a dome shape. Lightly oil a baking sheet. Shape dough in a rough cylinder. Roll dough back and forth firmly on work surface, pressing with your hands held flat and elongating the cylinder from center to edges as you roll, to form smooth rope about 28 inches long and 1¼ inches wide. Flour very lightly only if necessary, so dough won't stick. Wind dough around one end in spiral; tuck other end underneath and pinch to attach it to dough. Set bread carefully on prepared baking sheet and bake for approximately 40 minutes.

FLAVORING VARIATIONS

Light challah: Decrease oil quantity to 2 tablespoons. Increase the water by 2 or 3 tablespoons.

Rich challah: For a richer bread for dairy meals, substitute 6 tablespoons cooled melted butter for oil and warm milk for water.

Sweet challah: Increase sugar to 3 or 4 tablespoons. The dough will require a few tablespoons more flour. It will take longer to rise than basic challah dough and will rise less, especially if largest quantity of sugar is added. Let rise and shape as desired; if using loaf pan, use 8 × 4-inch size. Bake loaf at 375°F. for 15 minutes. Reduce oven temperature to 350°F. and continue baking according to shape chosen, adding 2 or 3 minutes to baking time. (If loaf browns too quickly, cover loosely with brown paper or foil.)

Large challah: For a fairly large challah, use these proportions: 4 cups flour, 1 cup lukewarm water, 2 envelopes active dry yeast, 2 tablespoons sugar, ½ cup vegetable oil, 2 large eggs, and 2 teaspoons salt. After letting rise, shape as a free-form braid. Bake at 350°F. for 1 hour.

SHABBAT BREAKFAST BREAD (KUBANEH)

This unique Yemenite bread, which is baked all night in a tightly covered dish, is prepared for Sabbath breakfast or brunch. It defies all the usual rules for bread baking—it bakes at a very low temperature rather than at high heat, and it is baked covered, so it steams, rather than uncovered. And it is absolutely delicious. When I prepared this for a cooking class on Jewish breads in California, the students were wild about it. Before baking, you can put a few eggs (in their shells) in the baking dish; they come out brown and are a good accompaniment for the bread. In some families, this bread is served with sugar for sprinkling; in others, it is accompanied by Yemenite Tomato Salsa (page 166) and Hot Pepper–Garlic Chutney (page 142).

1 envelope active dry yeast
⅓ cup lukewarm water
6 tablespoons plus 1 teaspoon sugar
1½ teaspoons salt
5 tablespoons margarine or butter, cut into pieces

¾ cup boiling water
3 cups all-purpose flour
½ cup (1 stick) very soft margarine or butter, for spreading on dough

Sprinkle yeast over lukewarm water and add 1 teaspoon sugar. Leave for 10 minutes until yeast is foamy.

In a mixing bowl, combine remaining sugar, salt, 5 tablespoons margarine, and boiling water. Stir until sugar and margarine are completely dissolved. Stir in yeast mixture. Add flour and mix with a wooden spoon until dough becomes difficult to stir. Knead in remaining flour.

Knead dough vigorously on a lightly floured work surface, adding flour by tablespoons if necessary, until dough is very smooth but still soft, about 10 minutes. Put dough in a clean, oiled bowl, cover with a damp cloth, and let rise in a warm place for 1 hour or until nearly doubled in volume.

Punch down dough, knead it briefly in bowl, cover, and let rise again in a warm place for about 1 hour; or refrigerate for 3 to 4 hours.

Generously rub a deep 2-quart baking dish with margarine or butter. Divide dough into 8 pieces. With a lightly oiled rolling pin, roll out one piece on a lightly oiled surface to a rectangle about ⅛ inch thick. Spread with about 2 teaspoons of butter or margarine. Roll up like a jelly roll. Flatten resulting roll by tapping it with your knuckles and spread it with about 1 teaspoon butter, then roll up in a spiral and place it in baking dish so that spiral design faces up. Continue with remaining pieces of dough, placing them one next to the other and touching each other in dish. If any margarine or butter remains, put it in small pieces on top. Cover with greased paper or foil placed on surface of dough and with a tight lid.

Prehead over to 225°F. Bake 3 hours or until golden brown. Turn out onto a plate, then reverse onto another plate and put back into baking dish, so it is now upside down. Cover and bake another hour; or reduce over temperature to 200°F. and bake overnight. (Bread can be baked ahead and reheated in its covered baking dish for about 45 minutes in a 225°F. oven.) Serve warm.

Makes 8 servings

ONION-PARMESAN BRAID

Although challah rarely contains dairy products so that it will be a suitable accompaniment for all types of foods, this delicious version, with cheese in the dough and sautéed onions enclosed in each braid, is perfect for a vegetarian or dairy dinner or party. Kosher parmesan cheese, which does not contain rennet, is made in both the United States and Israel.

Challah dough (page 289), made with 1 teaspoon sugar, ¼ cup oil, 1¼ teaspoons salt, and remaining ingredient quantities as in challah recipe
¾ cup (about 2½ ounces) freshly grated parmesan cheese

1 large onion, minced (2 cups)
3 tablespoons unsalted butter
2 teaspoons dried leaf oregano, crumbled
1 large egg, beaten with pinch of salt, for glaze

NOTE: When making dough, sprinkle teaspoon sugar over yeast mixture. Make dough by any method, adding cheese when ingredients are just mixed. Let dough rise twice.

While dough is rising, prepare onion mixture. Pat minced onion dry with several changes of paper towels. Melt butter in a large heavy skillet over medium-low heat. Add onion and oregano and cook, stirring often, until soft but not brown, about 10 minutes. Reduce heat to low and cook, stirring occasionally, until dry, about 20 minutes. Transfer mixture to bowl and cool.

After dough has risen a second time, lightly oil a baking sheet. Knead dough lightly on work surface, adding flour 1 tablespoon at a time only if necessary so that dough can be rolled out; it should still be soft and slightly sticky so that it can be easily pinched around onions.

Roll dough into a 13 × 9-inch rectangle. Cut dough into three 13 × 3-inch strips. Spoon onion mixture evenly down center of each strip. Spread mixture over strip, leaving a ½-inch border of dough free of onion on each side. Join long sides of strips by pinching together borders of dough, to form a rope enclosing the onions. Pinch ends and edges to seal very well. Turn over so that seams face down. Roll lightly on surface to smooth seams.

To braid dough, put ropes side by side, with one end of each closer to you. Join ends far from you, covering end of rope on your right side with end of center rope, then end of left rope. Press to join. Bring left rope over center one. Continue bringing outer ropes alternately over center one, braiding tightly. Pinch each end and tuck them underneath. Set braided bread carefully on prepared baking sheet.

Cover with warm, slightly damp cloth and let rise until nearly doubled in size, about 1 hour. Meanwhile, position rack in center of oven and preheat to 375°F.

Brush risen loaf gently with beaten egg. Bake until top and bottom of bread are firm and bread sounds hollow when tapped on bottom, about 40 minutes. Cool on rack.

Makes 1 medium loaf

PITA (POCKET BREAD)

Pita, also known as pocket bread, has become better known in America in recent years. Good pita should be slightly chewy but tender. Fresh pita can be found in some gourmet markets and in Israeli, Iranian, and Middle Eastern grocery stores. New varieties, such as small pita puffs and whole wheat pita, have been developed. Unfortunately, much of the packaged pita sold in our supermarkets is dry, stiff, and has a cardboardlike texture.

In Israel freshly baked pita is available everywhere but many people like to bake it at home. One of my in-laws has an authentic Yemenite round clay pita oven, resembling an Indian tandoori oven, that she built with her own hands. To bake the pita, she sticks the dough to the searing-hot sides of the oven, as Indian cooks do when baking naan. *Other cooks in Israel either use a special electric pita pan, which bakes the pita from above and below, or simply bake pita in a very hot oven.*

My mother-in-law adds about a tablespoon of aromatic black caraway seeds (also known simply as ''black seeds'') to the dough and they add a wonderful flavor. These can be found at Iranian and other Middle Eastern grocery stores or ordered from spice and baking supply houses. Sesame pita is made by rolling each ball of dough in sesame seeds before flattening it.

Pita tastes best fresh, but if it gets stale, it can be cut into quarters to make triangles and toasted.

2 envelopes active dry yeast
1⅓ cups lukewarm water

4 cups bread flour
2 teaspoons salt

To make dough in a food processor: Sprinkle yeast over ½ cup lukewarm water in a bowl and leave for 10 minutes. Stir to dissolve yeast. In a food processor, process flour and salt briefly to mix them. Add remaining water to yeast mixture. With blades of processor turning, gradually pour in yeast-liquid mixture. If dough is too dry to come together, add 1 tablespoon water and process again. Process for 1 minute to knead dough.

To make dough by hand: Sift flour into a bowl and make a well in center. Sprinkle yeast into well. Pour ½ cup water over yeast and leave for 10 minutes. Stir to dissolve yeast. Add remaining water and salt and mix with ingredients in middle of well. Stir in flour and mix well, to obtain a fairly soft dough. When dough becomes difficult to mix with a wooden spoon, mix in remaining flour by hand. If dough is dry, add 1 tablespoon water. Knead dough by slapping it vigorously on a lightly floured working surface until dough is very smooth and elastic. If it is very sticky, flour it occasionally while kneading.

Transfer dough to an oiled bowl and turn dough over to oil its entire surface. Cover with a damp towel and let rise in a warm place 1 to 1½ hours or until doubled in volume.

Knead dough again briefly on a floured surface until smooth. Roll it to a thick log. With a floured knife, cut dough in 8 or 10 equal pieces and, with cupped palms, roll each to a smooth ball on an unfloured surface; flour only if dough begins to stick. Put on a floured board or other surface. Cover and let rise about 30 minutes or until doubled in volume. Preheat oven to 500°F.

Lightly flour 2 baking sheets. Using a floured rolling pin, roll 4 balls of dough on a lightly floured surface to 6-inch circles, about ¼ inch thick. Try to keep them round, but do not worry if they are a little uneven. Transfer 2 rounds to each baking sheet.

Bake about 3 minutes until beginning to brown. Turn over and continue baking 2 or 3 minutes until firm. Repeat with remaining dough. If not serving pitas immediately, let cool on racks and keep them wrapped tightly in plastic wrap or plastic bags; freeze those that will not be used within 2 days.

Makes 8 to 10 pitas

NOTE: Sometimes one or two pitas don't puff enough to form a pocket, but they are still good to eat.

VARIATION: Sesame Pita
Roll each ball of dough in 1 teaspoon sesame seeds before rolling it out.

TIPS ON MAKING BAGELS

✗ Bagels should be chewy and therefore are best when made with bread flour. All-purpose flour can be substituted, but the bagels will be a little softer.

✗ Homemade bagels have a good, fresh flavor but are not as evenly shaped as commercial ones.

✗ In the recipes here, the instructions given are for mixing and kneading the dough by hand or for using a food processor. Either technique can be used for any of the bagel recipes. If you prefer to make the dough in a mixer with a dough hook, follow the instructions for mixing by hand; once the dough is mixed, let the machine run until the dough is very smooth.

BASIC BAGELS

The word bagel *entered the English language from Yiddish, and bagels are the best-known of Jewish rolls. Many a bar mitzvah or other Jewish party features bagels with cream cheese and lox or smoked white fish, accompanied by thin slices of red onion and tomato. In many families this combination is also a treat for a relaxed breakfast or brunch. The bagels are served warm or at room temperature. They are also popular lightly toasted and buttered, and make great sandwiches.*

The cooking procedure for bagels is unusual because they are boiled before they are baked. The dough is firmer than for challah or other breads, so the bagels will hold together during the boiling. There are two main types of bagels: egg bagels, as in this recipe, and water bagels, which are represented by our recipe for Garlic Bagels (page 300).

4 cups bread flour	**2 teaspoons sugar**
¾ cup lukewarm water	**¼ cup vegetable oil**
1 envelope active dry yeast	**2 large eggs**
	1¾ teaspoons salt

For Boiling and for Glaze

2 quarts water
1½ tablespoons sugar
1 large egg, beaten with a pinch of salt

Sift flour into a large bowl. Make a well in center. Pour in ¼ cup lukewarm water. Sprinkle yeast on top and add 1 teaspoon sugar. Leave for 10 minutes until yeast is foamy. Add remaining sugar, oil, eggs, remaining water, and salt. Mix with a wooden spoon until ingredients begin to come together to a dough. When mixing with a spoon becomes difficult, mix in remaining flour by hand.

Knead dough vigorously on a work surface until very smooth and no longer sticky, about 10 minutes. Put dough in a clean oiled bowl, cover with a damp cloth, and let rise in a warm place about 1 hour or until light but not doubled in volume. (Dough can be made 1 day ahead; it should be left to rise 30 minutes, then should be punched down and refrigerated overnight. Be sure it is covered with a damp cloth so it doesn't dry out; let it come to room temperature before continuing.)

To shape bagels, knead dough again lightly. Roll it to a thick log and cut it into 12 pieces with a floured knife. Roll each piece of dough to a very smooth ball by holding it under your cupped palm on an unfloured surface, and rolling it over and over on surface, pressing firmly. The more the dough is rolled, the more even in shape the final bagel will be. Flatten ball slightly. Make a hole by flouring your index finger and pushing it through center of round of dough. Twirl round of dough around your finger to stretch hole, then insert 2 fingers and continue twirling. Gently pull edges to even out shape of bagel. Cover and let rise on floured board 15 minutes.

Preheat oven to 400°F. Bring water and sugar to a boil in a wide pan. Add 3 or 4 bagels and boil 1 minute. Turn them over and boil 1 minute. If holes begin to close, force then open with handle of a wooden spoon. With a slotted spoon, transfer bagels to a cloth or to paper towels. Repeat with remaining bagels.

Put bagels on 2 lightly floured or greased baking sheets. Brush with egg glaze. Bake about 20 minutes or until browned; if both baking sheets don't fit on center oven rack, bake them one above other and switch their positions after 10 minutes. If not serving them right away, cool them on a rack and wrap them. They keep 2 days at room temperature. They can also be frozen and reheated before serving.

Makes 12 bagels

CHEESE AND HERB BAGELS

Most bagels are firm textured, but those made with cheese are more delicate and should be simmered instead of being boiled. I like these with cream cheese and tomato.

1 envelope active dry yeast
¾ cup lukewarm water
2 teaspoons sugar
4 cups bread flour
1½ cups grated Swiss cheese (6 ounces)

1½ teaspoons dried leaf oregano
½ teaspoon dried leaf thyme
1¾ teaspoons salt
6 tablespoons (¾ stick) unsalted butter, melted and cooled
2 large eggs

For Boiling and for Glaze

2 quarts water
1½ tablespoons sugar
1 large egg, beaten with a pinch of salt

To make dough in a food processor, sprinkle yeast over ¼ cup lukewarm water in a bowl, add 1 teaspoon sugar, and leave for 10 minutes until yeast is foamy. In a food processor, process flour, remaining sugar, cheese, oregano, thyme, and remaining salt briefly to mix them. Add butter and eggs and process with a few on/off turns to mix. Add remaining water to yeast mixture. With blades of processor turning, gradually pour in yeast liquid mixture. If dough is too dry to come together, add 1 tablespoon water and process again. Process for 1 minute to knead dough.

Put dough in a clean oiled bowl, cover with a damp cloth, and let rise in a warm place about 1 hour or until light but not doubled in volume. (Dough can be made 1 day ahead; it should be left to rise 30 minutes, then should be punched down and refrigerated overnight. Be sure it is covered with a damp cloth so it doesn't dry out; let it come to room temperature before continuing.)

Shape dough in bagels as in previous recipe. Cover and let rise on floured board 15 minutes.

Preheat oven to 400°F. To simmer bagels, bring water and sugar to a boil. Add 3 or 4 bagels and simmer them over medium heat for 1 minute. Turn them over and simmer 1 minute. If holes begin to close, force them open with handle of a wooden spoon. With a slotted spoon, transfer them to a cloth or to paper towels. Repeat with remaining bagels.

Put bagels on 2 lightly floured or greased baking sheets. Brush with egg and bake about 20 minutes or until browned.

Makes 12 bagels

GARLIC BAGELS

These are water bagels and are more chewy than those containing egg. Serve them buttered, with scrambled eggs or with cheese.

4 cups bread flour
1 cup plus 2 tablespoons lukewarm
  water
1 envelope active dry yeast

1 teaspoon sugar
6 tablespoons (¾ cup) unsalted butter
4 garlic cloves, minced
1¾ teaspoons salt

For Boiling and for Glaze

2 quarts water
1½ tablespoons sugar
1 large egg, beaten with a pinch of salt

Sift flour into a large bowl. Make a well in center. Pour in ¼ cup lukewarm water. Sprinkle yeast on top and add sugar. Leave for 10 minutes until yeast is foamy.

Melt butter in a medium saucepan, add garlic, and cook over low heat, stirring, about 1 minute or until softened but not brown. Let cool slightly.

To well in flour, add garlic and butter in which it was cooked, remaining water, and salt. Mix with a wooden spoon until ingredients begin to come together to a dough. When mixing with a spoon becomes difficult, mix in remaining flour by hand.

Knead dough vigorously on a work surface until very smooth and no longer sticky, about 10 minutes. Put dough in a clean oiled bowl, cover with a damp cloth and let rise in a warm place about 1 hour or until light but not doubled in volume. (Dough can be made 1 day ahead; it should be left to rise 30 minutes, then should be punched down, covered with a damp cloth, and refrigerated overnight. Let it come to room temperature before continuing.)

Shape, boil and bake bagels as in Basic Bagels (page 297).

Makes 12 bagels

WHOLE WHEAT BAGELS

Honey gives these bagels a touch of sweetness. They are good with smoked turkey or chicken, or for breakfast with cream cheese or butter. The bagels in the variation, made with cinnamon, nuts, and raisins, are best, I find, with butter and jam.

2 cups bread flour	4 tablespoons honey
2 cups whole wheat flour	¼ cup oil
¾ cup lukewarm water	2 large eggs
1 envelope active dry yeast	1¾ teaspoons salt

For Boiling and for Glaze

2 quarts water
1½ tablespoons sugar
1 large egg, beaten with a pinch of salt

Sift both types flour into a large bowl. Make a well in the center. Pour in ¼ cup lukewarm water. Sprinkle yeast on top and add 2 teaspoons honey. Leave for 10 minutes until yeast is foamy. Add remaining honey, oil, eggs, remaining water, and salt. Mix with a wooden spoon until ingredients begin to come together to a dough. When mixing with a spoon becomes difficult, mix in remaining flour by hand.

Knead dough vigorously on a work surface until very smooth and no longer sticky, about 10 minutes. Put dough in a clean oiled bowl, cover with a damp cloth, and let rise in a warm place about 1½ hours or until light but not doubled in volume. (Dough can be made 1 day ahead; it should be left to rise 45 minutes, then should be punched down, covered with a damp cloth, and refrigerated overnight. Let it come to room temperature before continuing.)

Shape, boil, and bake bagels as in Basic Bagels (page 297).

Makes 12 bagels

VARIATION: Walnut and Raisin Bagels

Add 1½ teaspoons ground cinnamon to dough with the honey. Add ½ cup coarsely chopped raisins and ¼ cup chopped walnuts to finished dough before letting it rise. Knead to distribute raisins and walnuts evenly. Bake these bagels at 375°F. for 20 to 25 minutes or until browned; watch them carefully so raisins don't burn.

SHABBAT PASTRY ROLLS (JIHNUN)

This rich Yemenite pastry is made of very thin, tender layers of dough rolled up in cigar shapes. In many Yemenite homes it is baked overnight for Shabbat *and served for breakfast or brunch, with sugar for sprinkling or with Yemenite Tomato Salsa (page 166) and Browned Eggs (page 205). Today it has become chic and enjoys great popularity in Israeli cafés. The menu items in a typical trendy café are coffee, cake, Melawah (a pancake made from a similar dough, page 202), Jihnun, and Cheese Filo Turnovers, or Cheese Bourekas (page 55).*

Most often the dough for Jihnun is enriched with margarine, but it can be flavored instead with samneh, *the aromatic Yemenite-style clarified butter that resembles Indian* ghee. *In Israeli grocery stores in some large American cities like Los Angeles, the dough is available frozen, already rolled into the cigar or the pancake shape.*

3¾ cups all-purpose flour	1 large egg
2 tablespoons sugar	1¼ cups water
1 teaspoon baking powder	¾ cup (1½ sticks) margarine, cut into
1½ teaspoons salt	6 pieces

Combine flour, sugar, baking powder, and salt in a food processor and process to blend. Add egg and 1 cup water and process with on/off turns to mix. With motor running, gradually add remaining water, about ¼ cup, adding enough so mixture comes together to a smooth, fairly stiff dough. It will be sticky.

Remove from processor. Knead dough well by slapping dough vigorously on the work surface. Divide into 6 pieces and knead each one with a slapping motion until smooth. Roll each in your palm to a ball. Put on an oiled plate or tray, cover with plastic wrap, and refrigerate at least 4 hours or overnight.

Oil your working surface and rolling pin. Let margarine stand at room temperature until very soft. Roll out 1 ball of dough on oiled surface to very thin 12-inch square. To help stretch dough, pull it gently from time to time by hand, until very thin. If dough tears, simply press it together. Spread with a piece of soft margarine. Fold in half, then in half again to make a long strip. Roll up strip from a short side in a tight cylinder. Repeat with 5 remaining pieces of dough. Put in greased, shallow 8-inch square baking dish. Cover with foil and a lid and refrigerate at least 2 or up to 8 hours.

Preheat oven to 200°F. Bake pastries 13 to 14 hours or until golden brown. Serve hot.

Makes 6 generous servings

17
DESSERTS, CAKES, AND COOKIES

 When I lived in Israel, my relatives, friends, and neighbors always had a pastry on hand during the weekends. "Come over for coffee and cake" was a frequent invitation. This practice enabled us to get together easily and at a moment's notice and to enjoy tasting each other's homemade desserts. French Jews liked to bake fruit tarts, Jews from the Middle East specialized in nut-filled filo pastries, and American Jews often served chiffon cakes.

Most of all, I noticed an Austro-Hungarian influence on Jewish Israeli baking. Thus, the most popular desserts are light nut cakes and tortes, and all sorts of Viennese pastries. Jews of every extraction also love Israeli-style Bavarian cream, which is prepared in a different way from the classic dessert but still is light, smooth, and creamy.

Since Jewish bakeries and delis are found in many American cities, they helped make several European pastries and desserts well known in the United States and these became associated with Jewish cooking. Strudel, rugelach, blintzes, and cheesecake, for example, originated in eastern Europe and were adopted by Jews, who continued to prepare them after they emigrated to the New World.

For serving after meals that feature a meat or poultry main course, Jewish cooks have developed a variety of desserts that do not contain dairy products. Many are based on fruit, and thus are light, refreshing, and relatively low in calories. Cakes and pastries are often made in two versions, depending on how they will be served: with nondairy margarine so they will be pareve and thus suitable for all meals, or with butter for dairy meals and for tea time.

Since cakes and other desserts are most often prepared for festive occasions, many of them appear in the holiday chapters of this book.

VANILLA POUND CAKE

Pound cakes are popular items at Jewish bakeries, and also are favorites for making at home, since many people prefer a freshly baked, simple, unfrosted cake of this type for enjoying with a cup of tea or coffee.

1⅓ cups all-purpose flour
1¼ teaspoons baking powder
¾ cup (1½ sticks) unsalted butter or margarine, at room temperature
1 cup plus 2 tablespoons granulated sugar

3 large eggs, at room temperature
2 teaspoons vanilla extract
5 tablespoons heavy cream, half-and-half, milk, or water
confectioners' sugar, for dusting (optional)

Preheat oven to 350°F. Butter and flour a nonstick 9 × 5-inch loaf pan, tapping pan to remove excess flour. Sift flour with baking powder.

Cream butter in a large bowl, if possible using paddle beater of mixer, at medium speed until butter is soft, smooth, and most of it clings to side of bowl. Gradually beat in sugar. Beat mixture at medium speed until it is very pale, smooth, and fluffy, about 4 minutes. Beat in 2 eggs, one by one, at medium speed, beating thoroughly after each. Beat third egg in small bowl. Add it to mixture gradually, beating thoroughly after each addition. Batter may look like it is beginning to separate but it will come together when flour is added.

With mixer at low speed, add about one-fourth of flour mixture to batter. Blend in vanilla and about 1 tablespoon cream. Blend in remaining flour in 3 batches, alternating with remaining cream. Stir at low speed just until blended.

Spoon batter carefully into pan. Smooth top with spatula. Tap pan a few times on work surface to level batter. Set pan in oven with a short side of loaf pan facing back of oven. Bake until cake tester inserted in center of cake comes out completely clean, about 50 minutes.

Cool cake in pan on rack 10 minutes. Run thin-bladed flexible knife around edges of cake and turn cake out onto rack. Carefully turn cake back over and cool it completely. (Cake can be kept, wrapped in plastic wrap or foil, up to 3 days at cool room temperature or up to 1 week in refrigerator; or it can be frozen about 2 months.)

Serve cake at room temperature. Sift confectioners' sugar over it if desired. Cut cake into ½- to ¾-inch slices with a serrated knife.

Makes 10 to 12 servings

CHOCOLATE-ORANGE MARBLE CAKE

Almost every Ashkenazic Jewish mother has her favorite recipe for marble cake, made with chocolate and white batters. This is a particularly rich version that makes use of a generous amount of chocolate for the dark batter and freshly grated orange zest to flavor the white batter.

4 ounces semisweet chocolate, chopped
1 cup (2 sticks) unsalted butter or nondairy margarine, at room temperature

1¼ cups sugar
4 large eggs, at room temperature
1¾ cups cake flour, sifted
1 teaspoon vanilla extract
2 tablespoons finely grated orange peel

Preheat oven to 350°F. Butter and flour a 9-inch springform pan with 2½-inch side, tapping pan to remove excess flour.

Melt chocolate in medium bowl set above hot water over low heat. Stir until smooth. Remove from above water and let cool.

Cream butter in a large bowl, if possible using paddle beater of mixer, until butter is soft, smooth, and most of it clings to side of bowl. Gradually beat in sugar. Beat mixture at medium speed until it is very pale, smooth, and fluffy, about 4 minutes. Beat in 3 eggs, one by one, beating thoroughly after each and scraping mixture down occasionally. Beat fourth egg in small bowl. Add it to mixture, a scant tablespoon at a time, beating thoroughly after each addition. With last few additions, batter will look like it is beginning to separate but it will come together when flour is added.

Sprinkle about one-fourth of flour over batter and stir it in, using rubber spatula. Stir in vanilla. Stir in remaining flour in 3 batches. Mix well; be sure there are no lumps.

Transfer 2 cups batter to a bowl and stir in grated orange peel. Stir cool melted chocolate into remaining batter.

Spoon about half the chocolate batter into prepared pan without spreading. Spoon about half the orange batter over chocolate batter. Spoon remaining chocolate batter on top. Spoon remaining orange batter over chocolate batter. Tap pan several times on work surface to level batter. Draw knife through batters several times with swirling motion to marble them slightly; chocolate batter should show only slightly at top. Tap pan again several times on work surface to level batter.

Bake until cake tester inserted in center of cake comes out completely clean, about 50 minutes. Cool in pan on rack 10 minutes. Release spring and remove sides of pan. Cool cake to lukewarm. Turn over onto another rack. Carefully remove base of pan with aid of metal spatula. (Cake can be kept, wrapped in plastic wrap or foil, up to 3 days at cool room temperature or up to 1 week in refrigerator; or it can be frozen.) Serve cake at room temperature.

Makes 10 to 12 servings

MERINGUE-TOPPED CHEESECAKE

A meringue topping adds to the impression of lightness of this cheesecake made in the eastern European style. The lemon-scented filling, made of cottage cheese and cream cheese, is also lighter than that of many cheesecakes. Perfect for Shavuot, it also makes a lovely summer dessert when accompanied by a mixture of strawberries, raspberries, and blueberries.

Sweet Pastry

2 large egg yolks
2 tablespoons sour cream
1⅓ cups all-purpose flour
1 teaspoon baking powder

⅓ cup sugar
pinch of salt
7 tablespoons unsalted butter or
   margarine

Lemon-Cheese Filling

1 pound (1 pint) cream-style cottage
  cheese
1 pound cream cheese, softened
¾ cup plus 2 tablespoons sugar

4 large eggs, separated
1 large egg yolk
grated rind of 1 lemon (1½ teaspoons)
2 teaspoons vanilla extract

Meringue Topping

3 large egg whites
¼ teaspoon cream of tartar
6 tablespoons sugar

For the sweet pastry, beat egg yolks with sour cream and set aside. Combine flour, baking powder, sugar, and salt in a food processor. Process briefly to blend. Scatter butter pieces over mixture. Mix using on/off turns until mixture resembles coarse meal. Pour sour cream mixture evenly over mixture in processor. Process with on/off turns, scraping down occasionally, until dough forms sticky crumbs that can easily be pressed together and just begins to come together in a ball. If mixture is dry, add ½ teaspoon water and process briefly again.

Pat pastry into a lightly buttered 9- or 10-inch springform pan to line it 2 inches up side. Prick base and sides lightly. Freeze 20 minutes. Preheat oven to 375°F. Bake pastry shell 15 minutes, until very light golden. Remove from oven. Reduce oven temperature to 350°F. Let pastry cool while making filling.

Force cottage cheese through a strainer, pushing with back of a spoon. Beat cream cheese with ¾ cup sugar in mixer until smooth. Beat in 5 egg yolks, one by one. Stir in cottage cheese, lemon rind, and vanilla. Whip 4 egg whites until soft peaks form. Beat in remaining 2 tablespoons sugar, and whip until stiff but not dry. Fold into cheese mixture. Transfer to pastry shell. Bake 50 to 60 minutes or until top is light brown, set, and beginning to crack. Remove from oven, set pan on rack, and let cool 30 minutes. Leave oven at 350°F.

For the topping, combine egg whites, cream of tartar, and sugar in bowl of mixer. Set bowl in a pan of hot water over very low heat and stir whites with whisk about 3 minutes or until mixture is slightly warm and sugar dissolves. Remove from pan of water and whip at high speed of mixer until whites are stiff. Spread over filling, using metal spatula to decorate it in a ridged design if desired. Return cake to oven and bake about 8 to 10 minutes or until meringue is light beige.

Cool cake to room temperature. Stick 5 toothpicks at edges of cake and 1 in center and cover cake loosely with paper towel; this keeps paper towel from sticking to meringue. Refrigerate cake 2 hours before serving. (Cake can be kept for 2 days in refrigerator.) Cut cake and serve cold.

Makes 8 to 10 servings

RASPBERRY ALMOND TART

Fresh fruit tarts are a beloved dessert among French Jews, because they are beautiful, enticing, and rich but do not require dairy products.

French Sweet Pastry (recipe follows),
  chilled until firm

Almond Filling

⅔ cup blanched almonds
½ cup sugar
6 tablespoons (¾ stick) unsalted
  margarine, at room temperature
1 large egg

1 large egg yolk
1 tablespoon raspberry brandy or
  kirsch
2 tablespoons all-purpose flour

½ cup red currant jelly
2 cups fresh raspberries

Butter a 10-inch round tart pan with removable bottom. Let pastry dough soften 1 minute before rolling it. Roll out dough on a cold, lightly floured surface to a round about ¼ inch thick. Roll up dough loosely around rolling pin and unroll it over pan. Gently ease dough into pan. Using your thumb, gently push dough down slightly at top edge of pan, so top edge is thicker than remaining dough. Roll rolling pin across pan to cut off dough. With your finger and thumb, push up top edge of dough all around pan so it is about ¼ inch higher than rim. Prick dough all over with a fork. Refrigerate 1 hour, or cover with plastic wrap and refrigerate overnight or freeze up to 2 weeks.

Position a rack in lower third of oven and preheat to 425°F. Heat a baking sheet on rack in oven.

Grind almonds with 2 tablespoons of sugar to a fine powder. Beat margarine until soft. Add remaining sugar and beat until mixture is smooth. In a small bowl, beat egg with yolk. Gradually add beaten eggs to margarine mixture. Add brandy. Stir in almond mixture and flour.

Spread almond filling in lined tart pan. (It will seem like a small amount but it puffs.) Bake tart on hot baking sheet for 10 minutes. Reduce temperature to 350°F. and bake another 30 minutes or until filling sets and is golden brown. Transfer to a rack to cool.

Melt jelly over low heat, stirring often. Brush about three-fourths of the jelly on tart. Arrange berries on top. If desired, dab berries very lightly with jelly. Serve tart at room temperature.

Makes 6 to 8 servings

FRENCH SWEET PASTRY

This cookielike dough makes a delicious base for fruit tarts.

1¼ cups all-purpose flour	½ cup (1 stick) unsalted margarine or
¼ cup cake flour	butter, very cold, cut into bits
6 tablespoons sugar	1 large egg, lightly beaten
¼ teaspoon salt	

To make pastry in a food processor: Combine both types of flour, sugar, and salt in a food processor. Process briefly to blend. Scatter margarine pieces over mixture. Mix using on/off turns until mixture resembles coarse meal. Pour egg evenly over mixture in processor. Process with on/off turns, scraping down occasionally, until dough forms sticky crumbs that can easily be pressed together but does not come together in a ball. If dough is too sticky, sprinkle with 1 tablespoon flour and process again. Transfer dough to a work surface.

To make pastry by hand: Sift both types flour onto a work surface and make a well in center. Add egg, sugar, and salt and mix using your fingertips. Pound margarine to soften it and cut it in pieces. Add it to well and quickly mix with other ingredients in well until partly mixed. Gradually draw in flour to make coarse crumbs. Toss mixture, rubbing it between your fingers, until crumbs begin to stick together.

Blend dough further by pushing about one-fourth of it away from you and smearing it with heel of your hand against work surface. Repeat with remaining dough in 3 batches. Repeat with each batch if dough is not yet well blended.

Using a rubber spatula, transfer dough to a sheet of plastic wrap, wrap it, and push it together. Shape dough in a flat disk. Refrigerate 4 hours. (Dough can be kept 2 days in refrigerator.)

Makes enough for a 10-inch round tart

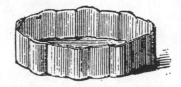

SOUR CREAM COFFEE CAKE WITH WALNUTS

When I was growing up, a slice of this tender cake with a ripple of cinnamon-nut filling running through it was a Shabbat morning treat that my brother and I looked forward to. This is the type of simple, homey cake that nobody can resist, whether it is served with a cup of coffee or a glass of milk. It is a favorite of American Jews; in Europe, coffee cakes usually are leavened with yeast.

1 cup walnuts, chopped
1½ teaspoons ground cinnamon
1 cup plus 3 tablespoons sugar
1¾ cups all-purpose flour
1½ teaspoons baking powder

½ teaspoon baking soda
1 teaspoon vanilla extract
1½ cups sour cream
½ cup (1 stick) unsalted butter
3 large eggs

Position rack in center of oven and preheat to 350°F. Generously butter a 9½-inch Bundt pan, kugelhopf mold, or fluted tube pan, taking care to butter tube and each fluted section. Mix walnuts, cinnamon, and 3 tablespoons sugar. Sift flour, baking powder, and baking soda into a bowl. Stir vanilla into sour cream.

Cream butter in a large bowl until light. Add 1 cup sugar and beat until smooth and fluffy. Beat in eggs, one by one. At low speed, stir in flour mixture alternately with sour cream mixture, each in 2 portions.

Pour slightly less than half the batter into prepared pan. Sprinkle with half the cinnamon-walnut mixture. Gently spoon dollops of batter over mixture, using just enough to cover it. Sprinkle with remaining walnut mixture. Gently drop remaining batter in dollops over it. Spread gently to cover nut mixture. Bake about 55 minutes or until a cake tester inserted in cake comes out clean.

Cool cake in pan 10 minutes. Run a thin-bladed flexible knife around tube but not around sides of pan. Invert cake onto a rack and cool completely. Transfer cake to a platter. (Cake can be kept, wrapped, up to 2 days at room temperature or 3 days in refrigerator.) Serve at room temperature.

Makes 10 to 12 servings

ASHKENAZIC POPPYSEED COOKIES

A favorite among Jews from central Europe and Alsace, these poppy seed–topped cookies are made from rich, tender One, Two, Three Dough.

One, Two, Three Cookie Dough
  (page 126)
2 to 4 tablespoons poppy seeds

Prepare dough and refrigerate. Use one-fourth of dough at a time, rolling it out on a lightly floured surface until slightly less than ¼ inch thick. Using a 3-inch cookie cutter, cut in circles. Sprinkle each with ⅛ to ¼ teaspoon poppy seeds, according to your taste. Press to make them adhere to dough. Put cookies on greased baking sheet, spacing them about 1 inch apart and refrigerate. Refrigerate scraps.

Roll remaining dough and scraps and shape more cookies. Refrigerate cookies at least 30 minutes before baking to firm dough. (They can be kept, covered, overnight in refrigerator.)

Preheat oven to 375°F. Bake cookies 8 to 9 minutes or until they are very light brown at edges.

Makes about 48 cookies

CRISP ALMOND SLICES (MANDELBROT)

Mandelbrot is a Yiddish word meaning ''almond bread,'' and indeed, the almond-studded dough is first shaped in a loaf and baked. It is then cut in slices and these are baked again, to make toasted cookies. The double baking dries the cookies so they keep well, and they therefore are best enjoyed with a drink.

During our travels in Europe my husband and I were surprised to find Mandelbrot by other names in various places—in Tuscany, Italy, biscotti di Prato *served for dunking in sweet wine, for example, and French* croquets de Carcassonne, *for dipping in tea, coffee or wine.*

3 large eggs
1¼ cups sugar
1 cup vegetable oil
2 teaspoons grated lemon rind
1 teaspoon vanilla extract
4 cups all-purpose flour

1½ teaspoons baking powder
¼ teaspoon salt
1 cup slivered almonds, chopped
1 tablespoon sugar mixed with 1 teaspoon ground cinnamon, for sprinkling

Grease a baking sheet. In a mixer bowl, beat eggs, sugar, and oil until blended. Beat in lemon rind and vanilla. Sift flour with baking powder and salt. Add to egg mixture. Stir on low speed of mixer just until blended. Stir in almonds on low speed.

Shape dough into 4 logs each about 2 inches in diameter; their shape will not be very even, as dough is sticky. Place on baking sheet. Refrigerate 30 minutes. Preheat oven to 350°F. Use spatula to smooth dough and to push again into log shape, since it will have relaxed and spread a bit. Sprinkle top with sugar and cinnamon and pat to make it adhere to sides as well.

Bake 30 minutes or until lightly browned and set. Transfer carefully to a board and let stand until cool enough to handle. With a sharp knife, carefully cut in diagonal slices about ½ inch thick; dough will be slightly soft inside. Return slices to cleaned baking sheets in one layer; you will need 2 or 3 baking sheets.

Bake about 7 minutes per side or until lightly toasted so they are beige and dotted in places with golden brown; side of cookie touching baking sheet will brown first. Watch carefully so cookies don't brown throughout. Cool on a rack. Keep in airtight containers. (They keep for about 2 weeks.)

Makes about 36 cookies

CHOCOLATE-FILLED WALNUT RINGS

I learned to prepare filled cookies of this type in Israel, where they are sometimes called "naughty children" for obvious reasons! They are made of a round base spread with filling and topped with a ring-shaped cookie, so that the filling peeks out. Instead of the chocolate filling, sometimes date filling or red jam is used.

Walnut Cookies

2½ cups (about 9¼ ounces) walnuts
¾ cup granulated sugar
½ cup plus 2 tablespoons all-purpose flour
6 large egg whites, at room temperature

4 teaspoons grated lemon zest
6 tablespoons (¾ stick) unsalted butter or margarine, melted and cooled

Chocolate-Walnut Filling

4 ounces bittersweet or semisweet chocolate, chopped
1 cup (about 4 ounces) walnuts

½ cup confectioners' sugar, sifted
¼ cup (½ stick) unsalted butter or margarine, softened

Preheat oven to 350°F. Butter and flour 2 baking sheets. Mark 16 circles, using a 2½-inch cutter and spacing them about 1½ inches apart.

Grind nuts with 6 tablespoons sugar in a food processor until as fine as possible, scraping inward occasionally; they should remain light and not pasty. Transfer to a large bowl. Sift flour onto nuts and stir until blended.

Whip egg whites in a large bowl until soft peaks form. Gradually beat in remaining 6 tablespoons sugar and whip at high speed until whites are stiff and shiny but not dry.

Gently fold lemon zest and walnut mixture into egg whites. When batter is nearly blended, gradually pour in cool melted butter while folding. Fold lightly but quickly just until batter is blended.

Using a pastry bag and medium star tip, pipe rings of batter in 8 of the marked circles: one ring at border of each circle and a second ring inside first and touching it. Pipe remaining batter in complete rounds in remaining marked circles by beginning at center and piping in a spiral motion from center to fill circle.

Bake cookies about 15 minutes or until light brown. Do not overbake or they will be bitter. Using a metal pancake turner, transfer them immediately to a rack.

Melt chocolate in a small bowl above hot water over low heat. Stir until smooth, then let cool. Grind nuts with 2 tablespoons confectioners' sugar in a food processor until as fine as possible.

Cream butter in a small bowl, add remaining 6 tablespoons confectioners' sugar, and beat until smooth and fluffy. Stir in chocolate, then nuts.

When cookies are cool, spread filling on full rounds, using about 1 tablespoon filling per cookie. Set rings on top. Refrigerate 30 minutes. (Cookies can be kept, covered, for 3 days in refrigerator.)

Makes 16 large cookies

STRAWBERRY PECAN SQUARES

This delicious Austrian-style bar cookie is popular in Israel. It uses a single cookie dough that serves both as a base and as a crumbly streusel topping. Generally a simple sweet dough is used, but I find these cookies even better with chopped pecans.

Pecan Cookie Dough

1 cup (about 3¾ ounces) pecans
3 large egg yolks
½ cup sugar
¼ teaspoon salt
2 teaspoons vanilla extract

2 teaspoons grated lemon zest
1 cup (2 sticks) unsalted butter or margarine, cut in 16 cubes, cold
1¾ cups all-purpose flour

Topping

½ cup strawberry preserves
2 tablespoons sugar

¼ cup all-purpose flour
¼ cup pecans, coarsely chopped

Chop nuts fairly fine in food processor, then transfer to a bowl. Combine egg yolks, sugar, salt, vanilla, lemon zest, and butter in processor. Mix using 10 on/off turns, then process continuously for 5 seconds until nearly blended. Add flour and pecans and process about 2 seconds. Scrape down and process about 3 seconds or until dough begins to form sticky crumbs but does not come together in a ball. Wrap dough, press together, and shape in a rectangle. Refrigerate 1 hour.

Preheat oven to 350°F. Cut off one-fourth of dough and reserve in refrigerator. Pat out remaining dough in an unbuttered 13 × 9-inch baking pan.

Stir preserves. Using a rubber spatula, spread gently over dough, leaving a ½-inch border. Cut reserved dough into 10 pieces. Return to cleaned food processor and add sugar and flour. Process with a few on/off turns until sugar and flour are blended in but dough is still very crumbly. Crumble dough quickly between your fingers to separate any lumps and sprinkle crumbs evenly over jam. Sprinkle with chopped pecans.

Bake about 33 minutes or until crumbs are firm and light brown. Cool in pan on a rack until lukewarm. Cut in 1½ × 2-inch bars in pan. (Cookies can be kept for 3 days in an airtight container at cool room temperature.)

Makes about 28 small bars

CHOCOLATE COCONUT RUM BALLS

These chocolate balls are fun to make because they taste different every time, depending on what type of cake or cookies you use to make them. They are a frequently made confection in Jewish homes. Although originally this was a way to use up leftover cake or cookies, now people even buy cookies in order to make these sweets. My mother prefers to use chocolate cake so the flavor is most intense, but almost any cake or cookies will give good results.

Many call these rum balls but they don't necessarily contain rum. They could be called chocolate wine balls or chocolate orange juice balls. The main thing is they contain chocolate, cake or cookie crumbs, and a variety of other goodies—raisins, nuts, coconut, or all three. These are rolled in coconut, but some people roll them in chopped almonds or chocolate sprinkles.

¼ cup raisins (optional)
2 tablespoons rum or brandy, or chocolate, orange, or chocolate-orange liqueur (optional)
4 ounces bittersweet or semisweet chocolate, chopped
2 tablespoons unsweetened cocoa
2 tablespoons sugar
½ cup sweet wine or orange juice

6 tablespoons (¾ stick) unsalted butter or margarine, at room temperature, cut into pieces
¼ pound simple cookies (1 cup crumbs)
¼ cup chopped pecans or walnuts
about 1½ cups flaked or shredded coconut

Combine raisins and rum in a jar and cover. Let stand about 1 hour for raisins to absorb flavor.

Heat chocolate, cocoa, sugar, and wine or juice in a heavy, small saucepan over low heat, stirring often, until chocolate melts. Remove from heat and add butter. Stir until melted. Crush cookies to fairly coarse crumbs, then stir crumbs into chocolate mixture. Add nuts and raisins with their rum. Mix well. Cover and refrigerate until firm enough to shape in balls, about 1½ to 2 hours.

Shape mixture into balls, using about 2 teaspoons for each. Put on plates and refrigerate 5 minutes to firm slightly. Put coconut in a shallow bowl or tray and roll balls in it. Set candies on plates. Refrigerate 1 hour before serving. (Candies can be kept in an airtight container up to 1 week in refrigerator.) Serve in candy papers.

Makes about 30 candies

CINNAMON-NUT-RAISIN CRESCENTS (RUGELACH)

Crescent-shaped rugelach, of eastern European origin, may be the best-known Jewish cookie in America—and for good reason. When made with a rich, flaky dough like this one, they are absolutely irresistible. Jewish bakeries like Canter's in Los Angeles present these in a variety of fillings, shapes, and colors: cinnamon-walnut, chocolate, cheese, apricot, and raspberry.

With this easy-to-handle cream cheese and sour cream dough, rugelach are a delight to prepare at home. Use the bar type of cream cheese for making the dough, not the soft type designed for spreading.

Cream Cheese Dough

6 ounces cream cheese
1 cup (2 sticks) cold unsalted butter
2 cups all-purpose flour

¼ teaspoon salt
⅓ cup sour cream
1 teaspoon water, if needed

Walnut-Raisin-Cinnamon Filling

½ cup sugar
1 tablespoon ground cinnamon

1 cup walnuts, finely chopped
½ cup dark raisins, chopped

Cut cream cheese into tablespoon-size pieces and let soften at room temperature. Cut butter into small pieces of about ½ tablespoon and keep cold until ready to use.

In a food processor combine flour, salt, and butter and process with on/off turns until mixture resembles coarse meal. Add cream cheese and sour cream, distributing them fairly evenly over mixture. Process with on/off turns until dough just holds together. Add 1 teaspoon water if necessary. Wrap dough, press together to a ball, and flatten to a disc. Refrigerate 4 hours or up to 2 days.

Lightly butter 2 or 3 baking sheets. Mix sugar and cinnamon for filling. Divide dough into 4 pieces. Press one-fourth of dough to a round, then flatten it. Roll it to a 9-inch circle about ⅛ inch thick. Sprinkle one-fourth of sugar-cinnamon mixture (about 2 tablespoons) all over circle, then sprinkle one-fourth of nuts and raisins near outer edge of circle. Press with rolling pin so they adhere to dough. Using a heavy knife, cut circle in 12 wedges, making each cut with a sharp movement of heel of knife. Roll up tightly from wide end to point; be sure filling is enclosed, since raisins can burn if exposed. Put cookies on baking sheets, with points of triangles facing down, spacing them about 1 inch apart. Curve each to a crescent, if desired. Refrigerate while shaping more cookies. Refrigerate all at least 20 minutes before baking. (Unbaked cookies can be frozen.)

Preheat oven to 350°F. Bake cookies 22 to 25 minutes or until light golden. Cool on racks. (Cookies can be kept 4 days in airtight containers.)

Makes 48 small cookies

CHOCOLATE CHIP RUGELACH

If rugelach are cousins of croissants, *these are petite relatives of the French* pain au chocolat. *They are shaped in a similar manner to the French pastry and are also rich and buttery, but are so much easier to make. And only one ingredient is needed for the filling.*

Cream Cheese Dough (page 316),
  chilled

about 1 cup miniature semisweet
  chocolate chips

Lightly butter 2 or 3 baking sheets. Divide dough into 4 pieces. Press one-fourth to a square, then flatten it. Roll it to a 9- to 9½-inch square and trim edges. Cut into 3 equal strips, then cut each strip crosswise into 3. You will have 9 squares.

Put 1 teaspoon chocolate chips on a square about ½ inch from edge nearest you. Spread chips in a row along the edge so they are as close together as possible but are in a single layer. Fold over edge of dough nearest you to cover row of chips. Roll up dough tightly toward other side, like a jelly roll. It will look like a thin cylinder. Cut cylinder in half.

Put cookies on baking sheets seam down, spacing them about 1 inch apart. Refrigerate while shaping more cookies, and refrigerate all at least 20 minutes before baking. (Unbaked cookies can be frozen.)

Preheat oven to 350°F. Bake cookies about 22 minutes or until light golden. Cool on racks. (Cookies can be kept for 2 days in airtight containers.)

Makes 72 small cookies

SEPHARDIC NUT-FILLED COOKIES

With a delicious, melt-in-your-mouth pastry moistened with orange flower water enclosing a filling of almonds and walnuts, these cookies are an exotic, wonderful treat. Pistachios are also a favorite filling ingredient and can be substituted for either of the nuts. Another well-liked filling for these pastries is made of ground dates. A special decoration made with pastry pinchers is characteristic of these cookies.

Orange Flower Pastry

2⅔ cups all-purpose flour
1 cup (2 sticks) unsalted butter, cut
  into pieces

5 or 6 tablespoons orange flower water

Nut Filling

1 cup walnuts
1 cup almonds
2 tablespoons granulated sugar
  (optional)

2 tablespoons orange flower water, or
  1 teaspoon ground cinnamon

confectioners' sugar, for dredging

In a food processor combine flour and butter and process with on/off turns until mixture resembles fine meal. Add 5 tablespoons orange flower water. Process until dough forms a ball. Dough should be fairly soft and pliable; if it is dry, add another tablespoon orange flower water and process briefly. Wrap dough and refrigerate 1 hour.

In food processor chop walnuts and almonds together, so there are still pieces; do not grind finely. Transfer to a bowl and stir in granulated sugar and orange flower water or cinnamon.

To shape pastries, make a ball from 1 tablespoon dough. Hold pastry ball in one hand and poke it with the index finger of your other hand to make a hole. Enlarge this hole, turning dough around your finger, until you have a thin shell for filling. Gently add enough nut filling to fill the shell. Pinch dough closed around filling. Press to a ball. Press top to flatten slightly. Put on a baking sheet with side that was open facing up. Shape more pastries.

Use pastry pincher to decorate each pastry all around with ridges going from top to bottom of pastry. Pinch once or twice on top also. Pinch firmly, or marks will disappear during baking. If you don't have a pastry pincher, make up-and-down ridges with the tines of a fork. Refrigerate at least 30 minutes or freeze 15 minutes.

Preheat oven to 375°F. Bake pastries 20 to 25 minutes or until color of dough changes only slightly, to light beige; do not let them brown. While they are still hot, dredge them generously with confectioners' sugar. (Cookies can be kept for 3 days in airtight containers.)

Makes about 25 to 30 cookies

MOIST COCONUT MACAROONS

A familiar Passover sweet, coconut macaroons are served as a snack or a treat with coffee or tea. I find fresh, home-baked macaroons clearly superior to those that come in cans or packages. And they are very easy to make. The unsweetened coconut needed for the recipe can be purchased at health food stores or in some supermarkets.

2 large egg whites
⅔ cup sugar
2 teaspoons lemon juice

grated rind of ½ lemon
1½ cups finely grated unsweetened coconut

Preheat oven to 300°F. Line a baking sheet with foil or wax paper and lightly grease paper.

Beat egg whites until soft peaks form. Gradually beat in sugar. Continue beating ½ minute or until very stiff. Gradually beat in lemon juice. Add lemon rind and one-third of the coconut and fold in lightly. Sprinkle in remaining coconut in 2 more portions, folding lightly after each.

Using a pastry bag fitted with a large tip, or 2 spoons, form mounds of mixture 1½ inches in diameter on lined baking sheet, spacing them about 1 inch apart. Bake 18 minutes or until macaroons are light beige. Leave in oven, with door wedged slightly open, 20 minutes.

Remove from oven and cool a few minutes on baking sheet. Carefully remove cookies from paper and cool on a rack. (Macaroons can be kept several days in airtight container at room temperature.)

Makes about 30 macaroons

NUT AND CHOCOLATE-STUDDED MERINGUES

Both Ashkenazic and Sephardic Jews love to serve meringues for Passover. These light, crunchy meringues can be made with pecans, walnuts, hazelnuts, or a mixture of nuts.

matzo cake meal, for flouring pan
4 large egg whites, at room
  temperature
¼ teaspoon cream of tartar (optional)
1 cup plus 2 tablespoons sugar
¾ cup coarsely chopped pecans
4 ounces bittersweet or semisweet
  chocolate, cut into tiny cubes
⅔ cup pecan halves

Preheat oven to 275°F. Lightly grease corners of 2 baking sheets with margarine and line them with foil. Grease and lightly flour foil with matzo cake meal, tapping baking sheet to remove excess.

Whip egg whites with cream of tartar in a large bowl until stiff. Gradually beat in ½ cup sugar at high speed and whip until whites are very shiny.

Gently fold in remaining ½ cup plus 2 tablespoons sugar in 2 batches, as quickly as possible. Quickly fold in chopped pecans and chocolate pieces. Spoon mixture in irregular mounds onto prepared baking sheets, using 1 mounded tablespoon for each and spacing them about 1½ inches apart. Set a pecan half on each meringue.

Bake 30 minutes, then reduce oven temperature to 250°F. Bake 30 minutes more or until meringues are firm to touch, dry at bases, and can be easily removed from foil. They will be light beige.

Transfer meringues to a rack and cool. Put them in airtight container as soon as they are cool. (Meringues can be kept in airtight containers at room temperature up to 1 week in dry weather. If they become sticky from humidity, they can be baked in a 200°F. oven for about 30 minutes to recrisp.)

Makes about 24 meringues

HONEY-GLAZED COOKIES WITH WALNUTS (TAYGLACH)

Tayglach are a sweet and sticky confection of pastry and nuts in a honey-flavored syrup, best served with coffee or tea. They are a specialty for the Jewish New Year, and many Jewish bakeries prepare them only for this holiday. Actually, there are three types of tayglach: those served in a thin syrup, those drained of their syrup, or as in this version, those left in thick syrup until firm, somewhat like French nougatine, and then cut. At bakeries I have also had tayglach that were formed into mounds and topped with maraschino cherries.

1⅓ cups all-purpose flour
¼ teaspoon baking powder
¼ teaspoon ground ginger
pinch of salt

2 large eggs
3 large egg yolks
2 tablespoons vegetable oil

Honey Syrup

1 cup honey (about ¾ pound)
1 cup sugar
1 teaspoon ground ginger

1 cup coarsely chopped walnuts
about 1 cup unsweetened coconut, for
   rolling (optional)

Preheat oven to 350°F. Oil 2 large baking sheets.

Sift flour with baking powder, ginger, and salt into a medium bowl. Make a well in center and add eggs, yolks, and oil. Stir until combined. Knead on a lightly floured surface to a soft, smooth dough. If dough is very sticky, knead in about 1 tablespoon more flour.

Cut dough into 8 pieces with floured knife. Using both hands, roll a piece of dough on a lightly floured surface into a thin rope about ½ inch in diameter. Cut rope into ½-inch lengths, using the heel of a floured heavy knife. Repeat with remaining pieces of dough. Place dough pieces on baking sheets without letting them touch each other. Bake about 10 minutes or until their bottoms are light brown. Remove from oven.

Combine honey, sugar, and ginger in large heavy saucepan. Cook over low heat, stirring occasionally, to dissolve sugar. Bring to a boil over moderate heat, taking care that mixture does not boil over. Cook over low heat about 5 minutes, or until syrup reaches 260°F. on a candy thermometer (hard-ball stage).

Carefully add baked tayglach and chopped nuts to syrup and simmer over medium-low heat, stirring occasionally, about 10 minutes or until tayglach are golden brown. Meanwhile, line a large baking sheet with foil and oil the foil.

Stir tayglach mixture to distribute nuts evenly and spoon mixture onto lined baking sheet. Flatten so that tayglach form one layer and let cool completely.

Turn tayglach over onto a board and carefully peel off foil. Cut into 1-inch squares or diamonds. Roll in grated coconut. Store in shallow airtight containers at room temperature until ready to serve. Serve in candy papers.

Makes about 30 pieces

NOTES: If tayglach stick together while being stored, cut them into pieces again; or, if making them to keep for some time, keep them in large blocks and cut them as needed. Alternatively, keep them in a large enough container so they do not touch one another.

ISRAELI–STYLE BAVARIAN CREAM WITH CHOCOLATE SAUCE AND PECANS

Judging by the number of restaurant menus on which it appears, Bavarian cream is the most popular dessert in Israel. But it is a special version of the dessert—a vanilla Bavarian cream topped with dark chocolate sauce or chocolate syrup and sprinkled with chopped nuts. Unlike the classic European Bavarian, based on a custard sauce enriched with egg yolks, the Israeli version usually includes the whipped egg whites too, and thus is lighter. It is served right from the dish instead of being unmolded.
SEE PHOTOGRAPH.

1½ cups milk
1 vanilla bean, split lengthwise; or 2 teaspoons vanilla extract
1 envelope plus 1 teaspoon unflavored gelatin
¼ cup water
5 large egg yolks, at room temperature

7 tablespoons sugar
1 cup heavy cream, well chilled
3 large egg whites
Chocolate Sauce (recipe follows)
½ cup pecans, diced, chopped, or whole

Bring milk and vanilla bean (but not extract) to a boil in a heavy medium saucepan. Remove from heat, cover, and let stand 15 minutes. Sprinkle gelatin over water in a small cup and let stand while preparing custard.

Whisk egg yolks lightly in a large heatproof bowl. Add sugar and whisk until thick and smooth. Reheat milk mixture to a boil, then remove vanilla bean. Gradually whisk hot milk into yolk mixture. Return mixture to saucepan, whisking. Cook over medium-low heat, stirring mixture and scraping bottom of pan constantly with a wooden spoon, until mixture thickens slightly and reaches 165°F. to 170F. on an instant-read thermometer; begin checking after 5 minutes. (To check without a thermometer, remove custard from heat, dip a metal spoon in custard, and draw your finger across back of spoon—your finger should leave a clear trail in mixture that clings to spoon.) Do not overcook custard or it will curdle.

Remove custard from heat and immediately add softened gelatin, whisking until it dissolves completely. Pour into a large bowl and stir for about ½ minute to cool. Cool to room temperature, stirring occasionally. Add vanilla extract.

Refrigerate mixture about 20 minutes, stirring often, or set bowl of mixture in a larger bowl of iced water about 10 minutes, stirring very often. Chill until mixture is cold and beginning to thicken but is not set.

Prepare eight ⅔-cup ramekins or other individual serving dishes or a 9-inch square serving dish.

Whip cream in a chilled bowl until nearly stiff. Set aside. In another bowl, whip egg whites until stiff. Gently fold cream into custard, followed by egg whites. Pour mixture into prepared dishes and smooth top. Cover and refrigerate at least 3 hours or until set. (Dessert can be kept up to 2 days in refrigerator.)

Serve dish in ramekins; or cut in 8 or 9 squares and use broad spatula to transfer to plates. Spoon a little cool Chocolate Sauce over each serving and garnish with nuts.

Makes 8 or 9 servings

Chocolate Sauce

Serve this with Israeli-Style Bavarian cream, or with Pear Strudel (page 89) and vanilla ice cream, or use it to make "Passover Profiteroles" using Passover "Rolls" (page 34).

8 ounces bittersweet or semisweet
  chocolate, chopped
¼ cup (½ stick) unsalted butter or
  margarine, cut into 8 pieces

½ cup water
1 teaspoon vanilla extract

Melt chocolate with butter and water in a medium bowl set above hot water over low heat. Stir until smooth. Remove from pan of water and cool 10 minutes. Gradually stir in vanilla. (Sauce can be kept, covered, up to 1 week in refrigerator.)

If preparing sauce ahead, even for serving cool, reheat it above hot water. If desired, cool it to room temperature. (If sauce is removed from refrigerator and brought to room temperature without reheating, it is too thick.)

Makes 1½ cups

SPICED APPLE BLINTZES

Apple blintzes, originally from eastern Europe, are one of the most prized of Jewish desserts. Although many recipes call for grated or sliced raw apples, I prefer to sauté the fruit first, so it is meltingly tender. These blintzes sprinkled with cinnamon and sugar are a lovely finale to a holiday dinner.

Apple Filling

2 pounds Golden Delicious apples
4 tablespoons (½ stick) unsalted
    margarine or butter

½ teaspoon ground cinnamon
6 to 8 tablespoons sugar, according to
    sweetness of apples

Basic Blintzes (page 198), cooked in an
    8-inch pan
3 to 4 tablespoons (½ stick) margarine
    or butter, for frying or baking

1 teaspoon ground cinnamon mixed
    with 1 tablespoon sugar, for
    sprinkling

Peel and halve the apples. Core them and cut into thin slices. Melt margarine in 2 large skillets or sauté pans. Add apples, sprinkle with cinnamon, and sauté over medium-high heat, turning pieces over from time to time, for 2 minutes. Cover and cook over low heat for 10 minutes or until apples are just tender. Raise heat to high and add 3 tablespoons sugar to each pan, turning apple wedges over so both sides are coated with sugar. Leave pan over high heat just until sugar dissolves.

Combine apples in one pan and heat briefly. Remove from heat. Taste and add more sugar or cinnamon if necessary; heat, tossing apples gently, just until sugar dissolves. (Filling can be kept 1 day in refrigerator.)

Spoon 2 to 2½ tablespoons filling onto brown side of each blintze along one edge. Fold over edges of blintze to right and left of filling so that each covers about half the filling; roll up, beginning at edge with filling. (Blintzes can be filled 1 day ahead and refrigerated, covered.)

Blintzes can be baked or fried. To bake them, preheat oven to 425°F. Arrange blintzes in one layer in a greased shallow baking dish. Dot each blintze with small pieces of margarine. Bake for about 15 minutes, or until heated through and lightly browned.

To fry blintzes, heat margarine in a skillet, add blintzes open end down, and fry over low heat 3 to 5 minutes on each side; be careful not to let them burn.

Sprinkle blintzes with cinnamon and sugar before serving. Serve hot.

Makes 6 servings

POLISH STRAWBERRY SOUP

Polish Jews brought their taste for creamy berry soups to Israel, where they are now enjoyed by people of many origins. Some cooks turn this easy-to-make soup into an appetizer by adding less sugar, but I like it best as a refreshing spring or summer dessert.

1 quart strawberries
2 cups water
10 tablespoons sugar

1 tablespoon potato starch or
   cornstarch, dissolved in 2
   tablespoons cold water
1 cup sour cream

For Garnish

about ½ cup sour cream
4 strawberry slices

Put half the berries in a saucepan with the water and bring to a simmer. Cover and simmer about 8 minutes or until berries are soft and liquid is red. Meanwhile, puree remaining berries in a food processor or blender until smooth and pour into a bowl. Remove cooked berries from saucepan with a slotted spoon and puree them in food processor or blender. Add to puree of raw strawberries.

   Add sugar and dissolved potato starch to liquid in pan and bring to a simmer, stirring. Remove from heat. Whisk sour cream until smooth in a bowl. Gradually whisk liquid into sour cream. Stir in strawberry puree. Chill thoroughly.

   To serve, garnish each serving with a dollop of sour cream topped with a strawberry slice.

Makes 4 servings

DRIED FRUIT COMPOTE WITH WINE

Jews from all over Europe prepare this simple but tasty dessert. Some cooks use water and lemon juice as the cooking liquid, others use tea, but I like to use wine, either red or white, because the wine and the fruit exchange flavors beautifully. I find that prunes are the best fruit for preparing this way, but a package of mixed dried fruit gives the dessert an interesting mix of colors and textures.

This dessert keeps very well. Since it uses no dairy products, it can be served after a meal containing meat. It also makes a good accompaniment for vanilla ice cream or for plain cakes like pound cake.

1 pound prunes (with pits) or mixed
   dried fruit (prunes, pears, apricots)
1 bottle (3 cups) dry red or white wine

½ to 1 cup water
1 cinnamon stick
½ cup sugar

Put fruit and wine in a glass bowl. Cover with a plate to help keep fruit submerged. Let soak overnight at room temperature.

Gently put fruit and its wine in a saucepan and add enough water to barely cover fruit. Immerse cinnamon stick in liquid, and sprinkle mixture with sugar. Very gently stir over low heat to dissolve sugar. Cover and cook over low heat 30 minutes or until tender. Transfer to bowl and let cool, spooning wine over fruit from time to time. Serve cold, as dessert. (Fruit can be kept, covered, 2 weeks in refrigerator.)

Makes 6 to 8 servings

SABRA SORBET

A Sabra is a person who was born in Israel, and also is the name of a famous Israeli chocolate-orange liqueur. Here, the liqueur is combined with orange juice as a refreshing sorbet, an ideal light dessert after a fleishig, or meat, dinner. If you like, serve it with slices of prickly pears, a fruit known in Israel as sabras. Israelis say this fruit is like them—tough and prickly on the outside but sweet on the inside!

¾ cup sugar
½ cup water
zest of 1 medium orange, pared in thin
   strips with vegetable peeler

2⅓ cups strained fresh orange juice
¼ cup Sabra chocolate-orange liqueur
1 tablespoon strained fresh lemon
   juice, or to taste (optional)

Combine sugar, water, and orange peel strips in small heavy saucepan. Heat over low heat, stirring gently, until sugar dissolves completely. Stop stirring. Bring to full boil over medium-high heat, then boil 30 seconds. Pour into heatproof bowl and cool completely. Cover and refrigerate at least 1 hour. (Syrup can be kept for 1 week in refrigerator.)

Remove strips of peel from syrup with slotted spoon. In a large bowl, add syrup to orange juice and mix thoroughly. Stir in liqueur. Taste, and add lemon juice if desired. Mixture should taste quite sweet; sweetness of sorbet will be less apparent when it is frozen.

Chill a medium metal bowl and airtight container in freezer. Transfer sorbet mixture to ice cream machine and process until mixture has consistency of soft ice cream; it should not be runny but will not become very firm. Transfer sorbet as quickly as possible to chilled bowl; it melts very quickly. Cover tightly and freeze until ready to serve. If keeping sorbet longer than 3 hours, transfer when firm to airtight container and cover tightly. (Sorbet is best served within 3 hours but can be kept up to 4 days.)

Soften slightly before serving. Serve in thoroughly chilled dessert dishes or wine glasses.

Makes about 3 cups sorbet; about 6 servings

APPLE CINNAMON ICE CREAM

Although I rarely use nondairy cream or milk substitutes, when it comes to ice cream I find it sometimes worthwhile to make an exception! This pareve ice cream gains a lovely flavor from cinnamon and apple juice. It is lighter than most ice creams because of its high proportion of fruit juice. Serve it on its own or with Apple Compote (page 116) or Strawberry Sauce (page 59).

2 cups apple juice
6 large egg yolks
6 tablespoons sugar

1 teaspoon ground cinnamon
1 cup nondairy creamer or light cream

Bring apple juice to a boil in a small heavy saucepan. Remove from heat.

Whisk egg yolks lightly in a medium bowl. Add sugar and cinnamon and whisk until smooth. Gradually whisk in hot apple juice. Return mixture to saucepan. Cook over medium-low heat, stirring and scraping bottom of pan constantly with a wooden spoon, until mixture thickens slightly and reaches 165 to 170°F. on an instant-read thermometer; begin checking after 4 minutes. (To check without thermometer, remove pan from heat, dip a metal spoon in sauce and draw your finger across back of spoon—your finger should leave a clear path in mixture that clings to spoon.) If necessary, cook another ½ minute and check again. Do not overcook mixture or it will curdle. Pour immediately into a bowl and stir about ½ minute to cool.

Stir nondairy creamer into mixture. Cool completely, stirring occasionally. Pour into ice cream machine and process until frozen. Meanwhile, chill bowl in freezer. Transfer ice cream quickly to chilled bowl, cover tightly, and keep in freezer until ready to serve. (Can be kept 1 week in freezer.) Soften slightly before serving.

Makes about 4 cups; about 8 servings

SUMMER FRUIT SALAD
WITH RASPBERRY SAUCE

Fruit salad is the natural choice to end a meal in many kosher homes and is especially popular today because it is a healthful dessert.

Strawberry Sauce (page 59) can be substituted for the Raspberry Sauce, if you like. For a simpler dessert, instead of using a berry sauce you can sprinkle the cut fruit with an additional tablespoon or two of sugar, two teaspoons of lemon juice, and two tablespoons of your favorite fruit liqueur. Or for a fancier finale, you can top this with ice cream, sorbet, or whipped cream.

3 peaches or nectarines
3 apricots (optional)
1 pint strawberries, lightly rinsed and
    hulled

1 pint blueberries, blackberries, or
    raspberries
1 kiwi (optional)
2 tablespoons sugar
Raspberry Sauce (recipe follows)

Slice peaches or nectarines in wedges. Slice apricots. Put slices in a bowl. Quarter strawberries lengthwise and add to bowl. Add blueberries. Peel kiwi, halve lengthwise, and cut into half slices.

Sprinkle fruit with sugar. Using a rubber spatula, mix ingredients as gently as possible. If desired, cover and chill for about 30 minutes.

To serve, add about half the Raspberry Sauce to fruit salad and mix gently. Divide salad among 4 to 6 dessert dishes or stemmed glasses. Serve remaining sauce separately.

Makes 4 to 6 servings

Raspberry Sauce

This sauce is wonderful with cheesecake, blintzes, vanilla ice cream, or fruit salad.

3 cups (about 12 ounces) fresh
raspberries; or one 10- to 12-ounce
package frozen unsweetened or
lightly sweetened raspberries,
thawed

¾ cup confectioners' sugar, sifted
1 to 2 teaspoons fresh lemon juice
(optional)

Puree berries in food processor or blender. Add confectioners' sugar and process until very smooth. Taste and add another tablespoon sugar if desired. Strain into a bowl, pressing on pulp in strainer; use rubber spatula to scrape mixture from underside of strainer.

Cover and refrigerate 30 minutes. (Sauce can be kept, covered, for 1 day in refrigerator.) Stir before serving and add lemon juice to taste. Serve cold.

Makes about 1 cup sauce

EASY CHOCOLATE-LADYFINGER PUDDING

Chocolate is a favorite flavor in Israel and among Jews in general. In my research for my book on chocolate desserts, Chocolate Sensations, *I learned that chocolate was brought from the New World to Spain but I was not aware of the major role played by the Jews in introducing chocolate to the rest of Europe. Parisian chef Alain Dutournier told me recently that in his home region in southwestern France, near the border with Spain, many of the master chocolatiers were of Jewish origin. Bayonne, a major city in the region, was the first city in France where chocolate was made, and remains a chocolate center to this day. And chocolate making in Bayonne was started by Jews who had settled in southwest France after being chased out of Spain during the Inquisition. The new product rapidly gained favor in the area and spread throughout France.*

This is a delicious, very simple chocolate dessert, with a base of cognac-dipped ladyfingers, a center of super-rich chocolate pudding, and a generous topping of whipped cream.

¼ cup cognac or brandy
¼ cup water
6 ounces ladyfingers
8 ounces semisweet chocolate,
  chopped

¾ cup (1½ sticks) unsalted butter
2 large egg yolks*

Topping and Decoration

1 cup heavy cream
2 teaspoons sugar

1 teaspoon cognac or brandy
½ ounce semisweet chocolate

Mix cognac and water in a shallow bowl. Quickly dip each ladyfinger in mixture and set it in a 9- or 10-inch springform pan; do not leave them in mixture too long or they will become soggy.

Melt chocolate and butter in a large bowl set above hot water over low heat. Stir until smooth, then remove from pan of water and let cool for 2 minutes. Beat yolks in a small bowl. Gradually beat 3 tablespoons of chocolate mixture into yolks. Return this mixture to pan of chocolate and mix quickly and thoroughly. Pour mixture over ladyfingers and refrigerate about 1 hour or freeze 30 minutes or until firm.

Whip cream in a chilled bowl until it begins to thicken. Add sugar and brandy and continue whipping until stiff. Spread whipped cream over chocolate mixture. Grate a little chocolate on top for garnish. Refrigerate at least 2 hours before serving. (Dessert can be made 1 day ahead and kept in refrigerator.)

To unmold, slide a thin-bladed knife carefully around dessert. Release spring and remove sides of pan.

Makes 6 to 8 servings

VARIATION: Chocolate-Ladyfinger No-Bake Pie
Instead of preparing this dessert in a springform pan, make and serve it in a 9- or 10-inch pie dish.

*If you are concerned about the safety of using raw eggs in a recipe, you may wish to choose another dessert.

CREAMY NOODLE KUGEL WITH ALMONDS

Cooking fine noodles in milk gives this kugel a wonderfully rich taste. It is a good dessert for winter or for Shavuot. Since this is a holiday for honoring the first fruits of the season, a fitting accompaniment for the dessert is slices of fresh summer fruit, such as peaches, nectarines, or apricots.

2½ cups milk
1 cup very fine noodles
pinch of salt
grated rind of 1 lemon
6 tablespoons sugar

2 tablespoons (¼ stick) butter or
  margarine
¼ cup coarsely chopped almonds
2 large eggs, separated

Bring milk to a boil in a heavy, medium saucepan. Add noodles and salt and cook over low heat, stirring occasionally, for 20 to 30 minutes or until noodles are tender and absorb most of milk. Do not drain.

Meanwhile, preheat oven to 350°F. Butter a 4- to 5-cup baking dish and sprinkle a little sugar on sides of dish. Set this dish inside a larger baking dish.

Stir lemon rind and 3 tablespoons sugar into hot noodle mixture. Cool several minutes. Stir in butter, almonds, and egg yolks.

Beat egg whites until soft peaks form. Beat in remaining 3 tablespoons sugar at high speed and whip until whites are stiff. Fold whites, in 2 portions, into noodle mixture. Transfer to baking dish. Add hot water to larger baking dish to come half way up sides of dish containing noodle mixture. Bake 40 to 45 minutes or until a small knife inserted into noodle mixture comes out dry. (Kugel can be kept, covered, for 2 days in refrigerator. Reheat in a medium oven.) Serve hot.

Makes 6 servings

MATZO AND APPLE KUGEL

Haroset gives this kugel from eastern France its special flavor. I like to use an orange-scented haroset, but you can use your favorite version.

4 matzos
4 large eggs, separated
1 teaspoon ground cinnamon
5 tablespoons sugar
¾ cup Orange-Scented Haroset with
  Wine (page 32)

1 large apple, peeled, cored, and cut
  into very thin slices
¼ cup (½ stick) margarine, melted and
  cooled

Preheat oven to 350°F. Grease a 7- to 8-cup deep baking dish. Break matzos into small pieces and put in a bowl. Cover with boiling water and let stand for 2 minutes. Drain and squeeze out as much water as possible.

Beat egg yolks with cinnamon and 3 tablespoons sugar until lightened. Beat in haroset until well blended. Stir in matzos, apple, and melted margarine.

Beat egg whites until just stiff. Add remaining 2 tablespoons sugar and beat at high speed another ½ minute or until glossy. Gently fold egg whites into matzo mixture.

Spoon mixture into greased dish. Bake about 40 minutes, or until browned and firm.

Makes about 8 servings

RUSSIAN BREAD PUDDING WITH ALMONDS AND RAISINS

This winter dessert is a good way to make use of extra challah left from the Sabbath. Warm Apple Compote (page 116) and sour cream are good accompaniments.

4 ounces stale challah (egg bread), crust removed
1¼ cups milk
6 tablespoons sugar
1½ teaspoons ground cinnamon
2 large eggs, separated

½ cup dark raisins, rinsed with hot water
½ cup chopped almonds
2 tablespoons (¼ stick) butter, cut into small pieces

Preheat oven to 400°F. Grease a 5-cup baking dish. Cut bread into cubes and put in a medium bowl. Bring milk to a boil and pour over the bread. Let stand a few minutes so bread absorbs milk. Mash bread with a fork, then stir in 4 tablespoons sugar, 1 teaspoon cinnamon, egg yolks, raisins, and almonds.

Beat egg whites to soft peaks. Beat in remaining 2 tablespoons sugar and whip until stiff and shiny. Fold whites, in 2 portions, into bread mixture. Transfer to baking dish. Sprinkle with remaining ½ teaspoon cinnamon and dot with butter. Bake 40 to 50 minutes or until a toothpick inserted in center comes out dry. Serve hot.

Makes 6 servings

─── 18 ───
MENUS FOR
CELEBRATIONS

Jewish cooking is much more than holiday food. Here are some kosher menus for festive occasions, and menus that turn everyday meals into celebrations.

Please note that in each menu the number of people each dish will serve varies according to the number of dishes you wish to prepare. In many menus there is a choice of preparing one or a selection of first courses, desserts, and sometimes even main courses. You can multiply the ingredient quantities in the recipes according to the number of dishes as well as the number of people you are serving.

A SPRINGTIME POLISH LUNCHEON MENU

Feasting on salmon, asparagus, and strawberries is a lovely way to welcome spring, and they are featured in this menu. You can serve it for a light lunch, with the salmon as a main course, or add a roast chicken and serve it with the kugel to make a more substantial menu. To make the cooking easy, the salmon, salad, and dessert are prepared ahead.

Beet Salad with Apples (page 84)
Sweet and Sour Salmon (page 210)
Potato Kugel with Asparagus and Broccoli (page 250)
Strawberry Pecan Squares (page 314), served with fresh strawberries

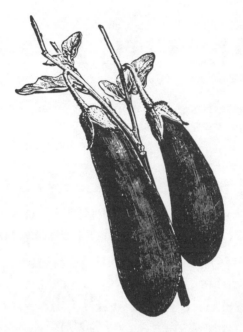

A SUMMER VEGETARIAN MENU

Kosher pareve and dairy meals fit in with the rules of many vegetarians. Thus, many Jews who keep kosher, whether they are vegetarians or not, often eat vegetarian menus. In Israel this style of dining is especially popular in the summer, when there are so many wonderful Mediterranean vegetables and fruits. Sephardic dishes, such as the eggplant dishes and the okra in this menu, lend themselves especially well to vegetarian meals.

Spicy Potato Salad (page 48)
Avocado and Egg Salad (page 162)
Easy Curried Eggplant (page 268)
Pita (page 295)
Okra with Tomatoes and Coriander (page 267)
Easy Rice Pilaf (page 145)
Raspberry Almond Tart (page 308);
Sabra Sorbet (page 326); or fresh fruit

A FALL FISH FEAST

Menus with a fish main course have been my favorite since I was a young girl. I think part of the reason is that fish goes with everything in a kosher menu, so I could look forward to a creamy dessert!

Spinach Pancakes (page 257), or Zucchini Pancakes with Garlic and Yogurt Mint Topping (page 117)
Moroccan Sea Bass with Red Peppers (page 211)
Spicy Couscous with Garlic (page 280),
or Aromatic Yellow Rice (page 278)
Israeli–Style Bavarian Cream with Chocolate Sauce and Pecans (page 322)

A SEPHARDIC SUPPER FOR A WINTER EVENING

A warming, slightly spicy soup of beef and beans is the center for this winter party menu, which is cozy, casual, and easy to serve. To turn this menu into a simple family supper, you can serve only one of the salad appetizers and omit the fish course.

Sephardic Beet Salad with Coriander (page 177)
Piquant Cooked Carrot Salad (page 174)
Sephardic Fish Steaks with Cumin and Garlic (page 217)
Hearty Meat Soup with Green Beans (page 193)
Nut and Chocolate-Studded Meringues (page 320)
Mint tea

A BARBECUE, ISRAELI STYLE

Our favorite barbecue menu, which we often serve when entertaining on short notice, features spicy chicken, aromatic mushrooms, and basmati rice. This is a delicious as well as "safe" menu—everyone seems to love these dishes, even picky eaters of all ages.

Tahini Sauce (page 164), served with Pita (page 295)
Israeli Grilled Chicken (page 228)
Savory Mushrooms with Thyme and Olive Oil (page 33)
Steamed white rice, preferably basmati
Israeli Vegetable Salad (page 20)
Fruit salad, or My Mother's Chocolate Applesauce Cake (page 91)

A MENU FOR A KIDDUSH

Kiddush is literally a blessing over wine, but also refers to the food that is sometimes served at the synagogue for this occasion. On Sabbath, after services, if someone is having a bar mitzvah, bat mitzvah, wedding, or other cause for celebration, the individual's parents or the individual might give a kiddush and invite the congregation to the party. It consists mainly of appetizers and desserts. In Jerusalem, it nearly always features Jerusalem Noodle Kugel. When I was growing up in Washington, D.C., the kiddush always featured bagels, lox, and cream cheese.

Creamy Eggplant Salad (page 173)
Hummus (Chickpea Dip) (page 163)
Tahini Sauce (Sesame Dip) (page 164)
Bright Red Cabbage Salad (page 119)
Challah (page 289), rolls, and crackers
Gefilte Fish (page 9)
Pickles, olives, and marinated herring
Jerusalem Noodle Kugel (page 138)
Chocolate-Orange Marble Cake (page 305)
Ashkenazic Poppyseed Cookies (page 311)
Chocolate Coconut Rum Balls (page 315)

AN EASY POTLUCK APPETIZER PARTY

This casual menu is popular for parties in Israel. Most of the appetizers will be salads and spreads, some of which can be brought by friends or purchased at a nearby deli. One or more homemade pastries is usually served, and is generally the item that disappears the fastest. A platter of cold meats is often available for heartier appetites.

Creamy Potato Salad with Dill Pickles (page 168)
Bulgarian Eggplant Salad with Grilled Peppers
(page 172)
Bright Red Cabbage Salad (page 119)
Bulgur Wheat and Parsley Salad with Mint and
Tomatoes (Tabbouleh) (page 180)
Mushroom Turnovers (page 156)
Sliced smoked turkey, turkey pastrami, salami, and
other cold cuts
Cocktail rye bread, pumpernickel, and Pita (page 295)
Chocolate-Orange Marble Cake (page 305)
Apple Cake with Pecans and Cinnamon (page 110)

A DESSERT PARTY

Having friends over for cake and coffee is a friendly and easy way to entertain instead of preparing a full dinner. This is also a convenient and welcome way to serve at a meeting of a club or organization. Dessert parties are best for late in the evening or in the afternoon. It's a good idea to offer some appetizer-type food as well, such as an eggplant salad with pita or perhaps some bagels with lox and cream cheese, in case someone is hungry for some "real food" before the sweets.

Roasted Eggplant Salad with Olive Oil and Garlic
(page 19)
Pita (page 295)
Creamy Cheesecake (page 60)
Pear Strudel (page 89)
Chocolate-Almond Cake with Chocolate-Honey Icing
(page 78)
Cinnamon-Nut-Raisin Crescents (Rugelach) (page 316)

A FALAFEL PARTY

Falafel and salads are fun to serve any time of the year, but especially in fall or winter. It's best to have a friend who will share in the work of frying the falafel. You can either serve the falafel in pita bread, or put it on platters together with several spreads such as hummus, tahini sauce, and eggplant salad.

Marinated Eggplant Slices (page 160)
Hot Pepper–Garlic Chutney (Zehug) (page 142)
Israeli Vegetable Salad (page 20)
Tahini Sauce (Sesame Dip) (page 164)
Eggplant Salad with Tahini (page 171)
Falafel (Chickpea Croquettes) (page 165)
Pita (page 295)
Pickles and olives
**Israeli-Style Bavarian Cream with Chocolate Sauce
and Pecans (page 322)**

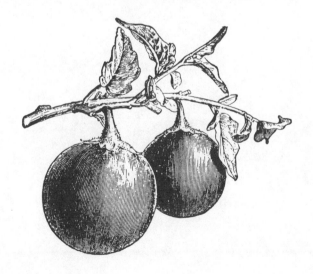

A COUSCOUS DINNER

A North African couscous menu is often quite lavish. The couscous itself, served with a meat or vegetable soup, is the center of attention; other accompaniments depend on the cook. There might be only a simple salad to start, but often there are stuffed vegetables and aromatic meat patties as well, so there is a variety of tastes and textures. At the end of such a feast, nobody has room for dessert, and so usually only mint tea or fruit is served.

Fresh and Tangy Carrot Salad (page 174)
Stuffed Celery in Quick Tomato Sauce (page 263),
or Stuffed Eggplant with Meat, Pine Nuts,
and Almonds (page 260)
Aromatic Meat Patties (page 241)
Couscous with Lamb and Seven Vegetables (page 244),
or Colorful Vegetable Couscous (page 281)
Fresh fruit
Mint tea

A BAR MITZVAH BRUNCH

A bar mitzvah or bat mitzvah is a special occasion and calls for a big party, to which relatives and friends are invited. If this will be a brunch party, dairy foods are the favorites, especially blintzes, luscious pastries, and noodle kugels. For the following menu, the filo pastries are Sephardic, and the piroshki, blintzes, and kugel are Ashkenazic specialties. The cake should be the favorite of the bar mitzvah boy or the bat mitzvah girl.

Creamy Eggplant Salad (page 173)
Potato and Lox Salad (page 169)
Grilled Pepper and Tomato Salad (page 176)
Challah (page 289), rolls, and Pita (page 295)
Cheese Filo Turnovers (Cheese Bourekas) (page 55)
Sephardic Spinach-Stuffed Filo Turnovers
(Spinach Bourekas) (page 154)
Browned Eggs (Huevos Haminados) (page 205)
Chive Blintzes with Cabbage and Sour Cream (page 200),
or Piroshki with Salmon and Cabbage (page 153)
Classic Cheese Blintzes with Strawberry Sauce (page 58)
Cinnamon-Scented Apple Noodle Kugel (page 139)
Chocolate-Nut Chiffon Cake (page 140)

A WEDDING PARTY, BUFFET STYLE

For weddings, the food should be lavish, be elegant, and make use of the best ingredients. It is a good idea to stick to familiar dishes—this is not the time to experiment with unusual combinations! Of course, the selection of dishes should be colorful and varied. In this menu, which features both Ashkenazic and Sephardic recipes, the food can be presented buffet style, which makes serving easy. There is a choice of three main courses, but the selection of dishes will still be ample if you choose to prepare only two of them. In the case of the roast chicken, the stuffing should be baked separately to facilitate serving.

Potato Salad with Smoked Turkey (page 170)
Grilled Pepper and Tomato Salad (page 176)
Chopped Liver and Eggplant Pâté (page 105)
Large braided Challah (page 289), rolls, and Pita (page 295)
Selection of olives, pickled vegetables, and cooked chickpeas
Baked Lamb with Orzo (page 243)
Crisp Turkey Schnitzel (page 236)
Roast Chicken with Pecan and Herb Stuffing (page 136)
Zucchini with Tomatoes and Dill (page 265)
Savory Mushrooms with Thyme and Olive Oil (page 33)
Easy Rice Pilaf (page 145)
Chocolate-Almond Cake with Chocolate-Honey Frosting (page 78)
Summer Fruit Salad with Raspberry Sauce (page 328)

19

COOKING TECHNIQUES

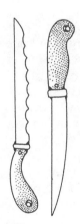

Following are ingredient preparation techniques that are required for several recipes.

PEELING AND SEEDING TOMATOES

To peel, cut the cores from the tomatoes. Turn tomatoes over and slit the skin in an *X* cut. Fill a large bowl with cold water. Put tomatoes in a saucepan with enough boiling water to cover them generously and boil them 10 to 15 seconds or until the skin begins to pull away from the flesh. Remove tomatoes with a slotted spoon and put them in the bowl of cold water. Leave for a few seconds. Remove tomatoes and pull off skins.

To seed, cut tomatoes in half horizontally. Hold each half over a bowl, cut side down, and squeeze to remove the seeds and juice.

ROASTING AND PEELING PEPPERS

Broil pepper on a rack under a preheated broiler, turning it often, for 15 to 20 minutes, or until skin is blistered and charred. Put pepper in a plastic or paper bag, close bag, and let it stand for 10 minutes or until it is cool enough to handle. Peel it with aid of a paring knife and discard top, seeds, and ribs. Drain pepper in a colander for 10 minutes.

PREPARING ARTICHOKE HEARTS

Squeeze juice of ½ lemon into a medium bowl of cold water. Break off stem of an artichoke and largest leaves at bottom. Put artichoke on its side on board. Holding a very sharp knife or small serrated knife against side of artichoke (parallel to leaves), cut lower circle of leaves off, up to edge of artichoke heart; turn artichoke slightly after each cut. Rub cut edges of artichoke heart with cut lemon. Cut off central cone of leaves just above artichoke heart. Cut off leaves under base. Trim base, removing all dark green areas. Rub again with lemon. Put artichoke in bowl of lemon water. Repeat with remaining artichokes. Keep artichokes in lemon water until ready to cook them.

To cook artichoke hearts, squeeze any juice remaining in lemon into a medium saucepan of boiling salted water. Add artichoke hearts, cover, and simmer over low heat until tender when pierced with knife, 15 to 20 minutes. Cool to lukewarm in liquid. Using a teaspoon, scoop out hairlike "choke" from center of each fresh artichoke heart.

CLEANING LEEKS

Discard very dark green parts of leeks. Split leeks lengthwise twice by cutting with a sharp knife beginning about 1 inch from root end and cutting toward green end, leaving root end attached. Dip leeks repeatedly in a sinkful of cold water. Check the layers to be sure no sand is left. Rinse well.

PREPARING RENDERED CHICKEN FAT (SCHMALTZ)

Chicken fat is firm and must be "rendered," or cooked, so it can be used in recipes. Rendered chicken fat can be purchased in jars but it's more economical to prepare your own, and then it has no preservatives. Save the fat from chickens (found near the tail) and fatty portions of skin in the freezer until you have fat from at least four chickens. The fat is rendered with a chopped onion, which gives it a delicate onion flavor. The chicken skin cooks to crisp bits that make tasty snacks and are sometimes added to chopped liver, noodles, or kasha.

Rinse the skin and fat, cut them in pieces, and sprinkle with salt. Heat a heavy skillet over low heat, add the skin and fat, and cook until the fat melts. Add one or two chopped onions and sauté until golden. Continue to sauté until skin and onions are crunchy. Strain fat, reserving onions and skins if desired. Pour the fat into jars and keep in the refrigerator.

MAKING CHICKEN SOUP OR STOCK

Follow the recipe for Ashkenazic Chicken Soup with Fresh Dill and Light Matzo Balls (page 84) or use your own recipe for any delicately flavored chicken soup or stock. When you don't have homemade soup, use packaged soup or stock, preferably unsalted or lightly salted.

BASIC TOMATO SAUCE

This sauce is a favorite accompaniment for stuffed vegetables, sautéed vegetables, fish, pasta, and white rice.

2 tablespoons olive or vegetable oil
½ medium onion, chopped
2 large garlic cloves, minced
2 pounds ripe tomatoes, peeled, seeded, and chopped; or 2 28-ounce cans plum tomatoes, drained and chopped

1 tablespoon tomato paste
1 bay leaf
½ teaspoon dried thyme, oregano, or basil (optional)
salt and freshly ground pepper

Heat oil in a large saucepan or deep skillet over medium heat. Add onion and sauté, stirring occasionally, about 5 minutes or until beginning to brown. Add garlic, tomatoes, tomato paste, bay leaf, thyme, salt, and pepper. Cook over medium heat, stirring often, about 15 to 20 minutes or until tomatoes are soft and mixture is thick and smooth. Discard bay leaf. Taste and adjust seasoning. (Sauce can be kept, covered, for 2 days in refrigerator or it can be frozen.) For a smoother sauce, puree in food processor or blender.

Makes about 2 cups

20

A BRIEF GUIDE TO KEEPING KOSHER

All the recipes in this book are kosher. But keeping kosher is a way of life that involves many rules regarding choice of foods, menu planning, and use of dishes and kitchen utensils.

Kosher foods are those that are permitted by the Jewish religion. Kashrut, the body of laws of keeping kosher, is extensive and involved. Following is a brief introduction, but anyone who would like to begin to keep a kosher kitchen can find many books dedicated to the subject.

The essentials of keeping kosher can be divided into three aspects: which foods can be eaten, how foods can be combined in a menu, and how certain foods should be "koshered," or prepared to make them kosher.

In the Torah, or Jewish bible, kosher animals are defined as those that chew their cud and have split hooves. Thus, beef, veal, and lamb are kosher, and pork is not. Poultry is also kosher.

Fish must have scales and fins. This includes most fish but, of course, excludes all shellfish.

The Torah prohibits cooking a kid in its mother's milk. From this have been derived the regulations against combining dairy products and meat or poultry in the same meal. In fact, dairy foods and meat foods are kept completely separate and require two sets of dishes. Different pots, pans, plates, and silverware are used for cooking, serving, and eating meals that include meat, called *fleishig* meals in Yiddish or *bsari* in Hebrew, and those that contain dairy products, which are called *milchig* in Yiddish or *halavi* in Hebrew.

Besides the two categories of dairy and meat foods, there is a third, known as pareve. Pareve, or neutral, foods go with everything. They can be eaten in a meal with either dairy or meat products. Included are fish, eggs, vegetables, fruits, breads, and grains, as well as vegetable oils and some margarines. Margarine sometimes contains dairy products, but if it is labeled pareve, it is suitable for all three types of meals.

For meat and poultry to be kosher, there are other special conditions that must be met. First, animals must be slaughtered in a certain manner; thus, game birds that have been shot are not kosher. Kosher meats can be purchased from a kosher butcher, or packaged at some supermarkets.

In addition, meat and poultry must be koshered to rid it of as much blood as possible, since blood is not kosher. This can be done at home or by the butcher. The process involves salting the meat, and because the meat absorbs a certain amount of salt, not much salt is needed when cooking it.

To kosher meat or poultry, rinse it well, then soak it in water for 30 minutes. Rinse the meat again, then put it on a board set at an incline so the juices can drip into the sink. Next sprinkle the meat with coarse salt, also known as kosher salt, and let it stand 1 hour. Then thoroughly rinse the meat again.

Livers are koshered in a different way. They are rinsed and broiled or grilled, which also cooks them completely. To do this, rinse the livers just before broiling them, then sprinkle them with salt and broil or grill, turning them a few times, so all sides become grilled. For broiling, put the livers on foil so they do not come in contact with the broiler pan.

Keeping dairy and meat separate also leads to avoiding certain products, such as cheeses that are made with an animal product called rennet, or yogurt made with animal-based gelatin. Kosher gelatin is vegetable based.

Kosher products are labeled with symbols to make them easy to recognize. The best-known one is Ⓤ, the seal of approval of the Union of Orthodox Jewish Congregations. Some products are labeled with *K* for Kosher. There are other kosher symbols for products in certain cities; a local rabbi can be consulted for a list of these.

CONVERSION CHART

LIQUID MEASURES

Fluid Ounces	U.S. Measures	Imperial Measures	Milliliters
	1 tsp.	1 tsp.	5
¼	2 tsp.	1 dessert spoon	7
½	1 T.	1 T.	15
1	2 T.	2 T.	28
2	¼ cup	4 T.	56
4	½ cup or ¼ pint		110
5		¼ pint or 1 gill	140
6	¾ cup		170
8	1 cup or ½ pint		225
9			250 (¼ liter)
10	1¼ cups	½ pint	280
12	1½ cups or ¾ pint		340
15		¾ pint	420
16	2 cups or 1 pint		450
18	2¼ cups		500 (½ liter)
20	2½ cups	1 pint	560
24	3 cups or 1½ pints		675
25		1¼ pints	700
27	3½ cups		750
30	3¾ cups	1½ pints	840
32	4 cups or 2 pints or 1 quart		900
35		1¾ pints	980
36	4½ cups		1000 (1 liter)

SOLID MEASURES

U.S. and Imperial Measures		Metric Measures	
Ounces	Pounds	Grams	Kilos
1		28	
2		56	
3½		100	
4	¼	112	
5		140	
6		168	
8	½	225	
9		250	¼
12	¾	340	
16	1	450	
18		500	½
20	1¼	560	
24	1½	675	
27		750	¾
28	1¾	780	
32	2	900	
36	2¼	1000	1
40	2½	1100	
48	3	1350	
54		1500	1½

OVEN TEMPERATURE EQUIVALENTS

Fahrenheit	Gas Mark	Celsius	Heat of Oven
225	¼	107	Very Cool
250	½	121	Very Cool
275	1	135	Cool
300	2	148	Cool
325	3	163	Moderate
350	4	177	Moderate
375	5	190	Fairly Hot
400	6	204	Fairly Hot
425	7	218	Hot
450	8	232	Very Hot
475	9	246	Very Hot

INDEX

Almond Cake with Orange
    Frosting, Passover, 23–24
Almond Matzo Balls, 26
Almond-Pine Nut Stuffing, 226
Almonds, 232, 260, 279–280
Alsace (France), xvii
Alsatian Almond-Raisin Matzo
    Kugel, 13

Appetizers, 149–166
    Artichokes with Lemon
        Dressing, 159
    Avocado and Egg Salad, 162
    Crisp Meat-Filled Pastries,
        157–158
    Falafel, 149–150, 165–166
    Hummus, 163
    Marinated Eggplant Slices,
        160
    Mushroom Turnovers, 156
    Piroshki with Salmon and
        Cabbage, 153–154
    potluck appetizer party,
        339
    Savory Cheese Knishes,
        150–151
    Savory Pastries with Buckwheat
        Filling, 151–152
    Sephardic Spinach-Stuffed Filo
        Turnovers, 154–155
    Tahini sauce, 165
    Yemenite Tomato Salsa,
        166
Apple Cake with Honey Frosting,
    72–73
Apple Cake with Pecans and
    Cinnamon, 110
Apple Cinnamon Ice Cream,
    327–328
Apple Compote, 116
Apple Filling, 324
Apples, 139, 237, 331–332
Applesauce, 91

Aromatic Beef and White Bean
    Casserole, 144–145
Aromatic Cornish Hens with
    Raisins, 106
Aromatic Lentil Soup, 191–192
Aromatic Meat Patties, 241
Aromatic Stuffed Onions, 95
Aromatic Yellow Rice, 278
Artichokes, 273, 346
Artichokes with Lemon Dressing,
    159
Ashkenazic Chicken Soup with
    Fresh Dill and Light Matzo
    Balls, 84–85
Ashkenazic cooking, xiv, xvi–xvii,
    4, 65–66, 83, 134
Ashkenazic Jews, xv
Ashkenazic Poppyseed Cookies,
    311
Ashkenazic Walnut Torte with
    Chocolate Glaze, 36
Asparagus, 250–251
Asparagus with Zehug Vinaigrette,
    264
Austria, xvii
Avocado, 178, 220
Avocado-Almond Rice, 279–280
Avocado and Egg Salad, 162

B

Bagels, 287, 297–301
Baked Eggplant with Tomatoes,
    Cheese, and Sesame Seeds,
    253–254
Baked Fish with Saffron and Red
    Bell Peppers, 39–40
Baked Lamb with Orzo, 243
Baked Sweet Potatoes with Dried
    Fruit, 255–256
Baking, xvii
Barbecue, 337
Bar mitzvah brunch, 343
Basic Bagels, 297–298
Basic Blintzes, 198–199
Basic Tomato Sauce, 348
Bass, 94, 211–212, 222

Bayonne (France), 329
Beans, 144, 179, 189–190,
    192–194, 239
Beef
    Aromatic Beef and White Bean
        Casserole, 144–145
    Aromatic Meat Patties, 241
    Beef and Sweet Potato
        Tzimmes, 70–71
    Beef Stew with Winter Squash
        and Raisins, 86
    Brisket, American-Jewish Style,
        102
    goulash, xvii, 240
    Hearty Meat Soup with Green
        Beans, 193–194
    Mediterranean Beef Stew with
        Chilies and Green Beans, 239
    Spicy Meat-Stuffed Peppers,
        259–260
    Yemenite Beef and Chicken
        Casserole, 43
Beef and Sweet Potato Tzimmes,
    70–71
Beef Stew with Winter Squash
    and Raisins, 86
Beet Borscht with Potatoes and
    Sour Cream, 194–195
Beets, 177
Beet Salad with Apples, 84
Black pepper, xvi
Blintzes, 58, 197–201, 324
Bombay (India), xx
Borscht, 194–195
Bourekas, 55–56, 155–156
Braised Cod with Chickpeas and
    Olive Oil, 216
Bread pudding, 332
Breads, 285–302
    bagels, 287, 297–301
    Shabbat Breakfast Bread,
        292–293
    tips on making, 288
    see also Challah
Bright Red Cabbage Salad, 119
Brisket, American-Jewish Style,
    102
Broccoli, 250–251
Broiled Salmon with Moroccan
    Seasonings, 221

Browned Eggs, 198, 205
Buckwheat *see* Kasha
Bulgarian Eggplant Salad with
    Grilled Peppers, 172
Bulgur wheat, 270
Bulgur Wheat and Parsley Salad
    with Mint and Tomatoes, 180
Bulgur Wheat Dough, 158
Bulgur Wheat Pilaf with
    Mushrooms, Peas, and Pine
    Nuts, 283–284

C

Cabbage, 97–98, 119, 153, 266
Cabbage Filling, 200
Cabbage Pletzlach, 274
Cakes
    Apple Cake with Honey
        Frosting, 72–73
    Apple Cake with Pecans and
        Cinnamon, 110
    Ashkenazic Walnut Torte with
        Chocolate Glaze, 36
    Cheesecake with Pine Nuts and
        Orange, 61–62
    Chocolate-Almond Cake with
        Chocolate-Honey Frosting,
        78–79
    Chocolate Hazelnut Gateau,
        14–15
    Chocolate Nut Chiffon Cake,
        140–141
    Chocolate-Orange Marble Cake,
        305–306
    Creamy Cheesecake, 60
    Hazelnut Honey Cake, 77–78
    Light Honey Cake with
        Cinnamon and Walnuts,
        71–72
    Meringue-Topped Cheesecake,
        306–307
    My Mother's Chocolate
        Applesauce Cake, 91
    Orange-Pecan Torte, 121
    Passover Almond Cake with
        Orange Frosting, 23–24

Passover Almond Cake with
Strawberry Sauce, 46
Pecan-Cocoa Torte with
Chocolate Cinnamon
Frosting, 29–30
Sour Cream Coffee Cake with
Walnuts, 310
Vanilla Pound Cake, 304–305
California, 24
Capers, 222
Carrot and Asparagus Salad, 42
Carrots, 64, 109, 174–175, 253
Casseroles
Aromatic Beef and White Bean
Casserole, 144
Moroccan Potato Casserole, 45
Yemenite Beef and Chicken
Casserole, 43
Zucchini Casserole with Dill, 12
Cauliflower, 143, 247, 258
Cauliflower and Green Bean
Salad with Lox Vinaigrette,
179
Cauliflower in Tomato Sauce, 28
Cauliflower Kugel with
Mushrooms, 252
Celebrations
barbecue Israeli style, 337
bar mitzvah brunch, 343
couscous dinner, 342
dessert party, 340
falafel party, 341
fall fish feast, 336
kiddush menu, 338
Polish luncheon menu, 334
potluck appetizer party, 339
Sephardic supper for winter
evening, 337
summer vegetarian menu, 335
wedding party buffet, 344
see also specific holidays
Celery, 263–264
Celery and Potato Pancakes with
Dill, 108
Challah, 289–292
Cheese-Walnut Challah, 57
dough, 286, 289, 290
flavoring variations, 292
Onion-Parmesan Braid, 294
Rosh Hashanah, 64, 66–67

Round Holiday Challah with
Raisins, 66–67
Sabbath, 132
shapes, 291
Cheese, 253–254, 272
Cheese and Herb Bagels, 299
Cheese blintzes, 58, 197
Cheese Bourekas, 55–56
Cheesecake, 53, 60, 306–307
Cheesecake with Pine Nuts and
Orange, 61–62
Cheese Filling, 56, 61, 150
Cheese Filo Turnovers, 55–56
Cheese Pancakes, 32
Cheese-Walnut Challah, 57
Chicken
Chicken Backed with Quinces
and Almonds, 232–233
Chicken Salad with Avocado
and Onions, 178
Chicken with Peppers and Rice,
231–232
Chicken with Tomatoes,
Peppers, and Coriander,
234–235
Easy Lemon Chicken, 233–234
Exotic Roast Chicken, 226–227
fat, 347
Israeli Grilled Chicken, 228
Roast Chicken with Noodle-
Mushroom-Walnut Stuffing,
225–226
Roast Chicken with Pecan and
Herb Stuffing, 136–137
Roast Chicken with Rice and
Fruit Stuffing, 75–80
Spicy Roast Chicken with
Matzo-Onion Stuffing,
230–231
Stuffed Chicken with Couscous,
Raisins, and Pecans, 229–230
Yemenite Beef and Chicken
Casserole, 43
Chicken Baked with Quinces and
Almonds, 232–233
Chicken Salad with Avocado and
Onions, 178
Chicken Soup, 84–85, 183–188,
347

Chicken Soup with Asparagus
and Almond Kneidlach, 26
Chicken Soup with Kreplach,
68–69
Chicken Soup with Rice,
Tomatoes, and Coriander,
187–188
Chicken with Peppers and Rice,
231–232
Chicken with Tomatoes, Peppers,
and Coriander, 234–235
Chickpea croquettes *see* Falafel
Chickpea dip *see* Hummus
Chickpeas, 216, 262, 281
Chilies, 239
Chive Blintzes with Cabbage and
Sour Cream, 200
Chocolate, 329
Chocolate-Almond Cake with
Chocolate-Honey Frosting,
78–79
Chocolate Chip Rugelach,
317–318
Chocolate-Cinnamon Frosting, 29
Chocolate Coconut Rum Balls,
315–316
Chocolate-Filled Walnut Rings,
313–314
Chocolate Frosting, 91
Chocolate Glaze, 36
Chocolate Hazelnut Gateau,
14–15
Chocolate-Honey Frosting, 78–79
Chocolate Mousse for Passover,
51
Chocolate Nut Chiffon Cake,
140–141
Chocolate-Orange Marble Cake,
305–306
Chocolate Sauce, 323
Chocolate-Walnut Filling, 313
Chopped Liver, 135
Chopped Liver and Eggplant Pâté,
105
Chutney, 142
Cinnamon-Nut Raisin Crescents,
316–317
Cinnamon-Scented Apple Noodle
Kugel, 139
Citron, 81–82

Citrus-Scented Almond Macaroons, 52
Classic Cheese Blintzes with Strawberry Sauce, 58
Cochin (India), xx
Cod, 216, 219
Coffee cake, 310
Cold Oven Poached Trout with Horseradish Sauce, 215–216
Cold Salmon Steaks with Herb Sauce, 8–9
Colorful Vegetable Couscous, 281–282
Cookies
    Ashkenazic Poppyseed Cookies, 311
    Chocolate-Filled Walnut Rings, 313–314
    Crisp Almond Slices, 312
    dough, 126
    Honey-Glazed Cookies with Walnuts, 321–322
    Moist Coconut Macaroons, 319–321
    Sephardic Nut-Filled Cookies, 318–319
    Soft Coconut-Chocolate Chip Cookies, 130
    Strawberry Pecan Squares, 314–315
Cooking techniques, 345–348
Coriander, xx, 177, 187–188, 214, 234–235, 267
Corn Cakes with Cumin, 118
Cornish hen, 106
Cornmeal kugel, 284
Country-Style Hummus with Tahini, 181
Couscous, 270, 280–283, 342
Couscous Stuffing, 229
Couscous with Lamb and Seven Vegetables, 244–246
Couscous with Raisins and Dates, 282–283
Cracked wheat *see* Bulgur wheat
Cream Cheese Dough, 316
Cream puffs, 50
Creamy Cheesecake, 60
Creamy Eggplant Salad, 173

Creamy Noodle Kugel with Almonds, 331
Creamy Potato Salad and Dill Pickles, 168
Crisp Almond Slices, 312
Crisp Meat-Filled Pastries, 157–158
Crisp Turkey Schnitzel, 236
Cucumber Salad with Yogurt and Mint, 175
Cumin, 44, 102, 118, 143, 217

D

Dairy, 30–31, 350
Date-Almond-Walnut Haroset, 39
Date-Filled Hamantaschen, 129
Daube, 43
Deep Fruit Compote with Wine, 326
Deep-frying, 112
Desserts, 303–332
    party, 340
    Passover, 29–30, 46, 50–52, 303–332
    Rosh Hashanah, 64
    Sephardic cooking, xviii
    see also specific types, e.g., Cakes; Cookies
Dill, xviii, 109, 213, 265
Dill Dumplings, 190–191
Dill pickles, 168
Dill Sour Cream, 120
Dough
    bulgar wheat, 158
    challah, 286, 289–290
    cookie, 126
    cream cheese, 316
    cream puff, 34
    orange-scented pastry, 61
    pastry, 151
    piroshki, 154
    pita, 295
    sour cream, 126–127, 150
Doughnuts, 102, 111
Dressings
    Lemon Dressing, 159

Lox Vinaigrette, 179
Mustard Vinaigrette, 170
Zehug Vinaigrette, 264
Duck, 87–88
Duxelles and Pasta Stuffing, 225

E

Easy Cauliflower Latkes, 258
Easy Chocolate Ladyfinger Pudding, 329–330
Easy Curried Eggplant, 268
Easy Lemon Chicken, 233–234
Easy Rice Pilaf, 145
Edot Hamizrach, xv
Egg barley *see* Farfel
Egg bread *see* Challah
Egg noodles, xvi–xvii
Egg Noodles for Soup, 275–277
Eggplant, 93–94, 105, 160, 172–173, 253–254, 260–262, 268
    Roasted Eggplant Salad with Olive Oil and Garlic, 19
Eggplant Salad with Tahini, 171
Eggs
    Browned Eggs, 198, 205
    Eggs with Peppers and Tomatoes, 204
    Lox and Eggs with Sautéed Onions, 203
    North African Baked Eggs with Tomatoes and Onions, 208
    Salami with Vegetables and Eggs, 206
    Scrambled Eggs with Spiced Mushrooms, 206
    Zucchini Frittata with Garlic, 207
Egg salad, 162
Eggs with Peppers and Tomatoes, 204
Egypt, xix
Esrog see Citron

Ethiopia, xx
Etrog see Citron
Exotic Roast Chicken, 226–227

F

Falafel, 149–150, 165–166, 341
Farfel, 269
Fasting, 80
Feast of the First Fruits *see* Shavuot
Festival of Lights *see* Hanukkah
Festival of the Torah *see* Shavuot
Figs, 128–129
Filo, 55–56, 99–100, 154–155
Fish, 209–222
  as appetizer, 150
  Baked Fish with Saffron and
    Red Bell Peppers, 39–40
  fall fish feast, 336
  Fish with Light Lemon and Dill
    Sauce, 213
  Italian-style Fish in Tomato-
    Garlic Sauce, 74–75
  Rosh Hashanah, 63
  Saffron Fish Balls in Tomato
    Sauce, 219–220
  Sephardic Fish Steaks with
    Cumin and Garlic, 217
  see also specific types of fish, e.g.,
    Gefilte fish; Sea bass
Fish with Light Lemon and Dill
  Sauce, 213
Flavorings, xix
Foie gras, 238
Four-Cheese Filling, 150
French Sweet Pastry, 309
Fresh and Tangy Carrot Salad,
  174
Fresh Mushroom Soup with Dill
  Dumplings, 190–191
Fried Cauliflower with Cumin and
  Turmeric, 143
Fried Matzo with Eggs, 33
Frittatas, 207
Fritters, 256, 258–259
Frosting, 23–24, 29, 72, 78, 91
Fruits

Deep Fruit Compote with Wine,
  326
  Rosh Hashanah, 63
  Succot, 81
  Summer Fruit Salad with
    Raspberry Sauce, 328–329
  see also specific fruits

G

Garbanzo beans *see* Chickpeas
Garlic, xviii, xx, 44, 207, 217,
  267–268, 280
Garlic and Yogurt Mint Topping, 117
Garlic Bagels, 300
Garlic-Chili Marinade, 160
Garlic Sauce, 220
Garlic-Scented Roast Potatoes,
  265–266
Gefilte Fish, 9–10
Gefilte fish, 209–210
Georgia (Soviet Union), xix
Germany, xvii
Goose, 237
Goulash, xvii, 240
Greece, xviii, xix
Green beans, 179, 193–194, 239
Green Bean Salad with Pecans,
  69–70
Grilled Pepper and Tomato Salad,
  176
Grilled Sea Bass with Caper
  Vinaigrette, 222
Gundi, 195–196

H

Haddock in Coriander-Green
  Onion Tomato Sauce, 214
Halibut, 213, 217
Halibut with Garlic Sauce and
  Avocado, 220
Hallah *see* Challah
Hamantaschen, 123–129

Hamantaschen with Fig Filling,
  128–129
Hamantaschen with Poppyseed-
  Raisin Filling, 125–127, 302
Hamantaschen with Prune Filling,
  127–128
Hamin, 144, 223
Hanukkah, 101–121
  latke party, 114
  menus, 104, 114
  recipes, 105–113, 115–121
Hanukkah Doughnuts, 111
Haroset, 4–5, 32, 39, 331
Haroset, Triple-Nut, 7–8
Haroset with Dates and Pine Nuts,
  17
Harvest Holiday *see* Succot
Hazelnut Honey Cake, 77–78
Hearty Meat Soup with Green
  Beans, 193–194
Herbed Bean and Pasta Soup,
  189–190
Herbs, xvi, xviii, 188
Herb Sauce, 8–9
Holidays *see* specific holidays, e.g.,
  Passover
Honey, 64, 72, 77, 78
Honey Glaze, 255
Honey-Glazed Carrots, 109
Honey-Glazed Cookies with
  Walnuts, 321–322
Horseradish Sauce, 215
Hot Pepper Garlic Chutney,
  142
Huevos Haminados *see* Browned
  Eggs
Hummus, 163, 181
Hungary, xvi, xvii

I

Ice cream, 327–328
India, xix–xx
Iranian Meatball Soup for Shabbat,
  195–196
Iraq, xx

Israel, xiii, 53, 81, 167, 337, 339
Israeli Bavarian Cream with Chocolate Sauce and Pecans, 322–323
Israeli Grilled Chicken, 228
Israeli Vegetable Salad, 20
Italian-Jewish Cold Noodles with Tomatoes and Parsley, 275
Italian-Style Fish in Tomato-Garlic Sauce, 74–75
Italy, xix

J

Jalapeño peppers, 239
Jerusalem Noodle Kugel, 138
Jewish Goulash, 240
Jewish New Year *see* Rosh Hashanah
Jihnun, 302

K

Kaita, 175
Kasha, 270
Kasha Knishes, 151–152
Kashrut, 349
Kiddush, 338
Kneidlach *see* Matzo balls
Knishes, 150–152
Kosher cooking, xiv, xv, 4, 349–350
Kreplach, 68–69
Kubaneh, 292–293
Kubeh, 157–158
Kugel, 35, 88–89, 138–139, 249–252, 269, 271–272, 284, 331–332
   Alsatian Almond-Raisin Matzo Kugel, 13

Potato and Vegetable Kugel, 22–23
Kurdistan, xx

L

Lamb, xviii
   Baked Lamb with Orzo, 243
   Couscous with Lamb and Seven Vegetables, 244–246
   Lamb and Rice Stuffing, 96–97
   Roast Lamb Shoulder with Spinach Stuffing, 27–28
   Roast Lamb with Garlic, Onions and Potatoes, 11
   Spicy Lamb Stew with Potatoes, 242
   Spring Lamb Stew with Many Vegetables, 48–49
   Stuffed Zucchini with Lamb, Almonds, and Raisins, 96–97
   Yemenite Braised Lamb with Cumin and Garlic, 44
Lamb and Rice Stuffing, 96–97
Latkes, 102, 108, 114–115, 250, 258
Lebanon, xix
Leek Fritters, 256
Leeks, 347
Lekach, 77–78
Lemon, xviii
Lemon-Cheese Filling, 307
Lemon-Dill Sauce, 213
Lemon Dressing, 159
Lemon-Scented Cheese Kugel with Raisins, 35
Lentils, 191–192, 278–279
Light Honey Cake with Cinnamon and Walnuts, 71–72
Liver, 105, 135, 238, 350
Lox, 169, 179
Lox and Eggs with Sautéed Onions, 203

M

Macaroni and Vegetable Kugel with Cheese, 272
Macaroons, 52, 319–321
Main-Course Chicken Soup with Vegetables, 184–185
Majadrah, 278–279
Mandelbrot, 312
Marble Cake, 305–306
Marinated Eggplant Slices, 160
Matzo, 3–4
   Alsatian Almond-Raisin Matzo Kugel, 13
Matzo and Apple Kugel, 331–332
Matzo and Onion Stuffing, 230
Matzo balls, 26, 85, 184, 188–189
Matzo brei, 33
Matzo-Mushroom Stuffing, 22
Meat
   kosher, 350
   see also specific types, e.g., Beef; Lamb
Meat and Pine Nut Filling, 157
Meatballs, 195
Meat Broth, 244
Meat Sauce, 273
Meat Stuffing, 259, 260, 263
Mediterranean Beef Stew with Chilies and Green Beans, 239
Mediterranean Vegetable Salad, 41
Melawah, 197–198, 202
Meringues, 320
Meringue-Topped Cheesecake, 306–307
Meringue Topping, 307
Middle East, xix
Middle Eastern Stuffed Cabbage Leaves, 97–98
Mint, 180
Moist Coconut Macaroons, 319–321
Moroccan Potato Casserole, 45

Moroccan Sea Bass with Peppers and Tomatoes, 211–212
Moroccan Sea Bass with Red Peppers, 94
Morocco, xviii
Mousse, 51
Msouki, 48–49
Mushroom-Barley Chicken Soup, 185–186
Mushroom Blintzes, 201
Mushroom Filling, 201
Mushrooms, 33–34, 190–191, 206, 218, 225, 252, 271, 283
Mushroom Turnovers, 156
Mustard Vinaigrette, 170
My Mother's Chocolate Applesauce Cake, 91
My Mother's Potato Pancakes, 115–116

N

Noodle kugel, 138–139, 269, 331
Noodle Kugel with Colorful Vegetables, 88–89
Noodle Kugel with Onions and Mushrooms, 271
Noodles, 275–276
Noodles with Sautéed Cabbage and Onions, 274
North Africa, xviii–xix
North African Baked Eggs with Tomatoes and Onions, 208
Nut and Chocolate-Studded Meringues, 320
Nut Filling, 99, 318

O

Okra with Tomatoes and Coriander, 267
Olive oil, xviii, 33, 216

Olives, 248
Onion-Parmesan Braid, 294
Onions, xvi, xvii, 95, 178, 203, 208, 230, 271, 274
Orange Flower Pastry, 318
Orange-Pecan Torte, 121
Orange-Scented Haroset with Wine, 32
Orzo, 243

P

Pancakes, 32, 76–77, 197–198
Rich Yemenite Pancakes, 202
Spinach Pancakes, 257
Vegetable Pancakes with Dill Sour Cream, 120
Zucchini Pancakes with Garlic and Yogurt Mint Topping, 117
see also Latkes; Potato pancakes
Paprika, 218
Pareve, 350
Paris (France), 6–7
Parsley, 180, 275
Passover, 3–52
in California, 24
dairy, 30–31
desserts, 29–30, 46, 50–52
festive, 47
in Jerusalem, 15–16
menus, 5, 16, 31, 47
in Paris, 6–7
primer, 3–4
recipes, 7–14, 17–30, 32–37, 39–46, 48–51
seder, 4–5
Sephardic seder, 38–39
Passover Almond Cake with Orange Frosting, 23–24
Passover Almond Cake with Strawberry Sauce, 46
Passover Cheese Pancakes, 32
Passover "Rolls," 34
Pasta, 189–190, 225, 269
see also specific types, e.g., Noodles

Pasta Shells with Tunisian Artichoke Meat Sauce, 273
Pastries
French Sweet Pastry, 309
Quick Hanukkah Pastry Puffs, 113
Raspberry Almond Tart, 308
Shabbat Pastry Rolls, 302
see also specific types, e.g., Filo
Pear Filling, 89
Pear Strudel, 89–90
Peas, 283
Pecan and Herb Stuffing, 136
Pecan-Cocoa Torte with Chocolate Cinnamon Frosting, 29–30
Peeling, 345–346
Peppers, 172, 176, 204, 211–212, 231, 238, 259–260, 346
Pepper Sauce, 234
Pickles, 168
Pine Nut-Almond Filo Fingers, 99–100
Pine nuts, 61, 157, 226, 260, 283
Piquant Cooked Carrot Salad, 174
Piroshki with Salmon and Cabbage, 153–154
Pita, xviii, 295–296
Pocket bread *see* Pita
Poland, xvi, xvii
Polish Strawberry Soup, 325
Poppyseed cookies, 311
Potato and Lox Salad, 169
Potato and Vegetable Kugel, 22–23
Potato and Walnut Fritters, 258–259
Potatoes
and borscht, 194–195
Garlic-Scented Roast Potatoes, 265–266
Moroccan Potato Casserole, 45
Potato Kugel with Asparagus and Broccoli, 250–251
Potato and Walnut Fritters, 258–259
Spicy Lamb Stew with Potatoes, 242

Spicy Potato Salad, 48
see also Sweet potatoes
Potato Kugel with Asparagus and
    Broccoli, 250–251
Potato pancakes, 102, 108,
    114–115
Potato salad, 48, 168–169
Potato Salad with Smoked
    Turkey, 170–171
Poultry
    kosher, 350
    see also Chicken; Turkey
Pound cake, 304–305
Prunes, 127–128
Pudding, 329–330, 332
Pumpkin, 76–77
Purim, 123–130
    sweets for, 124

Q

Quick Hanukkah Pastry Puffs,
    113
Quince, 232
Quince Compote with
    Cinnamon, 80

R

Raspberry Almond Tart, 308
Raspberry Sauce, 329
Rendered chicken fat, 347
Rice, 145, 187–188, 231, 262,
    270, 278–280
Rice Yemenite Pancakes, 202
Roast Chicken with Noodle-
    Mushroom-Walnut Stuffing,
    225–226
Roast Chicken with Pecan and
    Herb Stuffing, 136–137
Roast Chicken with Rice and
    Fruit Stuffing, 75–80
Roast Duck with Prunes and Red
    Wine, 87–88

Roasted Eggplant Salad with
    Olive Oil and Garlic, 19
Roast Goose with Apples, 237
Roast Lamb Shoulder with
    Spinach Stuffing, 27–28
Roast Lamb with Garlic, Onions
    and Potatoes, 11
Roast Turkey with Matzo-
    Mushroom Stuffing, 21–22
Romania, xvii
Romanian Cornmeal Kugel, 284
Rosh Hashanah, 63–80
    Ashkenazic, 65–66
    eclectic, 73–74
    menus, 66, 74
    recipes, 66–80
    sweet dishes for, 224
Round Holiday Challah with
    Raisins, 66–67
Rugelach, 316–318
Rum balls, 315–316
Russia, xvi, xvii
Russian Bread Pudding with
    Almonds and Raisins, 332

S

Sabbath, 131–144
    Ashkenazic menu, 134
    braised or stewed meats for,
        223
    fish for, 209, 210
    recipes, 135–145
    Yemenite menu, 144
Sabra Sorbet, 326–327
Saffron, xviii, 247
Saffron Fish Balls in Tomato
    Sauce, 219–220
Salads, 167–181
    Beet Salad with Apples, 84
    Bright Red Cabbage Salad, 119
    Bulgarian Eggplant Salad with
        Grilled Peppers, 172
    Bulgur Wheat and Parsley
        Salad with Mint and
        Tomatoes, 180

Carrot and Asparagus Salad,
        42
    Cauliflower and Green Bean
        Salad with Lox Vinaigrette,
        179
    Chicken Salad with Avocado
        and Onions, 178
    Country-Style Hummus with
        Tahini, 181
    Creamy Eggplant Salad, 173
    Creamy Potato Salad with Dill
        Pickles, 168
    Cucumber Salad with Yogurt
        and Mint, 175
    Eggplant Salad with Tahini,
        171
    Fresh and Tangy Carrot Salad,
        174
    Green Bean Salad with Pecans,
        69–70
    Grilled Pepper and Tomato
        Salad, 176
    Israeli Vegetable Salad, 20
    Mediterranean Vegetable
        Salad, 41
    Piquant Cooked Carrot Salad,
        174
    Potato and Lox Salad, 169
    Potato Salad with Smoked
        Turkey, 170–171
    Roasted Eggplant Salad with
        Olive Oil and Garlic, 19
    Sephardic Beet Salad with
        Coriander, 177
    Spicy Potato Salad, 48
    Zesty Pepper-Tomato Salad, 18
Salami with Vegetables and Eggs,
    206
Salmon, 153, 210–211, 221
Salmon Steaks with Herb Sauce,
    Cold, 8–9
Salsa, 166
Sautéed Chicken Livers with Red
    Peppers, 238
Sautéed Eggplant in Spicy
    Tomato Sauce, 93–94
Sautéed Spinach with Garlic,
    267–268
Savory Cheese Knishes, 150–151

Savory Lentils with Rice, 278–279
Savory Mushrooms with Thyme and Olive Oil, 33–34
Savory Pastries with Buckwheat Filling, 151–152
Schmaltz, 347
Schnitzel, 236
Scrambled Eggs with Spiced Mushrooms, 206
Scrod, 219
Sea bass, 94, 211–212, 222
Seasonings, xvi, xvii
Seder, 4–5
Seeding, 345–346
Sephardic Beet Salad with Coriander, 177
Sephardic cooking, xviii–xx, 4, 38–39, 92
Sephardic Fish Steaks with Cumin and Garlic, 217–218
Sephardic Jews, xv
Sephardic Nut-Filled Cookies, 318–319
Sephardic Pumpkin Pancakes, 76–77
Sephardic Spinach-Stuffed Filo Turnovers, 154–155
Sesame dip *see* Tahini Sauce
Sesame seeds, 253–254
Shabbat *see* Sabbath
Shabbat Breakfast Bread, 292–293
Shabbat Pastry Rolls, 302
Shabbos *see* Sabbath
Shakshuka, 204
Shavuot, 53–62
  menus, 55
  party, 54–55
  recipes, 55–62
Soft Coconut-Chocolate Chip Cookies, 130
Sole, 212
Sole with Mushrooms in Paprika Cream, 218
Soofganiyot, 102, 111
Sorbet, 326–327
Soups, 183–196
  Aromatic Lentil Soup, 191–192

Ashkenazic Chicken Soup with Fresh Dill and Light Matzo Balls, 84–85
Beet Borscht with Potatoes and Sour Cream, 194–195
chicken, 84–85, 183–188, 347
Chicken Soup with Asparagus and Almond Kneidlach, 26
Chicken Soup with Kreplach, 68–69
Chicken Soup with Rice, Tomatoes, and Coriander, 187–188
Egg Noodles for Soup, 275–277
Fresh Mushroom Soup with Dill Dumplings, 190–191
Hearty Meat Soup with Green Beans, 193–194
Herbed Bean and Pasta Soup, 189–190
Iranian Meatball Soup for Shabbat, 195–196
Main-Course Chicken Soup with Vegetables, 184–185
matzo ball, 184
Meat Broth, 244
Mushroom-Barley Chicken Soup, 185–186
Polish Strawberry Soup, 325
Spicy Winter Bean Soup, 192–193
Spring Vegetable Soup with Fresh Herbs, 40
vegetable, 183–185, 188
Vegetable Soup with Matzo Balls and Fresh Herbs, 188–189
Yemenite Chicken Soup, 186–187
Sour cream, 120, 126–127, 150, 194, 200
Sour Cream Coffee Cake with Walnuts, 310
Southern Europe, xviii
Spaetzle, 277
Spanish Jews, xv, 329
Spiced Apple Blintzes, 324
Spices, xvi, xviii
Spicy Couscous with Garlic, 280

Spicy Lamb Stew with Potatoes, 242
Spicy Meat-Stuffed Peppers, 259–260
Spicy Potato Salad, 48
Spicy Roast Chicken with Matzo-Onion Stuffing, 230–231
Spicy Sautéed Sole, 212
Spicy Tomato Sauce, 93
Spicy Winter Bean Soup, 192–193
Spinach, 267–268
Spinach and Matzo Stuffing, 27
Spinach Filling, 155
Spinach Pancakes, 257
Sponge cake, 36
Spring Lamb Stew with Many Vegetables, 48–49
Spring Vegetable Soup with Fresh Herbs, 40
Stews, 223–224
  Beef Stew with Winter Squash and Raisins, 86
  goulash, xvii, 240
  Mediterranean Beef Stew with Chilies and Green Beans, 239
  Spicy Lamb Stew with Potatoes, 242
  Spring Lamb Stew with Many Vegetables, 48–49
  Veal Stew with Saffron and Cauliflower, 247
Strawberry Cream Puffs for Passover, 50
Strawberry Pecan Squares, 314–315
Strawberry Sauce, 59
Strawberry Soup, 325
Strudel, 89–90
Stuffed cabbage, 97–98
Stuffed Celery in Quick Tomato Sauce, 263–264
Stuffed Chicken with Couscous, Raisins, and Pecans, 229–230
Stuffed Eggplant with Chickpeas and Rice, 262–263
Stuffed Eggplant with Meat, Pine Nuts, and Almonds, 260

Stuffed Zucchini with Lamb,
  Almonds, and Raisins,
  96–97
Succot, 81–100
  Ashkenazic, 83
  menus, 83, 92
  recipes, 84–91, 93–100
  Sephardic, 92
Summer Fruit Salad with
  Raspberry Sauce, 328–329
Sweet and sour, xvi
Sweet and Sour Cabbage, 266
Sweet and Sour Salmon,
  210–211
Sweet Carrot Kugel, 253
Sweet potatoes, 70, 255–256
Sweets, 64, 224
Syria, xix

T

Tabbouleh, 180
Tahini, 165, 171, 181
Tarts, 308
Tayglach, 321–322
Tchermela, 217–218
Thyme, 33
Tomatoes, 176, 180, 187–188,
  204, 208, 211–212, 234,
  248, 253–254, 265, 267,
  275, 345–346
Tomato sauce, 28, 74, 93, 214,
  219, 263, 348
Triple-Nut Haroset, 7–8
Trout, 215–216
Turkey (country), xviii, xix
Turkey (food), 236
  Roast Turkey with Matzo-
    Mushroom Stuffing, 21–22
Turmeric, 143
Tzimmes, 64, 70–71, 86

V

Vanilla Pound Cake, 304–305
Veal Stew with Saffron and
  Cauliflower, 247
Veal with Olives, Tomatoes, and
  Fresh Herbs, 248
Vegetable Pancakes with Dill
  Sour Cream, 120
Vegetables, 249–268
  Couscous with Lamb and
    Seven Vegetables, 244–246
  fillings for, 250
  Macaroni and Vegetable Kugel
    with Cheese, 272
  Noodle Kugel with Colorful
    Vegetables, 88–89
  pancakes, 102, 120
  Rosh Hashanah, 63, 64
  Salami with Vegetables and
    Eggs, 206
  Sephardic cooking, xviii
  soups, 183–185, 188
  Spring Lamb Stew with Many
    Vegetables, 48–49
  stuffed, 250
  Succot, 81
  Vegetable Pancakes with Dill
    Sour Cream, 120
  see also specific vegetables
Vegetable Soup with Matzo Balls
  and Fresh Herbs, 188–189
Vegetarianism, 335

W

Walnut and Raisin Bagels, 301
Walnut Cookies, 313

Walnut-Raisin-Cinnamon Filling,
  316
Weddings, 344
White beans, 144
Whole Wheat Bagels, 301

Y

Yemenite Beef and Chicken
  Casserole, 43
Yemenite Braised Lamb with
  Cumin and Garlic, 44
Yemenite Chicken Soup,
  186–187
Yemenite cooking, xiv, xx, 144
Yemenite Tomato Salsa, 166
Yogurt, 175
Yom Kippur, 80

Z

Zehug, 142, 166, 264
Zesty Pepper-Tomato Salad, 18
Zucchini, 96–97
Zucchini Casserole with Dill, 12
Zucchini Frittata with Garlic, 207
Zucchini Pancakes with Garlic
  and Yogurt Mint Topping,
  117
Zucchini with Tomatoes and Dill,
  265

ABOUT THE AUTHOR

Faye Levy has lived in the capitals of Israel, France, and the United States and has had the unique achievement of being the only author to have written cookbooks in three languages—English, Hebrew, and French.

Faye Levy spent seven years in Israel and is an honor graduate of the Hebrew University in Jerusalem and Tel Aviv University. She has been a biweekly cooking columnist of the *Jerusalem Post* for the past two years and the monthly culinary columnist of Israel's foremost women's magazine, *At*, for the past four years. In both columns she presents kosher recipes and articles on a variety of subjects, including Jewish holiday cooking. Faye has written four kosher cookbooks in Hebrew that were published by leading Israeli publishers.

In the United States, Levy's creative dishes have been featured on the covers of America's top cooking magazines. Faye Levy has written articles on Jewish cooking for *Gourmet*, *Bon Appétit*, and *Western Chef* magazines. She is one of the few recipe contributors to *Gourmet*'s *Golden Anniversary Cookbook*, featuring the fifty best recipes in half a century of the magazine's existence. For six years she wrote a highly acclaimed column, "The Basics," for *Bon Appétit* magazine.

A frequent contributor to major newspapers, Faye Levy has published recipes for Jewish holiday cooking in the *Boston Globe*, the *Washington Post*, the *Chicago Tribune*, the *New York Post*, the *Philadelphia Inquirer*, the *Detroit News*, the *Portland Oregonian*, the *San Francisco Chronicle*, the *Los Angeles Herald Examiner*, the *Cleveland Plain Dealer*, the *Atlanta Constitution*, and other newspapers across the country. Levy is now a nationally syndicated cooking columnist for the *Los Angeles Times* Syndicate, with a biweekly column called "Quick and Classy."

In 1986 two of Levy's books won prestigious Tastemaker/International Association of Culinary Professionals' cookbook awards, making her the only author in the history of the awards to have won top prizes for two books in a single year. *Classic Cooking Techniques* won as the Best Basic-General Cookbook and *Chocolate Sensations* was voted the Best Dessert and Baking Book of the Year.

Faye holds the "Grand Diplome" of the first graduating class of the famous Parisian cooking school La Varenne, where she spent nearly six years, and is the author of the highly regarded three-volume *Fresh from France* cookbook series.

Faye and her husband-associate Yakir Levy now live in Santa Monica, California. They return regularly to visit their family and friends in Jerusalem, Tel Aviv, and Paris and continue to explore the fascinating subject of international Jewish cooking.